RESPONSIBILITY IN LAW AND MORALITY

Responsibility in Law and Morality

PETER CANE
Australian National University

·HART·
PUBLISHING
OXFORD – PORTLAND OREGON
2002

Hart Publishing
Oxford and Portland, Oregon

Published in North America (US and Canada) by
Hart Publishing c/o
International Specialized Book Services
5804 NE Hassalo Street
Portland, Oregon
97213-3644
USA

Distributed in the Netherlands, Belgium and Luxembourg by
Intersentia, Churchillaan 108
B2900 Schoten
Antwerpen
Belgium

Hart Publishing is a specialist legal publisher based in Oxford, England.
To order further copies of this book or to request a list of other
publications please write to:

Hart Publishing, Salter's Boatyard, Folly Bridge,
Abingdon Road, Oxford OX1 4LB
Telephone: +44 (0)1865 245533 or Fax: +44 (0)1865 794882
e-mail: mail@hartpub.co.uk
WEBSITE: http//www.hartpub.co.uk

British Library Cataloguing in Publication Data
Data Available
ISBN 1–84113–321–3 (hardback)

Typeset by Hope Services (Abingdon) Ltd.
Printed and bound in Great Britain on acid-free paper by
Biddles Ltd, www.biddles.co.uk

In Honour and Loving Memory of
Phyllis and Stanley

Preface

In *The Anatomy of Tort Law* (1997) I argued for an understanding of tort law in terms of ideas and principles of personal responsibility. Referring to that book, Simon Deakin and Basil Markesinis have written that, although the development of liability insurance and vicarious liability means that individuals rarely pay tort damages, "one still finds tort lawyers who are willing to justify most tort rules by reference to rules of morality" (*Tort Law*, 4th edn. (Oxford, 1999), 6). In this book, I explore in more detail the relationship between law and morality. In the process I also reflect upon the relationship between legal reasoning and moral reasoning, and between philosophy and law as academic disciplines. While I discuss the nature of vicarious liability and the impact of liability insurance on tort law and the tort system, I simply assume that viewing tort law (as well as criminal law, contract law, administrative law, and so on) in terms of personal responsibility is a fruitful exercise, apt to reveal at least part of the truth about some very complex legal and social institutions. I certainly reject the idea—implicit in the comment of Deakin and Markesinis—that rules of law "regulating impersonal legal entities or the possible liability of innocent absentees" are not of "moral" significance. Readers must judge for themselves how well my initial assumption about the moral nature of law survives the scepticism of Deakin and Markesinis.

This book could not and would not have been written without the time for reading and reflection that my present post gives me. Equally important is the intellectual stimulation afforded by the vibrant multi-disciplinary environment of the Research School of Social Sciences at the ANU. I owe various other debts of gratitude. Tony Honoré's marvellous work on responsibility provided the initial stimulus for my interest in the topic. He was also kind enough to read the entire manuscript and to give me extensive and penetrating comments. I received great help from Niki Lacey, Declan Roche and an anonymous referee, who all read complete drafts and gave me the benefit of their wisdom. Declan was unfailingly encouraging. Allan Beever, Tony Connolly, Jim Evans, Desmond Manderson and Pete Morris read and commented perceptively on various chapters at various stages; and Tony Connolly gave more of his time teaching me about philosophy than I could decently have hoped for. I enjoyed and benefited much from stimulating discussions with Claire Finkelstein, Leo Katz and (as ever) Jane Stapleton. Andrew Ashworth helped me on several points of criminal law. I can only hope that none of these friends will feel that they wasted their precious time attempting to set me straight, or that the results are any of their responsibility!

Peter Cane
Canberra, 10 January 2002

Contents

1. Moral and Legal Responsibility 1

1.1 Prospectus 1

1.1.1 Starting points and themes 1

1.1.2. The structure of the book 4

1.2 The institutions of law and morality 6

1.2.1 Law 6

1.2.2 Morality 10

1.3 The relationship between law and morality 12

1.4 Moral reasoning and legal reasoning 15

1.4.1 Practical and analytical reasoning 16

1.4.2 Context and levels of abstraction 22

1.4.3 Deduction, induction and analogy 25

1.5. Summary 28

2. The Nature and Functions of Responsibility 29

2.1 Varieties of responsibility 29

2.1.1 Hart's taxonomy 29

2.1.2 The temporal element in responsibility 31

2.1.3 Personal and vicarious responsibility 39

2.1.4 Individual, shared and group responsibility 40

2.2 Responsibility and sanctions 43

2.3 Responsibility, evidence and proof 44

2.4 Responsibility as a relational phenomenon 49

2.4.1 Responsibility, agents and outcomes: three paradigms of legal responsibility 49

2.4.2 Responsibility and social values 53

2.4.3 Summary 56

2.5 Functions of responsibility practices 56

2.6 Responsibility, liability and the functions of law 60

2.7 Conclusion 63

3. Responsibility and Culpability 65

3.1 Responsibility, liability and culpability 65

3.2 Responsibility and luck 66

3.2.1 Limited sensitivity to luck 66

3.2.2 Limited sensitivity to circumstantial luck 69
3.2.3 Limited sensitivity to dispositional luck 72
3.2.4 Liability, sanctions and dispositional luck 76
3.3 Criteria of legal liability 78
3.3.1 Fault 78
3.3.2 Strict liability 82
3.4 The incidence of fault-based and strict liability 85
3.5 The nature and function of legal criteria of liability 88
3.5.1 Liability criteria are nested 88
3.5.2 Liability criteria are building blocks 89
3.5.3 Liability criteria and answers 89
3.5.4 Liability criteria and sanctions 92
3.6 Responsibility, fault and culpability 94
3.6.1 "Moral responsibility requires intentionality" 95
3.6.2 Some definitional preliminaries 96
3.6.3 The importance of choice 97
3.7 Summary 110

4. Responsibility and Causation 113
4.1 Causation, consequences and outcomes 114
4.2 The nature of causation in law 115
4.2.1 The scope of the causation question 115
4.2.2 The temporal orientation of causation 116
4.2.3 The meaning of "cause" 117
4.2.4 Causation as interpretation 118
4.2.5 Causation in the criminal law and civil law paradigms 119
4.3 Factual causation 120
4.3.1 The but-for and NESS tests 120
4.3.2 Causation, proof and uncertainty 123
4.4 Attributive causation 128
4.4.1 The relationship between causation and responsibility 128
4.4.2 Principles of causal responsibility 130
4.5 Causation in law and morality 136
4.6 Conclusion 140

5. Responsibility and Personality 143
5.1 Three issues of personality and responsibility 143
5.2 Approaches to the relationship between personality and responsibility 143
5.3 Legal personality and the corporation 145
5.4 Legal principles of group personality 148
5.4.1 Responsibility, personality and rules of attribution 148
5.4.2 Responsibility and capacity 150

5.4.3 Basic legal rules of attribution 151
5.5 Group responsibility and division of labour 158
5.6 The scope and functions of group responsibility 162
5.7 Legal and moral group responsibility 163
5.8 Modified humanistic approaches 165
5.9 Divided minds 169
5.10 Shared responsibility 171
5.10.1 The relationship between group and shared responsibility 171
5.10.2 Joint and concurrent responsibility 172
5.10.3 Contributory negligence 173
5.10.4 Secondary responsibility 173
5.10.5 Secondary and group responsibility 174
5.10.6 Vicarious responsibility 175
5.10.7 Assessing shares of responsibility 177
5.11 Conclusion 179

6. Grounds and Bounds of Responsibility 181
6.1 The basic argument and a prospectus 181
6.2 Responsibility, protected interests and the functions of law 181
6.3 Responsibility, distributive justice and the functions of law 186
6.4 Protected interests, proscribed conduct and distributive justice 190
6.5 Grounds of legal responsibility 191
6.5.1 Breach of promises and undertakings 191
6.5.2 Interference with rights 196
6.5.3 Uttering untruths 198
6.5.4 Breach of trust 200
6.5.5 Doing harm 202
6.5.6 Creating risks of harm 206
6.5.7 Making gains 208
6.5.8 Contemplating crimes 209
6.6 The bounds of legal responsibility 210
6.6.1 For breach of promises and undertakings 210
6.6.2 For interference with rights 211
6.6.3 For uttering untruths 213
6.6.4 For breach of trust 213
6.6.5 For doing harm 214
6.6.6 For creating risks of harm 221
6.6.7 For making gains 221
6.6.8 For contemplating crimes 223
6.7 Conclusion 224

7. Realising Responsibility 225
7.1 The “law in the books” vs the “law in action” 225
7.2 Settlement 226
7.2.1 The nature of settlements 226
7.2.2 The dynamics of the settlement process 229
7.2.3 For and against settlement 232
7.2.4 Settlement and responsibility 235
7.3 Selective enforcement 239
7.4 Spreading legal responsibility 241
7.4.1 The importance of insurance in civil law 241
7.4.2 Insurance and interpretations of tort law 242
7.4.3 A relational and functional account of the relationship between reponsibility and liability insurance 245
7.5 Conclusion 249

8. Responsibility in Public Law 251
8.1 The public law paradigm 251
8.2 The institutional framework of public law 254
8.3 The province of public law 256
8.4 Grounds of public law responsibility 258
8.4.1 Civil liability 258
8.4.2 Criminal liability 264
8.4.3 Judicial review 268
8.5 Bounds of public law responsibility 272
8.5.1 Civil liability 272
8.5.2 Criminal liability 273
8.5.3 Judicial review 273
8.6 Public law responsibility and “the problem of dirty hands” 275
8.7 Conclusion 278

9. Thinking about Responsibility 279

References 285
Index 297

1

Moral and Legal Responsibility

1.1 PROSPECTUS

1.1.1 Starting points and themes

LIKE "RIGHT", "DUTY" and "property", "responsibility" is a fundamental legal concept, a basic building block of legal thought and reasoning. It is even more abstract than these other concepts, and it tends to appear at a later point in chains of legal reasoning than its more concrete companions. It is rarely an "active ingredient" in legal rules—a notable exception being the problematic idea of "assumption of responsibility" in tort law.[1] Indeed, as a first reaction one might be tempted to say that "responsibility" is not a legal concept at all. "Liability" comes much more readily to the legal mind than "responsibility". But the two terms are certainly not synonymous. In tort law, for instance, a person may be responsible for harm in the sense that they caused it by their negligence, but be immune from liability for that harm. In many jurisdictions, judges and witnesses enjoy immunity from tort liability for reasons having to do with the functioning of the legal system as a whole.[2] Just as importantly, a person may incur legal liability even though they were not in any sense responsible for the event that triggered the liability. Restitutionary liability of an innocent, passive recipient of a mistaken payment[3] or beneficiary of a fraud[4] is a good example.[5] There may, in brief, be both responsibility without legal liability, and legal liability without responsibility. Responsibility is an important criterion of legal liability, but not the sole criterion.[6] Putting the point another way, liability is a trigger of legal penalties and remedies, whereas personal responsibility is one (but not the only) trigger of legal liability

On the other hand, it is true that "responsibility" is used much more commonly outside the law than in legal discourse to express ideas that underlie both it and "liability". Thus we tend to speak of "moral *responsibility*" and "legal *liability*". I think we do this partly because "liability" refers primarily to formal, institutionalised imposts, sanctions and penalties, which are characteristic of

[1] See 6.5.1.1.

[2] Cane (1996), 228–33. In some jurisdictions advocates, too, enjoy immunity from liability in negligence: *ibid.*, 233–7; but note *Arthur J.S. Hall & Co* v. *Simons* [2000] 3 WLR 543.

[3] Virgo (1999), ch. 8; Burrows (1993), ch. 3.

[4] *Foskett* v. *McKeown* [2000] 2 WLR 1299.

[5] Criminal offences of possession provide other instances: Ashworth (1999), 111–12.

[6] See further 2.6, 6.6.

law and legal systems but not of morality. "Responsibility", by contrast, refers to the human conduct and the consequences thereof that trigger such responses. This difference of usage does not, however, indicate that ideas of responsibility are less important in law than in morality.

"Responsibility" is a term that is used in many different senses, and it is no part of my project to stipulate how it should be used. This book offers an account of responsibility from a distinctively legal point of view. As a result, my basic concern is with a conception of responsibility that is bound up with (but distinct from) the idea of exposure to sanctions. This is a book about law, not a work of philosophy. Although it does not provide a detailed account of any particular area of the law, or of the law of any particular jurisdiction, the book is about particular areas of the law (those in which the idea of responsibility plays an important part), and about the law of actual legal systems. It is not about law and legal systems in general, or about "the idea of law", or even about "the idea of legal responsibility".

My decision to write the book was partly provoked by two casual observations and a conviction. One observation was that philosophers interested in concepts, such as responsibility, that play an important part in practical reasoning[7] in both law and morality (and which I shall refer to as "complex" concepts),[8] pay surprisingly little attention to the legal "version" of such concepts.[9] This is, perhaps, a result of the artificiality of the boundaries between academic disciplines. But it also reflects, I think, a certain view about law that seems to me to be implicit[10] in much philosophical analysis of complex concepts. To people who take this view, law and legal concepts often seem artificial and contrived, the product of political power and unprincipled compromise between opposing ethical positions, consisting of arbitrary rules designed to solve "practical" problems such as problems of proof. By contrast, "morality" is seen as "natural" and, at its best, the product of calm, rational and principled reflection on the nature of the world and of the place of human beings in it. According to this account, morality is in some sense prior to and independent of social practices in general, and of legal practices in particular. Whereas law is necessarily a social phenomenon, a matter of convention and practice, morality is ultimately non-conventional and critical, providing ultimate standards for the ethical assessment of law and other social practices.[11] Joel Feinberg puts the point well when he speaks, in relation to responsibility, of:

> "a stubborn feeling . . . even after legal responsibility has been decided that there is still a problem . . . left over: namely, is the defendant *really* responsible (as opposed to 'responsible in law') for the harm?"[12]

[7] i.e. reasoning about what to do and how to behave.

[8] Very many legal concepts are complex. An example of a non-complex legal concept is "tort".

[9] An exception is Wertheimer (1996), esp chs. 2 and 5.

[10] And sometimes explicit. See, for instance, the discussion of the views of Lewis in 2.5. Witness Nagel's much-quoted statement that strict liability "may have its legal uses but seems irrational as a moral position": Nagel (1979), 31; and the statement of Velasquez cited in 2.3 at n. 55.

[11] Coady (1991), 375; Sumner (1987), 90–1 (speaking of moral rights).

[12] Feinberg (1970), 30 (original emphasis). Feinberg goes on to cast doubt on the value of this way of thinking about responsibility. This attitude is not exclusive to philosophers. Consider, for

In this view, moral propositions can be "true" in a way that propositions of law cannot; and moral responsibility can be "real" in a way that legal responsibility cannot.

The second observation was that many theorists who call themselves "legal philosophers", and who are interested in complex concepts, tend to address their work to, and to engage the concerns of, philosophers rather than lawyers. They seek, first and foremost, to make contributions to debates in social, moral and political philosophy, not to debates about law, legal policy and legal practice. Their analyses often start with ideas found in philosophical literature that is, to a greater or lesser extent, unconcerned with and unaware of law; and their main aim is to interpret legal practices using "philosophical" ideas and modes of analysis. Some of the more abstract theorising about corrective justice in tort law provides a good example of this technique.

The conviction that provoked this book was that careful study of the legal concept of responsibility and of the legal practices associated with it could tell us a good deal not only about legal responsibility, but also about responsibility more generally. The idea is that by starting with a body of legal materials and with the legal version of the complex concept of responsibility, we can add to and enrich analyses of responsibility that more or less ignore the law. As I will argue in due course, this is because law possesses institutional resources that enable it to supplement extra-legal responsibility norms and practices, to influence thinking about responsibility outside the law, and to provide a way of managing, if not resolving, extra-legal disagreements about responsibility.

The analysis in this book has three main underlying strands that will, to some extent, be intertwined. One is concerned with the nature of law and "morality" respectively, and with the relationship between them. I do not mean this to be as ambitious as it sounds. I will not attempt to analyse the concept of law, or of a legal system, or of morality; and I will not attempt to give a thorough account of the relationship between them, or of their respective purposes and functions. But I do need to mark out two "normative domains"—that of law and that of morality—in order to be able to explore certain comparisons and contrasts between the versions of responsibility associated with each. The distinction between law and morality will also enable some comparisons and contrasts to be drawn between "moral reasoning" and "legal reasoning" as techniques for generating normative conclusions about responsibility.

The second strand is more substantive: what can we learn about responsibility more generally by analysing legal responsibility in particular? The analysis I offer of legal responsibility will be based on, and will elaborate, two related arguments. The first is that legal responsibility can fruitfully be understood as a set of social practices serving a number of social functions. The second argument is that legal responsibility is relational in the sense that it is concerned not

instance, the view that "[o]ne of the major distinctions between criminal law and other methods of constraining people's behaviour is that a criminal conviction often conveys a message of moral as well as legal censure": Arenella (1989), 61.

only with the position of individuals whose conduct attracts responsibility, but also with the impact of that conduct on other individuals and on society more generally. By contrast, much philosophical analysis of responsibility focuses on agents at the expense of "victims" and of society.

The reason for this concentration on agents provides the third underlying strand of my analysis. A common argument in the philosophical literature is that the essence of responsibility is to be found in what it means to be a human agent and to have free will. According to this approach, responsibility is a function or aspect of human agency and free will; and a proper understanding of responsibility requires a "naturalistic" or "quasi-scientific" account of "the facts" about human agency and freedom. There is disagreement amongst philosophers about what freedom means, about whether human beings are free in the relevant sense, and about the relevance of freedom to responsibility. The importance of this is that on one view, if human behaviour is unfree in the sense of "causally determined", humans "are not responsible" for their behaviour. Nevertheless, both in law and "morality" we regularly hold people responsible, and treat people in certain ways on the basis of our judgments of responsibility. Our responsibility practices have developed, and thrive, independently of "the truth" about human freedom. In this book, I am not concerned with whether a naturalistic account of responsibility is possible; or, if it is, with what the "truth" is about responsibility. My concern is with responsibility practices and with the concepts and ideas of responsibility on which they are based—in other words, with "conventional" responsibility.

Of course, those who believe that a naturalistic account of responsibility is possible, and that some naturalistic account is true, would argue that responsibility practices that conflict with the truth about responsibility (which, to adopt and adapt Rorty's phrase, do not "mirror nature")[13] should be abandoned. Because my concern is with responsibility practices that have developed independently of "the truth" about human freedom, I will not consider whether the moral and legal responsibility practices I examine and seek to illuminate are consistent with the natural truth about responsibility (whatever that might be).

1.1.2 The structure of the book

The structure of the book reflects its starting point in the project of seeking a better understanding of the relationship between legal and moral responsibility and between legal reasoning and moral reasoning. The analysis throughout is informed by seven recommendations for helpful ways of thinking about responsibility that are set out in chapter 9 by way of a summary of the main arguments of the book. In the spirit of these recommendations, chapter 2 deals with taxonomies of responsibility ideas, taking as its point of departure H L A Hart's

[13] Rorty (1979).

well-known catalogue of responsibility concepts. This chapter introduces two distinctions that are central to my analysis . One contrasts historic responsibility with prospective responsibility, identifying the former with the issue of "what it means to be responsible" and the latter with the issue of "what our responsibilities are". The other distinction introduced in chapter 2 is between three different paradigms of legal responsibility—the civil law paradigm, the criminal law paradigm and the public law paradigm. The distinction between the first two paradigms plays a particularly significant role in the discussion of responsibility and culpability in chapter 3.

The main issues tackled in chapter 3 are the relationship between responsibility and luck, the importance of outcomes (as opposed to conduct) as a ground of responsibility, and the moral status of negligence-based and strict legal liability in light of the emphasis on choice in many philosophical accounts of responsibility. Chapter 4 deals with causation. There are large philosophical literatures on both causation and responsibility, but less has been written that directly addresses the relationship between the two concepts. This is the focus of discussion in chapter 4.

The main topic of chapter 5 is a discussion of corporate responsibility against the background of philosophical accounts of the relationship between personality and responsibility. The analysis of grounds and bounds of responsibility in chapter 6 rests on the idea, first introduced in chapter 2, that a full account of responsibility requires analysis not only of what it means to be responsible, but also of what our responsibilities are. In other words, responsibility practices are concerned not only with allocating the costs of harm on an historic basis, but also with distributing risks of harm.

Chapter 7 explores various ways in which rules and principles of responsibility are used as resources to achieve practical objectives other than their straightforward application and enforcement. In particular, the chapter deals with settlement of civil claims and criminal prosecutions, selective enforcement of criminal law, and the impact of liability insurance on principles of legal responsibility. Chapter 8 examines the third of the three paradigms of responsibility introduced in chapter 2—the public law paradigm. The basic argument is that the distinctiveness of this paradigm resides in the answer it gives to the question of what our responsibilities are rather than to the question of what it means to be responsible. In terms of the relationship between moral and legal responsibility, the discussion explores the relevance of concepts of responsibility in public law to the philosophical debate about the distinction between public and private morality.

The present chapter lays the groundwork for the detailed examination in later chapters of various aspects of responsibility. I will first mark out the respective domains of "law" and "morality" in terms of their institutional landscape. Secondly, I will argue that by virtue of its institutional characteristics, law makes a distinctive contribution to our responsibility practices; and that, for this reason, it deserves careful attention in its own right, and should not be viewed as a distorted reflection of morality. Thirdly, I will explore some comparisons and contrasts between "legal reasoning" and "moral reasoning".

1.2 THE INSTITUTIONS OF LAW AND MORALITY

1.2.1 Law

The contrast between law and morality is deeply embedded in our thinking about responsibility. Neither of the contrasted concepts is straightforward, and the nature and content of both are contested.[14] For my purposes, however, it is not necessary to become involved in debates about such matters because my main concern is with responsibility understood as a set of social practices. Whatever view is taken about the value of positivism as a theory of law, no-one has any difficulty identifying the law of the state in which they live[15] as a set of social practices because the "domain of law"[16] is thick with formal institutions of three broad types: law-making institutions, law-applying institutions, and law-enforcement institutions.[17] There are two archetypal law-making institutions: legislatures and courts. Courts are also the archetypal institutions for applying general laws to particular cases. An important aspect of law-application is law-interpretation. Law-enforcement (which also involves law-application and law-interpretation) is primarily the province of "police" (understood in a very broad functional sense) and of courts (similarly understood).[18] In terms of responsibil-

[14] For a useful survey of approaches to the definition of "moral" and "morality" see Wallace and Walker (1970). The seminal jurisprudential discussion of the nature of morality is Hart (1961), 167–80.

[15] Although the discussion in this book focuses on law in this formal sense, much of the analysis could also be applied to less central instances of "law".

[16] The word "domain" is not ideal for describing the relationship between law and morality because it carries a general suggestion of separation and differentiation. It is important to note, therefore, that I use it only to bring out the significance of institutions. I certainly do not want to suggest that in terms of their subject matter, law and morality inhabit different domains. There may be some topics on which the one speaks and the other is silent, or vice versa; but there are very many topics on which both have something to say. And, of course, when both speak, they may or may not say the same thing. In terms of substance and subject matter, it may be helpful to picture our normative life in terms of a tapestry in which law, morality and so on, are intricately interwoven. So I use the imagery of domains in relation to institutional landscape, and of a tapestry in relation to the content of various normative systems.

[17] This is more true of "municipal" law than of international law. The main focus of this book is on municipal law, but I say a little about international law in 2.4.1.

[18] Courts, not "police", are the archetypal law-appliers because their interpretations of the law have an authority lacking in interpretations by police. On the other hand, police can typically exercise discretion in deciding whether and when to enforce the law. Such discretion to enforce the law selectively may be seen as conferring *de facto* law-*making* power. For instance, by limiting prosecutions for strict liability offences to cases of serious fault, environmental authorities may effectively change the nature of the offences in question (see Hawkins (1984), 161–2; Hutter (1988), 115–17; Hutter (1997), 9; the phenomenon is discussed in 7.3). Again, by the use of "extra-statutory tax concessions", revenue authorities can effectively modify the statutory rules of tax liability. In short, legal institutions typically exercise a complex mix of the three basic legal functions.

ity, law-making institutions make rules and enunciate principles about what our responsibilities are and about when we are responsible. Law-applying institutions bring those rules and principles to bear on concrete cases, in the process interpreting the rules and principles and resolving disputes about what our responsibilities are and about when we are responsible. Law-enforcement institutions apply various coercive techniques to maximise the incidence of "responsible behaviour" and to penalise and repair adverse consequences of "irresponsible behaviour".[19]

There is another very important sense in which law is highly institutionalised. Legal rules and principles are extensively documented. Legal literature falls into two broad categories which can be referred to as "legislation" and "common law" respectively.[20] Common law literature consists essentially of the reasons for decisions given by "superior" and, in particular, appellate courts. The analysis in this book is based on the legal literature of what might be called "Anglian" legal systems—that is, legal systems the conceptual structure of which is derived from that of English law. Legal literature provides us with a large amount of valuable source material for analysing legal responsibility that is lacking in the case of moral responsibility.

The two categories of legal literature I have identified—legislation and common law—reflect different methods of law-making which might be called "law-making through legislation" and "law-making through adjudication" respectively. The latter, as its name implies, is incidental to law-application and law-interpretation by courts.[21] Putting the point crudely, the legal legitimacy of legislation depends primarily on compliance with a complex set of rules governing the identity of the legislator and the procedures of law-making, and only secondarily on the content of the law. The content of legislation can affect its legal legitimacy to the extent that courts have the power to test that content for consistency with "superior" rules of law such as may be contained in a constitution or bill of rights. But the basic position is that while courts have the power

[19] For further explanation of the ideas of "when we are responsible", "responsible behaviour" and of "what our responsibilities are" see 2.1.2.1.

[20] The sense in which I am using the term "common law"—to refer to a body of legal literature—is closely related to another meaning of the term that refers to the judge-made law which is embodied in the documentary common law. "Common law" is used in at least two other senses: to refer to legal systems based on English law, in contrast to "civil law" legal systems based on Roman law; and in contrast to "equity". This last distinction is the product of a bifurcation in the English court system that no longer exists. However, the distinction between common law and equity is still conceptually important in English law and in many legal systems derived from English law.

[21] Judges make law in two senses: the enunciation of rules and principles, which have never been enunciated before, to cover situations with which the (written) law has not previously dealt; and the alteration of previously enunciated rules to cover situations formerly covered by the previously enunciated rule or principle. Typically, judicial law-making (in contrast to legislative rule-making) has retrospective effect. This principle should be distinguished from the so-called "declaratory theory" of judicial law-making which says that judges do not create or change the common law but only discover law that is, and in some sense always was, "out there" (Cane (2001)). Rejection of this absurd declaratory theory does not detract from the undoubted importance of historical continuity in the common law: Postema (1986), esp ch. 1.

to interpret and apply legislation, they do not have the power to disapply or amend it. The source of the legitimacy of the content of legislation is essentially political. In a democracy, the substance of legislation is a product of deliberation, consultation and debate (as well as of bargaining and compromise) conducted via the representative and participatory mechanisms loosely referred to as "the political system". The limited power of courts over the content of legislation is reflected in the fact that the very words of legislation are authoritative (or, in other words, the formulation of legislative provisions is canonical). The canonical authority of legislation is designed partly to promote certainty and stability in the law, and partly to limit the law-making power of unrepresentative, unelected and democratically unaccountable courts.

By contrast, the legal legitimacy of judge-made law depends heavily on its content and on the nature and quality of the reasoning used, and the reasons given, to support and justify that content. As a result, and because judicial law-making is typically incidental to the consideration of concrete cases, the terms in which the rules and principles of the common law are expressed are not canonical. Formulations of common law rules and principles are essentially provisional and open to reconsideration and revision in the light of further experience and of changes in values and outlook.[22] In this and other respects, judicial reasoning about complex concepts, such as responsibility, bears noteworthy similarities to "moral reasoning" about such concepts. I will explore this point in more detail in 1.4.

The importance of judicial reasoning to assessment of the legal legitimacy of the common law deserves to be emphasised. The legal legitimacy of legislation depends in no way on the reasoning supporting it—although, of course, it may be crucial to its political legitimacy. This is an important reason why courts are generally unwilling to have recourse to *travaux preparatoires* and records of parliamentary debates in interpreting statutes. Such materials rarely speak with a single voice. But more fundamentally, any force they might be given threatens to undermine the canonical status of the *ipsissima verba* of the legislative text.

There are certain other features of the judicial law-making process that deserve mention here. First, although debate, deliberation and consultation are just as important a feature of law-making by adjudication as of law-making by legislation, the participants in the adjudicative law-making process are predominantly lawyers—judges, advocates and attorneys, and (indirectly) legal academics.[23] The democratic credentials of the common law process are very weak, to say the least. Secondly, just as the canonical form of legislation promotes

[22] The conflict between the inflexibly canonical authority of legislation (including written constitutions), and the desirability of taking account of new experience and changes in values, lies at the heart of the deep theoretical and practical problems inherent in the judicial task of statutory (and constitutional) interpretation. Judicial interpretations of legislation have the provisional character of the common law, not the canonical quality of legislation.

[23] See Simpson (1973). For a normative theory of the role of academics as policy advisers see Kaplow and Shavell (2001).

certainty and stability in the law, so the principle of *stare decisis,*[24] the rules of precedent,[25] and judicial adherence to the values of coherence and consistency[26] promote certainty, stability and predictability in the common law. These rules, principles and values limit the provisionality of the common law. The features that limit its provisionality also, to some extent, make up for its lack of democratic legitimacy.[27] Another technique developed by courts for dealing with the "democratic deficit" of the common law is appeal to "common sense" and the values of the "ordinary" (or "reasonable") person as a basis for legal norms. This important feature of judicial reasoning is examined in more detail in 1.4.1.

Thirdly, even though the formulation of common law rules and principles is provisional and open to reconsideration and revision, nevertheless, the rules and principles are authoritative until they are revised by a court with the power to do so. By contrast, very many people recognise no external moral authority. Furthermore, when a court is confronted with a dispute or question about the meaning or application of a complex concept, the court must usually[28] make an authoritative decision to resolve the dispute or answer the question. By contrast, moral disputes can sometimes be left unresolved, and moral questions can often be left unanswered. This is one of the reasons why the legal versions of complex concepts are often thought "inferior" in some sense to their moral counterparts.[29] However, while we can sometimes leave moral issues unresolved, life constantly presents us with the necessity of moral choice. Moreover, it is by no means obvious that the quality of reasoning about complex concepts, and its conclusions, will necessarily be lower if the reasoning has a practical point. Indeed, reasoning that lacks a practical point (one might think) is likely to "miss the point".

A major claim of this book is that because of the nature of the judicial law-making process,[30] and because most of the basic conceptual building blocks of legal doctrine have been developed by courts, not by legislators, the literature of the common law provides extremely valuable (and, perhaps, indispensable) material for developing a thorough understanding of complex concepts such as responsibility, both in their legal versions and more generally.[31] Although legislation is now quantitatively a much more important source of law than the courts, the conceptual structure of much legislation is that of, or at least is derived from, the common law. More importantly, the legislative law-making process is not expected to conform to the rigorous standards of rationality and

[24] This principle tells courts to pay respect to relevant earlier decisions.

[25] These rules establish the hierarchy of authority of judicial decisions within the court system.

[26] This set of rules, principles and values helps define the "historicism" of the common law: Postema (1986), ch. 1.

[27] Reason-giving is also important in this regard.

[28] Unless the dispute is beyond the court's jurisdiction.

[29] Feinberg (1970), 26.

[30] Most notably because of the importance of the quality of judicial reasoning to the legitimacy of the common law.

[31] Similarly: Lloyd-Bostock (1983), 261.

reason-giving that apply in the judicial law-making process; and (consequently) the reasoning that underpins legislative rule-making is not as well documented, or as systematic and focused, as judicial reasoning in support of law making through adjudication. Because of the way the legislative process works, it is often notoriously difficult to ascertain the "purpose" of statutory provisions from the diverse documentary products of that process. Because my main concern in this book is with how people think and reason about responsibility in legal and non-legal contexts, the literature of the common law provides a much more fruitful basis for acquiring an understanding of legal concepts of responsibility than does the literature of legislative processes.

Although the details of the common law may vary from one Anglian jurisdiction to another, Anglian legal systems share a large body of basic concepts. The analysis in this book is pitched at the level of common concepts, and on the whole, differences from one jurisdiction to another in the detailed application and outworking of those concepts are not relevant to the analysis and will not be discussed. To the extent that the book has a jurisdictional focus, it is English. But this is only for the purposes of illustration and exposition. Jeremy Waldron draws distinctions between "general" and "special" jurisprudence, on the one hand; and between "general" and "particular" jurisprudence, on the other.[32] The first distinction refers to the difference between analysis of general concepts such as "right", "duty" or "property", and analysis of "specific topics in law such as tort liability". The second distinction refers to the difference between analysing ideas such as "law" and "legal system" without reference to any particular set of laws or any particular legal system, and analysing the legal institutions of a particular jurisdiction. In terms of the first of these distinctions, this book is a contribution to both general and special jurisprudence. Its broad topic is responsibility, but the discussion of that concept involves reference to specific legal topics. In terms of the second distinction, it is a contribution to particular jurisprudence, at least in the sense that it focuses on a family of legal systems the conceptual structure of which is based on English law.

1.2.2 Morality

From a sociological point of view, the moral domain may also be described as highly institutionalised. Indeed, John Searle invented the term "institutional facts" to describe social practices such as promising, and to account for their normative content.[33] More concretely, "institutional structures" such as families, schools, churches and interest groups play significant roles in establishing, maintaining and reinforcing extra-legal norms (as they do in the case of legal norms). Some of these institutions recognise individuals or bodies that perform

32 Waldron (1999), 4–8, 45–8.
33 Searle (1964); Searle (1995).

functions essentially similar to those performed by state legal institutions. There are religious courts, for instance, and many social groups have norm-making and norm-enforcing mechanisms and (a more or less rudimentary)"norm-literature". Such norm-related activities may generate normative systems in which concepts of"responsibility" play a part. On the other hand, from a normative perspective, the institutional aspect of the moral domain differs from that of the legal domain in at least two related ways. First, many people recognise no body or individual with the power to make moral norms.[34] For many people, there are no moral tribunals with power authoritatively to interpret and apply moral norms, and no moral police with power to enforce moral norms. Breaches of moral norms may be met by sanctions and moral obligations of repair, but typically these are not meted out or administered by formal morality-enforcing institutions.[35] For many people, morality is a purely matter of values, unclouded by claims of authority. Secondly, law and legal institutions of the four types discussed in 1.2.1 make a universal claim of legitimate authority over their subjects, to which the authority-claims of all other normative institutions recognised by those subjects are subordinate.[36] Moreover, this claim to universal authority is underwritten by the state's claim to a monopoly of legitimate force.[37] On the basis of these two observations we can say that law is institutionally based in a way and to an extent that morality is not.

My purpose in making this point is not sociological or descriptive but analytical. I am not concerned to map the relative degree of institutionalisation of the legal and the moral domains respectively. Instead, the contrast I want to draw is between two "ideal-type" normative domains in both of which responsibility norms play an important part, but one of which (law) is rich in the four types of institutions I have discussed, while the other (morality) is essentially devoid of such institutions. In other words, I will treat law and legal responsibility norms as institutionally based, but morality and moral norms of responsibility, by contrast, as not institutionally based.[38] The reason for drawing the distinction between law and morality in this stark way is this. While I assume that the

[34] In the law and economics literature, non-legal rules are called "norms": e.g. Posner and Rasmusen (1999). Hart's view was that the idea of a "moral legislator" was a contradiction in terms (Hart (1961), 175–8). This opinion was a corollary of his claim that the key to understanding "law" lay in the union of primary and secondary rules; or, more precisely, in the addition of secondary rules to primary rules. As a result, he drew a sharp distinction between law and morality, and gave relatively little attention to the common law which, as I will argue later (see esp 1.4), bears important structural similarities to morality. Although common law rules can be created by deliberate act, they are more like custom and conventional morality than like statutory legislation.

[35] Hart apparently believed that whereas the internal point of view was a condition of the efficacy of law, it was part of the definition of morality (Hart (1961), 179–80). Even if this is correct, it does not follow that sanctions play no role in the moral domain.

[36] Raz (1979), ch. 2.

[37] Sumner (1987), 70–9.

[38] For a similar approach see Sumner (1987), 87–90. To the extent that extra-legal normative systems possess institutions like those found in the legal domain, they can be treated as analogous to law for the purposes of the analysis in this book.

project of subjecting human conduct to the governance of (responsibility-generating) rules is shared by law and morality, one of the main aims of this book is to explore implications of the fact that for the purposes of furthering this project, law possesses institutional resources that morality lacks. This is not to say that morality and moral institutions do not play a crucial role in furthering the project, for they obviously do. But my aim is to focus on legal institutions and on their distinctive contribution to the project.

More particularly, I will argue that by reason of law's institutional resources, the legal "version" of responsibility has a richness of detail lacking in the moral "version" of responsibility. Because law is underwritten by the coercive power of the state, courts cannot leave disputes about responsibility (for instance) unresolved. A refusal by a court to find for a claimant effectively involves a finding for the person against whom the claim is made. And because moral sanctions are typically non-physical (censure and disapproval) and are not backed by institutionalised coercion in the way that legal sanctions are, there is much less pressure in the moral sphere than in the legal system to provide determinate answers to detailed questions about responsibility. The law does (and, indeed, must) provide determinate answers to many detailed questions about responsibility which may never explicitly arise outside the law or, which, if they do arise, may never (have to) be given a determinate answer. Morality can afford to be vague and indeterminate to an extent that law cannot. It is for this reason that law can make a contribution to thinking and judgement about responsibility outside the law as well as within it.[39] Law possesses the institutional resources needed to provide answers to many detailed questions about responsibility. Such answers are, of course, subject to critical assessment. But if they are found acceptable, they enrich our store of principles and practices of responsibility.

1.3 THE RELATIONSHIP BETWEEN LAW AND MORALITY

It was argued in 1.1.1 that many accounts of the relationship between law and morality (and between legal and moral responsibility) rest on the idea that morality is a source of ultimate values whereas law is purely conventional. This approach may involve no more than treating moral judgments as having a "certain priority" over law as "grounds for assessment" of human conduct in the structure of practical reasoning.[40] On this basis, although law may be criticised in moral terms, morality is not subject to criticism in legal terms. But Hart, for instance, seems to go further when he contrasts law with morality by saying that "morality is something "there" to be recognised, not made by deliberate human choice".[41] This state-

[39] Similarly Kenny (1978), 2.

[40] Pettit (2001b), 234–5.

[41] Hart (1961), 176. He seems to consider this formulation to be another way of saying that morality is not "made" in the way that statutes are "made". But these two propositions are obviously quite different in meaning. Morality could be the product of deliberate human choice without

ment apparently attributes to morality an "objective" quality that law lacks. Philip Pettit identifies three different notions of objectivity in ethics: semantic, ontological and justificatory.[42] To hold that morality is semantically objective is to believe that moral statements report "how things are" according to the speaker's "view of things".[43] The ontological objectivist additionally believes that moral judgments are like colour statements. Just as we see things as red because they are red, and not vice-versa, so we judge things as being morally good or bad because they are morally good or bad, and not vice-versa. Justificatory objectivism involves the further belief that there is a single set of values that everyone must use as grounds for assessing human conduct. From the perspective of justificatory objectivism about morality, there might seem little or no reason to concern oneself with legal responsibility concepts and practices. The important thing is to decide what it means to be morally responsible according to the set of values that is accepted as the proper basis for moral judgment. To the extent that legal rules and principles of responsibility coincided with morality, they could be viewed as a reflection and reinforcement of it; and to the extent that they diverged from standards of moral responsibility, they could be dismissed as immoral and unacceptable. This, I think, captures a common approach to the relationship between law and morality.

For my purposes, a problem with this approach is that it views law and morality as totally separate normative domains that exist side-by-side but do not interact with one another; and it implies that studying the law can teach us nothing about responsibility concepts and practices outside the law. On the contrary, my view (which is consistent with both semantic and ontological objectivity about morality) is that morality and law are both parts of a rich tapestry[44] of responsibility (and other normative) practices, and that all parts of the "responsibility tapestry" deserve and require careful attention if we are to make sense of the whole. It is not helpful, it seems to me, to treat law as an autonomous normative system, or to analyse the extra-legal meaning and use of complex normative concepts, which are found both inside and outside the law, without referring to the legal use of such concepts. Judges often assume that what they are doing in developing legal concepts is to bring into the law normative practices and understandings that already exist in society and outside the law.[45] For this reason

being made by a moral legislature. There is a world of difference between saying that morality is not legislated and saying that it is "out there waiting to be discovered".

[42] Pettit (2001b).

[43] Pettit (2001b), 236.

[44] See n. 16 above.

[45] Kaplow and Shavell argue that insofar as "social norms" (i.e. non-legal rules) are based on factors other than the well-being of individuals (the central concern of welfare economics) they provide an unsuitable basis for legal "policy-making" (Kaplow and Shavell (2001)). In their view, academic lawyers have an obligation to base their policy recommendations exclusively on welfarist considerations. This requirement does not apply so strongly to judges, they say, because they have competing role responsibilities (Kaplow and Shavell (2001), 1306–19). The authors provide no welfare-based criteria for choosing amongst competing rules (Kaplow and Shavell (2001), 988), no guide as to how to identify social norms that do not promote welfare, and no indication of when judges are justified in incorporating such norms into the law despite their failure to promote welfare.

alone, it seems worthwhile at least to allow of the possibility that legal concepts may embody social practices and understandings that exist outside the law; and that by studying legal concepts that have counterparts outside the law, we might learn something about those extra-legal social practices, as well as something about the law. In the process, of course, we must be alert to the possibility that the nature and content of extra-legal normative concepts may change when they are brought into the law. But this is no reason to ignore the law in seeking to understand widely used normative concepts.

Viewing the relationship between law and morality as being symbiotic in this way also opens up the possibility that just as we may appeal to morality to tell us what the law ought to be, so we may appeal to the law as providing a pointer to sound thinking in the moral sphere.[46] For instance, many would argue that by its rejection of capital punishment, English law takes a position superior to a strong strand in its favour in "popular morality". In other areas, too, some might want to argue that the law is, in some respects at least, a "moral exemplar". Anti-discrimination law and environmental law provide plausible examples. It is easy to think of instances when the law has been changed in response to changes in "popular morality". But equally, law can influence the way people think in the moral sphere. In Hart's words:

> "legal enactments may set standards of honesty and humanity which ultimately alter and raise the current morality; conversely, legal repression of practices thought morally obligatory may, in the end, cause . . . their status as morality to be lost; yet, very often, law loses such battles with ingrained morality, and the moral rule continues in full vigour side by side with laws which forbid what it enjoins."[47]

A second problem with the "separatist" approach to the relationship between law and morality is that it gives little or no weight to the fact of moral disagreement. As Jeremy Waldron puts it, moral discourse is characterised by "difference, controversy and disagreement".[48] Difference of opinion is endemic to the moral domain. If moral disagreements are deep and important, social conflict may result if people are free to act in accordance with their own moral opinions. One way of controlling such conflict is for the law to adopt a position on the issue in question and to use its institutional power to enforce compliance with that position.[49] Of course, the law's intervention does not resolve the moral disagreement, and it may not eliminate social conflict.[50] But in a democratic society, even those who think that the law is morally wrong have a (moral) reason (although, of course, not a conclusive reason) to respect and comply with it. By virtue of its institutional resources, the law can ameliorate the potentially negative social effects of moral disagreement.

[46] Similarly Raz (1982), 933–6.

[47] Hart (1961), 177. See also Robinson and Darley (1997).

[48] Waldron (2000), 43.

[49] Honoré (1993). See also Raz (1979), 50–2.

[50] Witness the instance of abortion law in the USA. Views about abortion are so polarised that there seems little prospect of legally-driven accommodation.

This argument can be pushed a little further and stated more positively. Productive and fulfilling social interaction is possible only within a framework of agreed norms and behaviour. When people disagree (as they frequently do) about the norms according to which social life ought to be conducted, law provides a mechanism for making and enforcing choices amongst competing views. The contribution it can make to facilitating cooperative and productive social life gives those whose views are not embodied in the law a reason to comply with it regardless of the dissonance between what it requires and their own vision of the ideal society. Even where there is widespread agreement in the moral domain, law can, by reason of its institutional resources, provide valuable reinforcement to morality. In other words, law can be (and is) used to make up for morality's institutional poverty. In this way, the law can be what Braithwaite calls a "moral educator".[51] The fact that the law may provide us with reasons for action in these ways reinforces the point that we should not ignore the law in seeking to understand complex concepts such as responsibility.

There is yet another respect in which law and morality are in symbiosis or, as Honoré puts it, in which morality may be dependent on law. Sometimes we *need* the law in order to identify the morally right thing to do.[52] The reason is that morality:

> "has to be based on values that can be defended as worth pursuing. But these values are so general that they do not by themselves determine how people should behave in a given instance. We can seldom proceed by a process of deduction from the values to the required behaviour".[53]

For example, says Honoré, although members of a community have a moral obligation to pay taxes, "apart from the law no one has a moral obligation to pay any particular amount of tax".[54] The underlying point is that law possesses institutional resources that morality lacks, and these enable it to answer detailed questions about responsibility, for instance.

To the extent that such answers are morally acceptable, they supplement and become part of morality. To the extent that such an answer is itself contentious, it can contribute to social stability and cooperation by providing an authoritative guide to behaviour for those who disagree with the answer as for those who agree with it.

1.4 MORAL REASONING AND LEGAL REASONING

The basic argument in 1.3 is that the relationship between law and morality is symbiotic. This is especially so in relation to complex concepts such as responsibility:

[51] Braithwaite (1987), 569. See also Robinson and Darley (1997).
[52] Honoré (1993). See also Finnis (1980), 284–9.
[53] *Ibid.*, 4.
[54] *Ibid.*, 5.

moral ideas about responsibility are absorbed into the law, and the law influences the way people think about responsibility in the moral domain. Because law is highly institutionalised and morality is not, there are certain obvious differences between the way legal and moral concepts of responsibility are developed. Nevertheless, the argument in this section will be that when courts develop rules and principles about responsibility, they are engaged in essentially the same reasoning processes as people use in the moral domain when developing rules and principles about responsibility.

1.4.1 Practical and analytical reasoning

For the purposes of this book, "legal reasoning" refers primarily to judicial reasoning directed to the formulation of common law rules and principles. Law-making is the prime function of appellate courts, whereas dispute resolution and law application is the prime function of "trial" courts. In many Anglian jurisdictions there are several levels of appellate courts. In the present context, the legal reasoning of "final" appellate courts is of the most importance and interest because such courts are least bound to give authoritative weight to decisions of other courts and to their own earlier decisions; and, consequently, most at liberty to base their law-making on arguments that they consider to be "the best", regardless of whether they can be found in the legal literature. In particular, final appellate courts are freer and more willing to appeal to "morality" in relation to issues such as responsibility. However, the degree of constraint imposed on lower-level appellate courts by the principles of *stare decisis* and the rules of precedent should not be exaggerated. Except in rare cases, relevant judicial reasoning exerts no more than a persuasive influence on any appellate court, and it usually leaves ample room for consideration of arguments not drawn from or developed in the existing "authoritative" legal literature.[55]

By "moral reasoning" I mean reasoning that takes place in the non-institutionalised environment of the domain of morality. It is useful to distinguish between what we might call "practical moral reasoning" on the one hand, and "analytical moral reasoning" on the other. By "practical reasoning" I mean reasoning directed towards developing moral rules and principles to govern one's own and other people's conduct.[56] By "analytical reasoning" I refer to analysis of moral rules, principles and practices. Analytical reasoning may be concerned, for instance, with understanding how we use moral language and how we understand moral concepts, both in general and in relation to particular moral language and concepts. It may also be concerned with the nature of practical moral reasoning in general, and with the quality of particular examples of moral reasoning—concerning responsibility, for instance. This distinction is

[55] Reasoning by analogy is important in this context. See 1.4.3.

[56] Jamieson (1991), 479–80.

important for my purposes because I want to suggest that insofar as legal reasoning appeals to morality as a source of legal rules and principles, it is in one way analogous to analytical moral reasoning, and in another to practical moral reasoning. It is analogous to practical moral reasoning by virtue of the fact that in laying down legal rules and principles judges are purporting to establish norms for their own and other people's behaviour. Judges, as well as citizens, are subject to the legal rules and principles they lay down.

However, for reasons related to ideas of democracy and separation of powers, it is not an acceptable justification for any particular judge-made rule or principle that the judge who made it thinks that it ought to be the law. This is one reason why *stare decisis* and precedent are important constraints on judicial law-making, and why ideas such as consistency and coherence play such an important role in judicial reasoning.[57] One way in which judges may attempt to justify their law-making is by reference to social practice and "community values". It is not unusual for judges to appeal to "commonsense morality", or "ordinary usage", or what "the ordinary person" thinks and does, in order to resolve normative controversies.[58]

In its emphasis on consistency and coherence, and in its appeal to community values, judicial reasoning designed to justify particular legal rules and principles bears notable similarities to philosophical analysis designed to provide an account of moral concepts. Philosophers, too, often start with "commonsense" assumptions and intuitions. For instance, Michael Bratman begins his well-known book on intention[59] by saying that "much of our understanding of ourselves and others is rooted in a commonsense psychological framework", and the word "commonsense" is used liberally throughout the book to describe the concepts Bratman is analysing. The philosophical technique of "reflective equilibrium" involves working such intuitions, convictions and judgments about a particular moral issue into a coherent analytical framework, discarding along the way any that do not "fit". At its best, legal reasoning by final appellate courts about complex concepts seeks a reflective equilibrium.[60]

An important difference between judicial and philosophical use of the technique (apart from the fact that philosophers tend to use it more self-consciously and rigorously) lies in the respective starting points. Courts have at their disposal a large literature containing rules, principles and judgments that provide raw materials for the equilibrium-seeking exercise. Because morality lacks an equivalent literature, and because few philosophers take advantage of the legal literature, the starting points for the philosophical equilibrium-seeking exercise tend to be self-generated, a product of the theorist's own observations and speculations. To the extent that any particular court is "bound" by precedents found in the literature, it may not be free to discard rules, principles or judgments that

[57] MacCormick (1994).

[58] I will use the term "commonsense" to cover this constellation of related ideas.

[59] Bratman (1987).

[60] See also Sunstein (1996), 17–19, 32–3.

cannot be fitted into a larger theoretical framework. But as I said earlier, the strength of this constraint should not be overestimated. Anyway, final appellate courts are typically free to discard any precedent they choose, and to follow the equilibrium-seeking procedure in essentially the same way as philosophers do.

Because the purpose of judicial law-making is different from the purpose of conceptual analysis, appeals to commonsense and social practice serve different purposes in the two contexts. In the context of judicial law-making the appeal to social practice is in pursuit of normative legitimacy, whereas in the context of conceptual analysis, it is in pursuit of epistemological validity. The assumption underlying judicial appeals to common sense is that the law ought to embody community values on matters such as responsibility; [61] whereas the assumption underlying philosophical appeals to common sense[62] is that widely-held ideas about responsibility, for instance, are likely to contain more than a grain of "truth" about the nature of responsibility.

The notion of "commonsense" is problematic for several reasons.[63] For one thing, it is ambiguous. It may mean no more than "widely held" or "shared". In that case, the word is used to make an empirical claim for which the judge or philosopher typically provides, and can provide, little or no support beyond their own intuitions and observations.[64] But "commonsense" is often also used evaluatively as a term of approval; and its use may act as a conduit to transfer that approval from the practice being analysed to the analysis itself, thus placing certain aspects of the analysis beyond debate, and begging questions about the truth or the normative desirability of the analyst's conclusions. Branding a particular view of the world as being "commonsense" at least raises a presumption that it is right and desirable. Unfortunately, the history of the human race is littered with empirical and normative propositions that were common sense to an earlier generation and nonsense to a later.[65]

A related problem with "commonsense" is that although, at a high level of generality or abstraction, there might be wide agreement about the nature and desirability of social practices, such as responsibility practices, there may be much less agreement about the details of such practices. This insight is particularly important for an understanding of common law concepts because they are bred of more-or-less small-scale disputes about legal liability. The existence of a dispute about the meaning of a normative legal concept proves that there is some level of disagreement about the concept; and provided the disputants can all make a "reasonable" argument in favour of the result they each desire, there seems no reason to prefer one result to the other on the basis that one deserves

[61] Bell (1983), ch. VII.

[62] As opposed to sociological or anthropological *descriptions* of "folk-morality".

[63] See also Lloyd-Bostock (1979) and (1984).

[64] The area of psychological research known as "attribution theory" is concerned with such empirical claims about responsibility. See e.g. Schultz and Schleifer (1983); Lloyd-Bostock (1983); Shaver (1985).

[65] Many values are also culturally specific. But this is not of great concern in the present context because so is a great deal of the law.

the description "commonsense" while the other does not.[66] However useful the language of "commonsense" may be to philosophers, we should be very wary of its use in legal contexts.

The analogy between judicial reasoning and *practical* moral reasoning is explored by Thomas Perry. Perry argues that there are several criteria of "reasonable reflection" on matters of morality: that all relevant facts should be taken into account; that our moral judgment should be made when we are in a psychologically normal state; that our judgment should be disinterested, i.e. impartial and universalisable; and that our arguments should be "sincere"—that is, the ones that we consider to be the "correct" ones, and not just arguments that allow us to reach the judgment "we want to defend".[67] These criteria he calls "the procedural requirements of moral rationality". Perry then suggests that "the major criteria of good reflection and argumentation" for judicial reasoning in cases in which the existing legal materials provide "no uniquely correct or true decision" are "practically identical" to the criteria of sound moral reasoning.[68] Cases of the sort Perry refers to are often called "hard cases", in order to distinguish them from "easy cases", which can be straightforwardly resolved by the application of an existing relevant rule of law to the facts of the case. In terms of the earlier discussion, the resolution of hard cases involves law-making through adjudication.

Cases can be hard for a number of reasons: because several intersecting or conflicting legal rules or principles are relevant to the facts of the case; because the existing legal materials contain no rule or principle relevant to those facts; or because, on reflection, existing relevant rules or principles seem no longer acceptable either at all or without some modification. Situations requiring moral judgment may, says Perry, present us with "hard" choices for similar reasons. In hard cases, judges should make themselves aware of all relevant facts and legal principles, they should be impartial and have no personal interest in the outcome; and they should reach the decision which they sincerely believe to be correct. Even so, argues Perry, as compared with individuals engaging in moral reasoning, judges deciding hard cases are less free to fashion new legal rules, and to modify and reject existing ones, because of their role-responsibility to respond to individual cases in ways that are consistent and coherent with the rest of the law, and because of the undemocratic nature of judicial law-making.

Perry's aim in comparing legal and moral reasoning is to provide support for an argument that if the procedure by which they were arrived at meets certain criteria, substantive judgments about difficult normative issues are "rationally justified" in a way that gives them a certain objectivity or validity. The success, or otherwise, of this project is of no immediate concern. It is not part of my

[66] In a normatively pluralistic society, appeals to shared values to resolve disputes at relatively low levels of abstraction are treacherous. A controversial concept from this point of view is "dishonesty": Ashworth (1999), 394–8.

[67] Perry (1976), ch. 2.

[68] Perry (1976), ch. 4.

argument that moral and legal judgments about responsibility are "objectively" valid in some sense. For my purposes, the interest of Perry's analysis lies in its suggestion that when judges engage directly in reasoning about normative issues relevant to the resolution of individual cases in the legal domain, they undertake essentially the same activity as people engaging in such reasoning in the moral domain; and that "reasoning performances" (as Perry puts it) can be judged by the same criteria in both domains. Of course, judgments about normative issues in the legal domain are authoritative, in a way that judgments in the moral domain are not, because they are underwritten by the coercive power of the state. This, no doubt, makes it all the more important that the reasoning performances of judges should satisfy the criteria of "good reflection and argumentation". But it does not, I think, weaken the analogy between normative reasoning in the legal domain and normative reasoning in the moral domain.

Do the constraints on judicial freedom mentioned by Perry seriously weaken the analogy? The three criteria of good argumentation suggested by Perry are adequate information, impartiality[69] and sincerity. The constraints on judicial freedom arise from the demands of consistency and coherence, and from the "democratic deficit" that afflicts judicial law-making. There is no obvious reason why either of these constraints should affect the ability of judges to be adequately informed or impartial. At first sight, however, sincerity may seem to present more difficulty. What sincerity basically requires is that our judgments should follow from what we sincerely believe to be the best arguments; and conversely, that we should not adopt what we think to be "second-best" arguments for the sake of justifying some desired judgment. The requirements of consistency and coherence need not impair sincerity in this sense because they are not absolutes. The law never requires a judge to sacrifice "justice" on the altar of consistency or coherence. Consistency and coherence are aspects of justice, but they do not exhaust it.

Suppose the reason that a judge gives for making a particular judgment is not that it is supported by what the judge considers to be the best arguments, but rather that (according to the rules of precedent and *stare decisis*) the "authority" of some earlier decision requires it; or because (considering the democratic deficit under which courts labour) the judgment supported by best arguments is beyond the law-making competence of the courts. In such cases, does the court contravene the requirement of sincerity? Surely not. On the contrary, the court sincerely acknowledges that it is not giving effect to what it considers to be the best arguments.[70] What these examples show is that certain values—notably predictability and stability—are more important in the legal domain than in the moral domain. There are, perhaps, three reasons for this. First, many conflicts

[69] I use this word as a shorthand for a cluster of desiderata: the judgment should be disinterested and universal in application, and the decision-maker should be impartial and have no personal stake in the outcome.

[70] I leave aside problems created by wicked legal systems. See Hart (1982), 150–1; Mureinik (1988), 206–14.

and disagreements that can be left unresolved in the moral domain have to be resolved once they enter the legal domain. Secondly, law is underwritten by the coercive power of the state. Thirdly, the lack of law-making institutions in the moral domain more or less rules out sudden changes in direction of the sort of which courts are capable. These differences both reflect and are reflected in the different institutional terrain of the two domains.

In fact, I think that the institutional constraints under which courts labour do create a problem of insincerity, but in a quite different sense from Perry's. They do not lead judges to use what they believe to be second-best arguments in order to support judgments that they want to defend. Rather they often lead judges to use second-best arguments to support judgments that they believe are actually supported by the best arguments. As a result of fears that they will be thought partial in their judgments, or that they will be accused of having trespassed into the policy-making and law-making domain of the executive and the legislature, judges (in jurisdictions such as England and Australia, at least) have traditionally been rather coy about expressing the "moral" or "policy" arguments that they believe best support their judgments, and have tended to fall back, whenever possible, on arguments from authority, and on the use of syllogistic reasoning using major premises derived from the legal literature. Indeed, it was only in 1966 that the English House of Lords freed itself (in principle at least) from the "obligation" to follow *its own* previous decisions. One result of this is that discerning the substantive (as opposed to the authority-based) reasons for judicial decisions often requires interpretation and speculation. For this reason, and because law-making through adjudication is necessarily piecemeal and episodic, "doctrinal analysis" of judicial decisions remains an enduringly important form of academic endeavour, designed to produce the best possible account (in terms of consistency and coherence) of the values underlying the rules and principles of the common law.

We may conclude that the criteria of good legal reasoning and of good moral reasoning about complex concepts are essentially similar in many respects.[71] On the other hand, judgments based on legal reasoning are authoritative in a way that judgments based on moral reasoning are not. Moreover, judges may, to some extent, be constrained by their institutional obligations to make decisions that are supported by authority but not by what they consider to be the best arguments independently of authority; and to support their decisions by authority-based arguments when better substantive arguments are available. However, we should not exaggerate the extent to which consistency, coherence, stability and predictability are more important in law than in morality. In the first place, consistency and coherence in normative reasoning are values of general application—they are not peculiar to law.[72] Secondly, the all-things-considered ideal of moral reasoning that underlies much moral theorising (in which authority, habit,

[71] Miller (1976), 56.

[72] Similarly: Lloyd-Bostock (1983), 277; Nussbaum (2000), 240–1, 246–7. But some particularists would not agree: Hooker (2000), 5–6 discussing Dancy's views.

tradition, past practice, and the like, play no role) is more preached than practised. Many people place importance on tradition in morality, and some even recognise moral authorities. Thirdly, the all-things-considered model gives an impractical and unrealistic account of day-to-day normative decision-making.[73] In real life, most aspects of the normative structure of our lives remain unexamined except when extreme circumstances occur that call them into question. Without a broad and thick normative bedrock, our moral lives would become intolerably unstable, uncertain and unpredictable, and moral decision-making would become inordinately time-consuming. For most people, most of the time, most moral questions remain firmly closed. In this respect, law mirrors morality.

1.4.2 Context and levels of abstraction

An important difference between much philosophical analysis of complex concepts on the one hand, and judicial reasoning on the other, is that the latter typically takes place in the context of a particular dispute between particular parties, whereas the former is more or less acontextual and abstract. In relation to responsibility, for instance, the question confronting a judge is never, what do we mean by "responsibility"? or even, "what are our responsibilities"? but rather "by what rule or principle should the dispute about responsibility, which has arisen between these two parties, be resolved"? In order to answer that question the judge must decide what are the respective responsibilities of the particular parties before the court in the particular circumstances of their dispute. Judicial reasoning about moral concepts is typically contextualised and concrete. By contrast, much philosophical analysis purports to provide a general or abstract account of a concept such as responsibility without reference to any particular social group, any particular point in time, or any particular set of human values or purposes.[74] The temporal, human and social context of much philosophical analysis is left more or less indeterminate.[75] This characteristic of philosophical analysis finds its most dramatic expression in the so-called "thought experiment". Thought experiments are the philosophical analogue of controlled scientific laboratory experiments. They are hypothetical fact situations stripped of any extraneous features that might get in the way of or confuse the analysis of the particular point the philosopher is seeking to establish. For this reason, the situations imagined in thought experiments are often deliberately bizarre and unreal; and like the economists' assumption of perfect rationality, this may raise questions about the validity, outside the precise frame of the analysis itself, of any conclusions drawn by the analyst.[76]

[73] Similarly: Dennett (1984), 70.

[74] According to Lloyd-Bostock (Lloyd-Bostock (1983)), much psychological research into attribution of responsibility suffers from a similar lack of attention to social context.

[75] Similarly: Lacey (1998), 14–17.

[76] For discussion of (the limitations of) this technique see Wilkes (1988), ch. 1; Jamieson (1991), 484–5.

Marion Smiley argues that the acontextual and abstract quality of what she calls "the modern concept of moral responsibility" is the result of looking for our understanding of responsibility in naturalistic ideas of "human agency" and "will" rather than in religious ideas of sin, or in social practices, such as allocating praise and blame.[77] The "modern" approach to responsibility is most often traced back to the work of Immanuel Kant, and it has very influential contemporary followers not only amongst philosophers but also amongst legal theorists such as Ernest Weinrib.[78] Their basic insight is that responsibility is not something we ascribe or attribute to human beings but is, rather, intrinsic to, and part of what we mean by, being a human agent with free will. Even if responsibility is not part of the furniture of the universe, it is certainly part of the constitution of human beings—a fundamental human characteristic, as it were. We are responsible, and only responsible, for conduct that is a "free" expression of our will. According to this account, responsibility is a matter of fact, not of social construction. It is natural, not conventional. Understanding responsibility, on this view, is an empirical, not an evaluative, exercise.

This concentration on agency and will as the source of responsibility creates a number of theoretical problems which, if taken seriously, cast doubts on the "rationality" of many, if not all, of our responsibility practices. One problem is causal determinism. On the one hand, it might seem that if the universe is deterministic, and everything we do is caused by some prior state of the world, we are not "truly" responsible for anything we do because nothing we do is an expression of our "free" (i.e. undetermined) will. In a deterministic world, agents, being deprived of "alternate possibilities", would always be able to say, "I could not have done otherwise". On the other hand, if the world is not entirely deterministic, and some of our conduct is uncaused and, in that sense, "random", this too might seem to undermine responsibility because uncaused events cannot be an expression of our free will either. A large philosophical literature addresses the problem of reconciling responsibility with the possibility that the universe is or is not deterministic. It contains a wide variety of views about whether the problem is soluble, and if so, in what way. Another problem for "modernists" is group responsibility. If responsibility is an expression of individual free will, it is hard to see how we can attribute responsibility to a group as opposed to individuals in that group. A third problem concerns the scope of responsibility. Some "modernists" argue that we can only be "truly" responsible for "intentional" conduct[79] because only such conduct is an expression of our free will. Others see liability for negligence as compatible with the modern review of responsibility.[80] All modernists have more or less difficulty with the idea of "moral" (i.e. "true" or "real") responsibility without fault.

[77] Smiley (1992).
[78] e.g. Weinrib (1995).
[79] Mackie (1977), 208–215.
[80] Weinrib (1995).

In practice, however, worries about whether or not the universe is deterministic do not prevent us from holding ourselves and others "truly" responsible. We do not attach to our practical judgments of responsibility a proviso about the truth of determinism. In practice, too, the ideas of group responsibility and responsibility without fault do not present insuperable problems either in law or morals. I will deal with each of these points in greater detail later.[81] There is a psychological reason why the issues of free will and determinism do not constrain our moral and legal responsibility practices in the way modernists suggest they should. Even if it were proved that the universe is deterministic, a psychological need[82] to feel a certain degree of control over our surroundings and our lives and not to surrender to fatalism would probably preserve our present responsibility practices more or less intact.[83] Because of the independence of our responsibility practices from the truth about determinism, it is valuable to examine and analyse those practices without reference to the problem of determinism; and that is what I will do in this book.

In contrast to the modernist approach to responsibility, my analysis is both contextual and concrete. It is rooted in and based on a specific body of literature, and that literature is the product of an identified set of social practices. These practices have an identifiable cultural and temporal context, and they perform social functions the general identity of which is a matter of wide agreement, even if the details are contested. Because one of the basic functions of our legal practices is dispute resolution, the literature of the common law contains myriad accounts of real-life fact situations. And because another of the basic functions of legal practices is law-making, the literature of the common law contains extensive discussion of concepts and principles (including responsibility) developed through reflection on real-life fact situations. Because they relate to a specific, identified set of social practices, accounts of legal concepts, such as responsibility, are often thought of as yielding "applied" rather than "pure" theory. In one sense, this is obviously true. However, we should be wary of claims to general validity made for analyses of complex concepts that are the result of acontextual reflection. The concept of responsibility, for instance, is used in various social contexts. It may be that there are some characteristics common to all of these usages which, in that sense, might be called "acontextual". But in order to identify such common characteristics, it would first be necessary to reflect on responsibility in its various contexts. And, of course, it is only by contextual reflection on a concept such as responsibility that we could identify context-specific usages and practices.

[81] Concerning determinism see 3.2; group responsibility, ch. 5; and strict responsibility, 3.6.3.5.

[82] Which may be partly natural and partly nurtured. Certainly, individuals and cultures vary by degree of fatalism.

[83] Similarly: Fischer (1999), 129–30; Fischer and Ravizza (1998), 14–16; Dennett (1984), 108. My approach here is well described by Young (speaking of Strawson) as focusing "on what is essential to the moral life and not on the intellectual niceties of metaphysics": Young (1991), 539.

Context-specific (or "context-determinate") reflection on responsibility is not only helpful, but indeed essential to a proper understanding of our responsibility practices and their associated concepts and language. We should allow of the possibility that the language of "responsibility" does not mark a homogeneous practice and concept best illuminated by context-indeterminate reflection, but rather that it marks a variegated and heterogeneous set of practices and concepts which can only be fully understood by context-determinate analyses. In this spirit, this book offers a context-specific analysis of the responsibility practices and concepts embedded in Anglian common law.

I am not suggesting that legal responsibility practices should be treated as in some sense more central or typical than other responsibility practices. Rather I am suggesting that responsibility might be a heterogeneous, context-specific practice and concept; and that if this is indeed the case, context-specific study of legal responsibility will enrich our understanding of responsibility more generally.

1.4.3 Deduction, induction and analogy

An important aim of both legal reasoning and moral reasoning is to develop rules and principles that can serve as the premises of deductive arguments on the basis of which individual cases can be dealt with in a consistent way. In the moral domain, we often attempt to derive and justify rules and principles by deduction from more abstract concepts such as equality, or liberty, or responsibility. By contrast, common law rules and principles are much more likely to be developed by induction than by deduction. Reasoning by analogy also plays a large role in the legal domain. Whereas deductive reasoning proceeds from the general to the particular, inductive reasoning proceeds from the particular to the general, and analogical reasoning proceeds from the particular to the particular by identifying similarities and differences.[84] In the common law, analogical reasoning is typically a prelude to deductive reasoning. The purpose of analogies is to classify particular cases as falling under one rule or principle rather than another.[85]

The emphasis in legal reasoning on individual cases—on the particular as opposed to the general—is explicable by the fact that judicial law-making typically takes place as an adjunct to the resolution of disputes between individuals. In the common law there is a constant tension between the desirability (for the sake of consistency and predictability) of developing rules and principles by extrapolation from individual cases, and the desirability of preserving flexibility to deal with new and unexpected circumstances. The pressure not to generalise

[84] White (1999).

[85] Reasoning by analogy plays an important role in enabling courts to escape the gravitational force of precedent. By finding a relevant difference between the case at hand and any previously decided case, the court may create space for itself to fashion a new rule or principle to decide the case; or, at least, to modify or qualify an existing one.

is reflected, for instance, in the principle that judicial rule-formulations should not be treated as if they had the canonical authority of statutes; and in the warning that decisions on standard of care in the tort of negligence should not be treated as creating duties of care.[86] Judges tend to be wary of laying down rules and principles that are wider than is necessary to resolve the dispute before the court, for fear that the precedential force of the rule (whatever that may be) might make it difficult or impossible for some other court to resolve some later dispute, with unforeseen features, in the way that seems best independently of precedent. Perhaps the absence of this institutional constraint on reasoning in the moral sphere makes us more ready to derive rules by deduction from concepts and principles that are even more abstract. It may be, too, that we are attracted to very abstract principles and concepts in moral argumentation partly because of a feeling that agreement is more likely at this level than at the level of individual cases, and because we can often afford to leave concrete moral disputes unresolved. In the legal domain, by contrast, disputes have to be resolved, and lawyers perhaps think that people are more likely to be able to agree about the right way of resolving a concrete dispute than about a general principle covering that and a range of other types of dispute. I am not arguing that induction plays no part in moral reasoning, but only that it plays a larger role in legal than in moral reasoning.

This feeling that people who disagree at the level of abstract principles may nevertheless agree about how to deal with individual cases perhaps also partly explains the prevalence of analogical reasoning in the common law.[87] Agreement that case B falls under rule X may be more readily forthcoming if it is agreed that case B is analogous in relevant respects to case A, and that case A falls under rule X, than if it were simply argued, deductively, that case B falls under rule X. Horizontal, analogical reasoning used as a prelude to deduction may be a more effective way of determining the agreed scope of rules and principles than vertical deductive reasoning on its own.

Historically, the significant role played by analogical reasoning in the common law has formed the basis of claims that the common law is autonomous and independent of other normative systems.[88] A modern exponent of this view is Charles Fried.[89] His basic argument is that pure philosophical analysis of concepts such as "rights" or "responsibility" operates at too high a level of abstraction to provide resources for the resolution of concrete disputes such as regularly confront the courts. His contention is that reasoning by analogy is needed to work out the detailed application of abstract normative concepts:

> "The picture I have, then, is of philosophy proposing an elaborate structure of arguments and considerations which descend from on high but stop some twenty feet above the ground. It is the peculiar task of law to complete it so that it is seated firmly

[86] Trindade and Cane (1999), 461–2.
[87] Sunstein (1996), ch. 3.
[88] See Postema (1986).
[89] Fried (1981).

> and concretely . . . The lofty philosophical edifice does not *determine* what the last twenty feet are, yet if the legal foundation is to support the whole, then values and ideals must constrain, limit, inform and inspire the foundation—but no more. The law really is an independent, distinct part of the structure of value".[90]

I agree with Fried that reasoning by analogy plays an essential part in working out how abstract "values and ideals" apply in concrete cases. Analogy, says Fried, is "the application of . . . intuition where the manifold of particulars is too extensive to allow our minds to work on it deductively". Analogy "fills in the gaps left by more general theory, gaps which must be filled because choices must be made and actions taken". However, I do not agree with his further conclusion that the prevalence of analogy in legal reasoning renders law "a relatively autonomous subject".[91] For one thing, reasoning by analogy is a much more characteristic feature of judicial reasoning than of reasoning that precedes and supports law-making by legislatures.

This contrast between reasoning of courts and legislatures perhaps points to the most fundamental reason why analogy is a characteristic feature of judicial reasoning, namely that the prime function of courts is to settle concrete disputes, not to make general rules. In other words, reasoning by analogy is characteristic of "low-level" normative reasoning. This might lead us to expect that analogy would play a larger part in practical than in analytical moral reasoning. People who are confronted with the need to resolve concrete disputes and problems in the moral domain are more likely to resort to analogy than theorists concerned with the grand architecture of morality, who have no responsibility to apply moral rules and principles to concrete cases in a timely fashion. Reasoning by analogy is likely to be a feature of everyday moral reasoning directed to the resolution of concrete problems and disputes, just as it is a characteristic feature of legal reasoning.

Even so, there is a practical reason why inductive reasoning and reasoning by analogy can play a more prominent role in the legal domain than in either everyday practical moral reasoning or in analytical moral reasoning. If reasoning by induction and analogy is to be at all complex, and if it is to have any chance of generating a coherent and consistent body of rules and judgments over time, there must be a well-documented body of "precedents" with which analogies can be drawn and against which the quality of rules derived by induction from concrete cases can be tested. The average human mind lacks the powers of memory that would be needed for a complex system of inductive and analogical reasoning, without the support of a reasonably comprehensive and reliable set of records of precedent judgments about concrete disputes. This would be true even in a system in which all decisions were made by one and the same decision-maker. It is all the more true in a system in which there are many decision-makers, and which persists for a period longer than the professional lifetime of

[90] *Ibid.*, 57 (original emphasis).
[91] *Ibid.*, 38.

any one generation of decision-makers. By virtue of being a highly documented system of reasoning, the common law possesses institutional resources for complex normative reasoning by induction and analogy that are lacking in the moral domain.

Far from making the common law an autonomous normative domain, its documentary character and its consequent capacity to support complex inductive and analogical reasoning make it capable of supplementing moral reasoning by working out the detailed implications of general rules and principles, and of abstract concepts. Just as the common law supplements legislation by interpreting and applying its general provisions in concrete cases, so the common law can show how general moral principles that have been absorbed into the law may apply in concrete cases. These detailed legal applications of moral principles may in turn influence thinking in the moral domain. The written materials of the common law provide a uniquely rich resource for studying the detailed application of complex concepts. For this reason alone, the common law deserves our close attention. Far from offering a distorted or tainted image of values and ideals developed in the moral domain, it may enable us to give concrete content and application to those values and ideals.

In sum, because of its focus on resolving disputes and its rich documentary resources, the common law is an important net contributor to the normative life of society, and an indispensable source of understanding about complex concepts such as responsibility. More particularly, while responsibility in law is not all there is to responsibility, no account of responsibility can be complete without it. Legal institutions play an important role in developing and maintaining society's responsibility concepts and practices.

1.5 SUMMARY

The discussion in this chapter has primarily been concerned with the relationships between law and morality and between moral and legal reasoning. It has been based on an institutional account of the domains of law and morality. I have argued that the relationship between law and morality (each being understood in this institutional way) is symbiotic. I have suggested that essentially similar criteria of sound reasoning about complex concepts apply in both the moral and the legal domains. By virtue of its institutional resources, law makes a distinctive and important contribution to the development of the rich tapestry of our responsibility concepts and practices. Consequently, study of responsibility in law is just as indispensable for a thorough understanding of responsibility as is study of moral responsibility. By focusing on responsibility in law, this book offers a contribution to our understanding of responsibility, full stop.

2

The Nature and Functions of Responsibility

IN CHAPTER 1 it was argued that studying legal responsibility concepts and practices can contribute to our understanding of responsibility more generally. In this chapter I begin the study of legal responsibility by considering some general issues about the nature and functions of responsibility in law.

2.1 VARIETIES OF RESPONSIBILITY

2.1.1 Hart's taxonomy

The most famous taxonomy of responsibility is that of Herbert Hart in *Punishment and Responsibility*.[1] Hart identifies five types of responsibility. Role responsibility refers to two related notions of responsibility: one, as in "the manager is responsible for making the players' travel arrangements"; the other as in "she is a responsible manager", meaning something like "she takes her responsibilities as manager seriously". Causal responsibility can be attributed not only to human beings but also to animals, events, and so on; in fact, to any causally efficacious factor. Legal liability responsibility refers to responsibility-based conditions of legal liability[2]—for instance, to pay compensation, or restitution, or to be imprisoned or pay a fine. Moral liability responsibility is analogous to legal liability responsibility, the differences between the two residing in the conditions for incurring each respectively. Capacity responsibility refers to the minimum mental and physical capacities a person must possess if they are to be properly made the subject of attributions of moral or legal liability responsibility. Hart's view was that liability responsibility—"answering or rebutting accusations or charges which, if established, carr[y] liability to punishment or blame or other adverse treatment"[3]—is the "primary sense" of responsibility.

For my purposes, Hart's account is unsatisfactory for several reasons. First, his discussion of legal responsibility is primarily focused on criminal law. It ignores both civil law (contract, tort, restitution, and so on) and public law (administrative law in particular). Secondly, he does not integrate the notions of

[1] Hart (1968), 211–30.

[2] Not all conditions of legal liability are responsibility-based: see 1.1 and 2.6.

[3] Hart (1968), 265.

role responsibility, causal responsibility and capacity responsibility into the discussion of legal liability responsibility and moral liability responsibility, or explain the relationships between the various types of responsibility. From this point of view, Kurt Baier's account is better because he sets out to demonstrate the part played by various notions of responsibility in a dynamic practice of bringing people to account.[4] For Baier, capacity (which he calls "accountability") and role responsibility (which he calls "task responsibility") are "presuppositions" of liability; while "answerability" (which is a function of accountability and failure to satisfy an "obligatory social requirement") raises a "presumption" of liability. "Culpability" is a "sufficient condition" of liability, and is present when a person is answerable "without adequate excuse". However, from my point of view, Baier's account suffers from being contextually indeterminate; and the practice he describes is hypothetical. A prime contention of this book is that study of actual and contextually determinate responsibility practices can contribute to our understanding of responsibility generally.

A third problem with Hart's account resides in his view that liability to incur a sanction[5] is the core sense of responsibility. Some writers[6] reject this view and find the essence of responsibility in the idea of having to answer for something, or of giving an account. Nevertheless, for them, as for Hart, responsibility is essentially backward-looking. The rejection of the centrality of sanctions seems right. People may rightly take responsibility and be held responsible even if no sanction will be incurred as a result.[7] However, putting the emphasis on accountability[8] also seems to me unduly restrictive. For one thing, it suggests a focus on bad outcomes; whereas a person can be responsible, and claim responsibility, for good outcomes as well as bad. More importantly, the backward-looking orientation of both sanctions and accountability tends to conceal the importance, both within the law and elsewhere, of what I shall call "prospective responsibility". In Hart's account, this finds its place in the idea of "role responsibility"; but he views this as a derivative form of responsibility. This approach ignores the fact that law is just as, if not more, concerned with telling us what our responsibilities are, and with encouraging us to act responsibly, as with holding us accountable and sanctioning us in case we do not fulfil our responsibilities. On the other hand, I do not want to deny the role of sanctions in the law. Indeed, I will argue later that the importance of sanctions in the legal domain provides one reason why legal practices are a fruitful subject of study for the analyst of responsibility.

[4] Baier (1970).

[5] Hart is, of course, famous for his attack on Austin's sanction-based theory of law: Hart (1961), ch. 2. But sanctions play an important part in Hart's theory of duty (Hacker (1973)), and in his account of responsibility.

[6] e.g. Haydon (1978), 55; Honoré (1999), 125, n. 11.

[7] Indeed, this is the force of the distinction between responsibility and liability. For instance, a person may be responsible for harm but immune from liability to repair the harm.

[8] In the sense of "answerability", not in Baier's sense of "capacity".

The aim in the first part of this chapter (2.1) is to give a taxonomic account of responsibility that can provide a more helpful framework for understanding legal responsibility concepts and practices than is provided by Hart. Then (in 2.2 to 2.4) I examine several aspects of legal responsibility practices that are of importance to understanding responsibility generally. The chapter ends (in 2.5 to 2.6) with discussion of the functions of law and legal responsibility practices.

2.1.2 The temporal element in responsibility

2.1.2.1 Historic and prospective responsibility

In a temporal sense, responsibility looks in two directions. Ideas such as accountability, answerability and liability look backwards to conduct and events in the past. They form the core of what I shall call "historic responsibility". By contrast, the ideas of roles and tasks look to the future, and establish obligations and duties[9]—"prospective responsibilities", as I shall call them. Accounts of legal responsibility tend to focus on historic responsibility at the expense of prospective responsibility. In 2.1.2.2 it will be argued that prospective responsibility is just as important as historic responsibility to an understanding of responsibility in law; and that the law is as much concerned with establishing prospective responsibilities (or as we might say, with telling us "what our responsibilities are") as with imposing historic responsibility. (I will refer to rules and principles of historic responsibility in terms of "what it means to be responsible".) But first, it will be helpful to explore the nature of prospective responsibility a little more.

Broadly, prospective responsibilities can be divided into two categories. Some prospective responsibilities are directed to the production of good outcomes ("productive" responsibilities) and others to the prevention of bad outcomes ("preventive" responsibilities). The law imposes such responsibilities, for instance, on employers in favour of employees, on trustees in favour of beneficiaries, on doctors in favour of patients, and on regulatory bodies in favour of the objects and beneficiaries of regulatory schemes. Such responsibilities are often created by contract or agreement. Obligations to pay taxes can also be

[9] Roland Pennock distinguishes between responsibilities on the one hand, and duties or obligations on the other. He argues that the core sense of responsibility involves the exercise of "judgment and discretion in the light of careful analysis and conscientious weighing of values", and that this is, in some contexts at least, inconsistent with the idea of a having duty or an obligation: Pennock (1960), 8–9, 27. In law, the distinction between duty and discretion is very important; and narrowly understood, duty and discretion cannot co-exist in the same person at the same time in respect of the same subject matter. However, there is no such inconsistency between duty and responsibility in either the historic or the prospective sense. A person under a legal duty has a prospective responsibility to fulfil that duty, and can be held historically responsible for failure to do so. Of course, the prospective responsibilities attaching to discretions are different from those attaching to duties. It is also the case that in law, very few discretions are absolute. Most are surrounded, structured and confined by a belt of legal duties and obligations.

seen as productive. To the extent that they may require those who bear them to take positive steps to achieve good outcomes or to prevent bad ones, prospective responsibilities of this sort can lay the foundation for historic responsibility for omission and what lawyers call "nonfeasance". Productive and preventive responsibilities play an important role in facilitating cooperative and value-generating human activity.

Prospective responsibilities of the second type are directed to the avoidance of bad outcomes. These we might call "protective responsibilities". The difference between protective and preventive responsibilities can be explained by distinguishing between harming someone and failing to prevent a person being harmed. Historic responsibility for harming is what lawyers call responsibility for "misfeasance" as opposed to nonfeasance, for acts as opposed to omissions. Protective obligations are directed against harming by misfeasance, whereas preventive obligations are directed against failing to prevent harm by nonfeasance. The distinction between acts and omissions (although controversial) is deeply embedded in both law and morality; and the incidence of legal protective responsibilities is wider than that of productive and preventive responsibilities.[10]

Two points need to be made about the relationship between the concept of prospective responsibility and Hart's idea of role responsibility. First, although Hart was prepared to extend the concept of a "role" to cover isolated "tasks", in two respects, it is still too narrow. On the one hand, there is some reason to think that Hart's idea of role responsibility was limited to productive responsibilities, and that it did not extend to preventive, let alone protective, responsibilities. Hart defines a "role" as involving duties "to provide for the welfare of others or to advance . . . the aims and purposes of [an] organization".[11] But there seems nothing wrong in describing as responsible a surf lifesaver who takes seriously the job of *preventing* surfers from drowning; or a driver who takes seriously the duty to take care to *protect* other road-users from harm by driving carefully. The other respect in which Hart's account is too narrow arises from the fact that not all prospective responsibilities attach to roles or tasks. Undertakings and agreements are another very important source of prospective responsibilities; and there is no reason to deny the accolade "responsible" to a person who takes their undertakings and agreements seriously. We may go even further. All human activities can have prospective responsibilities attached to them, whether or not we would think of them as involving the performance of some particular "role" or "task". Being a responsible person involves taking seriously the prospective responsibilities, whatever they are, attaching to whatever activity one is engaged in at any particular time.

The second (and related) point to be made about Hart's account is that it is very difficult to give the idea of a "role" any meaningful work to do.[12] In much,

[10] Honoré (1991).

[11] Hart (1968), 212. Similarly, Baier gives as an example of a task responsibility an obligation to promote the well-being of another: Biaer (1970), 104.

[12] Haydon (1978).

if not all, of our conduct we can be said to be performing some role or other. Hart attempted to solve this problem by defining a role as "a distinctive place or office in a social organization";[13] but he offered no justification or reason for restricting role responsibility to "social roles" that meet this description. The idea of a "task" is even more difficult: how are we to define "task" so as not to cover everything we do and every activity we engage in? Baier says that a person "is not task-responsible for any and all of his actions, but only for certain specific tasks".[14] But he gives no criterion for identifying those tasks to which task responsibility may attach.

These problems led Haydon to suggest that the idea of being responsible (which he called "responsibility as a virtue") is not related to roles or tasks, but connotes a particular desirable personal quality or "virtue" which is related to the idea of giving an account.[15] For Haydon, the responsible person is the person who is "likely to be in a position to give a satisfactory account of his conduct" because he realises "that an account of his conduct can be appropriately called for" and acts accordingly.[16] However, I prefer not to explain prospective responsibility in terms of accountability. Giving an account, whether or not it may lead to the imposition of some sanction in case the account is unsatisfactory, is a backward-looking and essentially negative process, whereas the idea of being a responsible person is forward-looking and positive.[17] The deficiency in Hart's analysis is not that it ties role responsibility to the future, but rather that it associates the idea of future-looking responsibility with roles and tasks. The concept of prospective responsibility has importance and value independently of accountability or liability to sanction. The law is as much concerned with telling us how to behave as with holding us to account for the way we have behaved.

In Hart's view, the idea of being a "responsible person"[18] requires reference to role responsibility for its elucidation:[19] a responsible person is someone who takes their role-responsibilities seriously. We should not conclude from this, however, that the accolade "responsible" should be reserved for what has been dubbed "high-quality compliance with norms—thoughtful compliance oriented toward achieving the objective of the norm or meeting one's obligations to others rather than toward avoidance of blame or superficial conformity".[20] The law does not aspire to generate the sort of virtuous behaviour describable as "high-quality compliance with norms". The law's ethic of responsibility is an

[13] Hart (1968), 212.

[14] Baier (1970), 104.

[15] Haydon (1978).

[16] Haydon (1978), 55.

[17] Mark Bovens captures this idea in his distinction between "passive" and "active" responsibility: Bovens (1998), 26–38. Passive responsibility involves being held responsible, whereas active responsibility involves taking responsibility.

[18] Haydon's "responsibility as virtue" and Bovens's "active responsibility".

[19] Hart (1968), 213.

[20] Heimer and Staffen (1998), 6.

ethic of obligation, not of aspiration; of acceptable behaviour, not virtuous or supererogatory behaviour.[21] The person who "goes the extra mile" may be more responsible and virtuous than the person who fulfils their obligations and no more.[22] But both are responsible people. Nor does it follow from the fact that the law is concerned only with minimum standards of acceptable behaviour that responsibility in law cannot be a matter of degree.[23] Just as a standard of conduct can be exceeded by degrees, so it is possible to fall short of a minimum standard of conduct by degrees. In the law, different degrees of responsibility are sometimes marked by the existence of different "heads of liability". In criminal law, for instance, the offences of murder and manslaughter represent different degrees of responsibility for homicide. Defences—especially partial defences, such as "diminished responsibility"[24]—can also be used to mark degrees of responsibility. Equally importantly, judgments about degrees of responsibility find expression in the type and severity of the sanction imposed. For instance, degree of responsibility is relevant to the sentencing of criminals,[25] and to the "apportionment of damages" between parties who share responsibility for harm.[26]

2.1.2.2 The importance of prospective responsibilities in law

Accounts of legal responsibility tend to focus much more on historic responsibility than on prospective responsibility. This is partly a result of emphasis on the activities of law-applying and law-enforcing institutions at the expense of the activities of law-making institutions, and on the resolution of disputes and conflict at the expense of prevention of disputes and the facilitation of cooperative and productive behaviour. By contrast, my contention is that the idea of prospective responsibilities is just as important as that of historic responsibility to an understanding of legal responsibility. It is true that the idea of responsibility does not provide a complete conceptual apparatus for analysing the law's productive, preventive and protective functions. We also need concepts such as rights and powers. For instance, legally recognised property rights and contracting powers provide an essential framework for the operation of competitive markets and the generation of wealth; and regulatory powers are central to

[21] In some philosophical usage, morality, too, is identified with "obligation" as opposed, for instance, to supererogation: Williams (1985), ch. 10; Taylor (1995). I take no stand on this issue—remember that I have defined morality in institutional, not substantive, terms. While the law does not encourage supererogatory behaviour, it does aim not to discourage it. So while it does not impose a general duty to rescue, it does, for instance, allow rescuers to recover compensation for harm suffered as a result of the negligence of the person who created the need for rescue; and in some contexts, it allows rescuers to claim the costs of rescue. See Cane (1996), 224–7.

[22] On the other hand, we would not say that a person "has a responsibility" to go the extra mile.

[23] *Pace* Bovens (1998), 33.

[24] Ashworth (1999), 288–92.

[25] One reason why mandatory sentences are controversial is that they deprive courts of the ability to discriminate on the basis of degree of departure from the law's demands.

[26] Trindade and Cane (1999), 756–8; see further 5.10.7.

the law's preventive and protective roles. But we should not conclude from this that as a form of legal responsibility, prospective responsibility plays second fiddle to historic responsibility. In fact, there is an important sense in which historic legal responsibility is parasitic on and subsidiary to prospective legal responsibility. Historic responsibility enforces, reinforces and underwrites prospective responsibility. Historic responsibility is not an end in itself, but only a means to the various ends the law seeks to further by creating and imposing prospective responsibilities. Historic responsibility, we might say, is the pathological form of legal responsibility.

I do not mean by saying this to deny the backward-looking orientation of historic responsibility. In other words, I do not mean that historic responsibility is not a matter of desert, or that it is purely concerned with encouraging certain sorts of behaviour in the future and of discouraging certain other sorts. But prevention is better than cure, and fulfilment of prospective legal responsibilities is more to be desired than punishment of nonfulfilment, or repair of its consequences. A well-functioning and successful legal system is one in which non-compliance with prospective responsibilities, and hence occasions for the imposition of historic responsibility, are minimised. Historic responsibility finds its role and meaning only in responding to nonfulfilment of prospective responsibilities; and in this sense, it is subsidiary and parasitic. Of course, imposition of historic responsibility may play a role in maximising compliance with prospective responsibilities. "Deterrence" is generally recognised to be an important function of the imposition of historic responsibility. But in a well-functioning legal system, most people will comply with their prospective responsibilities most of the time regardless of the possibility of imposition of historic responsibility for non-compliance.[27]

2.1.2.3 Causal responsibility and capacity responsibility

The discussion so far has dealt with the temporal aspect of Hart's categories of role responsibility and liability responsibility (both legal and moral). In Hart's account, a minimum level of mental and physical capacity is a precondition of historic responsibility. Lack of capacity immunises a person from historic responsibility. It does not follow from the fact that a person would be immune from historic responsibility for failing to fulfil a prospective responsibility that they are not subject to the prospective responsibility. However, in practical terms, capacity responsibility looks in both temporal directions, at least in relation to people whose lack of capacity is a continuing state rather than a momentary or temporary perturbation. The relevant capacity is the capacity to be guided by rules;[28] and the immunity from historic responsibility is a corollary

[27] This is the great insight that Hart captured in the idea of the "internal point of view". It is surprising, therefore, that he gave sanctions so central a place in his account of responsibility.

[28] Baier (1970), 103–4.

of lack of this forward-looking capacity. The relationship between capacity and responsibility is discussed in more detail in 3.2.3.

The temporal orientation of causal responsibility is complex. Causal responsibility is not a precondition of all forms of historic legal responsibility. In the legal context, the main role of causation is to trace a link between conduct and outcomes (4.1.3). Historic legal responsibility may attach to conduct as such regardless of its outcome. But when responsibility for harm is in issue (as it very often is in legal contexts), causal responsibility is typically[29] a precondition of historic responsibility. Causation may also have a forward-looking orientation, telling us how to achieve desired outcomes and to avoid bad outcomes—providing us with "recipes" for success in what we want or are obliged to do.[30] In one sense, this forward-looking aspect of causation is of great legal importance because the prime function of the law is to encourage fulfilment of productive, preventive and protective responsibilities. For this purpose, knowledge and understanding of causal processes is essential. However, the law does not reward people for success in fulfilling their prospective responsibilities, while it does penalise people for failing to fulfil their prospective responsibilities, and it imposes obligations to repair bad outcomes of such failure. As a result, legal concepts of causation are primarily concerned with the link between conduct and past bad outcomes, not between conduct and future good outcomes. The relationship between causation and responsibility is discussed in chapter 4.

2.1.2.4 *Reactive responsibility*

Brent Fisse finds a different temporal aspect of responsibility in the idea of "reactive fault", which he developed in the context of corporate criminal responsibility.[31] Fisse defines reactive fault as:

> "a corporation's fault in failing to undertake satisfactory preventive or corrective measures in response to the commission of the *actus reus* of an offense by personnel acting on behalf of the organization".[32]

The idea of reactive fault "extends the timeframe" of the responsibility inquiry. If a corporation could be shown to have committed the *actus reus* of an offence, proof of the appropriate *mens rea*, either in relation to the commission of the *actus reus* or in relation to the corporation's unsatisfactory preventive and corrective response to its commission of the *actus reus*, would justify a conviction for the offence. For Fisse, the concept of reactive fault has two main attractions. First, it "allows blameworthy corporate intentionality to be flushed out more easily than is possible when the inquiry is confined to corporate policy at or before the time of the *actus reus*".[33] This is because, according to Fisse, it is

[29] Concerning vicarious liability see 4.4.2.4; and concerning secondary responsibility see 5.10.4.
[30] Honoré (1995), 375.
[31] Fisse (1983), 1183–1213; Fisse and Braithwaite (1993), 46–9, 162–3, 210–13, 214.
[32] Fisse (1983), 1196–7.
[33] Fisse and Braithwaite (1993), 48.

often easier to establish *mens rea* in relation to the way a corporation reacts to harm it has caused than in relation to the causing of the harm. Secondly, when backed by judicial power to order a corporation that has committed the *actus reus* of an offence to take specific preventive action in the future (in addition to action to "correct" harm already caused), it can encourage the development of new and more effective harm-prevention procedures and technologies.[34]

In terms of traditional notions of criminal responsibility, reactive fault is a doubly radical concept. First, it would allow an accused to be convicted of an offence even though the relevant *mens rea* was not contemporaneous with the relevant *actus reus*. It is true that courts have applied the principle of contemporaneity flexibly;[35] but even so, there must be real doubt as to whether it would be satisfied in the typical sort of case Fisse has in mind. Secondly, it would allow an accused to be convicted of an offence even though the relevant *mens rea* did not relate to the relevant *actus reus*, and regardless of whether the conduct to which the *mens rea* related constituted the *actus reus* of any offence. Furthermore, by contemplating judicial power to order corporations to take positive action to prevent further harm in the future, Fisse's reactive fault regime challenges the law's traditional libertarian reluctance to go beyond penalising wrongful harm-causing, repairing the harm done, and either prohibiting or merely discouraging the repetition of harmful conduct. The fact that breach of such an order could attract criminal liability also challenges the law's traditional dislike (based on the presumption of innocence) of preventive criminal sanctions.

Under another version of reactive fault,[36] a party whose corrective or reparative response to their commission of the *actus reus* of an offence was "satisfactory" would be immune from criminal liability for that offence (although they might still be civilly liable for harm resulting from the offence). But a party guilty of reactive fault could be convicted of the relevant offence only if it could be proved that the accused had the *mens rea* of that offence at the relevant time and in relation to the *actus reus* of that offence. In certain respects, this version of reactive fault is less radical than Fisse's; but in another respect, it is more revolutionary. It allows a person's "satisfactory" response to their commission of an *actus reus* to immunise them from liability for that crime. Typically the law penalises bad behaviour. It does not offer rewards for good behaviour. This version of reactive fault also makes a person's "unsatisfactory" response to their crime "a more important determinant of penalty" than the crime itself. These two radical features signal an important difference in the institutional framework within which their respective proponents contemplate the two versions of reactive fault operating. Fisse's version seems designed to operate within the framework of traditional criminal law and criminal process. The truly radical features of Fisse's regime are substantive and doctrinal, not institutional. By contrast, the other version is designed to be part of a "restorative justice"

[34] Fisse and Braithwaite (1993), 210–13.
[35] Ashworth (1999), 163–5.
[36] Espoused by Braithwaite and Roche (2001), 72–4.

process of dealing with criminal offenders. A central feature of restorative justice lies in its attempt to replace punishment and retribution with more positive and forward-looking techniques for dealing with crime, focused both on empowering victims and reducing the risk of repeat offending. Thus, the radical features of the "restorative" version of reactive fault are procedural and institutional rather than doctrinal. Fisse's scheme entails a redefinition of criminal responsibility, whereas the restorative scheme offers new ways of dealing with people who are criminally responsible in orthodox terms.

In policy terms there is nothing especially radical in the idea of legal responsibility for the way a person reacts in the face of potential legal liability. Judicial power to make orders for costs and to award pre-judgment interest can be used to discourage delay on the part of civil defendants in responding to claims against them. In some jurisdictions, obstructive conduct on the part of insurers in handling damages claims can attract legal liability.[37] Being the object of a *bona fide* legal claim of historic responsibility can itself attract prospective responsibilities (to defend the claim in a timely fashion, for instance), and failure to fulfil such responsibilities can, in turn, attract historic responsibility. And while judicial power to make orders of the type Fisse advocates is rarely available or exercised in Anglian legal systems, it is not unknown.[38] The radical features of Fisse's proposals are, first, the idea that fault in reacting to harm one has caused may attract historic legal responsibility even if the harm-causing itself would not attract historic responsibility;[39] and secondly, that fault in the way a person reacts to harm they have caused may attract historic responsibility for the harm-causing itself. In other words, what is radical about Fisse's regime is not the idea that we might impose prospective legal responsibilities on people to react in certain ways to harm they have caused, but in the link it forges between "active" and reactive fault. Fisse's goals could be served in a conceptually simpler way by creating "reactive offences", the *actus reus* of which would consist of failure to respond in certain ways to commission of the *actus reus* of some other offence. In addition, it could be provided that commission by a corporation of the *actus reus* of specified offences would empower a court to order the corporation to take preventive measures, breach of the order being itself a criminal offence.

At all events, upon analysis it appears that neither version of reactive fault represents a third temporal dimension of responsibility but only a novel combination of prospective and historic responsibilities. On the other hand, both versions involve radical departures from traditional ideas of legal responsibility—Fisse's by allowing reactive fault to serve as a surrogate for "active"

[37] Fleming (1988), 181–4.

[38] Especially in the USA. The classic account is Chayes (1976). See also Cooper (1988). However, such orders are perceived as being an aspect of "civil" or "administrative" rather than "criminal" justice.

[39] Fisse does not apparently contemplate that proof of reactive fault would raise a presumption of fault in the causing of harm, but rather than reactive fault could itself satisfy the fault requirement of liability for the harm-causing.

fault, and the restorative version by allowing reactive virtue to attract immunity from legal historic responsibility for active fault. The aims of Fisse's reactive-fault scheme could be met without such radical departures from traditional ideas of criminal responsibility. By contrast, the restorative scheme presents a major challenge to traditional ideas of legal responsibility, and I consider this aspect again in 2.6.

2.1.3 Personal and vicarious responsibility

Personal responsibility is responsibility for one's own conduct,[40] and vicarious responsibility is responsibility for someone else's responsibility-attracting conduct. For those who hold what I earlier called "the modern view of responsibility"[41] and who think that responsibility is a function of human agency, personal responsibility is the only responsibility there is, because responsibility is a function of being a human agent. By contrast, vicarious responsibility plays a prominent role in the law. Vicarious responsibility must be distinguished from responsibility for (one's own) failure to prevent another's responsibility-attracting conduct, or for inducing, persuading or assisting someone to engage in responsibility-attracting conduct. In law, vicarious responsibility is a form of "strict" responsibility—that is, responsibility regardless of fault. Note the words "regardless of". Strict responsibility is not responsibility "without" or "in the absence of" fault. Absence of fault is never a precondition of legal responsibility. Many theorists maintain that in morality, unlike the law, there can be no strict responsibility. This view often rests on the false assumption that strict legal responsibility is responsibility in the absence of fault. Even so, strict legal liability may be imposed in the absence of fault, and many would regard this as out of step with notions of responsibility in the moral domain. I return to this point in 3.6.3.5.

Defining strict responsibility simply as responsibility regardless of fault says nothing about the basis on which strict liability can be imposed. There are broadly four categories of strict legal responsibility, which might be called "passive", "right-based", "activity-based" and "outcome-based" respectively.[42] In terms of this taxonomy, vicarious liability is activity-based: it attaches by virtue of the role played by the vicariously responsible person vis-à-vis the "personally responsible" party. The role that chiefly (if not exclusively) attracts legal vicarious responsibility is that of employer. Vicarious liability is much more controversial in criminal law than civil law,[43] but its justification is a matter of general

[40] Or for conduct of another to whom the performance of one's obligations has been "delegated" (see 5.4.3.4).

[41] See 1.4.2.

[42] See 3.3.2.1. In Cane (1997), 45–9 I use the term "relationship-based", but here the term "activity-based". The latter is better because more inclusive. As well as vicarious liability, it can capture, for instance, the strict liability of a licence-holder for breach of a condition attaching to the licence.

[43] Ashworth (1999), 118–19.

debate and disagreement. Many would say that it is not a form of responsibility at all, but rather an instance of liability without responsibility. I return to this issue in 5.10.6.

Vicarious responsibility performs two main functions in law. First, it facilitates the imposition of legal liability on groups, such as corporations and governments, which the law recognises as capable of bearing rights and responsibilities (5.4.3.3). Secondly, it promotes the reparative function of civil law by providing an injured person with an additional target for a compensation claim.

2.1.4 Individual, shared and group responsibility

According to the modern view of responsibility, individual responsibility is the only sort of responsibility there is. Adherents to the modern view need not deny that responsibility for an event can be shared by several individuals, but they would deny that groups can be responsible independently of the individuals who constitute them. Shared responsibility is a common legal phenomenon found in doctrines such as contributory negligence (5.10.3) and contribution amongst wrongdoers (5.10.2). Group legal responsibility attaches to corporations. Legal discussion of corporate responsibility is imbued with the distinction between "natural" and "legal" persons. The implication of this distinction is that human beings are "real persons" whereas corporations can only be "artificial persons". A corollary is that the responsibility of human beings is "real" or "inherent" responsibility, whereas the responsibility of corporations (for instance) is "artificial" or "attributed" responsibility. In this respect, the legal approach shares something with the modern view of responsibility.

In a physical and mental sense, we can reasonably say that human beings are "natural" in a way that corporations are not. However, *legal* personality is not a matter of physical and mental attributes. Human beings are not legal persons by virtue of their physical and mental characteristics, but by virtue of meeting the criteria for personhood laid down by the law. Some of these criteria refer to physical and mental characteristics or "capacities"; but this is precisely because they are not universal amongst human beings.[44] The legal personality of human beings is as much a social construct as the legal personality of corporations. To be a legal person is no more or less than to be subject to law; and it is the law, not nature, that tells us what entities are subject to law. Human beings (like corporations) can be subject to some laws and not others, have certain legal rights, powers, obligations (and so on) and not others. The same is true outside the law. To be a "moral person" is to be subject to morality; and it is morality, not nature, that tells us who its subjects are. Indeed, some human beings lack the capacities we consider necessary for moral personhood.

[44] The archetypal legal person is the human being "of full age and capacity".

Similarly with responsibility: all legal responsibility, whether that of humans or of groups, is "artificial" in the sense that it is the law, not nature, that tells us what legal responsibility is and when it arises. The same is true outside the law: it is morality, not nature, that tells us what moral responsibility is, who can be morally responsible, and when it arises. Neither in law or morality are there "natural persons" or "real responsibility". Moral and legal personality and responsibility are all human artefacts.

Concerning group responsibility, it is important to distinguish between legally institutionalised groups—that is, corporations—and groups that are not legally institutionalised. Groups of the latter kind can be divided into those that are structured and those that are unstructured. Being structured is a matter of degree according to the extent to which the membership of the group and its decision-making procedures are governed by rules (which may be legally enforceable) accepted by the members of the group. Corporations are both institutionalised and highly structured. An unincorporated group, such as a partnership, may be as highly structured as a corporation.

Corporations are treated for many purposes as if they were individual human beings rather than groups of human beings. Corporations can bear legal rights and obligations in the same way as individuals. Corporations can make contracts, own property, and commit torts, crimes[45] and other legal wrongs. Corporations, like individuals, can be held legally responsible, both vicariously and personally. There are complex sets of legal rules for determining when, for the purposes of attributing legal responsibility to a corporation, conduct and mental states[46] of individuals will count as conduct of the corporation. For proponents of the modern view of responsibility, the idea that a corporation could be personally responsible for conduct is deeply problematic. But in day-to-day life we have little difficulty attributing moral responsibility to corporations and other groups, and the law is not alone in recognising group responsibility.

The distinctive characteristic of a corporation that marks it out from unincorporated groups is that a corporation is separate from the human beings who constitute the corporation. Incorporation brings with it a set of legal rights, powers and obligations that do not attach to unincorporated entities, however highly structured they might be. However, it is important to distinguish legal institutionalisation (in the form of incorporation) from legal recognition. The law may recognise unincorporated groups that it does not treat as legal persons. For this purpose, what seems critical is that the collectivity should have a structure of membership and decision-making rules that enables it to generate decisions which are accepted by its members as decisions of the group that they, as individual members, are bound to accept whether they agree with them or not. This is illustrated in administrative law where groups may have "standing" to

[45] Indeed, there are crimes that can only be committed by corporations.

[46] Much discussion of corporate criminal responsibility is dominated by the difficulty of attributing mental states to corporations. But it is no less (or more) difficult to attribute conduct to corporations.

challenge government decisions in judicial review proceedings. The qualifications needed for "group standing" focus on the nature and activities of the group rather than on whether it is a corporation or not.[47] Seen from this perspective, the importance of incorporation is not so much that it confers "personality" but that it imposes legal structure on a group and subjects it to a particular set of rules for the attribution of human conduct to the group. In other words, incorporation should be seen primarily in terms of legal regulation of group activity rather than as involving ontological transformation of the group. It is better to conceptualise the corporation as a *group* of human beings than as a non-human *person*.[48] In this light, we could interpret the law's refusal to treat unincorporated groups in the same way as corporations as being designed to provide incentives for groups to structure themselves in a standard way, thus making it easier for the law to deal with groups than it would be if each group had to be dealt with on the basis of its own peculiar structure.

Issues of group legal responsibility loom large in public law and international law, both of which are centrally concerned with the legal rights, powers and obligations of governments, nation-states and "public bodies" of various sorts. Most difficulty arises in relation to the highest levels of government. In England, the legal status of central government is enormously complicated by its constitutional relationship with the monarch. This connection between a group governmental institution and an individualised constitutional entity persistently raises the question of the extent to which conduct of the government should be conceptualised as that of some individual (such as a minister), or, by contrast, as that of a group. The idea of "the government" in English law is still highly individualised.[49] In other Anglian legal systems, there has been less difficulty in treating "the state" as a corporate body even in the absence of formal legal provision to this effect. At lower levels, many governmental and public bodies are formally constituted as corporations, either under special statutory provisions or under general incorporation statutes. There is certainly no reason to think that the law is out of step with other normative systems in treating governments and governmental bodies as proper subjects of responsibility judgments. Indeed, without a complex set of rules about group legal responsibility, there could be no public law.

The importance of concepts of group legal responsibility is even greater in international law. Here, indeed, the priority of individual human beings that we find in domestic law is reversed. The archetypal international legal entity is the nation-state; and the entity with the most problematic status in international law is the individual human being. Adoption of this order of priorities, not surprisingly, generates intensely functionalist accounts of personality and responsibility. According to Brownlie:

[47] Cane (1996a), 51–5; Cane (1995), 285–6.

[48] Similarly: Posner (1992) §§14.1–3

[49] For instance, under the Crown Proceedings Act 1946, s. 2, the government ("Crown") is to be treated for certain purposes as a "person of full age and capacity". See generally Loughlin (1999).

> "All that can be said is that an entity of a type recognised by customary law[50] as *capable* of possessing rights and duties and of bringing international claims, and having these capacities conferred upon it, is a legal person".[51]

The dominant theory of responsibility in international law, the so-called "objective theory", is a neat corollary of such functionalist accounts of personality. As Brownlie puts it:

> "one can regard [state] responsibility as a general principle of international law, a concomitant of substantive rules and of the supposition that acts and omissions may be categorised as illegal by reference to the rules establishing rights and duties . . . in principle, an act or omission which produces a result which is on its face a breach of a legal obligation gives rise to responsibility in international law, whether the obligation rests on treaty, custom or some other basis".[52]

However plausible naturalistic accounts of responsibility may be as a starting point for analysis of domestic ("intranational") law, they can provide no help in understanding a system in which the archetypal agents are groups rather than human beings. Only conventional and functionalist accounts are likely to be of any use in this context.

Group and shared legal responsibility are discussed in more detail in chapter 5.

2.2 RESPONSIBILITY AND SANCTIONS

So much for taxonomy. I now turn to examine certain distinctive features of law that enable a study of legal responsibility to illuminate responsibility generally. One of the most important differences between law and morality is that law has much stronger and much more highly developed enforcement mechanisms and institutions than morality. Because morality lacks strong enforcement mechanisms and institutions, discussions of moral responsibility typically have little to say, in detail at least, about the relationship between grounds of responsibility and sanctions. Legal sanctions are of three basic types, punitive, reparative (or "corrective") and preventive. Punitive sanctions focus on the person held responsible, whereas reparative and preventive sanctions also take account of the interests of those for whose benefit responsibility is imposed. Legal sanctions that benefit identified individuals are called "remedies". Punitive sanctions include imprisonment and fines. Reparative sanctions include orders to pay monetary compensation and restitution, and to take other types of action; and orders depriving instruments and decisions of legal effect. Preventive sanctions

[50] International law is much less institutionalised than domestic law. In particular, there is no "world parliament" in any meaningful sense. Many of the most basic rules of international law are the product of customary practice amongst or agreement between states.

[51] Brownlie (1998), 57. See also O'Connell (1970), 81–2.

[52] Brownlie (1998), 436, 439. This objective theory finds clear expression in the International Law Commission's Draft Articles on State Responsibility: Crawford (1999).

include detention, and orders prohibiting future conduct that would contravene some law or requiring action to avoid some legal contravention.

Legal sanctions are a response to historic responsibility,[53] and some sanctions operate by creating prospective responsibilities in the person to whom they are directed. Sanctions that do not operate in this way are those that involve the use of physical force (imprisonment, and corporal and capital punishment, for instance); and those that are "self-executing" (such as an order depriving a decision of legal effect). Punitive sanctions such as fines, and remedies such as compensation and restitution, generate responsibilities (to pay money), the non-fulfilment of which can in turn generate historic responsibility. Further sanctions attach to historic responsibility for failure to satisfy "remedial" responsibilities, typically involving the application of physical force against the person or property of the defaulter. Remedies that generate responsibilities other than to pay a sum of money are called "specific" remedies. There are various types of specific remedies, and they fall into two broad categories—orders to take action (mandatory orders) and orders to refrain from action (prohibitory orders). Because of the libertarian orientation of the common law, courts are much less willing to make mandatory orders than prohibitory orders, and the conditions for awarding the former are more stringent that those governing the award of the latter.

The importance of remedies and sanctions to an understanding of historic legal responsibility must not be underestimated. This is obvious in the criminal context where the sentencing process is just as important a locus of responsibility judgments as the process of adjudicating guilt.[54] More generally, the process of deciding what remedy or sanction ought to attach to any particular finding of legal liability provides important opportunities for the law, by establishing "scales" or "degrees" of responsibility, to modify and fine-tune responsibility judgments made in adjudicating upon liability. Because the sanctioning and remedial stage is much more highly formalised and developed in law than in morality, study of legal rules and principles governing remedies and sanctions can provide us with a depth of understanding about responsibility that could hardly be obtained by reflection on and observation of systems of responsibility that lack formalised and well developed remedial and sanctioning mechanisms and institutions.

2.3 RESPONSIBILITY, EVIDENCE AND PROOF

Apart from impoverishing our understanding of responsibility, the lack of attention to matters of sanctions and enforcement leads many theorists largely to

[53] More precisely, legal sanctions respond to legal liability. Not all legal liability is responsibility-based (see 1.1); but the distinction between liability and responsibility is not important in the present context. See 6.6.5.2.

[54] Few offences carry mandatory sentences, which are controversial. The importance of the sentencing stage as a locus of responsibility judgments is related to the "breadth" of the offence in question. For instance, the offence of theft potentially catches conduct of widely differing degrees of seriousness. (I owe this point to Niki Lacey).

ignore an issue that is of the utmost importance to lawyers—the issue of evidence and proof of responsibility. It is one thing to know what we mean by "responsibility"; to know, in historic terms, when we are responsible; and to know what our prospective responsibilities are. It is quite another to determine, in particular cases, whether a person's conduct satisfies the criteria of historic responsibility and whether, in particular circumstances, the person was "actually" responsible. The first question is one of definition and prescription, the latter one of evidence and proof. For instance, if it is a condition of responsibility for harm that the harm was intended, we need to know not only what it means to say that the harm was intended, but also whether the person who is the subject of the responsibility judgment intended the harm according to those criteria. Appropriate and fair rules and principles of evidence and proof are a fundamental requirement of justice in the imposition of sanctions as a response to responsibility for conduct and outcomes. This is especially true in the law because legal sanctions are serious and intrusive, and because they are underwritten by state power.[55] But it is also true to a lesser extent in morality. The reason why it is true *to a lesser extent* in the moral than in the legal domain is not because of any difference in the nature of responsibility judgments in the two domains, but precisely because moral sanctions are different from legal sanctions, and because they are not underwritten by state coercion.

Even if it is conceded that matters of evidence and proof are important both within and outside the law, it might be replied that their importance is practical rather than theoretical or conceptual.[56] At one level, this is obviously true. It is perfectly possible and, indeed, necessary, to decide what we mean by "responsibility" before, and independently of, deciding whether, in particular circumstances, a person is responsible. On the other hand, one of the most important reasons why we are interested in responsibility and related concepts is because of the role they play in practical reasoning about our rights and obligations vis-à-vis other people, and about the way we should behave in our dealings with them. If analysis of responsibility is divorced from its role in practical reasoning, the danger is that the analysis will misrepresent the nature and content of responsibility judgments. It is in the law that problems of evidence and proof receive their fullest consideration, and this provides another respect in which study of the law can supplement, rather than just illustrate, non-legal analyses of responsibility.

Here is not the place for a detailed exposition of the law of evidence and proof. But it is worthwhile mentioning some of the more important and pervasive features of the law relevant to evidence and proof in order to show that they

[55] Similarly: Lloyd-Bostock (1979), 164–5: elaborate legal procedures of proof "would be pedantic (or irrational) and unnecessarily costly in most non-legal" contexts. See also Posner and Rasmusen (1999).

[56] "the classical (i.e., the nineteenth-century common law) notion of criminal responsibility . . . is often taken to be a legal rendition of our common understanding of moral responsibility, but one that is subject to the practicalities of legal enforcement": Velasquez (1983), 113.

are of fundamental, not marginal, importance to legal responsibility practices. Most obviously, for any and every issue that a court has to decide, the law allocates the onus of proof or persuasion on that issue to one party or the other. Allocation of the onus of proof is not a mere technical matter. This can be illustrated by reference to the so-called doctrine of *res ipsa loquitur*. In tort law, the burden of proof on the issue of whether the defendant was negligent or not rests on the claimant. But in some cases, where an accident has occurred which, in "normal experience", would not have happened unless the defendant had been negligent, it may be said that "the accident speaks for itself" (of negligence on the part of the defendant). On one interpretation, the effect of applying the maxim *res ipsa loquitur* is that the onus of proof on the issue of negligence is shifted from the claimant to the defendant. Instead of the plaintiff having to prove that the defendant was negligent, the defendant must prove lack of negligence on their part. The inherent difficulty of proving a negative proposition of this nature has led many to the conclusion that application of the doctrine of *res ipsa loquitur* effectively (although not in principle) imposes strict liability—that is, liability regardless of fault.

Successful invocation of the doctrine of *res ipsa loquitur* (as interpreted above) creates a rebuttable presumption that the harm caused was a result of negligence on the defendant's part. The use of presumptions, both rebuttable and irrebuttable, is a pervasive legal technique for dealing with conflicts of evidence and epistemological uncertainty—with what we might call "the cost of proof". The use of presumptions about responsibility reduces the cost of making responsibility judgments, while at the same time increasing the risk of misattributions of responsibility. This risk provides a reason why some people say that "responsibility in law" is not "real" responsibility. However, problems of proof are not unique to the law; and in the face of limited resources, such trade-offs between cost and accuracy are a necessary feature of any system that distributes benefits and burdens on the basis of responsibility. They tend not to be so acute or so obvious in the moral as in the legal domain only because moral sanctions are generally less severe and coercive than those meted out by the law. In one sense, a practical system for making responsibility judgments in the face of epistemological uncertainty is more "real" than a realm of pure responsibility concepts.

Equally important as the allocation of the onus of proof is the issue of burden of proof—generally "beyond reasonable doubt" in criminal law, and "on the balance of probabilities" in other areas. The traditional justification for the difference is that the stigma and sanctions attaching to criminal responsibility are greater and more serious than those attaching to non-criminal responsibility. Few people would view this as merely a matter of legal technicality. In the moral domain as much as in the legal domain our willingness to hold a person responsible, in the face of epistemological uncertainty, depends partly on the seriousness of the consequences of doing so.

Problems of proof are particularly acute in relation to responsibility predicated on some mental state or other, such as intention or recklessness. The traditional legal approach to proof of mental states is that while a person's mental states, unlike their conduct, cannot be directly observed by another, they can be indirectly observed.[57] However, I would argue that practical judgments of responsibility based on conduct accompanied by a mental state do not involve indirect *observation* of an agent's mental state. Rather they rest on an *interpretation* of what the agent said and did—viewed against a background of "relevant" circumstances—as manifesting or not manifesting the mental state in question.[58] Take responsibility for intentional conduct and intended consequences as an example. The legal starting point for proving intention is that in order to determine whether a person's conduct was intentional and whether its consequences were intended, we must rely either on that person's account of their frame of mind at the relevant time, or on "inferences" from their conduct and its surrounding circumstances ("circumstantial evidence").

Consider, first, testimony of the accused about their mental state. Even leaving aside the possibility of lies, defects of memory and *ex post facto* rationalisations, and assuming truthfulness, the agent's own account of their mental state will inevitably be mediated through their understanding of the concept of intention. In other words, the account is unlikely to consist merely of "raw" data about the agent's frame of mind. Rather, it will provide the accused's own interpretation of what they said and did in the relevant circumstances, couched in terms of their understanding of relevant concepts and norms.[59]

In the common case where the subject's mental state has to be inferred from behaviour and surrounding circumstances, the interpretative nature of findings of intention seems even clearer. In such cases, I would argue, a judgment that a person's conduct was intentional will be underpinned by an assertion about the "normal person", not about the agent. The (implicit) reasoning will go something like this: "the accused's conduct must have been intentional because what the agent did is not the sort of thing that people normally do unintentionally"; or "the accused must have intended these consequences because they are not the sort of thing that people normally bring about unintentionally". If I am right about this, "inferred intention" as we might call it, is not a frame of mind at all; rather it consists of a contextualised interpretation of what the accused did and said based on a judgment about the way people normally (ought to) behave.[60]

The argument is not that when a person is found, by inference, to have intended conduct or its consequences, they did not so intend. They may or may

[57] e.g. *Peters* v. *R* (1998) 192 CLR 493, 550–1 (para. 134) per Kirby J.

[58] My approach here (see further Cane (2000)) is similar to that of Kenny (Kenny (1978), 10–12) and (to a lesser extent) that of Duff, usefully summarised in Duff (1987) and developed in detail in Duff (1990). Whereas Duff wants to argue that the mental state of an actor can be directly observed in their conduct, I want to argue that practical judgments of responsibility rest on interpretation of conduct as manifesting a mental state, not on observation of conduct as involving a mental state. Duff is addressing an epistemological issue, whereas I am addressing an issue of proof.

[59] Similarly Shaver (1985), 41–3, 160. See also Blackman (1981).

[60] In Dennett's terms (Dennett (1993) esp 17, 25–6, 39–40), the law takes "the intentional stance" to understanding and explaining human behaviour.

not have. Rather my point concerns the nature of legal liability for intentional conduct and the role intention plays in our legal responsibility practices. Consider strict liability: an important justification for strict liability, first put forward by Justice Oliver Wendell Holmes, and taken over by modern economic analysts of law,[61] is that it increases the chance that those guilty of fault will be held liable in circumstances where proof of fault is difficult, albeit possibly at the cost of imposing liability in some cases in the absence of fault. Similarly, the "normal behaviour test of intention" is best seen as a concession to the difficulty of proving intention—a rebuttable presumption of intention,[62] in effect. Because it is rebuttable, the agent may escape liability by convincing the court that the conduct in question and its consequences were not intended. But if it be accepted that even the accused's report of his or her mental state will consist of a contextualised interpretation of his or her conduct, the way for the accused to rebut the presumption of intention is to persuade the court that the better contextualised interpretation of his or her conduct is that it was not intentional.[63]

The effect of the rebuttable presumption approach is that a legal finding of intention does not entail a proposition about the accused's (subjective) mental state at the relevant time, based on an indirect observation of the accused's mind. Rather it rests on an interpretation of the accused's conduct based on a statement about normal behaviour. It does not follow that the agent did not act intentionally. But it does follow that having acted intentionally is not a necessary condition of incurring legal liability for having acted intentionally. If the best interpretation of the accused's conduct is that it was intentional, then the accused can be held legally liable for having acted intentionally. In short, a legal finding that a person acted intentionally is a contextualised interpretation of their conduct.[64]

The argument, then, is that the difficulty of proving mental states requires us to give rather different accounts of mental states understood theoretically, on the one hand, and as elements in practical reasoning about responsibility, on the other. More generally, problems of evidence and proof suggest that we may need to distinguish between what might be called "theoretical responsibility", on the one hand, and "practical responsibility" on the other. This distinction is not relevant only to responsibility in law, but to judgments of responsibility in any normative domain where adverse consequences are attached to holding a

[61] See Rosenberg (1995), 126, 138–40; Shavell (1987), 26–32, 264–5.

[62] This should not be confused with an irrebuttable presumption such as "a person is presumed to intend the natural and probably consequences of their conduct". On the history of this presumption see Lacey (2001a), 367, 370.

[63] Shaver (1985), 130 suggests that agent's denials of intention are less likely to be believed than admissions of intention. The fact that a person has what philosophers call "privileged access" to their mental states is a relevant factor in this context.

[64] Beaumont (2000), 382, makes a similar point in relation to mistake: the more reasonable the belief on which the mistake is based, the more likely it is that the agent will be held actually to have been mistaken.

person responsible. As we have seen, a person may be practically responsible regardless of whether they are theoretically responsible. Some may want to say that practical responsibility is, for this reason, less "real" than theoretical responsibility. However, my argument is that the difference between the two concepts of responsibility lies not in their relative genuineness, but in the fact that one (theoretical responsibility) belongs to the world of normative concepts while the other (practical responsibility) is a normative component of a social practice of holding people responsible. Judgments of responsibility that result from the application of techniques to deal with epistemological uncertainty are just as "real", and just as central a part of our legal and moral lives, as the concepts and definitions of responsibility on which they are based.

2.4 RESPONSIBILITY AS A RELATIONAL PHENOMENON

In this section I explain another very important way in which paying careful attention to legal responsibility practices can add to and enrich our understanding of moral as well as legal concepts of responsibility.

2.4.1 Responsibility, agents and outcomes: three paradigms of legal responsibility

Philosophical analyses of responsibility are typically agent-focused. In agent-focused accounts of responsibility, being responsible depends primarily on what a person has done or failed to do, on their acts and omissions.[65] When applied to law, such an approach fits the contours of criminal responsibility reasonably well. The rules and principles of criminal law focus on the offender's conduct (*actus reus*) and mental state (*mens rea*). This is reflected in the fact that there are "victimless" crimes (such as possession offences) and inchoate crimes (such as conspiracy), and that attempting a crime is itself a crime. Victims are marginal to modern ideas of criminal responsibility, and they play a largely passive role in the criminal justice process.[66] The main criminal sanctions are offender-oriented. Reparation for harm done and restitution of the proceeds of crime are typically seen as being based on ideas imported from outside the criminal law rather than as being integral to its basic goals and purposes.[67]

But when we turn from criminal law to civil law—contract and tort, for instance—the picture looks very different. Responsibility in civil law is two-sided,

[65] A word on terminology. I shall use the term "conduct" to cover both acts and omissions, misfeasance and nonfeasance; and I shall use the term "agent" in relation to both.

[66] "the Crown and the defendant are the only proper parties to criminal proceedings": *R* v. *Seceratary of State for the Home Department, ex parte Bulger*, *The Times*, 7 March 2001 (http://www.thetimes.co.uk/article/0,,12–94847,00.html) (victim's father lacks standing to challenge sentence tariff set by Lord Chief Justice).

[67] Concerning reparation see Zedner (1994); Zedner (1996).

concerned not only with agent-conduct, but equally with the impact of that conduct on others. Victims[68] play a central role in the civil justice process. Responsibility in civil law is always *to* someone as well as *for* something. All civil law sanctions are victim-oriented. This is true even of "punitive damages", that is, damages designed to punish the agent rather than to compensate the victim. Although such damages are calculated by reference to the agent's conduct, they are payable to the victim rather than, as in the case of criminal fines, to the state. In civil law, the nature and quality of relevant outcomes and their impact on victims are just as important to responsibility as the nature and quality of the conduct that produced those outcomes.

I am not saying that outcomes are of no importance in criminal law. Such a statement would be obviously wrong. There are "result crimes" as well as "conduct crimes". The *actus reus* of the typical crime includes a reference to the impact of the criminal conduct on the victim.[69] As a general rule, the more serious the harm resulting from criminal conduct, the more serious the crime. Completed crimes may be punished more severely than attempts,[70] and victimless crimes may be controversial precisely because they offend the "harm principle", which is deeply embedded in widely-accepted liberal ideas about the proper scope of the criminal law. To that extent, agent-focused analyses of responsibility do not even fit what I shall call the "criminal law paradigm" of responsibility.[71] But they fit that paradigm much better than they fit what I shall call the "civil law paradigm" of responsibility. The nature and quality of outcomes and their impact on the victim are central to the civil law paradigm because it is only by paying attention to them that we can give an adequate account of, and justification for, victim-oriented remedies (which I shall refer to collectively from the agent's point of view, as "obligations of repair").[72] Conversely, agent-conduct is the focus of criminal law because penalties and punishments are its main sanctions.

One of the main arguments of this book is that the distinctions between the civil law and criminal law paradigms of responsibility, and between penalties and punishments on the one hand, and obligations of repair on the other, add an important dimension to accounts of responsibility that is likely to be lacking in accounts of responsibility that pay little or no attention to the law and to legal responsibility practices. The absence of this dimension is regrettable not only because legal responsibility practices are intrinsically and independently important, but also

[68] It is common in legal literature to refer to the person whose responsibility is in issue as "the defendant" and to the person to whom responsibility is owed as "the plaintiff" or "the claimant". In this book I will often refer to the former as "the agent" (see n 65 above) and to the latter as "the victim".

[69] Gardner (1998). For a victim-focused account of the proper scope of the criminal law paradigm of responsibility see Hampton (1992).

[70] Zedner (1996), 158.

[71] For a quite different (prescriptive) account of the relative significance of agency and harm in criminal law see Brudner (1993).

[72] This term is convenient but not ideal because I am using it to cover not only what (in 2.2) I called "reparative sanctions", but also victim-oriented preventive sanctions—notably injunctions.

because the distinctions we have found in the law are found, in less developed forms, in morality as well. These distinctions are not legal peculiarities, but are as deeply embedded in ideas of moral responsibility as in legal concepts of responsibility. Accounts of responsibility that ignore them are not unfaithful just to the law: they also neglect important aspects of moral reasoning. An advantage of studying legal responsibility practices is that it brings these different paradigms of responsibility much more clearly into view.

Besides what I have called civil law and criminal law, there is another similarly broad legal category that deserves some attention, namely public law. Does this category suggest a different paradigm that may be useful in analysing concepts and practices of responsibility? Public law is traditionally contrasted with private law; and the latter can, for present purposes, be treated as synonymous with "civil law" in the sense that term bears in the phrase "the civil law paradigm of responsibility". The conceptual and doctrinal core of private law is found in the law of (tangible and intangible) property, the law of trusts, the law of contract, tort law, and the law of restitution. These provide building blocks for "functional" legal categories such as company law, family law and environmental law. Private law is concerned with the rights and obligations *inter se* of individual "citizens". By contrast, public law focuses primarily on the rights, powers and obligations of governments and on the performance of what might be called "public functions". One concern of public law is whether and how rules of private law (such as the law of contract) should be modified in their application to governmental bodies and the performance of public functions. Private law can provide citizens with valuable resources for holding governments responsible for what they do. More importantly, however, public law is concerned with the accountability of governments, and with accountability for the performance of public functions, to citizens *qua* citizens, rather than citizens *qua* holders of rights recognised by private law.

As an accountability (or "responsibility") mechanism, public law complements, and to some extent competes with, "political" institutions such as parliament, public auditors and ombudsmen. The grounds of "public law" accountability are different from the grounds of responsibility applied by institutions of political accountability. In judge-made Anglian public law there are two competing models of the role of the courts in holding government responsible to citizens: a "private model" and a "public model". For our purposes, the most important characteristic of the private model is that it sees the role of the courts as being to protect rights and interests that were created and are recognised in private law, against certain interferences and harms which would not attract liability in private law. More concretely, public law, on this view, protects private law rights and interests against certain sorts of conduct that would not attract liability in contract or tort or any other area of private law. By contrast, the public model sees the role of the courts as going further than this to protect not only rights and interests created by and recognised in private law, but also to protect rights and interests of citizens *qua* citizens that are not recognised in private law. More concretely, on this view, the courts can protect rights and interests that citizens share with other citizens but to which no individual as such has a claim.

One way this last point is quite commonly put is to say that the role of the courts is not just to protect individual rights, but also to make sure that government does not act "illegally". This perhaps makes public law sound too much like criminal law. Even according to the view we are considering, public law is just as much about protecting citizens and providing them with accountability resources as with sanctioning government misconduct. Like civil law process, public law process is typically initiated and pursued by citizens, and public law sanctions are more analogous to civil law remedies than to criminal law penalties. What distinguishes the public model from the private model of the role of courts in providing accountability resources is that it is more amenable to the idea of group or non-individualised rights and obligations. The subjects of private law rights and obligations are human beings and institutionalised groups (i.e. corporations).[73] Under both models of the judicial function of holding governments to account, human beings and corporations are subjects of public law; but so is "the government" (or "the state" or "the Crown"), which is neither human being nor corporation. Moreover, under the public law model, groups of citizens that are bound together merely by shared purposes and interests can be recognised as legal subjects, regardless of whether they are also bound by the tie of incorporation.[74] This recognises the importance of the participation of unincorporated and relatively unstructured groups in the political process.

This last feature of the public model is reflected in the rules of "standing" that determine who may challenge government action in the courts on the ground that it is in breach of public law rules and principles. Under the private model, only human beings and corporations have standing, and only if their private law rights have been adversely affected by government action or if government action has affected them adversely in a different or greater way than it has affected other citizens. By contrast, under the public model, individual legal persons may have standing simply as representatives of "the public" or of "a section of the public"; and interest groups, for instance, may have standing regardless of whether they are incorporated or not, and regardless of whether the individuals who make up the interest group have been more harmed than other citizens or, indeed, of whether they have been harmed at all by government action.

This discussion of public law has added two new dimensions to the account of responsibility. First, it has introduced the idea of "political responsibility". Many of the rules and principles of political responsibility are, like morality, the result of organic growth rather than legislative activity. The enforcement of

[73] Corporations are groups either in the sense that at any one time, they are made up of more than one human being; or in the sense that different individual human beings constitute the (same) entity at different times (i.e. a corporation sole).

[74] See also 2.1.4 above.

political responsibility is less institutionalised and coercive than the enforcement of legal responsibility, but more so than the enforcement of morality. The resolution of disputes about political responsibility is less institutionalised than the system for resolving disputes about legal responsibility. Most importantly of all, it should not be assumed that the criteria of political responsibility are the same as those of either moral or legal responsibility. It may well be, for instance, that certain conduct that would not be considered contrary to norms of political responsibility would be seen to breach interpersonal morality, or that certain conduct that would attract political responsibility would not be contrary to law.

Secondly, and more importantly for present purposes, the discussion of public law has squarely raised the issue of responsibility of and to groups. As in the civil law paradigm, concern with the consequences of conduct has a more prominent place in what I shall call "the public law paradigm" of responsibility than in the criminal law paradigm. But the public law paradigm differs from both the civil law and the criminal law paradigms in its greater recognition of groups, and in its focus on interactions between government and "civil society" as opposed to interactions within civil society. All of these issues are discussed at greater length in chapter 8.

2.4.2 Responsibility and social values

Besides conduct and outcomes, there is a third important focus of legal responsibility practices which typically finds little or no (explicit) place in many philosophical analyses of responsibility—namely social values. Because responsibility practices rest on general principles according to which responsibility is allocated and distributed, holding any particular individual responsible in any particular set of circumstances has potential ramifications for other individuals who find themselves in similar circumstances. The point can be simply illustrated by referring to the famous case of *Donoghue* v. *Stevenson*,[75] in which it was decided for the first time in England that a manufacturer could be held liable to a consumer who suffers injury as a result of a defect in a product caused by the negligence of the manufacturer. At one level, the case concerned the responsibility of a particular manufacturer to a particular consumer. At another level, it dealt with much larger social questions about the relationship between manufacturers and consumers generally. In other words, the case was not only about the responsibility of one individual to another, but also about the distribution of rights and obligations in society generally. For this reason, in deciding how to resolve the case, the judges considered not only the issue of "fairness" as between the plaintiff and the defendant, but also the wider social and economic impact of a decision one way or another in relation to the two parties before it. Lawyers often use the word "policy" to refer to such wider social, political and economic considerations.

[75] [1932] AC 562.

Policy considerations are central to legal responsibility practices because law is a social phenomenon, and because the principles of legal responsibility are of general application. If an agent-focused approach to responsibility is adopted, social, political and economic considerations may seem to have little or nothing to do with responsibility. For example, Hart distinguishes between conditions of criminal liability that concern responsibility, and the question of whether any particular conduct is "punishable by law".[76] Hart identifies three categories of criteria of responsibility: "(i) mental or psychological conditions; (ii) causal or other forms of connection between act and harm; (iii) personal relationships rendering one man liable to be punished or to pay for the acts of another".[77] For Hart, the question of whether what was done was a crime is not one of responsibility.[78] This may be because the question of whether particular conduct is criminal or, in other words, of what we recognise as crimes, can only be answered by reference to legal (i.e. social) authority. Certainly it is not a question that can be answered by consideration only of the agent's identity, conduct and mental state, and of the harm caused.

But why should the issue of what amounts to criminal conduct not be treated as a criterion of responsibility? Certainly, without a catalogue of crimes, the concept of *criminal* responsibility has no meaning or content. Some might agree with this statement, and conclude that this is precisely why legal responsibility is a distorted or debased or tainted version of moral responsibility. But a similar point applies to morality. Morality is at least partly a social phenomenon; and in the absence of judgments about what sorts of conduct are "moral" or "immoral", worthy of praise or blame, the concept of *moral* responsibility has no meaning or content. As in the case of law, the question of what we mean by "moral" and "immoral" cannot be answered merely by reference to the agent's conduct and its consequences. Social values are relevant both to the question of what counts as a crime, and to the question of what is immoral. Views change from time to time about what sorts of behaviour are immoral, and about what sorts of behaviour ought to be criminalised or otherwise rendered contrary to law. It follows that what we might call the "normative structure" of moral responsibility is essentially similar to the normative structure of legal responsibility. Both have mental and causal components (for instance) and both have components derived from social values. Understanding responsibility, whether in law or morality, is not just a matter of knowing what it means to say we are responsible, but also of knowing what we are responsible for and what our prospective responsibilities are.

It does not follow, of course, that what the law approves or condemns will be approved or condemned outside the law; or vice versa. In other words, it does not follow that the social values embodied in morality will be the same as those

[76] Hart (1968), 217. This distinction is related to that traditionally drawn between the general and special parts of the criminal law. See Moore (1997), 30–35 and Lacey (2000).

[77] *Ibid.*, 217–18.

[78] However, Hart was not entirely consistent on this point: see Hart (1961), 179.

embodied in the law. It may be that law and morality have different social functions and purposes, and this may generate divergences between illegality and immorality. Consider, for instance, the distinction between so called "*mala prohibita*" and "*mala in se*". This contrast reflects the fact that by reason of its institutional geography and resources, law can make a distinctive contribution to the coordination of human social behaviour. For instance, our responsibility to drive on the left is a legal responsibility; and to the extent that it is a moral responsibility, it is so merely by virtue of the fact that it is a legal responsibility. Another important cause for divergence between our moral and legal responsibilities is the fact that legal sanctions are generally more severe than moral sanctions. This partly explains, I think, the perceived gap between law and morality in relation to the so-called "duty to rescue".[79] It is one thing to disapprove of or censure a person for failing to render aid, but quite another to impose a legal punishment or obligation of repair on them on account of the failure. For this reason, we should not be too quick to conclude (pejoratively) that the law is "out of step" with morality when it refuses to impose an obligation that morality recognises.[80] It may well be that institutional and functional differences between law and morality not only support but even require divergences between our moral and our legal responsibilities.

Knowing what we are responsible for will often require reference to the ideas of "role" and "task" which, although not exhaustive of the concept of prospective responsibilities, play an important part in it. A good illustration of this point comes from the earlier discussion of public law. One of the most important underlying issues in public law concerns the extent to which, and the ways in which, the responsibilities of governments are and should be different from those of citizens. These are questions which can be given both legal and moral answers. But they are also social and political questions; and an account of our responsibility concepts and practices would be incomplete without answers to them.

In summary, a full account of our concepts and practices of responsibility, both within the law and outside it, must refer to three matters: (i) the conduct and mental life of agents; (ii) the consequences of conduct and their impact on others; and (iii) what our (prospective) responsibilities are. The concept of responsibility shorn of any account of "to whom we are responsible" and "what we are responsible for" is a philosopher's dream—or, perhaps, a philosophical nightmare. Consider Mackie's "straight rule of responsibility: an agent is responsible for all and only his intentional actions".[80a] This rule makes no reference to what our responsibilities are or to the intended beneficiaries of those responsibilities. And from a practical point of view, there is obviously no such

79 See, for instance, Honoré (1966).

80 "We [moralists] can afford to have stricter standards of culpability than the lawyers since no formal punishment will follow as a result of *our* verdicts and we do not have to worry about procedural complexities": Feinberg (1970), 245–6.

80a Mackie (1977), 208–15.

rule. Both in law and morality, we are often held responsible for unintended conduct and consequences. A driver who unintentionally exceeds the speed limit and, as a result, causes harm to another road user may be held legally liable. But we might also say, in a non-legal way, that the driver "ought to have taken more care". Nor is it true, outside the law, that praise is attracted only by intended outcomes and the outcomes of intentional conduct. Some of our responsibilities may only require us to avoid doing harm intentionally, and sometimes we may attract praise for the good we do only if it was intended. But in order to be able to give a sound account of the scope of the rule of "intention responsibility", we need to know what our responsibilities are. An account of the concept of responsibility which pays no attention to what our responsibilities are is too short by half.[81]

2.4.3 Summary

The thrust of this section can be summarised by drawing a distinction between agent-focused accounts of responsibility and a relational account of responsibility. My argument is that responsibility in law is a relational concept and practice in the sense that it concerns the three-way relationship between agents, "victims" and the wider community. I would also argue, however, that responsibility in the moral domain is also relational in this sense; and that, for this reason, a study of responsibility in law, where the relational aspect of responsibility is manifest and extensively documented, can add significantly to our understanding of responsibility more generally.

2.5 FUNCTIONS OF RESPONSIBILITY PRACTICES

For people who think that giving an account of responsibility involves an empirical or quasi-scientific inquiry into the truth about human nature, responsibility practices and the functions of those practices are, at best, of secondary importance. Indeed, one might think that to attribute functions to features of the natural world would involve imposing value on brute phenomena in an unscientific way. Likewise, for people who think that moral responsibility is "real" while legal responsibility is "artificial" or conventional, inquiry into the functions of responsibility is likely to be of little interest or importance.

My focus in this book is on legal responsibility. Legal responsibility is, by common consent, a product of a complex set of social practices (see 1.2.1). It would, therefore, seem uncontroversial to say that legal responsibility practices have certain functions and have been developed to serve certain purposes.

[81] In Raz's terms, a complete theory of responsibility needs a normative as well as an ascriptive component: Raz (1975), 11–12.

However, in chapter 1 it was argued that responsibility in the moral domain itself has a significant conventional element, and in this chapter I have suggested several respects in which the "practical" concerns of legal responsibility practices are also relevant to responsibility in the moral domain. Regardless of the "empirical truth about responsibility", much of what we mean by "responsibility" outside the law is a product of social practices. Just as it makes sense to inquire into the functions and purposes of legal responsibility practices, so it makes sense to inquire into the functions and purposes of responsibility practices in other domains of life.

I suggest that responsibility practices serve four broad functions which I shall call the ontological, the explanatory, the evaluative and the normative. The ontological function of responsibility practices, which is essentially backward-looking, is to allocate "ownership" of conduct and outcomes. This ownership function contributes to the formation and maintenance of our identities as individuals, and to our sense of being able to influence the course of events and to achieve things in the world. It is discussed further in later chapters.[82] The explanatory function is concerned with the way things come about in the world, and is based on ideas of causation. It has both a backward-looking and a forward-looking aspect, the former concerned with the history of how things happened in the past, and the latter with what has to be done to make things happen in the future (with "recipes", as Tony Honoré felicitously puts it).[83] It is discussed in chapter 4. The normative function of responsibility practices is forward-looking, namely to specify how people ought to behave in the future. By contrast, the evaluative function of responsibility practices is concerned with whether past conduct was good, bad or indifferent. In the terminology used in 2.1.2, the normative function is concerned with prospective responsibilities, and the evaluative with historic responsibility.

Turning now to legal responsibility practices more specifically, the functions of law are many and various. The normative functions of legal responsibility practices are as multifarious as the content of our prospective legal responsibilities; and to the extent that historic legal responsibility reinforces prospective responsibilities, the evaluative functions of legal responsibility practices are equally multifarious. However, more narrowly conceived, we can say that the evaluative function of legal responsibility practices focuses on the allocation of legal sanctions. Judgments of historic legal responsibility provide the basis for the imposition of legal sanctions, whether punitive, reparative or preventive. Some would say that it is precisely this practical legal focus on sanctions that distinguishes responsibility in law from "real" (moral) responsibility. In the words of H.D. Lewis:

> "the mere fact of our liability to suffer a penalty is far too incidental a feature of conduct to constitute moral responsibility . . . responsibility . . . means simply to be a

[82] See 3.6.3.5, 4.2.2, 5.9 and 6.2.

[83] Honoré (1995), 375.

> moral agent, and this means to be an agent capable of acting rightly or wrongly in the sense in which conduct is immediately morally good or morally bad, as the case may be".[84]

On this basis, Lewis denies that "the legal meaning of responsibility provides any analogy to the meaning of the term in the ethical sense".[85] To the contrary, I would argue that the prime function of judgments of historic responsibility in the moral domain is analogous to their function in the legal domain, namely to provide the basis for the allocation of moral praise and blame. Lewis resists this conclusion by arguing that sanctions in the moral domain, like legal sanctions, may be "out of accord with ethical requirements" and that a person "may be morally guilty in respect of conduct to which no sort of penalty attaches". We can easily agree with both propositions. All that follows from them, however, is that the imposition of moral sanctions (like the imposition of legal sanctions) may sometimes be contrary to the rules and principles of moral responsibility. It does not follow that the sanctioning function distorts principles of responsibility, or that there is a domain of "real ethical responsibility" in which sanctions play no part.[86]

It might be argued that it is only the focus on sanctions that requires rules about such "practical" matters as proof of responsibility, and time limits on the enforcement of responsibility; and that the need to take account of such matters distorts sanction-focused responsibility judgments, rendering contingent their connection with "real" responsibility. However, it is difficult to make much sense of the idea of responsibility completely divorced from, and independent of, consideration, based on relevant information, of whether a person's conduct satisfied relevant criteria of responsibility. It is impossible to say whether "conduct is immediately morally good or morally bad" without considering whether the characteristics of the conduct in question match the criteria of moral goodness and badness. This is a practical matter, regardless of whether the purpose of classifying the conduct is sanction-focused. How can we rightly attribute moral goodness or moral badness to a person's conduct without satisfying ourselves that their conduct satisfies the criteria of moral goodness or badness?

But what about time limits? Aren't "limitation periods" arbitrary concessions to the practical need for legal closure? How can the expiry of a legal limitation period relieve a person of "real" responsibility? At one level, the answer to the last question must be that it cannot. The passing of three or six or twelve or twenty years does not alter what happened in the past. Indeed, this is recognised in the law by the fact that there is no limitation period for the prosecution of criminal offences. Limitation periods are a feature only of civil law. On the other hand, the reasons why closure is desirable in the legal domain are not irrelevant in the moral domain. With the passage of time, it tends to become

[84] Lewis (1948), 23.
[85] *Ibid.*
[86] For a philosophical version of this point see Rorty (1982), esp xli–xlii.

harder and harder to determine with confidence whether particular conduct satisfied relevant criteria for responsibility without unreasonable expenditure of resources on investigation. Although there is no limitation period for the prosecution of criminal offences, an important source of unease about the prosecution of old offences—for instance, trials at the start of the twenty-first century in respect of crimes against humanity allegedly committed during the Second World War—is the effect of the passage of time on our ability to discover the truth about what actually happened so long ago. The discretion to prosecute is exercised more and more sparingly as time passes precisely because reliable judgments of responsibility become harder and harder to make with the passage of time. And this is so regardless of whether such judgments are sanction-focused.

Closure is also important in its own right. For the sake of their financial and emotional well-being, people need to be able to get on with their lives without the constant threat of being subject to sanctions for long-past conduct. But even regardless of sanctions, a life in which one's moral ledger was never wiped clean would, for most people, be insupportable. The inability to draw lines and move on is a seriously dysfunctional characteristic for most people. There comes a point when the present tense—*is* responsible—must give way to the past tense—*was* responsible.[87] This is as true for victims as it is for agents. As Martha Minow puts it: "[t]hrough forgiveness, we can renounce resentment, and avoid the self-destructive effects of holding on to pain, grudges and victimhood".[88] This need for closure has a moral as well as a psychological dimension. In judging other people's behaviour, it is a moral failing never to let go of the past. We may not have a moral obligation "to forgive and forget", but forgiving and forgetting is a virtue, not just a prudential good.

Of course, there is a sense in which the precise point chosen at which to truncate legal liability (e.g. three or six or twelve or twenty years) is arbitrary. Instead of inquiring in every case whether the reasons that support the truncation of liability apply in that case, the law announces fixed limitation periods for different types of case, and applies them to cases of the relevant type. But this procedure is not as arbitrary as it might appear at first sight. Limitation periods are designed to strike a balance between the interest of claimants in being able to enforce their legal entitlements, and the interest of potential defendants in being able to plan their affairs without having the risk of incurring legal liability for past conduct indefinitely hanging over them. Different limitation periods for different types of case represent the law's attempt to assess this balance with appropriate sensitivity to context.[89] Treating every case as unique would introduce a degree of uncertainty that might not be to the overall benefit either of potential claimants or of potential defendants. Even so, fixed limitation periods

[87] This is the basic insight underlying the Rehabilitation of Offenders Act 1974 (UK).

[88] Minow (1998), 14.

[89] The choice of limitation period may be seen as instance of what Finnis, following Aquinas, calls "*determinatio*": Finnis (1980), 284–9.

are more advantageous to potential defendants than to potential claimants; and in certain contexts (as where the limitation period is relatively short or where the harm suffered was undiscoverable for a period after it occurred) the law gives courts a discretion to extend the limitation period on a case-by-case basis where this seems fair.

The foundations of Lewis's approach is a distinction between *being* responsible, and *being held* responsible (whether by oneself or by others). He apparently wants to define responsibility independently not only of sanctioning practices but also of any practice of holding oneself or others responsible and of being held responsible. While it is certainly true that being responsible and being held responsible do not necessarily coincide, it is difficult to make much sense of the idea of being responsible entirely independently of being held responsible. Significantly, Lewis's view is that "no answer is possible" to the question of "what we mean by rightness, moral worth, and their correlatives".[90] This, I would suggest, is because these ideas have no meaning independently of human practices of holding people responsible, whether in the legal domain or in some other normative domain. I would argue, therefore, that studying the evaluative function of legal responsibility practices may throw important light on our responsibility practices more widely.

2.6 RESPONSIBILITY, LIABILITY AND THE FUNCTIONS OF LAW

In 1.1 the point was made that in law, historic responsibility is neither a necessary nor a sufficient condition of legal liability. In this chapter I have argued that the prime aim of the "legal system of responsibility" is maximisation of the incidence of responsible (law-compliant) behaviour, not the imposition of liability for irresponsible (law-breaking) behaviour. But while the imposition of sanctions for irresponsible behaviour is not the *law's* prime aim, and while (historic) responsibility for conduct and outcomes is neither a sufficient nor a necessary condition of legal liability, an assumption of the discussion so far has been that the prime purpose of *legal liability*—of legal penalties and obligations of repair—is the sanctioning of those responsible for past conduct and outcomes, and that historic responsibility is normally a necessary condition of legal liability. Typically, historic responsibility and legal liability coincide.

Not everyone accepts this assumption. The most systematic challenge comes from so-called "economic analysts of law", who seek to explain, justify and evaluate legal liability as a mechanism for "enhancing the efficient allocation of society's resources".[91] From this perspective, what attracts legal liability is not responsibility for past conduct and outcomes, but ability to avoid inefficient outcomes, and to achieve efficient outcomes, in the future. This should be

[90] Lewis (1948), 23.
[91] Markesinis and Deakin (1999), 24.

distinguished from the view that imposing liability on the basis of historic responsibility for past conduct may provide incentives for people to fulfil their prospective responsibilities in the future. On this latter view, the forward-looking incentives for responsible behaviour are a by-product of the imposition of liability. According to the economic analysis, by contrast, the basis of and the justification for imposition of liability is forward-looking, and the fact that the person held liable was historically responsible is incidental.

The economic approach to law is essentially consequentialist. Other less systematic consequentialist approaches involve, for instance, interpreting and justifying tort law as concerned with compensation and fair loss distribution;[92] and arguing that the focus of the criminal law ought to be on social protection.[93]

It is important to distinguish the descriptive and the prescriptive versions of these various approaches. It is one thing to argue that the law should pursue economic efficiency, or fair loss distribution, or social protection, at the expense of giving practical expression to ideas of historic responsibility.[94] It is quite another thing to argue, as some of their proponents do, that such approaches provide the best explanation of what the legal system of responsibility actually is and does. There are two related points to be made here. The first is that the body of legal materials with which this book is primarily concerned—Anglian common law—contains a huge amount of evidence to support the idea that judges view large areas of the law primarily in terms of historic responsibility. There seems no good reason to doubt that what judges say about the role of historic responsibility in the law expresses what they think the law is really about. Secondly, there are crucial structural features of the common law and of common law adjudication that make very little sense except as reflections of a concern with issues of historic responsibility.[95] It does not follow, of course, that this concern with historic responsibility is exclusive of other concerns, or that judges and litigants may not use the law to pursue goals such as compensation, deterrence or social protection. Indeed, it is perfectly clear from the legal materials that pursuit of these and other goals is an important aspect of our legal responsibility practices. It does mean, however, that the pursuit of such goals is constrained by the responsibility-oriented structural and substantive features of the common law.[96] Put another way, achievement of the law's goal of maximising compliance with prospective responsibilities is constrained by the fact that its main tool for doing so is liability to incur penalties and obligations of repair. The design of this tool is based on ideas of historic responsibility. We must look to institutions other than those that apply and enforce the law, to promote law-abidingness by techniques not based on concepts of historic responsibility.

[92] Markesinins and Deakin (1999), 6.

[93] Hart (1968), 177–85, 193–209. Many of Barbara Wootton's ideas (discussed by Hart) find contemporary expression in restorative justice principles: see 2.1.2.4. See also 3.6.3.5.

[94] e.g. Braithwaite (1982).

[95] Weinrib (1995), ch. 1; Cane (1997).

[96] Cane (1997), ch. 7.

In fact, whereas the economic approach, if taken to its logical conclusion, renders historic responsibility and related concepts (such as intention and (backward-looking) causation) redundant, less systematic approaches tend to accept the uneasy co-existence in the law of backward-looking responsibility ideas with the pursuit of its forward-looking goals, while assuming that in case of conflict, fidelity to responsibility concepts will, and should, be sacrificed to a greater realisation of desired social goals. Such pragmatism seems to me to be faithful to the spirit of the common law; although I would challenge the assumed subjection, in practice, of personal responsibility to consequences. In this respect, it is important to distinguish between legal doctrine and legal processes. Ideas of historic responsibility continue to lie at the very core and base of much legal doctrine. As a mechanism for dealing with a wide range of social problems and conflicts, legal liability is based fairly and squarely on concepts of historic responsibility. The law, however, operates in a social environment in which competing models for dealing with such problems and conflicts find many adherents. In the past 100 years, the two main competing models have found expression in the welfare state on the one hand, and free-market individualism on the other. Litigants who support one or other of these models understandably seek the law's aid to resolve problems and conflicts in a way consistent with their own ideology; and judges who are sympathetic to one or other of these competing models are likely to want to oblige to the extent possible within the constraints imposed by the law's orientation to ideas of historic responsibility.

Some people think that the encounter with competing ideologies has affected the substance of the law in important ways. For instance, many have argued that an excessive (welfarist) concern with the needs and rights of victims has distorted the principles of historic responsibility underlying tort law, and has created (or widened) the gap between historic responsibility in law and moral responsibility.[97] On the other hand, it has been suggested that the extreme individualism underlying the economic approach to tort law (which has arguably affected the approach of courts to liability for economic loss) ignores the fact that agents have duties and that victims have corresponding rights.[98] The basic point, however, is that the concern with historic responsibility is ineradicably built into the substance and structure of the common law; and so there is a limit to the extent to which legal liability rules can be used to achieve forward-looking goals. Personal responsibility is not the only principle on which social relations could be (or are) organised, but it is the principle which is, to use the philosophical jargon, "immanent" in the common law.

[97] Atiyah (1997), chs. 3 and 4.
[98] Stapleton (1995).

2.7 CONCLUSION

In this chapter I have developed a taxonomy of responsibility concepts suited to an analysis of responsibility in Anglian common law. I have distinguished between historic and prospective responsibility, which tracks a distinction between accountability ("what it means to the responsible") and the idea of "what our responsibilities are". In terms of responsibility, the prime function of law (I have argued) is to tell us what our responsibilities are. Holding people accountable for failure to fulfil their prospective legal responsibilities is an important, but only secondary, concern. In other words, historic responsibility is (typically) a function of failure to fulfil one's prospective responsibilities. In law, as in morality, possession of a minimum level of physical and mental capacity (which Hart called "capacity responsibility") is a precondition of having prospective responsibilities. Although such capacity entails the ability to understand relevant causal processes, in law causation is primarily relevant to historic responsibility for causing harm. I have also distinguished between personal and vicarious responsibility, and between individual responsibility on the one hand and group and shared responsibility on the other. These distinctions cut across and add necessary detail to that between historic and prospective responsibility.

I have argued that because of its practical concern with sanctions, study of legal responsibility practices can illuminate our concept of responsibility more generally. I have also argued that by reason of its explicit concern with victims and with social values as well as with agents, study of legal responsibility can supplement understanding of responsibility that is derived by viewing it from an agent-focused perspective. These *functional* and *relational* aspects of responsibility in law give it much greater importance for our general understanding of responsibility than is commonly recognised by theorists who view responsibility in an agent-focused way. Central to this discussion, and to the analysis of responsibility in the rest of the book, are the distinctions I have drawn between the civil law, criminal law and public law paradigms of responsibility.

Finally, I have argued that historic responsibility is not the only basis for resolving the sorts of social problems to which law-applying institutions apply the criteria of historic responsibility. However, because ideas of historic responsibility are integral to the substance and structure of the common law, attempts to use it to regulate social interactions according to different criteria are bound to be of only limited success.

Having explored briefly and in general terms the distinctive contribution that the study of law can make, by virtue of law's institutional resources, to our understanding of responsibility, we are now in a position to analyse certain aspects of that contribution in more detail.

3

Responsibility and Culpability

3.1 RESPONSIBILITY, LIABILITY AND CULPABILITY

ONE OF THE strongest and most persistent themes in the philosophical literature dealing with responsibility is that responsibility requires culpability (or "blameworthiness"). It is generally agreed that a minimum level of mental and physical capacity is a precondition of culpability. A person should not be blamed if they lacked basic understanding of the nature and significance of their conduct, or basic control over it, unless their lack of capacity was itself the result of culpable conduct on their part. Beyond that, there is less agreement about what makes conduct (and its consequences) culpable. For some, conduct is culpable only if it is deliberate or intentional. Deliberation and intention are typically explained in terms of plans—intentional (or "deliberate") conduct and intended consequences are planned. Other theorists include conscious risk-taking ("recklessness") in their account of culpability. On this view, it may be blameworthy to take a known risk of an adverse outcome, even if producing the outcome was not part of the agent's plan. Yet other accounts of culpability embrace at least some cases of "negligence" or "carelessness".

Whatever view is taken of the relationship between responsibility and culpability, it is quite clear that not all legal liability is based on "fault". In the first place we have seen that some legal liabilities are not even based on responsibility for past conduct, let alone fault.[1] Secondly, strict liability—that is, liability based on responsibility regardless of fault—is an important and widespread legal phenomenon. This fact tends to elicit one of two responses from philosophers: either that strict legal liability is inconsistent with ideas of "moral" responsibility and is, for that reason, to be deplored; or that strict legal liability is to be explained in terms of certain "practical concerns" of the law that are not shared by morality.

The main purposes of this chapter are to explore the relationship between legal liability and culpability, and to challenge the popular argument that in imposing strict liability, the law parts company with morality. In the process, I will also address two major philosophical debates relevant to law: one concerning the relationship between responsibility and luck; and the other concerning the relationship between responsibility and the outcomes of conduct.

[1] See 1.1 and 2.6.

3.2 RESPONSIBILITY AND LUCK

3.2.1 Limited sensitivity to luck

In 1.4.2 it was suggested that for the purposes of analysing responsibility practices, the truth or falsity of causal determinism can be ignored. Even if causal determinism is true, the facts remain that although we feel our conduct to be subject to varying degrees of external and internal limitation and constraint, we experience freedom of choice and a fair degree of control over our conduct and the world around us; that people differ in terms of their capacities and abilities to achieve good outcomes and avoid bad outcomes; that people can change their behaviour patterns; and so on. Regardless of the truth or falsity of determinism, we hold ourselves and others responsible, and we accept responsibility, for at least some (of their and our) conduct and some of its consequences. Responsibility is a human construct; and facts about human psychology, and about the way we experience our relationship with the physical world, provide an appropriate basis for analysis and evaluation of our responsibility practices.[2] It is important not to confuse determinism, which is a belief about the way things are, with fatalism, which is a psychological response to the human condition. Fatalism would be corrosive of our responsibility practices in a way that determinism by itself is not.[3]

But while our responsibility practices assume (consistently with the way most people perceive their situation) that we have a certain freedom of choice and a certain degree of control over our conduct and its consequences, they also acknowledge (once again, consistently with the way we perceive our situation) that our freedom of choice, and our control over ourselves and the world around us, is limited.[4] In other words, our responsibility practices acknowledge the role of luck in our lives, understanding "luck" as referring to events and outcomes that are outside our control. Because the analysis in this book rests on no assumption (or argument) either way about the truth or falsity of causal determinism, "control", as used here, refers to the human experience of control, and to the presupposition of control that is fundamental to the psychology of responsibility. This "experiential" sense of "control" (and the corresponding experiential sense of "luck") is compatible with both the truth and the falsity of causal determinism.

[2] Similarly Wallace (1994), 147–9, 181–2; Fischer and Ravizza (1998). Wallace's project, it seems, is to establish that holding people (morally) responsible would be compatible with determinism (if it were true). The compatibility of responsibility with a deterministic world is irrelevant to my concern with responsibility *practices*, because we have developed these practices without knowing whether determinism is true or not. As McFee says, determinism is a philosopher's problem, not a lawyer's or a historian's or a psychologist's: McFee (2000), 144–5, 150.

[3] Similarly: Dennett (1984), 104; also 122.

[4] For a definition of control see Dennett (1984), 52.

We can usefully distinguish two types of control relevant to responsibility—internal and external. Internal control is the control that each of us has over our mental processes and bodily movements—"self-control", if you like. External control is the control we have over other people's conduct and behaviour and over the natural world. Corresponding to these two types of control are two types of luck. "Dispositional luck" refers to aspects of one's personality, temperament, emotions, desires, mental and physical capacities, and so on, which one cannot control. "Circumstantial luck" refers to aspects of the world around us, and of our situation in life, that are outside our control. People vary in their ability to control their own behaviour and the world around them. When things turn out well for a person despite their lack of control, we can say that they have good luck; and when things turn out badly for a person as a result of their lack of control, we can say that they have bad luck.

A basic issue for any responsibility system is the extent to which it ought to be "sensitive" (and, correspondingly, "insensitive") to the role of luck in human lives. All our conduct, and all the outcomes of our conduct, are, to a greater or lesser extent, affected by factors outside our control. If responsibility depended on control over all aspects of our conduct and its consequences, we would never be (fully) responsible for anything. Luck is ubiquitous. By acknowledging that we have a certain degree of control over our conduct and its consequences, but that this control is limited, our responsibility practices (we might say) exhibit "limited sensitivity to luck". In the law, such sensitivity to bad luck manifests itself in two different ways: sometimes it negatives liability (as in the case of the defence of frustration in the law of contract: 3.2.2) and sometimes it reduces liability (as when lack of capacity is taken into account in sentencing criminals: 3.2.4).

This feature of our responsibility practices can be explained psychologically. It is important to our sense of personal identity to feel that we can, by our own efforts, effect changes in ourselves and in the world around us—that we have some control over our conduct and its consequences.[5] In order to maintain this sense of being able to affect the course of events, we need to feel that some conduct and some consequences are within our control and our responsibility; but equally that other conduct and other consequences are beyond our control and our responsibility. There is a fine line between feeling that we are masters of our fate and that we are victims of circumstance. Feeling that we were responsible for all of our conduct and all its consequences, no matter how little control we seemed to have over them, would be just as destructive of our sense of ourselves as agents who can effect change as feeling that we were responsible for nothing, no matter how much control we seemed to have.

The fact that our responsibility practices make only limited allowance for luck may be explicable in normative terms. Because people accept and are thought deserving of praise for at least some good conduct and outcomes despite the role

[5] Attitudes to luck, and hence the strength of this psychological need, may vary between individuals and cultures. Dennett thinks that "free will is an almost exclusively Western preoccupation": Dennett (1984), 5.

of good luck in producing them, they should (we might think) also be prepared to accept blame for at least some bad conduct and outcomes despite the role of luck in producing them. As Honoré puts it:

> "We cannot take the credit without the discredit, since that would be to violate the principle of taking the rough with the smooth—a principle that possesses moral force and can perhaps be regarded as a form of distributive justice".[6]

Where to draw the line between sensitivity and insensitivity to luck is an issue to which philosophers have given surprisingly little attention. In the context of the allocation of resources, as opposed to the allocation of responsibility, the leading theorists opt either for total insensitivity to luck,[7] or total sensitivity to luck.[8] Dworkin distinguishes between "handicaps" (a person's "circumstances") and "preferences and ambitions" (which are "features of body or mind or personality").[9] The former, he thinks, should be taken into account in the distribution of resources, while the latter should be ignored. However, it is not clear whether Dworkin sees this distinction as cutting across that between luck and control, or as reflecting it (handicaps being outside a person's control, but preferences and ambitions within it). Nor is it clear what role it might play in relation to responsibility.

Rawls thinks that whereas luck should be ignored in distributing resources, it is relevant to the allocation of responsibility. The validity of this distinction has been questioned.[10] Certainly, from the perspective of the person "enforcing" the responsibility, as opposed to that of the person held responsible, legal responsibility, at least, can sometimes itself be viewed as a resource. For instance, when the House of Lords held, in *Donoghue* v. *Stevenson*,[11] that manufacturers of products owe a duty of care to consumers, this gave consumers a legal and financial resource that they previously lacked. Putting the point more abstractly, it is a mistake to think that responsibility—legal responsibility, anyway—is purely a matter of "corrective", as opposed to "distributive", justice.[12] If luck is relevant to the allocation of responsibility, it must also be relevant to the allocation of resources, or, at least, the resource of responsibility. This is obvious once we notice that if A causes harm to B (partly) as a result of factors outside the control of both of them, and on account of that bad luck, A is held not responsible, B must bear the cost of the harm even though the occurrence of the harm was, in some relevant respect(s), beyond B's control as well as A's. In such circumstances, to allocate responsibility is to distribute the costs of bad luck. It is for this reason that a crucial test of the acceptability of our responsibility practices is how they distribute those costs. As Ripstein argues:

[6] Honoré (1999), 9; also 134.
[7] e.g. Rawls (1972), 310–15.
[8] e.g. Cohen (1989).
[9] Dworkin (1981), 293.
[10] e.g. Scheffler (1992), 306 n. 7.
[11] [1932] AC 562.
[12] Cane (1996b), 480–1; Cane (2001b).

> "The idea that a person's life should depend only on the things he can control may make sense in the case of a particular individual if others are ready to devote their lives and resources to covering that person's losses. But it cannot be made sense of in the case of a plurality of persons living together on terms of mutual respect".[13]

Because of the ubiquity of luck in human affairs, we need, in law and morality alike, principles that determine when lack of control of the circumstances in which our conduct occurs and takes effect will negative or reduce responsibility, and when it will not. Such principles are an aspect of distributive justice.

3.2.2 Limited sensitivity to circumstantial luck

So far as circumstantial luck is concerned, there are various rules and principles that inject limited sensitivity to luck into the law. For instance, under the doctrine of "frustration" in the law of contract, a contracting party may be relieved of a contractual obligation if it becomes impossible to perform as a result of circumstances outside the party's control.[14] In the law of tort, it is relevant to whether a person will be judged to have acted negligently or not that they were confronted by an emergency that was not of their own making.[15] In both tort law and criminal law, the defences of necessity and duress recognise that a person may be excused, by reason of external circumstances over which they had no control, for having behaved in ways that would ordinarily be unacceptable. Various aspects of the law of causation—such as the distinction between a causal condition and an effective cause,[16] and the notion of an intervening cause[17]—reflect the fact that our control over the consequences of our conduct is limited.

On the other hand, it is equally clear that in certain respects the law is insensitive to circumstantial luck. For instance, completed crimes may be punished more severely than attempted crimes.[18] Another example is the principle of tort law and criminal law that an injurer must take the victim "as found". So, for instance, a driver bears the risk that a pedestrian injured by the driver's negligence might suffer abnormal damage by reason of being a haemophiliac. This rule is an application of a much wider implicit principle that agents must take the world as found. It is generally no answer to legal liability that the circumstances in which one's conduct occurred and took effect were beyond one's control. On the other hand, in judging whether a person has been negligent for the

[13] Ripstein (1999), 269–70.

[14] Collins (1997), 275–82.

[15] Trindade and Cane (1999), 458–9.

[16] Trindade and Cane (1999), 484.

[17] Trindade and Cane (1999), 493–7

[18] Ashworth (2000), 98, 104–5; see also 117 re causing death by bad driving. Whether attempts should be punished as harshly as completed crimes is a much-debated issue. See, for instance, Ashworth (1999), 463; Ripstein (1998), ch. 7; Duff (1996), ch. 4, 151–4, 180–2, 350–62; Brudner (1993), 38.

purposes of tort liability, the rule is that a defendant will be liable for the full extent of the abnormally vulnerable person's injury only if the defendant failed to take precautions that would have been necessary to protect the normal person from injury. In the absence of knowledge of the victim's abnormality, there is no duty to take special precautions to protect the abnormal victim from injury.[19] By combining this rule with the "take-as-found" principle, the law (as it were) distributes the luck between the tortfeasor and the victim.

In very abstract terms, the characteristic of liability-negativing unlucky circumstances seems to be extraordinariness. For instance, coincidences—unusual combinations of (unlucky) circumstances—may negative responsibility both in law and morality. In contract law[20] a person may be relieved of contractual obligations if they were induced to enter the contract by extraordinary pressure exerted by the other contracting party, but not if their entry into the contract or their acceptance of disadvantageous terms under it, was the result of common external circumstances (such as poverty) which put them in a relatively weak bargaining position.[21] In criminal law, pressure of external circumstances may found a successful plea of necessity or duress, but only if it is extreme and unusual. Within the range of "normality" agents are expected to adjust their behaviour to circumstances outside their control, and accept the consequences if they cannot or do not. So, for instance, poverty does not excuse theft, and homelessness does not excuse squatting.[22]

These last examples deserve a little more discussion. There are well-documented correlations between economic and social deprivation and certain types of crime. And yet, at least at the level of liability (as opposed to sanctions—see 3.5.4) social factors are ignored (in principle, at least) in assessing criminal responsibility for conduct and consequences. Instead, the law focuses on the agent's choices and their physical and mental capacities. Similarly, the rules of tort liability for interference with property rights pay no attention to wider issues of social justice concerning the way property rights are distributed within society. The law's disregard of "social justice" in its construction of concepts of personal responsibility has provoked various critiques, particularly of the criminal law.[23] Norrie, for instance, has argued that the criminal law (and much theorising about the criminal law) takes insufficient account of the

[19] Trindade and Cane (1999), 360.

[20] For a non-legal statement to similar effect see Hooker (2000), 9–10.

[21] See also Raz (1986), 89 ("The undesirable aspect of duress is not in the absence of choice but in the fact that it is engineered in order to exact consent"); 154–6.

[22] Dan-Cohen explains the difference between duress (etc.) on the one hand and poverty (etc.) on the other in terms that the latter is more integral to self-identity than the former: Dan-Cohen (1992), 997–9. For an argument that the law should recognise a wider defence of necessity see Wright (1996), ch. 3.

[23] See e.g. Zedner (1996), 131. In principle, it might be argued that because criminal law is concerned primarily with protection of society's interests rather than those of individual victims, social inequality should be more relevant to criminal liability than to civil liability. The civil claimant can disclaim responsibility for social inequality in a way that sounds less acceptable coming from state authorities enforcing the criminal law.

"relational" nature of responsibility.[24] His basic argument is that agency is a function not solely of individual choice and capacity but also, to some extent, of social forces outside the agent's control.

Norrie's analysis is complex and raises many issues that will not be discussed here.[25] There is one strand of his discussion which does deserve comment, and that is the pervasive (and largely implicit assumption) that morality is more sensitive to circumstantial luck than the criminal law.[26] Yet at the same time, Norrie detects ambivalence in criminal law theory and doctrine which, in his view, acknowledges and reflects the interplay between individual agency and social context.[27] Putting this observation together with his view that a truly "moral" approach to responsibility takes account of both individual agency and social context, it seems that Norrie would not dissent from the plausible proposition that thinking about responsibility in both the legal and the moral domains recognises the impact of external circumstances on people's behaviour and choices. In criminal law, for instance, pressure of external circumstances can be taken into account in sentencing even when it would be ignored at the level of liability.

Whether morality is more sensitive to circumstantial luck than the law is a difficult question to answer in the abstract. As in other contexts, a careful survey of moral thinking about the relevance of social factors to personal responsibility would, no doubt, reveal considerable disagreement and difference of opinion. So far as the law is concerned, detailed analysis might reveal that the balance between sensitivity and insensitivity to circumstantial luck varies from area to area because different areas of law have different purposes and perform different functions. More generally, to the extent that the functions of law are different from the functions of morality, one might expect that the balance would be struck differently in the two domains. For instance, attitudes to the relevance of circumstantial luck might depend partly on the nature of the various sanctions available to enforce judgments of responsibility. What seems clear, however, is that it is a mistake to assume that unlike the law, morality is entirely sensitive to circumstantial luck. Thinking in both domains displays sensitivity, but only limited sensitivity, to circumstantial luck.

[24] Norrie (2000). See also Nicolson (2000), 171, 174–9.

[25] It is worth mentioning Norrie's tendency not to distinguish between motive, character (by which, I think, he refers to a type of dispositional luck—see Norrie (2000), 127–8) and the impact of social factors on individuals' conduct (circumstantial luck). In particular, he tends to conflate motive and social factors. But a person may be "led to a life of crime" by social deprivation without that deprivation being their reason for committing any particular crime.

[26] See e.g. Norrie (2000), 25–6, 38–9, 115–19, 166. Similarly, in relation to the consequences of conduct, Ashworth's view is that arguments of "moral principle" require complete sensitivity to luck, at least in the allocation of punishment: Ashworth (1993). The problem with this approach is that circumstances are always outside our control to a greater or lesser extent. In fact, Ashworth seems to support reasonable foreseeability as the basic test of liability for consequences.

[27] e.g. Norrie (2000), 46–9.

3.2.3 Limited sensitivity to dispositional luck

As is to be expected, the law also strikes a balance between sensitivity and insensitivity to dispositional luck. Sensitivity finds expression, for instance, in defences such as insanity, diminished responsibility and automatism; and also in rules and principles that relieve young children of legal liability. More generally, possession of a minimum of physical and mental capacity is a precondition of legal liability.[28] However, this minimum is set at a low level,[29] and there can be large variations amongst those who rise above it in their ability to avoid behaving in ways that may attract legal liability.

A clear manifestation of legal insensitivity to dispositional luck is found in the "reasonable person" (or "objective") standard of care in the law of negligence.[30] Under the objective test of negligence it is not open to a person to say that they could not have met the standard of the reasonable person because of their own mental, physical or financial abilities and resources. In setting the standard of the reasonable person, the law's starting-point is to establish a relevant universal standard of conduct by constructing a sort of model person, with commonly possessed characteristics, abilities and resources,[31] and asking what that person would have done in the circumstances in which the defendant was placed. The word "relevant" refers to the fact that there are different categories of average person for different types of case. For instance, in a road accident case, the average person is the average driver; in a medical negligence case against a surgeon, the average person is the average surgeon; and so on. In certain cases, however, negligence law does take account of the agent's own abilities and resources, regardless of whether they are commonly possessed,[32] thus making limited allowance for dispositional luck.

In analysing the relationship between luck and the objective test of negligence, a distinction needs to be drawn between what might be called "personal"

[28] Arenella (1992). The discussion in this section focuses on mental and physical capacity. In the theoretical criminal law literature there is also much discussion of the relevance to responsibility of "character", which is related to emotions, motives and reasons for action. Character is often assumed to be beyond the individual's control (see e.g. Norrie (2000), 36–7, 108–9, 127–8). For discussion see 3.6.3.3.

[29] Witness the recent abolition in England of the rebuttable presumption that children aged between ten and fourteen are incapable of committing crimes: Crime and Disorder Act 1998 (UK), s 34. For discussion see Bandalli (1998).

[30] For a criminal law example see *R* v. *Stone* [1977] QB 354 (negligent manslaughter). The defence of provocation is another prime site for debates in the criminal law about the appropriate balance between sensitivity and insensitivity to dispositional luck: Gardner and Macklem (2001).

[31] There is, of course, much room for controversy in constructing the profile of the reasonable person. An issue that has been much discussed in recent years is whether and how gender ought to be taken into account. See, for instance, Conaghan (1996). Taking gender into account could have dramatic effects in criminal law since men are much more likely to commit crimes than women. In England, gender has been relevant to the defence of provocation since the decision of the House of Lords in *DPP* v. *Camplin* [1978] AC 705.

[32] Trindade and Cane (1999), 446–7.

and "interpersonal" standards of conduct. In applying a personal standard to particular conduct, the question is whether the agent measured up to their own individual level of competence—i.e. their abilities and resources. By contrast, applying an interpersonal standard involves asking whether the agent's conduct displayed a level of competence defined, to a greater or lesser extent, independently of the agent's own level of competence. The reasonable person test of negligence imposes an interpersonal, not a personal, standard of conduct, i.e. a standard of conduct defined by reference to the characteristics, abilities and resources of the reasonable person, not those of the agent.[33] It follows that there may be people who, through bad luck, lack abilities or resources attributed by the law to the model person; but who, nevertheless, are subject to the reasonable person standard because they possess the minimum capacity that is a precondition of legal liability. Provided the standard of the reasonable person is set at a level that most people are competent to meet most of the time,[34] such people (for whom Honoré has coined the tag "shortcomers"),[35] will be a minority. Even so, by adopting an interpersonal test of negligence, the law is insensitive to the shortcomer's bad luck of lacking the characteristics, abilities and resources attributed to the reasonable person.

The law's insensitivity to the shortcomer's unlucky lack of competence may be explained and justified in several ways. The first rests on the observation that in order to set personal standards of care we would have to be able to observe and measure differences in competence between individuals. While some differences in competence may be obvious, many will be difficult and costly to observe and measure. In order to avoid this cost, the law is justified in setting impersonal standards.[36] This argument assumes that in principle, personal standards of conduct are preferable; but that in practice, they may be unacceptably costly to achieve.

A second explanation of the law's use of impersonal standards rests on the argument that by holding shortcomers to standards beyond their competence, it gives them an incentive to improve their abilities and increase their resources or, alternatively, take steps to prevent their lack of competence producing adverse consequences. Andrew Simester argues that the law's insensitivity to dispositional luck should extend only to corrigible characteristics—such as lack of knowledge and memory-power—and not to incorrigible characteristics such as

[33] The question of whether the agent ought to be judged against a personal or an interpersonal standard is central to criminal law defences such as provocation (see e.g. *R* v. *Smith* [2000] 3 WLR 654) and duress.

[34] If the law set its standards so high that most people would be incapable of meeting them most of the time, it could be considered unfair as a system of personal responsibility. In theory, the law avoids this criticism by equipping the model person with commonly possessed abilities and resources. In practice, it is often alleged that the law attributes to the model person abilities and resources which most people simply do not have. My view, for what it is worth, is that such criticism is generally unjustified.

[35] Honoré (1999), 16.

[36] Shavell (1987), §§ 4.1.1 and 4.1.3; Posner (1992), 167–8; Honoré (1999), 24, but see *ibid.* 19–20.

lack of intelligence.[37] This argument suffers from two defects. First, it seems possible, in principle at least, that what Simester classes as "corrigible" characteristics might, in some people, be incorrigible. If so, would it then be unfair to treat people uniformly in relation to memory, for instance, even if the powers of memory attributed to the model person were within the grasp of most people most of the time? An affirmative answer to this question would be unwelcome because it suggests that it would not be fair to treat people uniformly in relation to *any* characteristic, ability or resource that, as a result of bad luck, some people lacked incorrigibly. Secondly, Simester's argument ignores the possibility that even if the incapacity is not corrigible, it may be reasonable to expect the incapable person to take steps to avoid situations in which their lack of capacity might produce adverse consequences.[38]

Unlike the first explanation of the law's adoption of interpersonal standards, the second assumes that such standards are preferable, both in principle and in practice, to personal standards. The same is true of the third explanation, which rests on the argument that personal standards of care would strike the balance between our interest, as agents, in freedom of action, and our interest, as victims, in security of person and property, too heavily in favour of our interest in freedom of action. As we have seen, the interests of victims are given greater weight in civil law than in criminal law. Thus it is that in civil law, unlucky lack of ability to meet interpersonal standards of care is generally ignored both in imposing liability and in assessing sanctions. In criminal law, because the interests of victims are given less weight, and because criminal liability carries more stigma than civil liability, more allowance is made for the personal characteristics of agents in defences such as insanity and diminished responsibility, and in sentencing.[39] For the same reasons, there is a view that criminal liability for negligence should be based on personal rather than interpersonal standards.[40] According to this third argument, then, interpersonal standards provide a mechanism for allocating bad dispositional luck to agents rather than victims. The more personalised the standards of conduct imposed on agents, the greater the burden of dispositional bad luck imposed on victims. Making only limited allowance for dispositional luck in favour of agents distributes the burden of such luck between agents and victims, for the benefit of victims.

It is often assumed that morality[41] is much more sensitive than the law to dispositional luck, and that a person will not be held morally responsible for doing what they could not have avoided, or for failing to do what they could not have done: "ought implies can", as the common aphorism goes. In assessing the validity of this assumption, it is important to note that in the phrase "ought implies

[37] Simester (2000)

[38] Similarly: Shavell (1987) §§ 4.1.2 and 4.2. For Dennett, the "elbow room" created by foreknowledge of features of the world and of ourselves that are outside our control is the form of "free will" "most worth wanting": Dennett (1984), 54–5, 62–3.

[39] See further 3.2.4.

[40] Ashworth (1999), 197–8.

[41] Or "the courts of Heaven" as Oliver Wendell Holmes put it: Holmes (1881), 86.

can", "can" is ambiguous. Tony Honoré captures two senses of "can" in his distinction between "can (particular)" and "can (general)".[42] If a person fails to meet a standard on a particular occasion, we can say that on that occasion they could not (particular) have met the standard. But if the person typically succeeds in meeting the standard when they try, we can say that they can (general) meet the standard; and occasional failure to meet the standard does not cast doubt on the validity of such a statement.[43] It is a normal part of human experience that people do not always succeed in exercising abilities and skills that they undoubtedly have, even when they try. Once a person has failed to meet a standard on a particular occasion, there is no way that we can know whether they could have met it *on that occasion*, even if they normally meet the standard when they try.[44] This is as true of personal standards as of interpersonal standards. Displaying practical sensitivity to dispositional luck is a matter of designing standards of conduct that make appropriate allowance for dispositional differences. For instance, it would be uncontroversially unfair to hold blind people to standards of conduct that require sight for compliance. On the other hand, within a very broad range, differences of intelligence are treated as irrelevant to standards of safe driving. But once an appropriate standard of conduct has been agreed upon, it makes no practical sense to exempt a person to whom the standard applies from responsibility on the ground that on the particular occasion in question they could not have complied with it.

The practical question, then, is whether morality is more sensitive than the law to unlucky lack of the resources and abilities needed in order that an agent can (general) meet interpersonal standards of conduct. In other words, are moral standards of conduct more personalised than legal standards? Even leaving aside the fact of disagreement about moral issues, this is a very difficult question to answer in the abstract.[45] As in the case of circumstantial luck, it may be that our attitude to the relevance of dispositional luck varies with context. In law, for instance, it is widely thought that principles of criminal responsibility are, or ought to be, more sensitive to dispositional bad luck than principles of civil responsibility. However, there is no reason to think that the arguments in favour of the use of interpersonal standards in the legal domain do not also play a part in moral thinking. Perhaps the argument based on the difficulty of observing and measuring differences of competence has less force in the moral domain than in the legal domain. But this is only because legal sanctions are, in general, more onerous than moral sanctions; and because many issues of responsibility that can be left unresolved in the moral domain must be resolved once they enter

[42] Honoré (1999), ch. 7. "Can" is also ambiguous in respect of the relationship between responsibility and determinism: Wallace (1994), 223; Glover (1970), ch. 4, esp 79–81.

[43] See also Pettit (2001), 95–7; Pettit (2001a): the notion that an agent could have done otherwise should be interpreted as concerned not with the causal process leading to what was done but on the nature of the agent. For Pettit, an agent who has "discursive control" over an action is fit to be held responsible for it even if the action was the result of a causal sequence that made it inevitable.

[44] Honoré (1999), 35–6, 139; Dennett (1984), 136–7, 147–8; Pettit (2001), 96.

[45] For a positive answer see Pettit (2001), 15–17.

the legal domain. Certainly, morality is as much concerned with influencing future behaviour as the law; and it is only the excessive focus on agents found in many discussions of moral responsibility that conceals morality's concern with our interest, as victims, in security of person and property.

Honoré's account of responsibility suggests that interpersonal standards may be justified by appealing to the principle of taking the rough with the smooth. According to this principle, it is fair to hold people responsible for the bad outcomes of their conduct if they are able, in aggregate over a lifetime, to produce a surplus of good outcomes over bad outcomes.[46] Restated in terms of interpersonal standards, it is fair to hold people responsible for breach of interpersonal standards provided they are able, more of often than not, to comply with such standards when they try. People who are unable to do so should be exempted from moral responsibility (and legal liability) for breach of interpersonal standards on the ground that they lack minimum capacity. People who possess minimum capacity are able, more often than not, to comply with interpersonal standards;[47] and people of greater competence can comply more often than people of lesser competence, especially shortcomers. Because even shortcomers are able, over their lifetime, more often than not to comply with interpersonal standards, it is not unfair to require them to take responsibility for instances of non-compliance, for the sake of protecting the interest in security of person and property of those adversely affected by their behaviour. If this argument is successful, it supports the conclusion that morality, as much as law, makes only limited allowance for dispositional bad luck; and that interpersonal standards find a place in the moral domain as well as in the legal.

3.2.4 Liability, sanctions and dispositional luck

The law absolves certain categories of persons from responsibility for failure to meet its standards because they lack minimum general capacity; but it sets the level of minimum capacity needed for legal responsibility very low. People whose capacities exceed that minimum level are held responsible regardless of the extent to which their general capacities exceed the minimum. This is not to say that differences in abilities and resources are irrelevant; but they are relevant to deciding how to treat responsible persons, not to attributing responsibility. In legal terms, differences in capacity are relevant to sanctions, not liability. Outside the law, even if it is the case that the minimum level of capacity required to attract responsibility for failure to meet interpersonal standards of conduct is

[46] Honoré (1999), 26–7; Dennett (1984), 94–7.

[47] The empirical basis of this proposition is insecure (Cane (2001a), 80 n. 60). In Perry's view, the proposition is "simply false" (Perry (2001), 67. In a reply to Perry, Honoré bolsters his position by saying that because nearly everyone (even the shortcomer) wants to be treated as a "rational person", being held outcome-responsible according to interpersonal standards is itself a benefit: Honoré (2001), 226–7.

set higher than the law sets it, some people will exceed that minimum level of capacity to a greater extent than others. And as in the law, so in morality, differences in capacity may be taken into account in determining sanctions rather than in the attribution of responsibility.[48] For instance, if two young siblings of different ages commit the same moral misdemeanour, their parents may feel justified in punishing the elder more harshly than the younger.

Attending to this distinction between responsibility and sanctions reveals a very important contrast between what (in 2.4.1) I called the criminal law paradigm and the civil law paradigm of legal responsibility. The civil law paradigm gives much greater weight to victims' interests than the criminal law paradigm, which focuses primarily on the agent's conduct. In the criminal law paradigm, sensitivity to the bad luck of lacking a minimum level of (general) capacity may lead to denial of criminal liability. But also, sensitivity to unlucky differences in capacity amongst those who possess minimum capacity may find expression in sentencing practice.[49] Degrees of capacity to avoid incurring responsibility can be expressed as degrees of fault by penalising less harshly those of lesser capacity. The principle that punishment should be relative to individual fault is one source of misgivings about mandatory sentencing. This is not to say that the sentencing process is finely tuned to individual differences of capacity. Differences between the capacities of individuals may be difficult to observe and measure. The most courts can do is to give effect to the principle in a rough and ready way.

In the civil law paradigm, by contrast with the criminal law paradigm, sanctions typically take the form of victim-oriented remedies, not agent-oriented penalties. The basic measure of civil law sanctions is the negative impact of the agent's conduct on the victim (the victim's "loss" or the agent's gain at the victim's expense), not the faultiness of the agent's conduct. In assessing civil sanctions, differences of capacity amongst those who possess minimum capacity are generally ignored. Only in those rare cases in which a civil sanction is punitive in nature does the civil law paradigm pay attention to the agent's fault in matters of sanction as opposed to responsibility. In this way, the civil law paradigm is less sensitive to dispositional luck than the criminal law paradigm.[50] Both display limited insensitivity to dispositional luck at the level of attributing responsibility (although even here, the criminal law makes more allowance for dispositional bad luck than the civil law). But the criminal law paradigm is more sensitive to luck than the civil law paradigm at the level of sanctions. I hypothesised in 2.4.1 that the civil law and criminal law paradigms of legal responsibility broadly reflect moral principles of responsibility. If this hypothesis is

[48] Similarly: Shaver (1985), 82–3.

[49] Ashworth (2000), 123–8, 139–40; Walker and Padfield (1996), 50–1, 55, 314; Morse (1993), 242. The reduction of murder to manslaughter on grounds of diminished responsibility illustrates the same point.

[50] For the suggestion that criminal law ought to be more sensitive to circumstantial luck than civil law see Law Commission (1996), para. 4.33; Ashworth (1993).

correct, it supports the earlier conclusion that our moral responsibility practices, like our legal responsibility practices, make only limited allowance for dispositional luck.

3.3 CRITERIA OF LEGAL LIABILITY

3.3.1 Fault

3.3.1.1 Components of fault criteria

Legal criteria of fault have two types of components: mental elements and standards of conduct. Legal fault consists either of failure to comply with a specified standard of conduct, or of failure to comply with a specified standard of conduct accompanied by a specified state of mind.[51] Legal fault criteria may relate to conduct or to outcomes (or to both). The term "conduct" refers to both acts and omissions; and it connotes acts and omissions described not in terms of bodily movements (or their absence), but in terms of some legal category. In other words, "conduct" connotes acts and omissions plus what might be called their "definitional" consequences.[52] For instance, trespass to land may consist of the bodily movements involved in walking onto land, plus the definitional consequence of entering the land of another without their consent. "Outcomes" refers to what might be called "extrinsic" consequences. So, for example, if a person crashes their car into someone's house without the house-owner's consent, the person's relevant acts and omissions have trespass to land as a definitional consequence, and damage to property as an extrinsic consequence. It can be seen from this example that extrinsic consequences, as much as definitional consequences, may figure in the description of conduct. We could describe the driver's acts and omissions in terms of damaging property. So the distinction between definitional and extrinsic consequences does not reside in the fact that the former are part of the description of conduct while the latter are not. In law, the distinction lies in the respective relationships of definitional and extrinsic consequences with acts and omissions. The relationship between acts and omissions and extrinsic consequences is causal, but the relationship between acts and omissions and definitional consequences is not. A person will be liable for an extrinsic consequence of their acts or omissions only if it can be proved that their acts or omissions "caused" the consequence. The relationship between responsibility and causation is discussed in more detail in chapter 4.

[51] I am using this phrase in a purely descriptive way. I do not intend to enter the debate about whether states of mind are non-physical entities that can be "indirectly observed". As I argued in 2.3, for the purposes of understanding our responsibility practices, legal mental-state requirements are best understood as involving the interpretation of conduct against criteria of normal behaviour couched in terms of plans, knowledge of risk, and so on.

[52] Terry (1924), 123.

3.3.1.2 Intention

The mental elements of legal fault criteria are "intention", "recklessness", "knowledge/belief" and "malice". Intention may relate either to conduct (in which case we would describe the conduct as "intentional" or "deliberate") or to outcomes (in which case we would describe the outcome(s) as "intended"). In its core sense, intention involves "aiming at" as part of a plan. If a person's conduct is aimed at producing a certain outcome, then that conduct will necessarily be deliberate. But the converse is not true. A person's planned, deliberate conduct may produce an unintended outcome.

In law, a person may be liable for deliberate conduct regardless of outcome. Attempting a crime is an example: attempt is, by definition, deliberate. By contrast, some forms of legal liability arise only when a person's deliberate conduct produces an intended outcome. Murder is the classic example: the killing (or, at least, grievous bodily harm) must have been the intended outcome of an act of personal violence. Yet other forms of legal liability may attach to unintended outcomes of deliberate conduct. An example is tort liability for fraud ("deceit") in cases where the deliberate conduct consists of making a statement known (or believed) to be false.

3.3.1.3 Negligence

Legal negligence consists of breach of a standard of conduct—namely, the requirement that reasonable care be taken. It has no mental element. In particular, legal negligence does not involve inadvertence or inattention, understood as states of mind.[53] Negligence is failure to meet a standard of conduct *regardless of* accompanying mental state. Thus, for instance, deliberate, harm-causing conduct will satisfy the legal definition of, and may be actionable as, negligence if it can be described in terms of failure to take reasonable care. Negligence has a conduct-related element and an outcome-related element. The outcome-related element is foreseeability, and the conduct-related element is the taking of an unreasonable risk. Negligence is failure to take reasonable precautions against a foreseeable risk of injury. The function of the concepts of "foreseeability" and "unreasonableness" is to provide a normative criterion for the distribution of risks within society. In other words, they are principles of distributive justice. They strike a balance between the interests in freedom of action and freedom from adverse consequences that we all share.[54]

A foreseeable risk is one that the reasonable person in the agent's position would foresee. There are two standards of unreasonableness, which might be called "ordinary" and "extraordinary". The test of ordinary unreasonableness asks whether the reasonable person would have behaved as the agent did; while

[53] Similarly: Hart (1968), 148.
[54] Ripstein (1999).

the test of extraordinary unreasonableness is satisfied only if the agent behaved in a way that no reasonable person would (or could) have. The test of extraordinary unreasonableness tips the balance further in favour of freedom of action than does the test of ordinary unreasonableness. In civil law, the main areas of its operation are in relation to the application of bodies of professional knowledge,[55] and the exercise of discretionary powers by public authorities.[56] In criminal law, in the guise of "gross negligence", the function of tests of extraordinary unreasonableness is to justify the imposition of stiffer penalties than a holding of ordinary negligence would justify. For instance, causing death by gross negligence may qualify as manslaughter. In this context, gross negligence is characterised by the taking of risks that are "obvious", not merely "foreseeable", and which could have been avoided at relatively little cost to the agent. An obvious risk is one that would be obvious to the reasonable person in the agent's position.

3.3.1.4 Recklessness

In its core sense, recklessness consists of a mental element and breach of a standard of conduct. The mental element has two aspects: deliberation, and knowledge or "awareness". Reckless conduct is deliberate. The required knowledge is of a risk: either that certain conduct may produce a certain adverse outcome (as in the case of reckless homicide), or that a certain proposition may not be true (as in the case of tort liability for fraud, which can arise if the speaker knew or believed that the statement might be false). In the former case, the knowledge relates to an outcome; and in the latter case, it relates to the definitional consequence of the utterance—namely making a false statement. The relevant standard of conduct proscribes the taking of unreasonable risks: it is not reckless knowingly to take a reasonable risk (such as is typically involved in surgery, for instance). Reckless conduct is conduct done in the knowledge that it carries with it an unreasonable risk of some adverse consequence. One way of putting this is to say that recklessness involves "indifference". This might suggest that a person could be reckless only if they took a known risk "not caring" whether it would materialise, in other words, that "indifference" refers to a mental state. However, while a reckless person might be indifferent in this sense, it is not a necessary condition of legal recklessness. "Indifference" in the legal context should be understood simply in terms of deliberately taking a known risk.[57]

The difference between recklessness (in its core sense) and negligence resides in the fact that the former has a mental element (deliberation and knowledge of risk) that the latter lacks. The distinction is blurred, however, in the idea (which plays some part in the criminal law) of "inadvertent recklessness". Inadvertent recklessness involves deliberation as to conduct, but does not require knowledge

[55] Trindade and Cane (1999), 453–6.
[56] Cane (1996a), 246–7.
[57] Similarly: Galligan (1978), 62–3, 71–3.

of a risk attaching to the conduct. Deliberate risk-taking can be reckless if the risk is "obvious". In this respect, inadvertent recklessness is akin to gross negligence.

3.3.1.5 Intention and recklessness in the law of homicide

There are those who insist that "intention" should be understood only in its core sense (3.3.1.2)[58] in order to preserve a fundamental moral distinction between planned events and side-effects. In the English law of homicide, however, intention is given a wider meaning according to which outcomes that were foreseen but not planned may count as "intentional". Courts have vacillated on the issue of how high the probability of the foreseen event must be in order for it to count as an intended outcome of the conduct that causes it. But "indirect" or "oblique" intention is firmly entrenched in the law as a form of intention even though it encompasses cases that fall within the core meaning of "recklessness" (3.3.1.4). The effect of "stretching" the meaning of "intention" in this way is to extend the boundaries of the offence of murder and, hence, the incidence of the unique moral and social stigma and the severe penalty (life imprisonment or even death in some jurisdictions) that attach to it. A corresponding effect is to shrink the boundaries of the lesser offence of manslaughter, which is left to cover taking foreseen risks of lower probability.

Motive may provide a ground for treating a person who brings about a foreseen but unplanned outcome as harshly as if they had planned it (3.6.3.3). We may well think that a person who takes a high-probability foreseen risk for a bad reason is as culpable as if they had planned for the risk to materialise.[59]

3.3.1.6 Knowledge and belief

Knowledge and belief, as mental elements of legal criteria of fault,[60] relate to the definitional consequences of legally proscribed conduct, not to extrinsic consequences.[61] Whereas it is possible to believe something that is false, it is only possible to know things that are true. And whereas a person either knows a certain truth or does not know it, there can be different qualities of belief. More precisely, beliefs may be (more or less) reasonable or unreasonable. A function of the distinction between knowledge and belief, and of the concept of (un)reasonableness as applied to beliefs, is to distribute the risk of uncertainty about the existence of conditions of liability. Take rape, for instance. Rape is sexual intercourse without

[58] e.g. Finnis (1991).

[59] Similarly Norrie (2000), ch. 8.

[60] Knowledge and belief lie at the core of the difficult concept of dishonesty. Whether conduct is dishonest or not depends on the knowledge and beliefs of the agent.

[61] This is not to say that knowledge and beliefs may not be indirectly relevant to liability for extrinsic consequences. For instance, we would not normally say that a person intended to produce an outcome that they did not believe to be possible. But as criteria of fault in their own right, knowledge and belief relate to definitional consequences.

consent. The law could (but does not) interpret this to mean that a defendant was liable to be found guilty of rape unless the victim actually consented. Such a rule would put the risk of uncertainty about the existence of consent on the defendant. In practice, a defendant can be acquitted of rape even if the victim did not actually consent, provided the defendant believed there was consent. This raises the issue of whether the defendant's belief must be reasonable. A requirement of reasonable belief would put the risk of uncertainty about the state of the victim's mind on the defendant. Conversely, a requirement of genuine (even if unreasonable) belief would put the risk on the victim.[62]

3.3.1.7 Bad motives

Motives are reasons for action. In law, bad motives are sometimes referred to as "malice". It is important to distinguish motive from intention. The two may coincide, of course. The execution of a plan of action may be the agent's reason for embarking on the plan. But equally, they may not coincide—a thug's motive for inflicting a deliberate beating may be the facilitation of robbery, not the infliction of physical harm. The role in the law of malice and other components of fault criteria is discussed in 3.4.

3.3.2 Strict liability

3.3.2.1 Varieties of strict liability

Strict legal liability is liability regardless of fault, that is, liability regardless of whether the defendant engaged in conduct that breached a legally specified standard of conduct, and regardless of whether the conduct was accompanied by any particular mental state. Four varieties of strict legal liability can be distinguished, which I will call passive strict liability, right-based strict liability, activity-based strict liability and outcome-based strict liability. Passive strict liability is exemplified by the liability of the recipient of a mistaken payment, or of the proceeds of a fraud. The recipient may be liable to give up the benefit received regardless of whether the receipt of the benefit was in any sense the recipient's fault, and even regardless of whether it was the result of any conduct on the recipient's part.

Right-based strict liability is exemplified by liability for trespass to land. Legal rights (metaphorically) define the boundaries of legally protected spaces. Crossing such a boundary into a protected space may attract legal liability regardless of whether the crossing was in any sense the intruder's fault. Trespass to land involves crossing the boundary defined by the legal concept of "possession", by interfering with the possessor's legal rights over the land without consent. Two

[62] Similarly: Ripstein (1999), chs. 5 and 6.

points of explanation deserve to be made here. The first addresses a possible objection to the claim that liability for trespass to land (and strict liability more generally) is liability regardless of breach of legally specified standards of conduct. Could we not say (it might be objected) that entering another's land without consent (for instance) breaches the legally specified standard of conduct that proscribes entering another's land without consent? This objection confuses conduct with standards of conduct. Standards of conduct are concerned with the quality of conduct, that is, with whether for instance, physical harm was caused *negligently* or *recklessly* or *intentionally*. In this sense, the concept "entering another's land without their consent" does not express a quality of conduct, but rather a definitional consequence that turns certain acts and omissions into legally proscribed conduct. In just the same way, the concept of "creating a risk of harm" does not express a quality of conduct, but a definitional consequence that turns certain acts and omissions into legally proscribed conduct. All legal liabilities are based on some legally specified event; in most cases, that event consists of some specified conduct (that is, acts or omissions plus definitional consequences); and in some cases, legal liabilities depend on that conduct having a certain quality, namely that of satisfying a criterion of fault.

The second point of explanation concerns the concept of "rights". The point can be rendered salient by contrasting legal liability for wrongful arrest with legal liability for false imprisonment. Both wrongful arrest and false imprisonment are forms of "trespass to the person", and involve interference with the "right" to personal liberty. They differ, however, in that imprisonment will be illegal[63] unless it is actually authorised by some legal provision, whereas an arrest may be legal if the arrester had reasonable grounds to believe that a valid ground for arrest existed. In such cases, it follows that although wrongful arrest is a tort that protects rights, it is a fault-based tort, not a strict liability tort. Only some right-based liabilities are strict. When liability for fault is right-based, the fault element relates to a definitional consequence of the relevant act or omission, not to an extrinsic consequence. As a result, in cases where the arrester lacked reasonable grounds to believe that the arrest was lawful, no issue arises about whether there was a causal connection between the arrest and that lack of reasonable grounds. In effect, it is presumed in the plaintiff's favour that the arrester believed that a valid ground of arrest existed, and that if the arrester had believed the contrary, the arrest would not have occurred.

The third type of strict liability is activity-based. In the case of vicarious liability, the relevant activity is defined primarily in terms of a relationship with another person, for whose breach of the law the first person is held strictly liable by virtue of that relationship. Non-relational activity-based strict liability is common in the criminal law. Strict liability for breach of regulatory statutes is, perhaps, the prime example.

[63] In this context, both "wrongful" and "false" are synonyms for "illegal".

Fourthly, there is outcome-based strict liability. This form of liability rests on causation of adverse outcomes (i.e. extrinsic consequences) regardless of fault. The relationship between responsibility and causation is discussed in chapter 4.

3.3.2.2 Strict liability and luck

Before examining the incidence of fault-based and strict liabilities in law, it is necessary to say something about the relationship between strict liability and luck. I have defined strict liability as liability regardless of fault. By contrast, in philosophical discussions of responsibility, strict liability is often equated with liability regardless of bad luck. This is a mistake (so it seems to me). I would not argue, of course, that liability that is insensitive to bad luck may not be called "strict liability". What needs to be avoided is a confusion (which such terminology may bring in its wake) between liability regardless of fault and liability regardless of bad luck. This confusion arises partly from a failure to distinguish between liability regardless of fault, and liability in the absence of fault. It is often assumed that strict legal liability is liability in the absence of fault. In fact, absence of fault is never a precondition of legal liability; and it is perfectly consistent with holding a person liable regardless of fault that they actually were at fault. Because regimes of strict liability are typically created in order to improve the protection of the interests of potential plaintiffs, it would make no sense to build absence of fault into such regimes as a precondition of liability. An important justification for strict legal liability is to increase the chance that those at fault will be held liable in the face of difficulties of proof.

Having made the assumption that strict liability is liability in the absence of fault, the conclusion is then (often implicitly) reached that there is nothing that the person held strictly liable could have done to avoid the liability—or, in other words, that the events that gave rise to the liability were (in some relevant respect) outside their control and, therefore, a matter of bad luck. Unfortunately, this conclusion is false even allowing the premise. Of course, if the person held strictly liable was actually at fault, the liability-attracting events may have been relevantly under their control. But even if they were not at fault, it does not follow that the occurrence of the liability-attracting event was beyond their control. Whereas fault criteria are social and normative, control—on which the notion of luck is based—is an empirical concept. It does not follow from the premise that an event was not a person's fault that they could have done nothing to prevent it. All that we can conclude is that there is nothing they *ought* to have done, but did not do, to prevent it. This point is reflected in the insight provided by economic analysis that a strict liability regime may reduce the amount of harm an activity generates by reducing the incidence of the activity rather than affecting the way the activity is conducted.

There is another reason to resist the equation of insensitivity to fault with insensitivity to luck. In important respects, criteria of fault are themselves insensitive to bad luck.[64] First, people may vary in their ability to meet interpersonal standards of conduct for reasons entirely outside their control. In other words, variations in people's ability to meet specified standards of conduct (and, hence, to conduct themselves without fault) may themselves be a matter of luck. But such variations in ability may not be fully reflected in judgments of responsibility. In the law of negligence, for instance, individual differences of skill and ability, amongst adults who possess the minimum capacity needed for legal liability, are generally ignored for the purposes of allocating liability.

Secondly, a person who has the ability to meet a specified standard of conduct may be said to have been at fault in relation to a particular breach of that standard regardless of whether they could have exercised their abilities so as to prevent that breach of the standard. As we saw in the discussion in 3.2.3 of Honoré's distinction between "can (general)" and "can (particular)", once a person has failed to meet an applicable standard of conduct on a particular occasion, they cannot avoid responsibility for that failure by arguing (even if it is true) that they could not have met the standard on that occasion. The reasons why we do not allow such a plea were explored in 3.2.3. The point to be made here is simply that criteria of fault are not entirely sensitive to luck.

It follows from all this that the task of justifying insensitivity to fault in the allocation of responsibility is different from the task of justifying insensitivity to luck in the allocation of responsibility. In order to justify strict responsibility for conduct,[65] we need to justify holding people responsible for their conduct and its outcomes regardless of whether their conduct was in breach of any specified standard of conduct. This is typically done (in the legal domain, at least) by pointing to some *other* characteristic of the conduct, such as its impact on the interests of another person—perhaps that it infringed that person's rights, or that it subjected them to a "special risk of harm".

3.4 THE INCIDENCE OF FAULT-BASED AND STRICT LIABILITY

It is obviously out of the question to provide, in this book, a detailed map of the role of fault and strict liability in the law. However, it will be useful to provide a rough sketch of the main features of the terrain. The area in which mental elements are most important (in a qualitative, if not a quantitative, sense) is the criminal law.[66] There are two main reasons for this. One is that of all types of legal liability, criminal liability carries the greatest social stigma. Indeed, there is a widely-held view (especially amongst academics) that there should be no criminal liability without a mental fault element. A second reason is that the focus of criminal law is on punishing and deterring offenders rather than on

64 See 3.2.3.

65 Passive strict liability calls for agent-neutral justification in terms of fair distribution of resources.

66 On the quantitative issue see Ashworth and Blake (1996).

compensating victims. This focus has led to the adoption of choice and autonomy as the basis of notions of desert in the criminal law. Nevertheless, there are some criminal offences in which the fault element is defined purely in terms of standards of conduct; and certain defences (such as provocation and duress) rest, in part at least, on ideas of reasonable (or acceptable) conduct. Many criminal offences involve strict liability or have elements of strict liability.[67] It is noteworthy, too, that many strict-liability criminal offences are subject to a "due diligence" defence which allows the accused to avoid liability by proving compliance with standards of reasonable conduct. But even in cases where the conditions of criminal liability do not include a mental element, the accused's mental state can be taken into account in sentencing.[68]

Mental fault elements play a smaller role in tort law than in criminal law.[69] Tort law does not distinguish between intention and advertent recklessness: either will satisfy a requirement of intentionality.[70] This is because tort law is more concerned than criminal law with the interests of victims and, consequently, less concerned with degrees of fault; and because acting intentionally and acting with advertent recklessness both imply deliberation and choice. In (what might be called) its "ancillary" function in tort law, intention[71] justifies the awarding of remedies that would not be available in the absence of intention. The most obvious example of a remedy attracted by intentional conduct is punitive damages. In its "independent" function, intention justifies liability where none would attach in its absence. The main area of independent operation of intention in tort law is that of the so-called "economic torts". The requirement of intention serves to limit the intrusion of tort law into competitive market activity, and into the relations between capital and labour in the context of industrial action. The dominant criterion of fault liability in tort law is negligence. Strict liability plays a central role in those torts that protect property (and related) rights;[72] but it plays a relatively small role in liability for the infliction of physical and economic harm.[73]

In English contract law,[74] mental states play no function at all, not even at the level of remedies. Liability for breach of contract is either strict, or based on negligence; and contract remedies serve exclusively to protect and vindicate the interests of victims. This is because those interests are conceptualised as rights,

[67] Ashworth and Blake (1996).

[68] Ashworth (1996); *R* v. *F. Howe & Son (Engineers) Ltd* [1999] 2 Crim App R(S) 37 (negligence); *R* v. *Milford Haven Port Authority* 16 March 2000, CA (accessible on Casetrack) (strict liability).

[69] For a more detailed account see Cane (2000a).

[70] Similarly, in the tort of deceit, it is a condition of liability that the defendant either knew that the statement was false, or did not honestly believe it to be true. In tort law, inadvertent recklessness is assimilated to negligence, as are honest but unreasonable beliefs.

[71] By which, in this context, is meant "intention-or-advertent-recklessness".

[72] Cane (1996), ch. 2.

[73] Cane (2000b).

[74] The position in Canada, for instance, is different: *Royal Bank of Canada* v. *W. Got & Associates Electric Ltd* (2000) 178 DLR (4th) 385.

the invasion of which, *per se*, attracts liability. Nor do mental states play a large part in other areas of the law (such as restitution (or "unjust enrichment") and trusts).

At a general level, the distinction drawn in 2.4.1 between the criminal law and civil law paradigms of legal responsibility is central to understanding the role of mental states as conditions of legal liability. Mental states are of most importance in criminal law because criminal liability is essentially agent-oriented. Victims, of course, are not invisible in criminal law. The impact of the consequences of criminal conduct on victims is an important criterion of the seriousness of an offence. Nevertheless, as it is traditionally understood,[75] criminal law is not primarily concerned with victims but with offenders. By contrast, civil law exists primarily to protect rights and to compensate for harms. In terms of fault, the centre of gravity of civil law is negligence, not intention or recklessness; and strict civil liability does not attract the criticism that strict criminal liability does. Indeed, in some contexts, strict liability is seen as essential for giving proper weight to the interests of victims. For instance, maintaining the integrity of property rights is a major function of tort law. To this end, tort liability for taking another's property ("conversion") is basically strict; and, in addition, it is normally no answer to such liability that the owner failed to take reasonable care of the property. These rules are necessary for preserving the distinction between *meum* and *tuum*—what is mine and what is yours. By contrast, the criminal counterparts of tort liability for taking of property ("theft", for instance) typically require proof of intention and knowledge.[76]

Finally, a word about motives. The law's starting point is that liability should depend on conduct and mental states, not on reasons and motives for action. It is not the case, however, that motive is never relevant to legal liability. In tort law, for instance, a bad motive ("malice") can render conduct unlawful that would not be unlawful in the absence of a bad motive; and, conversely conduct that is *prima facie* unlawful can be "justified" by a good motive.[77] In the criminal law, whether a demand constitutes blackmail depends on the reason it was made; and offences of doing X "without lawful excuse" also make reasons for conduct relevant to criminality. Certain "defences" to liability, such as necessity, duress and self-defence, allow a person to avoid liability by pleading that although what they did was *prima facie* unlawful, they had an acceptable reason for doing it.[78] Motives may also be relevant to sanctions. For instance, in criminal law, reasons for action, both good and bad, can be taken into account in sentencing;[79] and in tort law, bad motive can be taken into account in assessing punitive damages.

[75] The "restorative justice" approach to criminal responsibility puts considerable emphasis on dealing with the effects of crime on victims: Braithwaite (1999).

[76] Ashworth (1999), ch. 9

[77] Cane (2000a), 539–42.

[78] For a general theory about the bounds of such defences see Horder (2000). See also Kahan and Nussbaum (1996) and Lacey (2000a).

[79] Walker and Padfield (1996), 49; Norrie (1993), 45–7. See 3.5.4.

3.5 THE NATURE AND FUNCTION OF LEGAL CRITERIA OF LIABILITY

The purpose of this section is to point out various features of legal criteria of liability that are typically unobserved in philosophical discussion of responsibility, or the significance of which is not fully appreciated. An understanding of these features is important for analysis of the relationship between legal criteria of fault and moral concepts of culpability.

3.5.1 Liability criteria are nested

By saying that criteria of legal liability are nested, I mean to capture the fact that conduct which attracts strict liability may satisfy the legal definitions of negligent, reckless or intentional conduct; that conduct which attracts liability for negligence may satisfy the legal definitions of reckless or intentional conduct; and that conduct that attracts liability for recklessness may satisfy the legal definition of intentional conduct. The same is true, I believe, of criteria of moral responsibility. However, much non-legal analysis of such criteria treats them as discrete rather than nested. For instance, outside the law it is often assumed that strict liability is liability in the absence of fault rather than liability regardless of fault.

There are two important reasons for this difference of approach. The first is concerned with proof. Take intention, for instance. It is one thing to know what intention is, but quite another to prove that a person acted intentionally. It may be easier to prove that the person's conduct was reckless or negligent even if, in fact, it was intentional. As we saw in 3.2.3, one of the suggested justifications for interpersonal standards of conduct is that they overcome difficulties of observing and measuring differences in competence between individuals. And a justification for some instances of strict liability is that they facilitate imposition of liability for fault in the face of difficulties of proving fault.[80] Non-legal discussions of criteria of responsibility rarely address issues of evidence and proof, and are concerned primarily with defining responsibility criteria.

A second reason why non-legal discussion of responsibility criteria tend to ignore the nested nature of such criteria is because they focus on agents. Consideration of strict liability brings out this point. In criminal law, strict liability is typically rationalised in terms of "social protection"; and in civil law, strict liability is a feature of heads of liability that are seen as protecting (victims') "rights". These justifications for strict liability direct attention away from the agent and onto the victim or society more generally. In this light, it would make no sense at all to require absence of fault as a precondition of the imposition of

[80] Leigh explains the development of strict and vicarious criminal liability in terms of "practical difficulties of enforcement" of regulatory laws: Leigh (1982), 15 and ch. 2 generally.

strict liability. Similarly with negligence: since the core idea here is lack of consideration for others, it would make no sense to define negligence so as to exclude intentional and reckless conduct.

3.5.2 Liability criteria are building blocks

The point to be made here can be well illustrated by reference to tort liability for fraudulent misstatements—"deceit" as it is called. The elements of liability for deceit are: (1) making a false statement; (2) either knowing it to be false, or not honestly believing it to be true;[81] (3) with the intention that another rely on it to their detriment. Liability for deceit extends to (4) harm caused by the making of the false statement, regardless of whether the harm was intended, foreseen or foreseeable. The elements of the tort of deceit, then, are an amalgam of knowledge, belief, intention, recklessness and cause-based (strict) liability.[82] This shows that the various components of legal responsibility judgments (intention, negligence, knowledge, and so on), are building blocks that can be put together to produce complex and subtly different liability criteria. The example of deceit draws attention to an important legal distinction between conduct and extrinsic consequences. It is by no means uncommon for the criterion of liability for conduct to be different from the criterion of liability for the extrinsic consequences ("outcomes") of that conduct. For example, the criterion of liability for conduct might be intention, while the criterion of liability for the outcomes of that conduct might be foreseeability. The effect of this combination of criteria is that there will be no liability unless the agent acted deliberately with the aim of producing some specified adverse outcome; but that once liability has been established, it extends to all foreseeable outcomes of the deliberate conduct. Similarly, a criterion of responsibility regardless of fault in relation to conduct may be combined with a fault-based criterion of responsibility for outcomes.

There is no reason to think that such combining of responsibility criteria is peculiar to the law. It is more common in the law than outside because the serious business of imposing penalties and obligations of repair requires finer responsibility discriminations than are often required in the moral domain.

3.5.3 Liability criteria and answers

The discussion so far has been concerned with what might be called "*prima facie*" liability. Equally important to judgments of legal responsibility are what

[81] i.e. in the awareness that it might be false; or as it is sometimes put, "recklessly, not caring whether it is true or false".

[82] An example in the criminal law is manslaughter by unlawful act: Simester and Sullivan (2000), 177.

might be called "answers"[83] to *prima facie* liability judgments. Such answers take a variety of forms. Most answers fall into one of two categories, that might be called "agent-relative" and "victim-relative" respectively. Certain victim-relative answers, such as contributory negligence and illegality, deny the agent's responsibility, either in whole or in part, by attributing it to the victim. Other victim-relative answers, such as consent and assumption of risk, admit the agent's responsibility for what happened, but deny that the victim has cause for complaint about what happened; in other words, they deny wrongdoing. Agent-relative answers fall into three broad categories: justifications, immunities and excuses. Justifications deny wrongdoing but not responsibility; immunities deny neither wrongdoing nor responsibility;[84] and excuses deny responsibility but not wrongdoing.[85] Examples of justifications can be found in tort law where, for instance, conspiring to cause economic loss by use of lawful means (a *prima facie* wrong) can be justified by pursuit of self-interest.[86] Conduct that *prima facie* constitutes trespass to the person may be justified by pointing to a lawful ground for arrest; and conduct that *prima facie* amounts to a nuisance[87] may be justified by pointing to statutory authorisation for what was done. Self-defence and consent are recognised as justifications in both tort law and criminal law, as is assumption of risk in tort law. As for immunities, judges and witnesses cannot, for instance, be held liable in tort (whether for negligence, defamation, or whatever) as a result of statements made in court proceedings; and children under a certain age are immune from criminal liability.[88]

Most excuses deny responsibility by denying that the agent had (full) control—either over their mind (as in the case of insanity or diminished responsibility), or over both body and mind (as in the case of automatism, somnambulism or hypnotism),[89] or over external circumstances (as in the case of frustration, necessity, provocation and duress). In this way, excuses play a crucial role in injecting into the law sensitivity to circumstantial and dispositional luck. The excuse of mistake negatives responsibility by negativing knowledge or belief of some definitional element of the wrong, such as lack of the victim's consent in rape.

No account of criteria of legal liability (or, for that matter, of moral responsibility) is complete without reference to answers. Answers are an integral part

[83] I have deliberately avoided the narrower term "defences".

[84] In other words, justifications and immunities negative liability, not responsibility. See also 6.6.5.3.

[85] Fletcher blurs the distinction between justifications and excuses by distinguishing between two theories of justification. According to the theory he favours, justifications do not deny wrongdoing: Fletcher (1993).

[86] This is an example of the relevance of motive to legal liability.

[87] Trindade and Cane (1999), 628–9.

[88] This is not to say that all of these excuses are similarly grounded. While ideas of capacity are central to defences that deny control over mind or body, defences such as provocation and duress (as well as the "justification" of self-defence) rest, in part at least, on ideas about reasonable or acceptable conduct in the face of exceptional circumstances (3.4).

[89] It may be argued that rules exempting children from liability are properly viewed as surrogates for judgments about the mental and physical capacities of individuals.

of judgments of responsibility.[90] The division between elements of *prima facie* liability and answers provides a technique for distributing between the agent and the victim the burden of doubt (or, positively, the onus of proof) as to whether particular components of relevant responsibility criteria were present in particular circumstances. This is not merely a technical matter. Consider contributory negligence, for example. Contributory negligence is a defence available in cases, for instance, of negligently inflicted personal injury. The onus of proving contributory negligence rests on the person whose negligence allegedly inflicted the personal injury, just as the onus of proving negligence on that person's part rests on the victim. The result of a successful plea of contributory negligence is reduction of the compensation that would otherwise be payable by the person whose negligence allegedly caused the injury, to reflect the victim's fault. By contrast, up until the middle of the twentieth century, the effect of a successful plea of contributory negligence was to relieve the injurer entirely of liability. The concept underlying the "defence" of contributory negligence also underlies the rule that a person, who causes financial loss to another by making a false statement on which the other relies, will be liable only if the reliance was "reasonable". The victim bears the onus of establishing that the reliance was reasonable; and if this cannot be proved, the loss-causer is not liable at all. The effect of this rule is that the defence of contributory negligence has no practical operation in relation to liability for negligent misstatement.

In the case of liability for negligent misstatement, the all-or-nothing requirement of reasonableness, coupled with the imposition on the victim of the onus of proof on this issue, gives expression to a judgment that in respect of the risk of suffering financial loss as a result of relying on false statements, people should take more care to protect their own interests than is required in cases in which contributory negligence is available as a defence. The interests of the party to whom the onus of proof on any particular issue is allocated are less well protected by the law than those of the party who enjoys the benefit of this allocation because in the face of uncertainty that cannot be resolved on the available evidence, the latter's interests will be preferred by the law to those of the former. Allocation of the onus of proof provides a technique by which the law can express and give effect to value judgments about the strength of the various interests to which responsibility judgments relate. Matters are further complicated by the fact that whether the onus of proof has been "satisfied" is ultimately a matter of judgment. As a result, the weight given to evidence adduced by the party who bears the onus of proof on a particular issue may be affected by whether the other party offers any evidence in reply. In technical terms, this is sometimes expressed by saying that the latter bears an "evidential onus" (i.e. a

[90] The point made in 3.5.2—that liability criteria are building blocks—can be extended to the relationship between liability criteria and answers. A good illustration is provided by the interaction of strict liability and the defence of contributory negligence: Cane (1997), 59–60.

tactical requirement to adduce evidence) even though they do not carry the "persuasive onus" (which rests on the other party).[91]

The interaction between answers and the onus of proof is clearly illustrated by a class of agent-relative defences that do not neatly fall into any of the three categories of defences introduced earlier, namely fault-based defences to *prima facie* strict liabilities. For instance, a statute may impose (strict) liability for the escape of a noxious substance into a waterway, but provide a defence that "all practicable precautions" were taken, or that "due diligence" was exercised by the defendant. In theory, such a provision creates a fault-based liability. The legal effect of including fault as a matter of defence rather than *prima facie* liability is to shift the onus of proof on the issue of fault to the defendant, thus making it easier for *prima facie* liability to be established. In practice, it may be very difficult for the defendant to disprove fault, thus rendering the liability effectively strict, even though theoretically fault-based.

Clearly, this evidentiary element of responsibility practices is a feature that a purely agent-focused account is unlikely to capture. There is a greater need to resolve evidentiary uncertainty in the legal domain than in the moral domain. But the difference is only one of degree, related to the fact that in the moral domain we can live with more uncertainty than we can in the legal domain. The allocation of burdens of proof is neither a technicality nor a mere practicality of the law. It is essential for dealing with epistemological uncertainty about the past, which pervades all domains of life.

3.5.4 Liability criteria and sanctions

As noted in 2.2, a central feature of legal responsibility practices which tends to be ignored in philosophical discussions of responsibility is that of sanctions. The liability criteria identified in 3.3 play a part not only in determining when legal liability arises,[92] but also in determining sanctions. This is most notably true in the criminal law, where the nature and quality of the defendant's conduct and mental state can be taken into account in determining sentence. Indeed, the offender's mental state is relevant to sentencing even in cases where mental state is irrelevant to the existence of liability (3.4). In addition, however, the impact of the crime on the victim and on society, as well as the offender's motives and the social context of the crime, can all be taken into account in determining sentence even when they are irrelevant to liability.[93]

The allocation of matters such as motive and social context to the sentencing stage is not a mere technical detail. It leaves these issues much more in the

[91] Cross and Tapper (1995), 121–9.

[92] And when responsibility-negativing answers are available.

[93] Motive is also relevant to the defences of duress and necessity. But even when the agent's reason for action does not satisfy the requirements of such a defence, it may be taken into account in sentencing.

discretion of the court than is the issue of liability. Except at the margins, liability criteria ignore individual differences of capacity and opportunity to comply with the law, and treat everyone alike. At the sentencing stage, by contrast, each offender is treated much more as an individual, and ideas of culpability and desert are given much more individualised interpretation.

Norrie believes that the abstractness and generality of the criteria of criminal liability (intention, recklessness, and so on), juxtaposed with individualised assessments of culpability for sentencing purposes, make the law internally incoherent.[94] He also detects tension in the law's rejection of the relevance of motive to *prima facie* liability and its admission in defences (such as duress and necessity) and at the sentencing stage. At first sight, this view has considerable force. How can it make sense for the law to announce, on the one hand, that motive is irrelevant (as a matter of *prima facie* liability), but on the other hand that it is relevant after all (as a matter of defence, and in the sentencing process)? Or how can it make sense for the law to announce, on the one hand, that fault is irrelevant (as a matter of liability), but on the other hand that it is relevant after all (as a matter of defence, and in the sentencing process)? Surely the law cannot have it both ways. Either motive is relevant or it is not. Either fault is relevant or it is not.

It seems to me, however, that the force of Norrie's argument rests largely on an assumption that the only, or at least a predominant, function of the criminal law is to make and enforce assessments of individual responsibility. This is certainly one of its purposes, and an important one at that. But it has other important functions as well, such as deterrence of undesirable behaviour, expression and reinforcement of social norms, and education in desirable patterns of behaviour. The performance of such functions would be difficult, if not impossible, without the use of rules and principles of general application. Putting the point another way, the criminal law is as much concerned with telling us what our responsibilities are as with deciding whether, in particular cases, we should be subject to sanctions for not performing those responsibilities. The law gives us goals to aim at, while at the same time offering reassurance that failure to meet those goals will not necessarily attract legal sanctions. No doubt this multiplicity of functions introduces complexity into the law, but not incoherence or, as Norrie seems to think, unproductive tension.

In fact, Norrie seems to object not to general principles of responsibility, as such, but rather to the general principles embodied in the current law, in particular that they are predominantly based on concepts of individual human agency and will at the expense of qustions of motive and social context. So, for instance, he apparently thinks that the general criteria of liability for theft should refer to the reason why the property was taken in addition to the fact that the agent's

[94] Norrie (2000), 25: issues of motive "continually irrupt within the law . . . contradictorily as between the stages of conviction and punishment"; 134; ch. 8. His position bears some affinities to moral particularism, as to which see Crisp (2000), 24–32. The theoretical underpinning of my position is akin to "Rossian generalism": Hooker (2000), 2–7.

conduct displayed a certain mental attitude.[95] He also thinks, for instance, that the general rules of liability for homicide should allow for exculpation of the mercy killer.[96] These are controversial views, but they do not cast doubt on the utility of distinguishing between the issue of liability—whether a person should be subject to sanctions at all—and the question of appropriate sanction; or of deciding the issue of liability according to general principles while taking a much more individualised approach at the sentencing stage. The distinction between responsibility and sanctions is much less prominent in morality, not because (as Norrie seems to suggest) moral ideas of responsibility are more individualised than legal liability concepts, but because morality lacks the institutional resources to utilise sanctions to fine-tune responsibility judgments based on general principles.

Under the civil law paradigm, the relationship between liability and sanctions is rather different than that under the criminal law paradigm. The main criterion for the assessment of civil law remedies is the impact of the breach of law on the interests of the victim. This explains why the quantum of damages (for instance) is generally insensitive to the degree of the defendant's fault.[97] Civil law is much more concerned with victims than criminal law. One context in which the defendant's fault is relevant to remedy in civil law is that of punitive damages in tort. Although such damages are payable to the plaintiff, they are assessed as if they were a fine, taking account, amongst other things, of the degree of the defendant's fault. It is only in this context, too, that the financial means of the defendant are relevant to the assessment of compensation. In criminal law, by contrast, the offender's means are more generally relevant to the assessment by criminal courts of monetary fines and (in England, at least) compensation orders.[98] This difference between the assessment of criminal and civil sanctions is, no doubt, partly to be explained by the fact that people are rarely sued civilly unless they are insured against liability or can afford to pay substantial damages out of their own resources. But the agent-focus of the criminal law, and the civil law's concern with the interests of victims, provide principled support for the different approaches to the relationship between culpability and sanctions.

3.6 RESPONSIBILITY, FAULT AND CULPABILITY

So far, the discussion has skirted the issue of the relationship between responsibility and culpability, and that between culpability (understood as a notion belonging to the moral domain) and fault (understood as belonging to the legal domain). The time has now come to confront these issues head-on.

[95] Norrie (2000), 101–2.
[96] Norrie (2000), 175–6.
[97] For a more detailed discussion in relation to tort law see Cane (1998), 160–70.
[98] Cane (1999), 251.

3.6.1 "Moral responsibility requires intentionality"

To repeat the opening sentence of this chapter, one of the clearest and most persistent themes in philosophical discussions of responsibility is that responsibility requires culpability (or "blameworthiness").[99] In such discussions, "responsibility" is typically glossed as "moral responsibility", and culpability is commonly equated with intentionality. This produces the conclusion that moral responsibility requires intentionality. A further conclusion is sometimes then reached: to the extent that legal liability can attach to conduct and consequences that are not intentional, the law is out of step with morality. To that extent, law is to be explained by reference to its own special goals and purposes rather than by reference to ideas of moral responsibility.

The requirement of intention is the product of an agent-relative perspective that grounds responsibility in autonomy and choice.[100] As Wallace puts it: "the [moral] demands we make of people regulate not just bodily movements but also the quality of will expressed by such bodily movements".[101] Conduct and consequences that are part of the agent's plan are the paradigm of intended phenomena. When assessed against this paradigm of deliberate conduct and planned consequences, all other suggested criteria of responsibility appear more or less problematic. For instance, Finnis objects to the extension of the legal definition of "intention" to cover cases of awareness of a virtually certain risk of harm (advertent recklessness) by asserting that there is a fundamental moral distinction between the planned consequences and "side-effects" of deliberate conduct.[102] For Wallace, by contrast, "recklessness can itself be a blameworthy quality of will" because doing something "in the awareness that there was some risk" that harm would occur as a result "is an aspect of choice that is subject to being controlled directly by reason".[103] In terms of the choice paradigm, the legal concept of inadvertent recklessness is more difficult because while it involves deliberation as to one's conduct, it does not require awareness of the risk attached to the conduct. Negligence is doubly problematic in requiring neither deliberation as to conduct nor awareness of its possible consequences, but only failure to meet specified standards of (reasonable) conduct in one's bodily movements and mental awareness. Liability without fault does not even require failure to meet such standards.

[99] e.g. Hart (1961), 173, 178.

[100] Wallace (1994), 128, 132–3; McFee (2000), 4. The account of moral responsibility in Fischer and Ravizza (1998) in terms of "reasons-responsiveness" is a choice-based theory.

[101] Wallace (1994), 119.

[102] Finnis (1991).

[103] Wallace (1994), 138–9.

3.6.2 Some definitional preliminaries

Before proceeding further, a couple of definitional points need to be addressed. First, it should be noted that there are certain senses of the word "responsibility" in relation to which it is untrue, by definition, that responsibility requires culpability. Most obviously, the word "responsibility" may be used in relation to conduct and consequences that attract praise rather than criticism.[104] Again, a person (or an animal, or a state of affairs) may, for instance, be the cause of some event and, in that sense, called "responsible" for it, regardless of whether they were culpable in relation to it. Similarly, talk of a person's prospective "responsibilities" carries with it no implication of culpability. In fact, the word "responsibility" in the phrase "responsibility requires culpability" typically seems to refer to what Hart called "moral liability responsibility".[105] This entails having to account for past conduct and consequences, and running the risk of incurring a sanction if the account is judged unsatisfactory.

The second definitional point concerns use of the word "moral" in the phrase "moral responsibility". As was noted in 1.2.1, there is no agreement amongst theorists about how to delimit the domain of morality. Wallace argues that conduct will attract moral responsibility if a "reactive" emotion would be an appropriate response to it.[106] The reactive emotions "principally" include "resentment, indignation and guilt".[107] In Wallace's view, what distinguishes moral assessment of a person's conduct and its consequences from non-moral assessment is that the former "has a quality of opprobrium"[108] lacking in the latter. This suggests that in his view, moral reasons for action are reasons non-compliance with which would be culpable and would rightly attract blame. Under this approach, a person could not be morally responsible for any conduct or consequences that would not rightly attract blame. According to the choice-based account of moral responsibility, conduct rightly attracts blame when it is at fault, fault being understood in terms of choice.[109]

Even accepting, for the sake of argument, that culpability requires choice, the fundamental problem with such an approach is that it defines fault and culpability entirely in terms of "quality of will". But quality of will is only half the subject-matter of a theory of culpability. Many of the things we choose to do are not culpable. Some are praiseworthy rather than blameworthy, and some are neither praiseworthy nor blameworthy. Similarly, deliberately taking a known

[104] The distinction between praise and blame may be important in other ways, too. It has been suggested that unintended good outcomes are less likely to attract praise than unintended bad outcomes are to attract blame: Schultz and Schleifer (1983), 58.

[105] See 2.1.1.

[106] Wallace (1994), 80–3. This approach derives from Strawson (1962). For a useful discussion of Strawson's approach and of objections to it see Fischer and Ravizza (1993), 4–25.

[107] Wallace (1994), 20.

[108] Wallace (1994), 81.

[109] Wallace (1994), §5.2

risk is only blameworthy if the risk is an unreasonable one to take. A theory of moral responsibility needs not only to specify the quality of will that attracts responsibility, but also to give an account of the sorts of conduct that attract responsibility. Putting the same point another way, an account of moral responsibility needs to tell us not only what counts as breach of a moral obligation, but also what our moral obligations are.

3.6.3 The importance of choice

3.6.3.1 Moral obligations of care

The importance of the objection just made (at the end of 3.6.2) is this: by focusing attention on quality of will as the basis of moral responsibility, approaches such as that of Wallace implicitly invite us to compare law and morality in terms of their respective approaches to quality of will, at the expense of considering the equally important issue of what our moral obligations and our legal obligations respectively are. Such approaches tell us nothing about the conduct that attracts responsibility, either in terms of its nature or of its impact on other individuals. As I argued in 2.4, one of the lessons law teaches us is that our responsibility practices have important relational aspects; and there is no reason to believe that moral responsibility practices differ from legal responsibility practices in this respect. Theories of moral responsibility that focus exclusively on the quality of the agent's will, and ignore the nature of the agent's conduct and its impact on other individuals, invest the quality of the agent's will with a centrality and importance, in explaining the nature of responsibility, that it does not deserve. Moral responsibility is not a function solely of the quality of the agent's will any more than legal liability is.

In one respect, Wallace acknowledges this point. He is at pains to say that what makes conduct blameworthy (and, therefore, a proper subject of a judgment of moral responsibility) is not that it evokes a reactive emotional response, but that such a response would be appropriate; and such a response will be appropriate if the conduct breaches some moral expectation or obligation. Once this position has been reached, it becomes unclear why choice should be a precondition of moral responsibility. Take negligence, for instance. In law, negligence consists of failure to take reasonable precautions against foreseeable risks of injury.[110] It has no mental element. According to the "choice theory of moral

[110] Some criminal law theorists attempt to reconcile criminal liability for negligence with the traditional concept of *mens rea* by what Ashworth (Ashworth (1999), 197) calls "a form of 'capacity theory' ". This theory is derived from the point made by Hart (Hart (1968), 153–5) that there is a difference between asking whether a person failed to meet a standard of care and whether they could have done so. The idea seems to be that liability for failure to meet a standard *that one had the capacity to meet* justifies imposition of liability on the basis that one could have met the standard if one had *chosen* (or, perhaps, "tried")—a hypothetical choice, we might say. But, of course, a hypothetical choice is no choice at all. Obviously a person may deliberately flout a legal standard of conduct; but the essence of negligence is failure to comply with a legal standard, full stop. The second

responsibility", therefore, there is no moral obligation to take reasonable precautions against foreseeable risks of injury. It follows that the law is out of step with morality in imposing liability to pay compensation for negligently inflicted injuries. And yet it is far from obvious that it would be considered inappropriate (for instance) for a pedestrian, badly injured when a speeding car mounts the pavement, to feel indignation (or some other reactive emotion) against the negligent driver. Wallace attempts to meet this point by locating the culpability of negligence in some prior choice (for instance, to drive in the first place). A major problem with this move is that the pedestrian's reactive emotion is an appropriate response not to the decision to drive, but to the speeding that causes the accident.

More importantly, however, the notion of a moral obligation to take care appears problematic only because of the initial explication of moral culpability in terms of choice. This approach arises from concentration on the quality of the agent's will at the expense of the nature of the agent's conduct and of its impact on other individuals and on society at large. Once account is taken of the fact that the driver took an unreasonable risk and, as a result, inflicted serious personal injuries on the pedestrian, the notion that the driver did not breach a moral expectation and has no obligation to compensate the victim, seems preposterous. Indeed, from the pedestrian's point of view, such a conclusion might seem downright immoral. Putting the point more generally, an account of moral responsibility that condemns infliction of harm and interference with the interests of others only if they result from the agent's choice, puts far too much weight on our interest, as agents, in freedom of action, and takes far too little account of our interest, as victims, in security of person and property. In imposing liability for negligent infliction of personal injury, the law is not out of step with morality. Nor is it pursuing its own peculiar goals that find no place in practical reasoning outside the law. Rather, it is giving expression to widely held expectations about how individuals should behave towards one another. I am not suggesting that all of the expectations recognised and protected by the law, through the mechanism of imposing liability for negligently inflicted harm, are recognised and protected in the moral domain. Law and morality may differ in terms of the obligations and (prospective) responsibilities they recognise and impose. What I am questioning is that responsibility in the moral domain is limited by the notion of choice.[111]

My argument is not that the quality of the agent's will is unimportant to responsibility (either in the legal or the moral domain), but that it is only one factor relevant to responsibility. The interplay of the various interests that we all share as agents, victims and citizens is well reflected in the criminal law and

limb of Hart's distinction (as he notes) deals with the issue of (dispositional) luck as it affects capacity (as opposed to choice). As I have argued, the issue of luck is all-pervasive, and is in no way relevant only to liability for negligence. Injecting sensitivity to luck into capacity-based liability does not turn it into a form of choice-based liability.

[111] Wallace (1994), §3.3

civil law paradigms of legal liability. The quality of the agent's will plays an important role in the criminal law paradigm of liability for two main reasons. One is that the focus of this paradigm is on the offender rather than the victim. However, victims are not invisible in the criminal law. Although there are conduct crimes, the typical criminal offence is the result crime. As a general rule, the more serious the impact of the offender's conduct on the victim, the more serious the offence and the heavier the penalty. An important function of the criminal law is to discourage victims from "taking the law into their own hands" by providing them with diversionary vindication.[112] Because the interests of victims are not unimportant in the criminal law, the agent-focus of the criminal law paradigm does not support an objection of fundamental principle to offences of negligence.

However, such offences may be contingently objectionable on the basis of the second main reason why choice is important in the criminal law paradigm, namely the stigma that attaches to criminal liability and punishments. The greater the punishment, the greater the stigma. So the greater the penalty attaching to an offence, the less justified are departures from the choice principle in fixing the liability criteria for that offence. Although the choice principle does not exhaust the concept of fault, conduct that is faulty according to that principle is more blameworthy than conduct that merely breaches a standard of conduct. The most severe punishments should, therefore, be reserved for conduct that displays a bad will. But while it would be inappropriate for the most serious criminal penalties to attach to offences of negligence, it is not obvious that criminal offences that lack a mental element (intention or recklessness) are morally objectionable in themselves. Certainly, the choice theory of moral responsibility does not establish this conclusion because it pays little or no attention to factors, other than the quality of the agent's will, that are as important to practical reasoning in the moral domain as in law. In both domains, our responsibility practices have a relational character that the choice theory fails to capture.

When we move to the civil law paradigm of liability, the inadequacies of the choice theory of responsibility become even more obvious. In the civil law paradigm, the interests of victims are given at least as much weight as those of agents. This is reflected in the fact that the basic measure of civil law remedies is the impact of the proscribed conduct on the victim, not the nature of the agent's conduct or the quality of the agent's will. Take the law of contract, for example. According to the choice theory, the law of contract is, to all intents and purposes, completely out of kilter with morality because liability for breach of contract is either strict or negligence-based. It is true that typically, a person will not incur liability for breach of contract without first having made a choice to undertake contractual obligations. But many contractual obligations are imposed rather than undertaken. More importantly, in Wallace's terms, the choice to enter the contract is not the conduct to which a reactive emotion is an

[112] Gardner (1998).

appropriate response. The basic point is that the civil law paradigm of liability is essentially relational, and this is the main reason why the choice theory of responsibility, focusing as it does on the quality of the agent's will, cannot give an adequate account of it.[113] There is no reason to think that the ideas of responsibility underlying the civil law paradigm are peculiar to the law. Rather they have close analogies in the moral domain.

3.6.3.2 Choice and automaticity

There is, it seems to me, another important reason why the choice theory fails as an account of our responsibility practices. It can readily be conceded that free choice is the strongest basis for responsibility; and that various (mental, physical and environmental) factors, which deprive us of the faculty of choice or of the ability to give effect to our choices, or which render our choices less than fully free, may weaken the case for holding a person responsible. Such an approach seems based on the idea that a person either consciously chooses to act or they do not, and that the question of whether the agent made a free choice can meaningfully be asked in relation to each and every piece of conduct for which a person might be held responsible. If some piece of a person's conduct was freely chosen, then they can rightly held responsible for it. But if that piece of conduct was either not chosen, or was chosen under certain constraints, then they can rightly held either not responsible at all, or responsible to a lesser degree than they would be if their choice had been free of relevant constraints.

An important feature of human conduct missing from this account is what might be called "programmed choice". By this term I refer to what is more commonly called "automatic" behaviour. Automatic behaviour is behaviour in relation to which the power of free choice is available to the agent, but has been programmed (and, hence, suppressed), typically in the interests of efficiency.[114] Automatic behaviour is different from addictive behaviour, which is a product of some internal physical or mental constraint on freedom of choice. Both programming and addiction can typically be traced back to consciously chosen conduct; but programmed behaviour remains within the agent's power of control in a way (or, at least, to an extent) that addictive behaviour does not. Programmes can be overridden much more easily than addictions can be resisted, and may need to be overridden in the interests of efficiency and safety. A useful analogy is with the automatic pilot device on a large jet. Under stable conditions, the automatic pilot is at least as reliable and efficient as the (conscious) human pilot. But when flying conditions no longer fall within the parameters of the automatic

[113] For an agent-focused account of the difference between criminal law and tort law see Moore (1996): "wrongdoing, and not culpability, is the main trigger of tort liability" (331); "[t]ort law relies centrally on . . . the culpability of unexercised capacity [rather than] [t]he culpability of choice" (332).

[114] For a useful philosophical discussion of automatic behaviour taking account of neuropsychological data see Goldman (1994). See also Pettit (2001), 37–9, 90–3.

pilot's operation, safety and efficiency demand that the programmed behaviour of the electronic pilot be replaced by the more responsive choices of the human pilot.

Automatic behaviour is typically the result of repetition of tasks and the acquisition of skill. An experienced driver, for example, will do many things automatically or "without thinking" or "inadvertently" that a learner would do deliberately and attentively. The good driver is one who knows when it is necessary to pay attention and when doing things automatically will be safe. The good driver also knows which tasks can safely be programmed and which need attention on every occasion. Automaticity is not pathological, but a pervasive and functional form of human decision-making. At the same time, of course, automatic behaviour can be dysfunctional: not all tasks are suitable for programming, and sometimes programmes need to be overridden in the interests of safety and efficiency.

Because automaticity is a pervasive and functional mode of human decision-making, a good theory of responsibility will accommodate it. The choice theory, it seems, does not.[115] This is reflected in the difficulty that the choice theory has with negligence. Much behaviour that satisfies the legal definition of negligence—i.e. failure to meet the standard of reasonable care—is automatic. One of the functions of the reasonable care standard is to set the acceptable limits of automaticity. From this perspective, (inadvertent) negligent conduct occurs when tasks are inappropriately programmed, or when a programme is left running in inappropriate circumstances.[116] By its apparent exclusion of automatic behaviour from the realm of moral responsibility, the choice theory carries the unattractive and implausible implication that morality has nothing to say about such behaviour, despite its important role in human decision-making. The law is not out of step with morality in treating "automatic failure" to meet the standard of reasonable care as a species of fault. In morality, too, people may attract blame (or praise) on account of what they do "without thinking". And if this is correct, there is no reason to deny that negligent conduct that is not programmed may attract moral blame.

The choice theory of moral responsibility imposes an implausible and unattractive limitation on our moral obligations. By excluding failure to meet standards of reasonable conduct from the catalogue of moral faults, it deprives morality of resources to deal with inappropriate and dysfunctional automaticity.

[115] It was noted in 3.6.3.1 that Wallace attempts to integrate responsibility for failure to take care into the choice theory by relating the failure of care to some temporally prior choice. Searle adopts a similar strategy in relation to automatic behaviour, which he thinks can be described as "intentional" if it is a means to an end which the agent has consciously chosen (e.g. changing gear in the process of executing a conscious decision to drive to work): Searle (1983), 84–5. This account reduces the distinction between doing something deliberately and doing it voluntarily (understood as the opposite of "involuntarily") to the point where the phrase "intentional act" becomes (almost) pleonastic. Automatic conduct is voluntary, but it is not planned in the way that intentional conduct is.

[116] Killingley (1997). But I am not suggesting that all inadvertent behaviour is automatic in the sense of programmed.

In imposing obligations of reasonable care, the law is not departing from morality but reinforcing it.

3.6.3.3 Culpability, mental states and reasons

The choice theory of moral responsibility locates culpability in mental states, such as intention and recklessness, rather than in motives or reasons. As Wallace puts it:

> "At least for the purposes of apportioning blame, we generally do not care so much why people comply with the moral obligations to which we hold them, so long as they do comply with those obligations in fact . . . a person can be said to have complied with the obligation [of mutual aid] if she acted out of a choice to save me from harm—even if the choice was based on reasons of self-interest rather than a moral nature".[117]

One assumes that Wallace would also support the converse proposition: a person can be said to be morally culpable for having chosen not to comply with a moral obligation (to keep a promise, for instance) even if they had a good reason for doing so. However, Wallace adds (in a footnote), "it is of course otherwise when questions of assessment of character are at issue: there we do care very much what an agent's reasons for acting really were".[118]

Wallace's approach—that distinguishes between choices and reasons for choices, and between moral culpability and bad character—can be contrasted with Finnis's view:

> "the claim that . . . bad motives cannot delegitimate lawful means . . . sophistically ignore[s] one of morality's most elementary principles. . . . One's conduct will be right only if *both* one's means *and* one's ends are right . . . *all* the aspects of one's act must be rightful for the act to be right".[119]

On this basis, Finnis approves of certain decisions which are usually taken to establish that a person can be liable in the tort of nuisance for maliciously interfering with the use and enjoyment of a neighbour's land even if, in the absence of malice, the interference (though deliberate)[120] would not be actionable as a nuisance. He also supports a principle accepted in some US jurisdictions, but rejected in England, that intentionally inflicting economic harm is actionable if done for a bad reason, but not if done for an acceptable reason. Simester and Sullivan seem to go even further than Finnis by arguing that culpability is a function of motives, and that the quality-of-will elements of criminal offences are "technical" requirements of the law.[121] Norrie strikes a middle course, arguing that both quality of will and quality of reasons can be relevant to culpability.[122]

[117] Wallace (1994), 130–1, 132.

[118] Wallace (1994), 131 n. 19.

[119] Finnis (1995), 238 (original emphasis).

[120] The basic criterion of liability for nuisance is whether the interference was unreasonable, not whether it was deliberate.

[121] Simester and Sullivan (2000), 264, 280; also 113, 133.

[122] Norrie (2000).

This variety of approaches to the relevance of motives suggests a certain instability in thinking about the relationship between responsibility, quality of will (mental states) and quality of reasons for action. In the law, this instability is reflected in the fact that the general principle of the irrelevance of motives is subject to exceptions that form no clear pattern. As was suggested in 3.3.1.5, it is also reflected in judicial "stretching" of mental-state (i.e. quality of will) elements of criminal offences, so that a requirement of "intention" may be satisfied where the offender was aware of the risk of a bad outcome, but did not plan it; and so that a requirement of awareness of risk may be satisfied where the risk was so obvious that (in the court's view) any reasonable person would have been aware of it. One basis on which we might think that a person who takes a known risk deserves to be treated as if they had planned the outcome is the reason why they took the risk. Many people would have no difficulty concluding that a person who plants a bomb in a railway station solely in order to cause disruption and dislocation would be rightly treated as a murderer when it explodes, causing death and injury in addition to property damage. A motive of causing disruption to train timetables is a very bad reason for creating a risk of death. And one basis on which we might think that a person who fails to notice an obvious risk deserves to be treated as if they did notice it is the reason for their unawareness. A young driver who is not aware of the risk to a pedestrian he hits and kills should not be treated more leniently because his mind was focused on impressing his friends with daring antics.

The truth seems to be that both in law and morality, reasons sometimes matter, but not always. The association between motives and character alerts us to this. The notion of "character" is a vague and difficult one.[123] In Wallace's dichotomy between culpability and character, knowing someone's character tells us "the sort of person they are"; and this is related as much to their reasons for action as to the actions themselves.[124] For some criminal law theorists,[125] "character" refers to aspects of our personality that are beyond our control. For them, a person's character is a matter of "attitudes, concerns . . . values"[126] and dispositions as opposed to capacity and choice. This distinction between conduct

[123] For a recent judicial discussion see *Ryan* v. *R* [2001] HCA 21. For an historical account of the role of character as a basis of criminal liability see Lacey (2001).

[124] It is, however, important to distinguish between motives and reasons on the one hand, and character on the other. Failure to do so is, I believe, the source of some of the shortcomings of "character" theories of criminal responsibility discussed in Duff (1993). Duff's own account would also benefit from drawing this distinction. For instance, he explains the defence of duress in terms of the reasonable person's character (350–1, 357–9). It seems to me more straightforward to say that a defence of duress will succeed if the accused acted reasonably in yielding, i.e. if, objectively judged, the accused had a good reason for yielding. The law may be concerned with the reason why a person acted as they did on a particular occasion without being interested in their "character". Duff's discussion of "out-of-character" conduct (374–8) would also benefit from drawing the distinction between character and reasons. Character is an evaluative inference based on a person's behaviour, or an interpretation of their behaviour. Unlike reasons for action, it does not provide a causal explanation of that behaviour.

[125] See Norrie (2000), 127–8.

[126] Duff (1993), 361.

and character reflects an important strand in our thinking about responsibility in both the legal and the moral domains to the effect that sanctions should be imposed on people for what they do, not for what they are (thought to be).[127] We may well object to punishing a "bad person" for doing what we would not punish a "good person" for doing, or to imposing a sanction for doing a blameless act for a bad reason.[128] There is also a danger that if the distinction between quality of will and character is not maintained, we might too easily attribute responsibility for particular conduct and outcomes on the basis of an adverse judgment about a person's character rather than on an assessment of their behaviour on the relevant occasion. There are complex rules of evidence designed to avoid precisely this result.[129] On the other hand, "good character" is recognised as a mitigating factor in sentencing.[130]

The correct conclusion seems to be that in both the moral and the legal domains, judgments of responsibility and culpability are a function of complex amalgams of proscribed conduct, quality of will, and quality of reasons. Nor is it obvious that the respective weights given to these factors in the legal domain is systematically different from those given them in the moral domain.[131]

3.6.3.4 *Culpability, knowledge and belief*

Knowledge and belief are elements of certain legal fault criteria (3.3.1.5). As such, they relate either to the definitional consequences of the legally proscribed conduct, or (indirectly) to its extrinsic consequences.[132] As a general[133] rule, however, it is not a condition of legal liability that the person held liable knew, at the time of the conduct in question, that what they were doing, or its consequences, could attract legal liability. Ignorance of the law is no excuse. It is sometimes assumed that in this respect, law and morality are out of step. This assumption seems to me to be questionable.[134] It is certainly true that we do not expect young children, for instance, to understand the difference between moral right and wrong. They need to be educated. Ability to understand this difference is a precondition of fair judgments of moral responsibility and culpability. This is one of the reasons why the law, too, exempts children from legal liability. But in both the legal and the moral domains, adults who possess a certain minimum mental capacity are presumed to know the difference between right and wrong.

[127] Stein and Shand (1974), 132.

[128] This explains, for instance, why malice does not defeat a defence of justification in the law of defamation—the value of telling the truth is not destroyed by a bad motive.

[129] Keane (2000), chs. 15 and 16

[130] Walker and Padfield (1996), paras. 4.24–7. For Dan-Cohen, character is relevant to responsibility because a person's character (as much as their choices) is part of what they are: Dan-Cohen (1992), 973–7.

[131] *Pace* Norrie (2000), 232.

[132] See n. 61 above.

[133] But not absolute: Ashworth (1999), 243–8; Husack and von Hirsch (1993).

[134] Similarly: Smiley (1992), 42; Moore (1996), 327.

Any other approach would not only be impractical.[135] It would also undermine the whole project of subjecting human conduct to the governance of interpersonal standards; and it would set the balance between freedom of action and security far much too in favour of the former.

Knowledge and belief are sometimes associated with intention and recklessness, respectively. Ashworth says that "[in] general terms, the requirement of knowledge is regarded as having the same intensity as that of intention"; and "[r]eckless knowledge", he says, "bears the same relation to knowledge as recklessness to intention . . . the general common law meaning of reckless knowledge is that [the agent] believes that there is a risk that [X], and goes on to take that risk".[136] These formulations invite confusion. Intention, and the deliberation involved in taking a known risk, are qualities of will directed towards conduct; whereas knowledge and belief are cognitive states about the world which cannot, in themselves, be blameworthy. Even unreasonable beliefs are not culpable as such. What may be culpable is the conduct that led to the unreasonable belief being held (failure to make reasonable inquiries, for instance); or conduct based on knowledge or belief. Of course, intention and recklessness are related to belief. Normally, we would not say that a person intended some conduct or outcome X unless the person believed X not to be impossible. Similarly, we would not normally say that a person was (advertently) reckless in relation to a particular outcome unless the person believed the outcome not to be impossible. But to intend X is to plan it, not to know or believe it to be possible; and recklessness consists in the deliberate taking of a known risk, not the awareness of the risk. Knowledge and belief may be an element, in the sense of a precondition, of culpability; but culpability itself is a function of proscribed conduct, quality of will and quality of reasons.

3.6.3.5 Strict liability

Non-criminal liability

In terms of the agent-focused choice theory of responsibility, liability without fault (which I shall loosely call "strict liability" in this section)[137] lacks moral foundation.[138] From this perspective, if it is to be explained at all, this must be done in terms of "practical" or prudential concerns peculiar to the law, or by some teleological rationale that sacrifices personal autonomy to "social protection" or some such goal. An important attempt to provide an agent-focused justification for strict liability is that of Tony Honoré.[139] It is based on his concept

135 *Pace* Velasquez (1983), 114.

136 e.g. Ashworth (1999), 191 and 195 respectively.

137 Remember that strict legal liability is liability regardless of fault, not liability in the absence of fault.

138 Bodenheimer (1980), 9–10. In Hart's view, there are "conceptual barriers" to strict and absolute liability in morality but not in law: Hart (1968), 225–6.

139 Honoré (1999), esp ch. 3. For a more detailed discussion see Cane (2001). See also Dan-Cohen (1992), 982–5.

of "outcome responsibility". This is responsibility for the good and bad outcomes of conduct, regardless of luck. Outcome responsibility has an ontological function of establishing and maintaining our individual identity as persons. But it also has a normative basis in the principle of taking the rough with the smooth. The idea is that since people get (and take) credit for the good outcomes of their conduct regardless of whether they were the result of good luck, they must be prepared to accept responsibility for bad outcomes regardless of whether they were the result of bad luck. According to Honoré, outcome responsibility is fair to those people whose conduct, in aggregate over a lifetime, will produce more good outcomes than bad—who, in his view, are the vast majority.

Although Honoré's account of outcome responsibility stresses its insensitivity to luck,[140] it is clear that he also considers it to be insensitive to fault. It could not perform its ontological function if it was dependent on fault, because not only what we do culpably, but also what we do faultlessly, contributes to our personal identity. Apparently for this reason, he thinks that it is a short step from justifying outcome responsibility to justifying strict legal liability. Before considering that argument, however, it is worth looking at Honoré's discussion of moral responsibility. His views here seem to be internally inconsistent. On the one hand, he subscribes to the common opinion that moral responsibility requires blameworthiness, although he is prepared to classify failure to meet standards of care as blameworthy. On the other hand, however, he accepts that a person may be under a moral obligation to repair a bad outcome of their conduct even if they were not at fault in causing it. Thus, he thinks, if a child breaks a neighbour's window while playing ball, the parents are under a moral obligation to pay for the repair of the window even if they were in no way at fault.[141] Such moral responsibility is analogous to legal vicarious liability, which is a form of strict liability. He also thinks that if, through no fault of mine, I knock someone over in the street, I incur a moral obligation to repair the situation, perhaps by helping them up, or calling for assistance, or apologising, or replacing the bottle of wine that was broken when they fell.[142]

In this regard, it seems to me that Honoré's second thought is better than his first. It is certainly true that in the moral domain we would probably not think it right to punish a person unless they were to blame. On the other hand, these examples show that even in the moral domain, a person may be under an obligation to do something to repair a bad outcome even if they were in no way to blame for it.[143] Certainly, the person knocked over in the street could be thought

[140] Indeed, he tends to confuse insensitivity to luck with insensitivity to fault by taking strict liability to be liability regardless of luck.

[141] Honoré (1999), 126. For the view that such responsibility to compensate is not moral responsibility see Wolf (1985), 276–7. Dan-Cohen agrees, and bases such responsibility on a conception of "the self that extends to one's children": Dan-Cohen (1992), 960 and 981–2.

[142] Honoré (1999), 127

[143] For some empirical evidence supporting this conclusion see Lloyd-Bostock (1984).

justified in feeling a reactive emotion, such as indignation, toward me, if I did nothing to make good the harm done. This is not because harmful outcomes of an agent's conduct are in some part constitutive of their identity, but rather because our responsibility to repair bad outcomes can extend further than our responsibility to avoid faulty conduct.[144] So long as we focus on the agent, it is hard to see how this can be so. This is why it seems difficult to justify agent-focused punishment regardless of fault. But once we take account of the interests of the victim, it seems less clear that victim-focused obligations of repair should always depend on fault. In some situations, lack of fault seems a less than conclusive response to the harm suffered by a faultless victim.[145]

Support for this conclusion is found in cases of necessity, where a person damages another's property in order to protect some more valuable interest, such as life or personal safety. Feinberg gives the example of a backpacker, caught in a freak blizzard, who stumbles across an unoccupied hut, breaks in, consumes the owner's food, and uses their furniture for firewood. Surely, says Feinberg, the backpacker is "justified in doing all these things", and is blameless for doing them. And yet, he says, the rights of the hut owner have been infringed; and, we might add, the backpacker ought to pay for the damage done and the food consumed.[146] The classic legal example is *Vincent* v. *Lake Erie Transportation Co*,[147] in which a shipowner left its ship tied to the plaintiff's dock, after completion of unloading, in preference to putting out to sea in a storm. The ship repeatedly rammed the dock, causing it considerable damage. Although the court's holding that the shipowner's action was justified has been questioned,[148] the principle that justification does not extinguish property rights is generally accepted as not only legally correct, but also fair.

Because of his first thought about moral responsibility—namely, that it requires blame—Honoré does not see the potential of this line of reasoning to justify at least some instances of strict legal liability. Rather, he seems to think that the principle of taking the rough with the smooth, which, in his view, gives a moral grounding to outcome responsibility, can also provide a justification for strict legal liability. He says that once outcome responsibility has been justified, it involves "no great extension" to justify strict legal liability;[149] and he explicitly justifies vicarious liability by appealing to the principle of taking the rough with the smooth.[150] In my view, however, while this principle can provide a moral justification for a form of responsibility the function of which is to establish and maintain our individual identity as persons, it can hardly justify strict

144 Similarly: Herman (1993), 97–9.

145 "it would be a kind of insanity . . . to insist . . . that we might, if we conducted ourselves clear-headedly enough, entirely detach ourselves from the unintentional aspects of our actions": Williams (1976), 125.

146 Feinberg (1978), 102; discussed by Thompson (Thompson (1984), 112).

147 (1910) 124 NW 221.

148 Brudner (1987), 365–8.

149 Honoré (1999), 40.

150 Honoré (1999), 81.

legal liability, the function of which is the allocation of punishments and obligations of repair.[151] It is one thing to say that the outcomes of our conduct contribute to our personal identity even if the conduct was not faulty, but quite another to say that a person deserves to be punished for the bad outcomes of their conduct, or is under an obligation to repair such outcomes, even though the conduct was faultless.

It seems to me, therefore, that viewing responsibility in a relational, as opposed to an agent-focused, way provides a more promising foundation for strict non-criminal liability than the principle of taking the rough with the smooth. The examples considered above[152] illustrate how taking account of the interest in security of the faultless victim of harm can justify the imposition of an obligation of repair on the author of the harm in the absence of fault. Adopting the terminology introduced in 3.3.2.1, such cases involve outcome-based strict responsibility, i.e. responsibility for causing harm by one's conduct. Of course, the examples only show that obligations of repair may arise in the absence of fault. They do not support the proposition that causing harm will always generate an obligation of repair in the absence of fault. Indeed, in law, strict outcome-based liability is rare. This may be partly because the obligation of repair that the law imposes (normally to compensate the victim in full for the harm suffered) is onerous compared with the sort of obligations of repair that morality would impose in the absence of fault—to apologise, perhaps, or to make good minor damage, such as a broken window or bottle of wine.

In order to explain (in general terms) when strict outcome-based liability may arise it is necessary to look beyond the relationship of agent and victim of harm, and to ask questions, at a social level, about how risks of harm ought to be distributed. Indeed, consideration of such distributional issues is necessary in order to determine not only the scope of strict responsibility for harm. Once it is accepted that responsibility (for harm) may have more than one basis—intention, recklessness, negligence, and so on—criteria are needed to determine the scope of each of these bases of responsibility.[153] The key to doing this resides in the recognition that these various bases of responsibility for harm distribute the risks of harm differently. For instance, making intention a precondition of liability for harm gives greater protection to our interest in freedom of action than resting responsibility on negligence. Conversely, strict liability for harm gives more protection to our interest in personal security than negligence-based liability. Determining the scope of the various bases of responsibility is not a

[151] John Gardner (Gardner (2001) offers a different moral justification for responsibility regardless of fault based on the idea of reasons for action. We may have a moral reason to achieve or avoid a particular outcome independently, and even in the absence, of reasons to take steps to achieve or avoid that outcome—where, for instance, we know we could not succeed even if we tried. And if we have a moral reason to achieve or avoid an outcome, we may also have a "categorical, mandatory" reason—i.e. an obligation—to do so. However, Gardner explicitly acknowledges that this argument does not justify the imposition of sanctions for breach of such an obligation (140–1).

[152] Leaving aside, for the moment, the case of the broken window.

[153] These points are discussed in detail in ch. 6.

question of what it means to be responsible, but rather part of the specification of what our responsibilities are.

It might be argued that my analysis so far fails to distinguish between responsibility and obligations of repair. The argument would be that a person may be morally obliged to repair a bad outcome even though they are not morally responsible for it—moral liability without moral responsibility, we might say. It is certainly true that the distinction between liability and responsibility plays a role in moral thinking as it does in the law. The passive strict liability of the recipient of a mistaken payment provides an example of liability without responsibility that is as well grounded in morality as in law. But in my view, neither outcome-based strict liability (i.e. strict liability for causing harm) nor right-based strict liability (i.e. strict liability for interference with rights) is usefully analysed as an example of liability without responsibility because unlike passive strict liability, both attach to conduct of the person held responsible. However, for present purposes it is not necessary to press this point. My argument in this chapter is more concerned with the role of culpability in moral reasoning than with the precise scope of the concept of responsibility. Acceptance that there can be moral liability without moral responsibility, and that there can be moral liability without moral culpability, would be enough to challenge the view that strict legal liability is inconsistent with morality. For this reason, too, it is not necessary at this point to examine further the case of the child who breaks a neighbour's window and to consider whether vicarious liability is responsibility-based or whether it is, rather, an instance of liability without responsibility. This issue is dealt with in 5.10.6.

The law is not out of step with morality in recognising strict obligations of repair. The idea that it is arises from viewing moral responsibility in an excessively agent-focused way. Responsibility is not just a function of the quality of will manifested in conduct, nor of the quality of that conduct. It is also concerned with the interest we all share in security of person and property, and with the way resources and risks are distributed in society. Responsibility is a relational phenomenon. Herein lies the key to explaining and justifying obligations of repair regardless of fault.

Criminal liability

Whatever one might think of strict obligations of repair, punishment in the absence of fault is generally considered extremely difficult to justify. And the more severe the punishment, the more difficult is the justificatory task. How, one might ask, could we ever be justified in imprisoning a person regardless of fault? But the problem exists no matter how severe the punishment, because punishments carry a stigma and an implication of blameworthiness that obligations of repair do not. This point is most starkly illustrated by the fact that the restitutionary obligation of the passive recipient of a mistaken payment is not only strict, but arises regardless of whether any conduct of the recipient was causally related to the transfer, however indirectly. In other words, both in law and outside it, an obligation to repair an undesirable outcome can arise independently not only of fault, but even of conduct.

The responsibility-based objection to strict criminal liability[154] rests not directly on its disregard of fault, but rather on the fact that punishment carries with it an implication of blameworthiness that is inappropriate in the absence of fault. The problem is not that responsibility requires blameworthiness and fault, but rather that punishment does. Strict criminal liability is objectionable not because it is inconsistent with the fault principle, but because the sanction that attaches to criminal liability is punishment. A common strategy for justifying strict criminal liability and punishment in the absence of fault is an appeal to "social protection". The argument is that whereas the requirement of a mental element expresses the value of individual autonomy, strict liability protects society's interest in freedom from harm, especially (but by no means exclusively) diffuse harm such as environmental pollution. The force of this approach relies on diverting attention away from the agent and on to the victim—i.e. society. But so long as the response to social harming is punishment of the offender rather than imposition of an obligation of repair, the re-orientation does not overcome the basic responsibility-based objection to strict criminal liability.

It may be that in the case of some strict liability criminal offences (such as "minor", "regulatory" offences) fines are generally perceived to be a form of tax rather than punishment. This seems to be the way that some people view parking fines.[155] Many taxes, of course, are levied on activities and outcomes (such as wealth-generation) that are considered to be positively desirable, for purposes such as facilitating wealth redistribution. But some taxes (such as so-called "green taxes") are designed to discourage the pursuit of certain activities or reduce their incidence. The crucial difference between such an "activity tax" and a fine is that the latter carries an implication of wrongdoing that the former does not. For this reason, strict liability fines are problematic from a responsibility point of view in a way that activity taxes are not.

3.7 SUMMARY

This chapter has dealt with the relevance to responsibility of luck on the one hand and fault on the other. Its main aim has been to undermine the widely held view that the law is out of step with morality in its willingness to impose liability regardless of culpability. It has been argued that because of the ubiquity of

[154] On which see also Dan-Cohen (1992), 1001–1003. Even if strict criminal liability is objectionable in terms of principles of personal responsibility, it does not follow that it may not be justifiable on some other ground. Enforcing principles of responsibility is not the only value pursued either in the legal or the moral domains. See further ch. 6.

[155] The view that strict liability crimes are not "real crimes" (Norrie (1993), 89–95; Wells (2001), 5–8, 21–31 (discussing the relative roles of police and regulatory agencies as enforcers of the criminal law)) reflects uneasiness about punishment regardless of fault and suggests a re-interpretation of penalties for such offences as taxes.

luck, and because of our psychological need to feel a degree of control over our lives and the world around us, every responsibility system must incorporate limited sensitivity to luck. I used the example of reasonable person tests of negligence to illustrate the way in which the law does this. The elements of legal criteria of fault were then analysed and juxtaposed with what was termed the choice theory of moral responsibility. The conclusion reached was that morality, like law, recognises that failure to comply with standards of conduct can be culpable regardless of choice. More radically, it was then suggested that in certain circumstances, morality, like law, imposes obligations of repair regardless of fault. But the law is arguably out of step with morality in punishing regardless of fault. This may help to explain why regulatory authorities tend to prosecute strict liability offences only in cases where the offender was actually culpable. This point is discussed further in 7.3.

4

Responsibility and Causation

THE AIM OF this chapter is to elucidate the part played by principles of causation in the allocation of (historic) legal and moral responsibility or, in other words, the relationship between causation and responsibility. As in previous chapters, the starting point will be the law. In the philosophical literature, responsibility and causation tend to be treated in relative isolation from one another.[1] This is another result (so it seems to me) of the focus of many philosophical discussions of responsibility on the conduct and mental states of agents. Causation concerns the link between conduct and outcomes. To the extent that outcomes are ignored by (and in the analysis of) concepts of responsibility, causation is ignored, too.

It will be recalled that causal responsibility was one of the elements of Hart's five-fold taxonomy of responsibility.[2] In this sense, according to Hart, events, animals and inanimate objects may be responsible. For present purposes, an important omission from Hart's account is an analysis of the relationship between causal responsibility and what he termed "legal liability responsibility" and "moral liability responsibility".[3] It is clear from the discussion so far that being causally responsible for some harmful event is not a sufficient condition of legal liability; and it will become clear in the course of this chapter (in 4.1 particularly) that it is not a necessary condition either.

The argument of this chapter starts with the proposition that concepts of causation perform various functions. In law, their function is to justify the imposition of sanctions in respect of bad outcomes. Principles of causation link agents to outcomes (4.1). This explains various features of legal causation, and it needs to be borne in mind when comparing legal with extra-legal concepts of causation (4.2). Legal rules and principles of causation are concerned with two issues: as a matter of fact did the agent's conduct play a part in bringing about the outcome in question? (4.3); and if so, ought the agent to be held liable for that outcome? (4.4). By virtue of law's institutional resources, study of the legal answers to these questions can deepen and enrich our understanding of how they might be answered in extra-legal contexts. It also provides resources to meet the objection that responsibility for outcomes should not depend on causation (4.5).

[1] Shaver (1985) and Smiley (1992) are notable exceptions.

[2] See 2.1.1.

[3] Hart and Honoré (1985) (the first edition of which was published in 1959) provides detailed discussion of the role of causation in establishing legal liability, but it does not address the issue explicitly in terms of analysis of concepts of responsibility.

4.1 CAUSATION, CONSEQUENCES AND OUTCOMES

At this point, we need to return to an issue that was raised earlier (in 3.3.1.1) about the distinction between definitional consequences and extrinsic consequences (the latter of which I am calling "outcomes" to distinguish them from definitional consequences). Human behaviour—both acts and omissions—can be described in terms of (the presence or absence of) bodily movements—mechanically, as it were. Thus, the event of A hitting B could be described in terms of the movement of A's arm through space into contact with B's body. From A's point of view, we might describe the event in this way if, for instance, C had overpowered A and used A's arm as a weapon to hit B. Except under circumstances such as (or analogous to) this, descriptions of a person's bodily movements normally rest upon and reflect an assumption that the person is motivated by reasons, purposes and knowledge. This is certainly true in the context of attributing historic responsibility, because we only attribute responsibility to people who possess a minimum capacity for practical reasoning, and in circumstances where it is judged that the opportunity to exercise that capacity was not blocked by circumstances beyond the person's control. The shift, from describing the event purely in terms of the movement of A's arm to describing it as A hitting B, rests on an assumption that A possesses a minimum degree of what might be called "general" capacity to control the movement of the arm. "General capacity" corresponds to Honoré's concept of "can (general)", which was explained in 3.2.3. If a person can (general) control the movement of their arm, and their arm comes forcefully into contact with another person's body, we would normally describe their conduct in "teleological" terms such as "hitting" the other person, not in "colourless" mechanical terms such as "physical contact between two bodies".

In this example, the hitting of B is a consequence of the movement of A's arm, but it is a definitional consequence, not an extrinsic consequence (or "outcome"). To say that A hit B with his arm is to describe A's conduct, not an outcome of A's conduct. It provides a purposive, as opposed to a mechanical, description of A's conduct. In the labelling of criminal offences, the distinction between definitional and extrinsic consequences is sometimes made explicit. "Causing death by dangerous driving" provides an example: "dangerous driving" is a purposive description, in terms of a definitional consequence, of certain acts and omissions; whereas "death" specifies the proscribed outcome of that (proscribed) conduct. The definitional consequence supplies a description of the means by which the proscribed outcome came about. Criminal responsibility attaches not to the driver's bodily movements as such, but to those movements under a particular purposive description, i.e. "dangerous driving". That description contains an evaluation of the agent's conduct, chosen in order to justify the imposition of criminal liability. By contrast, "murder" describes an outcome (i.e. causing a person's death), and it implies a mental state (basically, intention), but it provides no description of conduct in terms of definitional consequences (such as "stabbing" or "poisoning"). Whereas the means by which death is caused are of the essence of the offence of causing death by dangerous driving, it is the mental state of the killer rather than the means of causing death that constitutes the essence of murder. These examples confirm the point, made in 3.3.1.1, that the distinction between definitional consequences and outcomes is not that the former figure in the description of conduct while the latter do not. The difference is that for the purposes of attributing legal responsibility, the relationship between conduct and outcomes is treated as being causal, whereas that between definitional consequences and conduct is not. For instance, the law does not ask whether the driver's bodily movements caused the dangerous driving; but it does ask whether the driver's bodily movements, under the description of "dangerous driving", caused the death.

Definitional consequences, then, transform mechanical descriptions of human behaviour into purposive descriptions. Purposive descriptions are evaluative interpretations of human behaviour. Acts and omissions ("conduct") are bodily movements—or their absence—under a purposive description, evaluatively interpreted. Acts are "voluntary" bodily movements, and omissions are voluntary abstentions from bodily movement. For the purpose of attributing responsibility, we are inclined to describe human behaviour mechanically only when we judge that the person had no control over their bodily movements because they were unconscious, for instance, or physically overpowered. Our normal assumption is that a person's bodily movements are under their purposive control. Voluntary conduct is a precondition of most forms of legal liability. Some forms of legal liability attach to purposive conduct regardless of outcomes. A classic example is trespass to land. Here, the relevant purposive description of human behaviour is something like "entering or encroaching upon land". If the land is in another's possession, and if the entry or encroachment is done without the consent of that person, the conduct can constitute trespass to land regardless of any extrinsic consequence ("outcome") of the conduct, such as damage to the land or to buildings on it, or financial loss to the person in possession. In civil law, such forms of liability are described as "*per se*" liability. In criminal law, conduct crimes (such as attempts, possession offences and many "regulatory" offences) are of this form. Causation is irrelevant to *per se* liability.

4.2 THE NATURE OF CAUSATION IN LAW

4.2.1 The scope of the causation question

In relation to some proscribed conduct C and some proscribed outcome O, the causal question in law is not "what caused O?", but "did C cause O?". The legal causation inquiry is never at large because the purpose of the inquiry is the attribution of (legal) responsibility for outcomes. It does not follow, of course, that "C caused O" is synonymous with "C is responsible for O". Both in law and morality, a person may be held not responsible for some outcome that their conduct caused because, for instance, they lacked the minimum capacity needed to be a subject of judgments of responsibility. Conversely, "C did not cause O" is not synonymous with "C is not responsible for O". For instance, a person may have an obligation to repair an outcome even though they did not cause it. The restitutionary obligation of the passive recipient of a mistaken payment provides a clear example.[4] More importantly, perhaps, even in cases where causation is a necessary condition of moral or legal responsibility, it is not a sufficient condition. Causing a harmful outcome by one's conduct will not attract liability, either in law or morality, unless the conduct is in breach of some rule or principle of conduct, and unless the outcome is of a proscribed type. Causation merely provides the necessary link between proscribed conduct and proscribed outcomes.

4.2.2 The temporal orientation of causation

In law, causation is primarily concerned with the past, with allocating punishments and obligations of repair in respect of adverse outcomes that have already occurred. Even in cases where the law seeks to prevent an adverse outcome in the future by issuing an injunction, for instance, it does so on the basis of a judgment that if the outcome had occurred in the past, the person to whom the injunction is addressed would have been held to have caused it. As traditionally understood, legal causation is not concerned with identifying "recipes" for preventing adverse outcomes in the future. By contrast, according to one version of the economic analysis of legal liability rules the purpose of such rules is to impose obligations of repair on the "cheapest cost-avoider", i.e. the person who could, at least cost, have prevented the adverse outcome in respect of which liability is imposed. Under this approach, principles of "causation" perform the forward-looking function of identifying that person so as to minimise the future incidence of outcomes of the type in question.[5] However, it is difficult to explain why the search for the cheapest cost-avoider should be limited in range to the agent and the victim. Why should an agent be liable on the basis that they could have avoided the outcome more cheaply than the victim if some third party could have avoided it more cheaply than either of them? And why should the ability of this victim in particular to avoid the adverse outcome in question be relevant when the aim is to minimise the future incidence of adverse outcomes generally, not just in relation to this victim?

A significant part of the traditional answer to such questions is found in the nature of the historic link between D's conduct and the adverse outcome suffered

[4] See further 4.4.2.4.
[5] Calabresi (1975). On consequentialist approaches such as Calabresi's see Smiley (1992), 170–1.

by P. The significance of this link for ideas of responsibility can be explained psychologically. It is important to our sense of personal identity to feel that by our conduct, we can achieve effects in the world. What we are is partly a function of what we achieve, of the changes we bring about in the world, both good and bad. Because of the ubiquity of luck, we cannot fairly claim credit for all the good outcomes of our conduct; and neither, conversely, do we fairly attract discredit for all the bad outcomes of our conduct. Still less do all the bad outcomes of our conduct attract moral sanctions, or legal punishments and obligations of repair. But our moral and legal responsibility practices play a central role in establishing our identity and standing as moral agents and as members of a community bound together by moral and legal norms and practices. In those practices, principles of causation play a central role in linking us with events in the world.

This is not to say that our identity as persons is entirely a function of the outcomes, both good and bad, that our conduct produces. We are also partly defined by our abilities and capacities—our "potential" we might say, as opposed to our "achievements". Our responsibility practices assess people primarily according to their achievements. As we have seen, both law and morality make only limited allowance for differences in abilities, capacities and potentialities. This is not because giving people incentives to exercise their abilities and capacities and to realise their potential is not important, but only because our responsibility practices are not primarily designed to create such incentives. This is one reason why the "cheapest cost-avoider" approach provides an unconvincing interpretation of our legal responsibility practices: that approach is, as it were, "potential-based", whereas our legal responsibility practices are predominantly "achievement-based". It is not implausible to think that our legal and moral responsibility practices have incidental incentive effects that may minimise the sort of bad outcomes with which they are concerned. But if one were setting out to construct an efficient system for generating incentives to minimise such outcomes, it is highly unlikely that the result would be our moral and legal responsibility practices. It is, therefore, extremely ironical that economic analysts should offer an account in terms of incentives as the best interpretation of legal liability rules.

4.2.3 The meaning of "cause"

In their seminal work on causation,[6] Hart and Honoré identify the "central notion" of causation with events such as moving one thing by striking it with another, breaking glass by throwing stones, causing injury by blows, and heating things by putting them in a fire.[7] They treat other types of link between conduct and outcomes, such as providing the opportunity for an outcome to occur,

[6] Hart and Honoré (1985) (first published 1959).

[7] Hart and Honoré (1985), 27–8.

failing to prevent an outcome, and inducing or encouraging or assisting a person to bring about an outcome, as being, at best, marginal forms of causal connection.[8] So, for instance, they consider vicarious liability to be a "non-causal ground of responsibility".[9] Much of their analysis is affected by this approach to defining causal link, which is part of their larger project of showing that causation in the law is closely related to "commonsense" notions of causation used in everyday life. Their basic view was that "the ordinary person" uses the word "cause" in the narrow sense they called its "central notion".

For present purposes, it is satisfactory and even preferable to define causation simply in terms of a link between conduct and outcome. This leaves open the question of whether, to what extent, and in what respects, ideas of causation within the law are similar to or different from those outside the law. I share with Hart and Honoré[10] the view that there are important continuities between ideas of responsibility in law and in morality. Their procedure for establishing this is to begin with what they take to be the "commonsense" idea of causation outside the law, and to look for its reflection in the law. They point out, as I have done, that because legal sanctions are, on the whole, more severe than moral sanctions, and because responsibility issues that must be resolved by the law can often be left unresolved in the moral domain, legal concepts of causation and responsibility are often richer and more detailed than their moral counterparts. But their account can be interpreted as suggesting that to the extent that the law goes beyond morality, it parts company with it. By contrast, my argument has been that when it goes beyond morality, the law often supplements it by working out the detailed implications of principles and purposes that figure in a more abstract way in moral thinking. For this reason, it is better first to examine what the law says about the relevance to responsibility judgments of the conduct-outcome link, unencumbered by unsupported assumptions as to what "common sense" has to say on this topic.

4.2.4 Causation as interpretation

There is an important sense in which a statement that particular conduct C caused a particular outcome O is an interpretation of events that could be described without using the concept of causation.[11] Take a typical tort action arising out of a collision between two cars. Such an event could be described in terms of the direction, speed and trajectory of the cars, the state of the cars

[8] See also Shaver (1985), 102–6, esp 105. Unfortunately, the research cited by Shaver in support of the view that the "essence of causality" is found in cases where the last instant of the relevant conduct coincides with the first instant of the relevant outcome, does not distinguish between these different types of connection between conduct and outcomes. See also Solan and Darley (2001).

[9] Hart and Honoré (1985), 64.

[10] Hart and Honoré (1985), 62–8.

[11] Particularly in this section and in 4.3 I am greatly indebted to Stapleton (2000), Stapleton (2001) and discussions with their author.

before and after the collision, and so on, without making any statement about the "cause" of the collision. We can describe events in terms of what happened without saying anything about what caused what. Interpretation is a purposive activity, and causal interpretations of events are informed by the purposes for which the interpretation is being made. In this respect, there is an analogy between causal statements on the one hand, and descriptions of bodily movements in terms of their definitional consequences on the other. To say that C caused O is to give a purposive interpretation of physical events, just as saying that A hit B provides a purposive interpretation of bodily movements in terms of human motivations, and saying that A assaulted B provides a purposive interpretation of bodily movements in terms of a category of legally proscribed conduct. The typical purpose for which causal statements are made in legal contexts is the attribution of responsibility with a view to the allocation of sanctions. For this reason, legal statements about causation are always made in relation to human conduct (acts and omissions) described in terms of some category of legally proscribed conduct. Thus, statements about causation in legal contexts are interpretative in two respects: they relate to human conduct under some legal description, and they provide an interpretation of a sequence of physical events involving legally proscribed conduct and outcomes.

4.2.5 Causation in the criminal law and civil law paradigms

Although a very significant proportion of crimes are result-crimes as opposed to conduct-crimes, issues of causation tend to be less prominent in the criminal law paradigm than in the civil law paradigm. This is a reflection of the fact that whereas the civil law paradigm is as much concerned with the effects of conduct on victims as with the nature and quality of that conduct, the criminal law paradigm focuses primarily on agent conduct and mental states. Thus in criminal law, issues about the connection between conduct and outcomes tend to be treated under the single heading of "causation"; whereas in tort law, for instance, the topic is divided between "causation" and "remoteness of damage". In this dichotomy, principles of causation are concerned with tracing a link between the agent's conduct and a proscribed outcome. By contrast, principles of remoteness of damage focus more closely on the effects of the proscribed conduct on the victim in order to determine in detail which of those effects should be attributed to the agent's conduct. Principles of remoteness of damage enable judgments of causation to be "fine-tuned", as it were.[12] In the labelling of criminal offences, proscribed outcomes are typically described in a quite general way because the basic question is whether the offender, by proscribed conduct, has produced an outcome deserving of punishment. If that is so, the precise nature and extent of the effects of the outcome on the victim are not of great importance for labelling

[12] See also 4.4.2.1.

purposes. On the other hand, the impact of the criminal conduct on the victim may be taken into account in sentencing. Sentencing is a much more a matter of discretion than attribution of criminal responsibility; and as a result, sentencing criteria tend to be quite abstract, instructing the sentencer to take account, for instance, of the "impact of the crime on the victim".

The civil law paradigm, by contrast, is concerned primarily with the justification of obligations of repair, not punishment. The basic principle for determining appropriate punishment is that it should "fit" the criminal conduct, whereas the basic principle for determining an appropriate obligation of repair is that it should fit the harm done to the victim. Thus rules for determining the extent and financial cost of the relevant harm are more detailed and developed in civil law than in criminal law.

4.3 FACTUAL CAUSATION

The legal concept of causation has two elements that may be called the "factual" and the "attributive" respectively. The factual element is concerned with whether the legally proscribed conduct in question played a part in the transition from a state of the world in which the outcome in question did not exist, to a state of the world in which the outcome in question did exist. As the discussion in 4.2.4 suggests, the term "factual causation" is misleading to the extent that it suggests that causal statements merely describe what happened. The "facts" about what happened can be described without recourse to concepts of causation.

4.3.1 The but-for and NESS tests

The standard legal test used for answering the factual causation question is the so-called "but-for" test: the legally proscribed conduct in question was a factual cause of the outcome in question if (holding everything else constant) the outcome would not have occurred but for that conduct.[13] The but-for test tells us whether the relevant, legally proscribed conduct was a necessary condition of the outcome in question. In one case, for instance, a hospital was held not liable for failing to treat the victim of a poisoning because the treatment would have done no good.[14] Another test of factual causation is the so-called "NESS" test. The acronym "NESS" stands for "necessary element of a sufficient set". The NESS test is seen by its proponents as being superior to the "but-for" test because of the result it produces in cases of causal over-determination.[15] Suppose that A negligently

[13] The factual causation question concerns what would have happened if the agent's conduct had been in compliance with the law rather than in breach of it.

[14] *Barnett* v. *Chelsea and Kensington Hospital Management Committee* [1969] 1 QB 428.

[15] The NESS test may also provide a better explanation than the but-for test of criminal liability for aiding and abetting: Ashworth (1999), 136–7.

collides with B's car, resulting in damage that requires certain repairs to be done to the car at a cost of £2,000.[16] Suppose, further, that independently of A, C negligently collides with B's car, resulting in damage that requires precisely the same repairs to be done at precisely the same cost. Because the basic measure of damages for physical damage to property is the cost of repair, one's initial reaction might be that A and C have each played a part in the transition to the situation in which B's car needed the repairs in question. Both the conduct of A and the conduct of C are sufficient conditions of the need for repairs. The but-for test, however, produces the odd and unattractive result that neither A nor C is part of the history of that transition. Because of C's negligence, A can say that B's car would have needed the repairs even if A had not collided with it; and because of A's negligence, C can say that B's car would have needed the repairs even if C had not collided with it. By contrast, the NESS test implicates both A and C in the relevant historical transition because the negligence of each was a necessary element in a set of conditions that together were sufficient to necessitate the repairs.

The way the law deals with cases of causal over-determination is complex. A distinction is drawn between cases in which both of the relevant factors are legally proscribed human conduct, and cases in which only one of the factors is legally proscribed human conduct. In cases of the former type, if the relevant factors operated independently but simultaneously, each is treated as a cause of the outcome in question. Thus in the earlier example, both A and C would be liable to B for the cost of repairs, and B could sue either (or both) to recover that cost. If the relevant factors operated independently but successively, the earlier is treated as the cause (and alone attracts liability) on the basis that the relevant outcome had already occurred at the time the later factor operated. In cases where only one of the factors is legally culpable human conduct—where, for instance, one is a "natural" event (i.e. an event not traceable to human agency)—the latter will be treated as the cause. In one case, for example, a person suffered a back injury at work as a result of negligence of his employer. Some time later he contracted a condition that would have produced the same back injury even if the work accident had not occurred. It was held that the employer's liability for the worker's injury was limited to the period between the work accident and the onset of the illness.[17]

The result in the case of successive legal wrongs follows from application of the legal principle of "taking the victim as found", which is, in turn, an application of a wider, and typically unarticulated principle of "taking the world as found". The "take-as-found" principle is central to the way the law distributes the risk of circumstantial luck. So, for instance, a person who injures another by legally proscribed conduct cannot complain if the impact of the injury is aggravated by some unusual susceptibility of the victim, such as

[16] This example is derived from *Performance Cars Ltd* v. *Abraham* [1962] 1 QB 33.

[17] *Jobling* v. *Associated Dairies Ltd* [1982] AC 794.

haemophilia.[18] Conversely, however, the principle may work to an injurer's advantage if their conduct did not make matters any worse because the victim had already been harmed by legally proscribed human conduct. In cases where only one of the factors is legally proscribed human conduct, the perpetrator of that conduct is allowed to take advantage of the other factor, whether it is contemporaneous with, precedes or follows the conduct: the law treats the other factor as the cause in preference to the legally proscribed conduct.

The but-for test interprets physical events in terms of necessity, whereas the NESS test interprets them essentially in terms of sufficiency.[19] Given that the NESS test explains some results that the but-for test cannot, it is not clear why courts continue to espouse the but-for test as the basic approach. It may simply be that that necessity is seen as more appropriate to explaining and assigning responsibility for single outcomes in the past, while sufficiency is more associated with the achievement of generic outcomes in the future.[20] Honoré suggests that whereas the but-for test provides a generally adequate heuristic device for identifying causes, the NESS test captures what we really mean when we call something "a cause".[21] Honoré also believes that NESS captures the meaning of cause in both legal and non-legal reasoning. So far as non-legal contexts are concerned, he provides no evidence for this view. So far as legal usage is concerned, it should be observed that neither NESS nor but-for explains all the results that the law produces. For instance, in cases of causal over-determination where both factors are legally proscribed human conduct, the but-for test denies the status of cause to both, while the NESS test classifies both as causes. By contrast, where the factors operate successively, the law treats the first in time as the cause to the exclusion of the later; and where only one of the factors is legally proscribed human conduct, the law treats the other factor as the cause to the exclusion of the legally proscribed conduct. Honoré apparently endorses such results, but explains them as resting on principles of "risk-allocation" rather than causation.[22]

It is certainly possible to argue that for the sake of analytical clarity, the law should restrict the use of causal language to applications of the but-for and NESS tests; or, even more narrowly, to describing the role of legally proscribed conduct in transitions from states of the world in which a legally proscribed outcome did not exist to ones in which it does.[23] That the law does not currently do

[18] This is the so-called "egg-shell skull" rule, and its cousin, the "egg-shell personality" rule. There are limits to the take-as-found principle. For example, an injurer might not be liable if a victim refused treatment for personal religious reasons.

[19] As Honoré puts it, but-for is a test of strong necessity, whereas NESS is a test of strong sufficiency and weak necessity: Honoré (1995), 364–5.

[20] Similarly: Schultz and Schleifer (1983), 59. Honoré thinks that the basic use of concepts of causation is to provide "recipes", and that this explains why the but-for test gives "intuitively wrong answers" in some cases: Honoré (1995), 375, 385.

[21] Honoré (1995).

[22] Honoré (1995), 380.

[23] Stapleton (2000). According to this view, but-for and NESS should be treated not as tests of causation but as criteria of responsibility. See further 4.4.2.2.

this raises the question of whether the legal usage of causal language, and the causal concepts reflected in it, are different from extra-legal usage and concepts. Lack of empirical evidence makes it impossible to answer this question other than speculatively. Two points deserve to be made, however. First, the prime purpose of causal statements in the law is the attribution of responsibility and the allocation of sanctions. In comparing and contrasting legal and extra-legal concepts of causation, it is important to compare like with like: responsibility-oriented causal statements within the law, with responsibility-oriented causal statements outside the law. In my view, Honoré's assertion that "[t]he same concept of cause is used for discovering recipes, for explaining events, and for assigning responsibility for outcomes"[24] gives too little weight to the interpretational and purposive nature of causal statements.

Secondly, I would suggest that because of the functions of law, and by virtue of its institutional resources, legal principles of causation are likely to be richer and more detailed than those in common use outside the law for the purpose of making responsibility judgments. In order to fulfil their social functions, courts may be forced to make causal interpretations of sequences of events that would not need to be interpreted causally in the moral domain. If this is right, the appropriate question is not whether ideas of causation in the law are the same as those in the moral domain, but rather whether the ideas of causation at work in the law are normatively acceptable. If they are, they may be added to our store of responsibility concepts for use outside the law as well as within it.

4.3.2 Causation, proof and uncertainty

It is one thing to adopt either but-for or NESS as the test of causation, but quite another to determine whether the chosen test is satisfied in a particular case. This distinction is of less importance in criminal law than in civil law because in criminal law, the onus of proof on the issue of causation typically rests on the prosecution;[25] and to discharge this onus, causal connection between the proscribed conduct and the proscribed outcome must be established "beyond reasonable doubt". This heavy burden of proof may be seen as a reflection of the agent-orientation of notions of responsibility in the criminal law paradigm, and as a protection for alleged offenders against the severe penalties and stigma attaching to criminal responsibility. In civil law, by contrast, the burden of proof on the issue of causation (as on all other issues) is "on the balance of probabilities". This lighter burden may be seen as a compromise between our interest as agents in freedom of action, and our interest as victims in security of person and property and the repair of adverse outcomes.

[24] Honoré (1995), 385.

[25] Where the onus of proof rests on the accused, it can be discharged on the balance of probabilities.

In theory, the balance of probabilities test can be satisfied by evidence that there was more than a 50 per cent chance that the conduct in question caused the relevant outcome. In practice, however, reliable evidence is typically unavailable to support assigning a numerical value to causal factors in this way; in which case, what matters is not whether the conduct more probably than not caused the outcome, but whether the court is satisfied that it did.[26] In this light, the only course open to a party bearing the onus of proof is to present all available evidence to the court and leave the court to decide whether it generates such satisfaction. This, perhaps, is the reason why the balance-of-probabilities criterion operates in an all-or-nothing way; and why, in other words, liability is not proportional to contribution to risk. If the court is satisfied that the onus of proof has been discharged, then no matter how far short of certainty this satisfaction falls, the conduct in question will be treated as having been the cause of the outcome in question, and the defendant will (provided all other conditions of liability are satisfied) fall under an obligation to repair that outcome. Conversely, if the court is not satisfied that the onus of proof has been discharged, then no matter how close the court thinks the evidence comes to discharging it, the conduct in question will be treated as not having been the cause, and the defendant will fall under no obligation of repair to the claimant.

Proving causal connection is complicated by reason of the fact that it requires an answer not only to a question about what actually happened, but also to a hypothetical question about what would have happened if the agent's conduct had been in accordance with the law rather than in breach of it. The all-or-nothing balance-of-probabilities approach applies to (1) questions about what happened in the past; (2) hypothetical questions about what sequence of physical events would have happened in the past if the conduct in question had been in compliance with the law rather than in breach of it; and (3) hypothetical questions about how the person bearing the onus of proof would have behaved in the past (for instance, what they would have done if they had known the truth). But it does not apply to (1) questions about what will happen in the future; (2) hypothetical questions about what would have happened in the future if the conduct in question had been in compliance with the law rather than in breach of it; or (3) hypothetical questions about how a person, other than the person bearing the onus of proof, would have behaved in the past (for instance, what they would have done if they had known the truth). Questions of the three latter types are answered in terms of proportional contribution to risk, regardless of whether that contribution was less or more than 50 per cent.

So far as concerns what actually happened in the past, this approach no doubt reflects a feeling that no matter how uncertain we may be about the past, it is theoretically more accessible to us than the future. This feeling may also explain the approach to hypothetical questions about past sequences of physical events—what actually happened at least gives us a reference point for considering what

[26] For some interesting research on this issue in relation to criminal trials see Zander (2000).

might have happened if one event had been other than it was. The distinction, between questions about how the person bearing the onus of proof would have behaved and how other people would have behaved, no doubt reflects an assumption of "privileged access"—that a person is more likely to be able to establish what they would have done than what someone else would have done; and an assumption that predicting human behaviour is harder than predicting other events.

I suggested earlier that the all-or-nothing balance-of-probabilities rule can be seen as a compromise between our interests as agents and victims. The proportional-contribution-to-risk approach can be viewed in the same way. This approach is not used on its own, but as an adjunct to the all-or-nothing, balance-of-probabilities approach. Whereas the all-or-nothing approach is used to determine whether conduct was or was not a cause of an outcome, the proportional-contribution approach is used in quantifying obligations to repair bad outcomes by paying compensation. The proportional-contribution approach does not, of course, entail that there are degrees of causation. Rather it acknowledges that there may be uncertainty about whether conduct was a cause or not. Like the all-or-nothing approach, the proportional-contribution approach distributes the costs of such epistemological uncertainty. The difference between the two approaches resides in the way each distributes those costs.[27] In one respect, the proportional-contribution approach is more advantageous to agents because it reduces the quantum of liability in cases where the probability that the agent's conduct was the cause is judged to be more than 50 per cent but less than 100 per cent. In another respect, the proportional-contribution approach is more advantageous to claimants because it allows damages to be recovered in cases where the probability that the agent's conduct was the cause is judged to be between zero and 50 per cent.[28]

The crucial point is that both the all-or-nothing balance of probabilities approach to causation, and the proportional-contribution approach to the assessment of damages, distribute the costs of epistemological uncertainty. Furthermore, because the two approaches operate side-by-side, the way the costs of uncertainty are distributed can be understood only by considering the cumulative operation of the two approaches. For instance, a defendant's legally proscribed conduct may be held, on the balance-of-probabilities approach, to have been the cause of injuries that result in the claimant suffering loss of earnings into the future. It does not follow, however, that the defendant will be ordered to pay damages for loss of earnings on the assumption that but for the conduct, the claimant would have continued to earn at the pre-accident rate. Indeed, in assessing damages for future loss of earnings, allowance is always

[27] Of course, the beyond-reasonable-doubt criterion also distributes the costs of epistemological uncertainty, but in a different way from the all-or-nothing balance-of-probabilities approach and the probabilities approach.

[28] In practice, a court would be unlikely to award compensation if the probability was judged to be less than, say 10–15%.

made for the possibility that even if the defendant had not injured the claimant, thus reducing P's earning capacity, P's earning capacity would have been reduced by some other "contingency" or "vicissitude" in the history of which the legally proscribed conduct of the defendant played no part.

A different technique for achieving results similar to those reached by the combined operation of the all-or-nothing approach to causation and the proportional-contribution approach to assessment of damages, is to define the legally proscribed outcome (to which a causal link with proscribed conduct must be traced) in terms of a lost chance to avoid harm rather than in terms of the harm itself. Under this approach, the obligation of repair is quantified in terms of a proportion of the harm equivalent to the percentage chance of avoiding the harm of which the legally proscribed conduct deprived the claimant. This approach has been widely adopted in relation to financial harms, but not in relation to personal injury.[29] At first sight, this differential might seem explicable in terms of an unwillingness to redistribute the costs of uncertainty to the disadvantage of personal injury victims. However, on reflection, it is clear that the differential cuts both ways. While the loss-of-a-chance approach disadvantages claimants in cases where the lost chance is judged to be greater than 50 per cent but less than 100 per cent, it advantages them in cases where the lost chance is judged to be 50 per cent or less.

Yet another technique for dealing with epistemological uncertainty is found in cases of cumulative causation, where part of the total harm suffered is attributable to one cause, and another part is attributable to another (as a result, for instance, of successive periods of exposure to the same toxic substance, such as asbestos). Suppose that the proportion of the harm attributable to each cause respectively is known, and that each cause is legally proscribed conduct. In such a case, each responsible party will be liable in proportion to their contribution to the harm. But suppose that the relative proportions are not known. In that case, either or both responsible parties can be held liable for the whole loss provided the court is satisfied that each caused *or materially contributed to* the total loss. Despite the fact that it cannot be proved on the balance of probabilities that either party caused the whole loss, either or both can be held liable for the whole loss because it can be proved on the balance of probabilities that each made a "material contribution" to it. The same principle applies in cases where one of the causes is legally proscribed human conduct and the other is not. Provided the court is satisfied that the legally proscribed human conduct more probably than not materially contributed to the harm, the party responsible for it can be held liable for the total harm even though it is known that they did not cause all of the harm.

The all-or-nothing balance of probabilities approach has come under particular strain in cases involving harms allegedly caused by environmental pollution and pharmaceutical drugs, where the harm is known, as a result of epidemiological

[29] Cane (1996), 139–40.

research, to be caused, in 50 per cent of cases or less, by legally proscribed conduct of the type engaged in by the defendant. English courts have resisted invitations to reduce the proof threshold to 50 per cent or less. It may be that the balance-of-probabilities criterion is intuitively felt to strike the fairest possible balance between our competing interests as agents and victims. On the other hand, there is no logical reason why the proof threshold should not be lowered if this were thought desirable, as a matter of distributive justice, in the interests of shifting more of the costs of uncertainty onto agents and away from victims. This has been done in some jurisdictions.

In this section, I have discussed certain rules of evidence as they apply to proof of causation. These are not the only legal rules that perform the function of distributing the costs of epistemological uncertainty; nor do they apply only to issues of causation. They apply to any question about what happened in the past, or about what may happen in the future, that is relevant to legal liability. We can define our legal responsibilities and the conditions of legal liability without recourse to such rules. But because of the pervasiveness of epistemological uncertainty, such rules are essential when the issue to be decided is whether or not a person has breached their legal responsibilities, and whether or not their conduct satisfies the conditions for legal liability. By virtue of the operation of such rules, a person may, for instance, be held to have caused harm to another in breach of their legal responsibilities even though, in fact, they did not cause that harm. Conversely, a person may be held not to have caused harm to another in breach of their legal obligations even though, in fact, they did cause the harm. In other words, by virtue of the operation of such rules, a person may be held legally liable for harm even though they were not responsible for it according to the rules defining their legal responsibilities; and conversely, a person may be held not legally liable for harm even though they were responsible for it according to the rules defining their legal responsibilities.

Should we conclude, therefore, that the rules of evidence that can produce such results mark a divergence between legal and moral notions of responsibility? Surely not! Epistemological uncertainty affects judgments of moral responsibility as much as judgments of legal responsibility. It is a greater practical problem in law than in morality because many issues of responsibility that can be left unresolved in the moral domain need to be resolved in the legal domain. As a result, the law has developed much more detailed techniques for dealing with epistemological uncertainty than are in use outside the law. In this respect, the law makes a net contribution to our responsibility practices. It does not follow, of course, that the legal rules and principles distribute the costs of epistemological uncertainty in an acceptable way. In order to make a judgment on that issue we need a relevant theory of distributive justice. Just as a theory of responsibility is incomplete unless it states what our responsibilities are, as well as what it means to be responsible; and unless it contains a set of principles about how the costs of luck ought to be distributed; so too it is incomplete without a set of principles about how the costs of epistemological uncertainty ought to be distributed.

4.4 ATTRIBUTIVE CAUSATION

The second element of the legal concept of causation is what I have called "attributive causation". Both the but-for and the NESS tests are very indiscriminate because for any given outcome, there is an indefinitely large set of necessary conditions, and an indefinite number of sets of sufficient conditions. It must be remembered, however, that in law, the causal inquiry is always focused on particular conduct of an individual or on a particular event.[30] The legal question is, "did the conduct or event in question cause this outcome?", not "what caused this outcome?". If the defendant's conduct satisfies the but-for or the NESS test (as the case may be) in relation to a particular outcome, the next question is whether any other event that satisfies the test in relation to that outcome ought to be treated as the cause of the outcome in preference to the defendant's conduct. It is this second question to which I have attached the label "attributive causation".

4.4.1 The relationship between causation and responsibility

The use of the term "causation" in this context is controversial. "Causal minimalists" argue that the term "cause" should be applied to all events that satisfy the but-for or NESS tests. According to this view, other rules and principles concerning the link between conduct and outcomes (i.e. rules and principles of legal or proximate cause) are not about causation but about distribution of the risk of adverse outcomes; or, in other words, responsibility for outcomes. By contrast, Hart and Honoré argued that this approach is at odds with "common sense" and "the ordinary usage of causal language".[31] They purported to identify non-legal principles *of causation* that allowed *the* cause of an event to be picked out from amongst its but-for or NESS conditions. More recently, Stapleton has argued that even adoption of the but-for and NESS tests rests on principles of responsibility, as is shown by the fact that they produce different results in some cases.[32] As tests of causation, but-for and NESS provide purposive interpretations of physical phenomena, not mere descriptions. Stapleton suggests that the language of causation should be reserved for descriptions of the physical transition from one state of the world to another, and that all other issues (including the application of the but-for and NESS tests) should be seen as resting on principles of responsibility (or matters of policy) that should be spelled out explicitly and not concealed beneath the language of causation.

[30] The causal relationship between one event and another is often an issue in insurance law. For instance, after the devastating earthquake that hit the Hawkes Bay region of New Zealand in 1931 many properties were damaged by fire. Insurers declined to pay out under fire policies on the ground that damage to the properties was caused by the earthquake, not by fire: McDonald (1995).

[31] Hart and Honoré (1985).

[32] Stapleton (2000).

To the extent that these differences of opinion concern linguistic usage, they need not concern us unduly. For responsibility purposes, we can define causation adequately in terms of the link between conduct and outcomes without prejudging any of the issues in dispute. Hart and Honoré's disagreement with the causal minimalists rested on the premise that in its approach to causation, the law should (and does) take its lead from non-legal thinking. This view suffers from three major defects. First, Hart and Honoré established the "ordinary usage of causal language" by assertion rather than evidence. It is unlikely that the views of two such highly skilled lawyers about the "ordinary" usage of causal language were unaffected by their knowledge of the law. In other words, whereas they thought they saw non-legal usage reflected in the law, they might, in fact, have been reading legal usage into "ordinary" usage. The fact, that legal usage is highly documented whereas ordinary usage is not, supports this speculation. Secondly, because of the institutional landscape of the legal domain and by virtue of law's institutional resources, legal rules and principles of causation are more detailed and developed than their non-legal counterparts. To this extent, at least, the denotation of causal terms is more likely to be established by legal than by ordinary usage. Thirdly, in cases of genuine dispute about causal issues in the legal domain, recourse to non-legal usage is unlikely to provide resources for their resolution.

The main point that the causal minimalists (and, more recently, Stapleton) were concerned to make is that some of the issues dealt with by the law under the rubric of causation were normative issues about the distribution of the risk of adverse outcomes between agents on the one hand and victims on the other. To the extent that the language of causation suggests that they are factual issues about what happened, it conceals the prescriptions involved in attributions of causal status. In the interests of clarity and transparency, the normative nature of the issues should be acknowledged, and their resolution should be subjected to normative evaluation. Whereas causal minimalism accepted that application of the but-for and NESS tests was a matter of description rather than prescription, Stapleton argues that even the use of these tests may rest on normative assumptions about the fair distribution of risks of adverse outcomes.[33] These assumptions (some of which are explicit and many of which are implicit) are discussed in 4.4.2.

In order to accommodate the "minimalist" insights (which seem to me to be essentially valid) I have defined causation simply as being concerned with the link between conduct and outcomes. Distributive principles relevant to this link I call principles of "causal responsibility". This term acknowledges their normativity, but at the same time it distinguishes principles of responsibility that are concerned with the link between conduct and outcomes from principles of responsibility concerned, for instance, with mental states and the quality of conduct.

[33] Stapleton (2000), 65–6, 79–80.

4.4.2 Principles of causal responsibility

4.4.2.1 The distinction between causation and remoteness of damage

The legal principles of causal responsibility are traditionally dealt with under two headings: "legal" (or "proximate") causation and "remoteness of damage". Although both categories are concerned with the link between legally proscribed conduct and legally proscribed outcomes, principles of causation are agent-focused, while principles of remoteness of damage focus on the victim or, more precisely, on the impact of the legally proscribed conduct on the victim. This explains why the distinction between "causation" and "remoteness of damage" does not figure in the criminal law, where the link between conduct and outcomes is dealt with under the single rubric of "causation". Even in civil law, the distinction is only one of perspective which can, for this reason, be ignored in what follows.

4.4.2.2 But-for and NESS

As we have seen, in cases of causal over-determination, the but-for test is generally thought to produce unacceptable results for the purposes of attributing legal responsibility. In cases where the several sufficient causes are all legally proscribed human conduct, it seems unfair that a person who suffers harm as a result of several independent breaches of the law should be denied a legal remedy (on the ground of lack of causal link) when they would be entitled to a remedy if they had been harmed by only one of the law-breakers. Where the several breaches of the law are contemporaneous, there seems no reason to treat them differently in terms of causal link; and so both are treated as causes. Where the several breaches of the law are separated in time, the first in time is treated as the cause of the harm on the basis that the second is allowed to take the victim as found, i.e. already harmed. In cases where one of the several sufficient causes is not a breach of the law but, for instance, a "natural" disease, no matter whether that cause precedes, is contemporaneous with, or succeeds the relevant breach of the law, it will be held to be the cause of the harm in preference to the breach of the law. In the context of causal over-determination, a law-breaker will be relieved of liability if there is another independent sufficient cause of the relevant harm that is not itself a breach of the law. These principles show that in cases of causal over-determination, whereas the but-for test is judged to be under-inclusive, the NESS test is, in some instances, judged to be over-inclusive. The principles used to give effect to these judgments all distribute the cost of circumstantial luck between the causal factors and between the causal factors and the victim.

4.4.2.3 Eliminating causal factors

Whereas but-for is thought to be under-inclusive in cases of causal over-determination, in other cases both it and NESS are obviously grossly over-inclusive for the purposes of attributing legal responsibility. Every outcome has an indefinitely long causal history of but-for and NESS conditions, most of which would not even be considered as candidates for responsibility in law. In 4.4.2.4 to 4.4.2.7 we examine legal principles of causal responsibility that are used to determine whether legal responsibility will attach to human conduct that satisfies the but-for and NESS tests.

4.4.2.4 The meaning of "cause"

As was noted in 4.2.3, Hart and Honoré considered that the law reflected ordinary usage in treating certain linkages between conduct and outcomes as being "non-causal". For example, they classified vicarious liability as being a non-causal form of responsibility because it was based on providing the opportunity for harm to occur. In their view, ordinary usage did not treat provision of the opportunity to do harm as causation of the harm. They also thought that it was only in a modified sense that persuading or inducing a person to do harm could be said to be a cause of the harm.[34]

Even if Hart and Honoré are right about the "ordinary usage" of the word "cause", it is unclear what is gained by treating the link between the conduct that attracts vicarious liability and the relevant harmful outcome as being non-causal. Suppose an employer is held vicariously liable for a collision between the employer's vehicle and that of a third party caused by the negligence of the employee driving the employer's vehicle. Conduct of both the employee and the employer figure in the causal history of the collision, along with an indefinite number of other factors. For the purposes of attributing legal responsibility, the relevant question to be asked about the conduct of each is precisely the same: should that conduct, being a but-for or NESS condition of the harm, be singled out for legal responsibility? If the answer is positive, there is no obvious reason to baulk at applying the term "causal" to the employer's vicarious liability, as much as to the employee's personal liability. For the purposes of attributing legal responsibility, various types of linkage between conduct and outcomes satisfy the requirement of causation. The type of linkage relevant in any particular case is not a function of "the ordinary" or, indeed, of any "usage of the language of causation". Rather it is determined by the nature of the relevant legally proscribed conduct. For example, the causal link relevant to liability for negligent driving is different from that relevant to liability for inducing another to act to their detriment in reliance on a negligently false statement, and from that relevant to liability for negligently failing to control a third party, and from that relevant to vicarious liability; and so on.

[34] See also Honoré (1995), 384; contrast Davidson (1963), 696–9.

Once it has been decided that negligently making a false statement, for instance, or failing to control a third party, ought to attract liability, it follows that in appropriate cases the type of causal link relevant to such liabilities will, and indeed must, be recognised by the law. The point can be well illustrated by reference to liability for "omissions". It is sometimes baldly said that "omissions cannot be causes"; or, less starkly, that one of the reasons why the law hesitates to impose liability for omissions is a worry about whether omissions can be causes. In fact, the problem about omissions has nothing to do with causation, but is the product of unwillingness to limit individual freedom of action by imposing obligations (i.e. prospective responsibilities) to take positive action. Even in the absence of such an obligation, a person's inaction can qualify as a but-for or NESS condition of harm; but in the absence of such an obligation, we are unwilling to attribute legal responsibility to the inactive person by picking out their conduct as the legal cause of the harm. By contrast, where such an obligation is imposed, and the inaction qualifies as a but-for or NESS condition of the relevant harm, the mere fact that the relevant conduct is an omission provides no reason to deny it the status of cause of the harm. There may be some other reason not to pick it out from the set of but-for or NESS conditions as legally responsible for the harm, but its status as an omission does not, by itself, provide such a reason. Put briefly, there is a direct relationship between what our legal responsibilities are and what can count as causes for legal purposes. If there is a legal obligation to do or not to do X, then not doing X, or doing X (as the case may be), may count, for the purposes of attributing legal responsibility, as the cause of harm of which that not-doing or that doing is a but-for or NESS condition.

This point can be put more positively by saying that whether a person whose conduct was a but-for or NESS condition of a harmful outcome will be picked out as "the cause" of that outcome depends, in part, on what the person's legal obligations were and whether the conduct was a breach of such an obligation. This link between obligation ("what our responsibilities are") and causation is also a feature of causal judgments in the moral and political domains.[35] In the context of responsibility for bad outcomes, the reason why cases such as "injuring by blows" seem to lie at the core of causation, while cases such as "failing to prevent harm" and "inducing a person to do harm" seem to be marginal cases of causation, is that, both in law and morality, obligations of the type breached by a person who injures another by blows are more widespread and general in their incidence and application than obligations of the type breached by a person who fails to prevent harm or induces another to do harm.

There are few forms of legal liability for outcomes that can meaningfully be called "non-causal". In civil law, an example is the restitutionary liability of the passive recipient of a mistaken payment or the passive beneficiary of a fraud. Even in this case, the recipient is part of the history of the transition to

[35] Smiley (1992), 185–95.

the relevant outcome (i.e. receipt of the payment). If the recipient had not existed, and had not been in the right place at the right time (as it were), they would never have received the payment. On the other hand, since, by definition, the recipient did nothing to attract the payment, and was under no duty to prevent its being made, there seems no causal reason to single out the recipient as legally responsible for the making the payment. In other words, the reason why this form of liability is not cause-based is that it is not conduct-based. Causes link legally proscribed conduct with legally proscribed outcomes. Here there is a legally proscribed outcome, namely the receipt of a payment as a result of mistake or fraud. But that outcome is not traceable to any legally proscribed (or even any legally relevant) conduct of the person under the obligation to repair the outcome, i.e. the recipient.

In the criminal law, liability for possession may arise independently of relevant conduct on the part of the possessor.[36] This is an example of what has been more generally called "situational liability".[37] Certain cases of secondary criminal liability exemplify the rarer phenomenon of *conduct-based* non-causal liability.[38]

4.4.2.5 Agents, victims and causation

A fundamental respect in which the but-for and NESS tests are over-inclusive is that they attribute the same causal status to the sufferer of a legally proscribed outcome, who is guilty of no relevant legally proscribed conduct, as they do to legally proscribed conduct that satisfies the tests in relation to that outcome. Suppose a car mounts a pavement and injures a pedestrian as a result of negligence on the part of the driver, and in the absence of negligence on the part of the pedestrian. Both the driver's conduct and the pedestrian's presence on the pavement satisfy the but-for and NESS tests in relation to the harm to the pedestrian. But for the purposes of allocating legal responsibility to repair the harm, we would not pick the pedestrian out as a legal cause. This simple example illustrates two important points about principles of causal responsibility. One is that they play an important role in distributing the cost of circumstantial luck. The presence of the pedestrian on the pavement was (it is assumed) beyond the driver's control just as the driver's negligence was (it is assumed) beyond the pedestrian's control. Someone must bear the cost of the unlucky combination of circumstances. Secondly, the example shows the centrality to judgments of causal responsibility in law of the rules defining proscribed conduct. A reason why we pick out the driver as the sole cause of the accident is that the driver was, but the pedestrian was not, guilty of legally proscribed conduct. If the pedestrian had been guilty of legally proscribed conduct (such as "contributory negligence"), the pedestrian's conduct might be picked out, either alone or in combination with that of the driver, as having caused the harm.

[36] Ashworth (1999), 111–12.

[37] Glazebrook (1978) discussed in Ashworth (1999), 109–11.

[38] See 5.10.4.

The principle in play here is that as between legally proscribed conduct and "innocent" conduct that are both but-for or NESS conditions of harm, the former is more likely than the latter to be treated as the cause of the harm for the purposes of legal responsibility. A related principle is that the more culpable the legally proscribed conduct, the more likely it is to be treated as the cause of an outcome of which it is a but-for or NESS condition. For instance, the basic principle in relation to liability for harm resulting from negligent conduct is that only the foreseeable outcomes of the conduct attract liability. By contrast, liability for harm resulting from intentional conduct can extend to unforeseeable outcomes. Relative culpability is an important determinant of the distribution of the burden of bad circumstantial luck.

4.4.2.6 *The ordinary and the extraordinary*

Besides culpability, the most important and general idea underlying causal responsibility is the distinction, in relation to causal factors outside the agent's control, between the ordinary and the extraordinary. In relation to outcomes, human conduct takes place against a background of, and is embedded in a dense network of, other but-for and NESS conditions. In relation to other conditions operating at the same time as legally proscribed conduct to produce a proscribed outcome, the conduct is likely to be treated as the cause of the outcome unless one, or a combination, of those other conditions was quite out of the ordinary. There is, however, an extremely important qualification that must be added to this statement, which is encapsulated in the principle of taking the victim as found. Suppose that at the time the harm was inflicted, the victim suffered from a rare condition, and that as a result, the harm was more serious than it would not have been if they had not had the condition. Still, the agent will be liable for the harm suffered unless a court is prepared to say that the harm attributable to the condition was not only more serious than it would otherwise have been, but also that it was of a different kind than would have been suffered in the absence of the condition. This distinction between kind and seriousness of harm is explained in the next paragraph.

In relation to factors operating after the legally proscribed conduct but before the occurrence of the outcome, the same distinction between the ordinary and the extraordinary applies. In this context, it is often put in terms of "foreseeability": "ordinary" outcomes are foreseeable, while extraordinary outcomes are unforeseeable. In many contexts, only foreseeable outcomes attract legal liability.[39] However, the concept of foreseeability is qualified by the idea that an outcome will be classified as foreseeable if it was of a foreseeable "kind", even if it was the result of an unforeseeable sequence of events, and even if the harmful impact of the outcome on the victim was much greater than was foreseeable.

[39] Unless, of course, the outcome was either intended or actually foreseen, in which case it will attract liability however extraordinary.

Because events can be described in greater or lesser detail, the distinction between "kind" of outcome, on the one hand, and "manner of occurrence" and "extent" on the other, can be manipulated to produce results that are thought desirable in terms of fair distribution of the burdens of bad circumstantial luck.[40] Especially in cases where the later event is human conduct, the causal issue may be framed in terms of whether that event "broke the chain of causation" between the agent's legally proscribed conduct and the relevant outcome. Although put in a number of ways, the test of whether an event breaks the chain of causation is basically whether it was out of the ordinary. For example, if an injured person requires medical treatment for harm inflicted by legally proscribed conduct, and that treatment causes the person further harm, the person whose conduct inflicted the initial harm will probably be held liable for the further harm if the medical treatment was merely negligent, but not if it was grossly negligent or reckless.

Hart and Honoré were of the view that intentional conduct is particularly likely to "break the chain of causation" linking the initial conduct to the harm.[41] But once again, this seems to depend on whether, in the circumstances, the intentional conduct is classified as out of the ordinary.[42] For instance, if an employer sends an employee to deliver the day's takings to a night safe in the early hours without adequate protection, it is only to be expected that the employee will face a high risk of being mugged.[43] In determining what would ordinarily be expected to happen in any particular case, attention must be paid to what the relevant legally proscribed conduct is; or, in other words, what obligation has been breached by the party whose liability is in issue. If a person agrees to close and lock a door when leaving a building, but fails to do so, a break-in through the door would not be treated as an extraordinary outcome for which the person should be held not liable.[44] Similarly, if prison authorities negligently allow inmates to escape, a court would be unlikely to relieve them of liability for car theft committed by the escapees in the vicinity of the prison on the ground that this was not to be expected.[45] On the other hand, the prison authorities might not be held liable if an escapee went to ground for two years and only then "resumed a life of crime". Such a sequence of events might not be thought extraordinary. But we might well think that in such a case, the harm caused by the escapee should be treated as a cost of living in society, or as the responsibility of the criminal, but not of the prison authorities. This example suggests that the factors relevant to judgments of causal responsibility, that are designed to distribute the burden of circumstantial bad luck, are likely to be context specific and as various as the circumstances in which such judgments fall to be made.

40 For a particularly strong statement of this point see Moore (1993).

41 Hart and Honoré (1985), 42.

42 *Empress Car Co (Abertillery) Ltd* v. *National Rivers Authority* [1998] 2 AC 22.

43 *Chomentowski* v. *Red Garter Restaurant Pty Ltd* [1970] 2 WN (NSW) 1070.

44 *Stansbie* v. *Troman* [1948] 2 KB 48.

45 *Home Office* v. *Dorset Yacht Co Ltd* [1970] AC 1004.

Of course, the concepts of the ordinary and the extraordinary are evaluative, and drawing the distinction between them requires judgment. At the end of the day, adjudicators make such judgments, and such judgments are themselves proper subjects for critical evaluation. The basic point, however, is that the distinction between the ordinary and the extraordinary is one of the most important mechanisms by which the law allocates the burden of bad circumstantial luck between agents and victims.[46]

4.4.2.7 *Types of harm*

In tort law there is a general principle that people are expected to take greater care to protect themselves from financial harm than from physical harm (whether to person or tangible property). Application of this principle sometimes leads to denial of liability. For instance, although there can be liability for negligently making a false statement on which another relies to their financial detriment, such liability will not arise if the person suffering the financial harm acted "unreasonably" in relying on the statement.[47] The principle also operates at the level of causation. There is some support for not applying to financial harm the distinction between kinds of harm, on the one hand, and the extent and manner of occurrence of harm, on the other, which was explained in 4.4.2.6. Under this approach, financial harm would be treated as "foreseeable" only if the manner of its occurrence and its extent were foreseeable.

4.5 CAUSATION IN LAW AND MORALITY

The function of causal principles in the law is to allocate (historic) responsibility for outcomes. It is normally a precondition of legal responsibility for outcomes that there be a link between some legally proscribed conduct of the person to be held responsible and some legally proscribed outcome such that the conduct can be said to have been a but-for or NESS condition of that outcome. Both the but-for and the NESS tests of causal link classify as causally relevant many conditions that are not credible candidates for legal responsibility. So these tests need to be supplemented by rules and principles designed to isolate the condition(s) of the relevant outcome to which legal responsibility should be allocated. Such rules and principles of responsibility can be characterised as causal because they are concerned with the link between conduct and outcomes. But they are principles of responsibility nonetheless.[48] Just as an important function of interpersonal standards of conduct, for instance, is to distribute the

[46] Refer back to 3.2.2 for discussion of circumstantial luck.
[47] Note, however, that this requirement of reasonable reliance does not apply where the false statement is made knowingly, with the intention of inducing reliance.
[48] Stapleton (2000).

burden of dispositional luck, so an important function of causal principles of responsibility is to distribute the burden of circumstantial luck.

Hart and Honoré set out to show that concepts of causation in the law reflect "ordinary" usage of causal language outside the law. Unfortunately, they offered little evidence of ordinary usage, and it seems likely that their views about it were considerably influenced by legal materials. At all events, since concepts of causation perform several different functions, it seems important, in considering the relationship between legal and extra-legal ideas, to limit the analysis to the function that causal principles perform in the law, namely the allocation of responsibility for outcomes and, on that basis, the impositions of sanctions—punishments and obligations of repair. It is because the imposition of legal punishments and obligations of repair is such a serious business that legal rules and principles of causation are more developed and detailed than their counterparts in morality. This is surely an area in which the law can make a net contribution to society's store of responsibility principles. The legal literature contains many real-life examples of complex chains of events that are every bit as bizarre as the most colourful philosophical thought experiments. The institutional imperative to allocate responsibility *and sanctions* for the outcomes of such chains justifies the thought that the direction of influence on matters of causation is likely to be from the law to morality rather than vice versa.[49]

The most fundamental assumption underlying the legal approach to causation is that responsibility to repair bad outcomes should depend on causation. Does this assumption reflect moral thinking? An argument (of John Fischer and Robert Ennis) that it does not rests on the observation that whether conduct causes harm is often a matter of luck. For example, most instances of negligent driving cause no harm to anyone; and when negligent driving does do harm, this is typically the result, in part, of factors outside the control of the driver. A person's responsibility for what they do, so the argument goes, should depend on factors within their control, not on factors outside their control. But, say Fischer and Ennis, such a system of responsibility

> "is obviously impractical; whereas it is often possible to identify the person who has *caused* a harm, it is difficult to identify the class of people who acted negligently (in the relevant respect) toward the victim. Since negligence often leaves no trace, it is more difficult to isolate the pertinent class of negligent people than the class of actual harm-causers . . . there may be good reasons of efficiency to adopt [a cause-based system of responsibility]".[50]

The argument, then, is that the legal requirement of causation can be explained in terms of practicality and efficiency, even though it is not "ideally fair". This argument was put in answer to Judith Jarvis Thompson's contention

[49] Similarly: Lloyd-Bostock (1984), 159–60.
[50] Fischer and Ennis (1986), 34.

that the requirement of causation can be justified in terms of avoiding undue encroachment on freedom of action.[51]

A first point to make about the approach of Fischer and Ennis concerns luck. There is a strong strand of thought in criminal law theory to the effect that outcomes are irrelevant to culpability.[52] Those who take this view oppose (for instance) the imposition of lighter sentences for attempts than for completed crimes, and treating seriousness of outcome as relevant to sentencing. This approach is sometimes based on the idea that outcomes are often a matter of luck—and apparently on the false assumption that conduct and mental states are unaffected by (dispositional) luck. Once the role of dispositional luck in people's lives is understood, the role of circumstantial luck in relation to the outcomes of conduct ceases to provide a convincing rationale for ignoring outcomes when determining responsibility and culpability. If circumstantial luck negatived culpability in relation to outcomes, then equally dispositional luck would negative culpability in relation to conduct and mental states. Because circumstantial luck, like dispositional luck, is ubiquitous, it is necessary, both in morality and law, to adopt principles to determine when people can fairly be held responsible for outcomes that are, in some respect(s) or other, outside their control.

Secondly, it seems to me that the approaches both of Thompson and of Fischer and Ennis suffer by being too agent-focused. So far as that of Fischer and Ennis is concerned, there is certainly an argument for not distinguishing between instances of equally culpable conduct on the basis of outcome if the issue is whether the agent should be blamed, censured or punished. This is why many criminal law theorists think that unsuccessful attempts should be punished as harshly as completed crimes, and why severity of harm inflicted should not be taken into account in sentencing. However, when the question is whether an agent should repair a bad outcome by paying compensation for harm, the argument for ignoring whether the agent's conduct caused that outcome seems very much weaker. It is true, of course, that an obligation to repair a bad outcome can be justified in the absence of causal connection between the outcome and conduct of the person(s) under the obligation. For instance, contracts of insurance, indemnity and guarantee give rise to such obligations; and there are sound moral arguments supporting no-fault accident compensation schemes such as that in New Zealand. But if the basis of the obligation to repair a bad outcome is that the person under the obligation was responsible for the outcome, it is difficult to see how the obligation could be justified if the person had not caused the outcome.

Suppose that A and B both shoot at C at the same moment with the intention of injuring C; and that A's shot misses while B's shot hits and injures C. Fischer and Ennis think that A and B "should be considered equally liable for" the

[51] Thompson (1984). For criticism see Kagan (1986); and for a reply see Thompson (1986).
[52] e.g. Ashworth (1993).

injury.[53] If the issue were whether A and B should both be punished, it would certainly arguable that they deserve to be treated similarly. It would also be arguable that A and B should be punished equally. But if the issue were whether A or B should be liable to compensate C, the agent-focused arguments from fairness and circumstantial luck by themselves would arguably provide as much support for holding neither A nor B liable as for imposing liability on both. The best way of avoiding this extremely unattractive no-liability conclusion, it seems to me, is to point to the harm done to C and to the causal connection between B's conduct and C's injury. The fact that B's shot hit C while A's shot missed is relevant to their respective liabilities because it connects B with C's injury in a way that A is not implicated in that injury. It is the causal link between B's conduct and C's injury that explains why B in particular should compensate C in particular, and why A need not: while A is responsible for bad conduct, B is responsible for bad conduct *and* a bad outcome. The reason why B should compensate C, and why A need not, is not (as Thompson thinks) because such an obligation to compensate would unduly interfere with A's freedom of action. A deserves no more freedom than B to shoot at C with intent to injure; and the equal liability of both to punishment reflects this judgment. The reason why an obligation to compensate C should not be imposed on A is that A is not responsible for C's injury, because A did not *cause* C's injury. To the extent that obligations to repair harm rest on responsibility for the harm, causation is a precondition of such obligations.

Fischer and Ennis reject the link between causation and responsibility for outcomes on the ground that it is not "ideally fair". It might also be attacked on consequentialist grounds. If the prime aim of our responsibility practices were to provide people with incentives to avoid causing harm in the future, there would be a good case for targeting all those who engage in potentially harm-causing conduct, and not just those who have caused harm by such conduct. If this were the prime aim, however, holding people responsible for past harm that they did not cause would not seem a likely candidate for the most efficient and effective way of generating such incentives. Much more promising than imposing sanctions in respect of past outcomes would be the adoption of techniques for directly regulating and controlling future, potentially harm-causing conduct. In order to develop such techniques, we would ideally need to understand the causal links between targeted conduct and the outcomes we were seeking to prevent. Causation is obviously relevant to this exercise; but it would be unwise to assume that causal principles developed for the purpose of allocating responsibility for past bad outcomes would serve well as recipes for preventing bad outcomes in the future. This is equally true in the moral and the legal domains.

This point deserves some elaboration. If our aim is to minimise harmful outcomes of a certain type in the future by imposing legal or moral obligations, the relevant causal question is whether doing so is likely to achieve this aim. In

[53] Fischer and Ennis (1986), 39.

answering this question, our practice of holding people who engage in certain sorts of conduct causally responsible for outcomes of the relevant type that have already occurred is of no direct assistance. Such a practice is relevant only to the extent that it identifies causal factors that we might be able to control in such a way as to minimise the incidence of harmful outcomes in the future. One reason to doubt the value of historic-responsibility practices for this purpose is what psychologists call the "fundamental attribution error" of giving too much weight to human conduct in explaining events, and too little weight to other factors. As Hamilton suggests, this error has serious negative implications for predicting and controlling the future; but it is clearly less problematic in the context of the allocation of moral and legal responsibility and sanctions for past outcomes.[54] Moral and legal sanctions are directed only at human beings. This is why human conduct is much more central to ideas of causation in the sanctioning context than they might be when the aim is to identify factors, whether human or not, that can be controlled in such a way as to prevent harmful outcomes in the future. Indeed, the fact that law and morality focus on human conduct helps to explain why they are of only limited utility in "making the world a better place".

The points that emerge from consideration of these challenges to the legal requirement of causation are these. First, if the question being asked is whether A ought to repair a bad outcome suffered by B, the answer, "if (but only if) B caused the outcome" seems as appropriate in the moral domain as in the legal. Secondly, in deciding whether A ought to be punished for bad conduct, and if so, how severely, the question of whether that bad conduct caused a bad outcome is arguably relevant in both the legal and the moral domains, but not conclusive. On the one hand, for instance, views differ about whether unsuccessful attempts ought to be punished as severely as completed crimes. On the other hand, if the aim of the punishment is to minimise the incidence of bad outcomes in the future, there is reason to think that targeting those who have caused bad outcomes in the past may be a second-best technique, whether in law or morality.

4.6 CONCLUSION

The aim of this chapter has been to explore the relationship between responsibility and causation. Causal concepts perform a variety of functions. In the legal domain, their prime function is to allocate responsibility for bad outcomes. Legal principles of causation specify the link between conduct and outcome required for the allocation to the conduct of (legal) responsibility for the outcome. The but-for and NESS tests identify events that played a part in the history of the outcome. Other rules and principles of causation identify the but-for or NESS condition(s) to which legal responsibility for the outcome may

[54] Hamilton (1980).

be allocated. These rules and principles are part of the definition of what our legal responsibilities are in relation to harmful events. Thus, the content of the obligation breached by the relevant conduct defines the nature of the relevant causal connection between that conduct and the outcome; and causal principles play an important part in allocating the burden of circumstantial luck. In short, whereas the principles of responsibility examined in chapter 3 related to the nature and quality of responsibility-attracting conduct, the responsibility principles analysed in this chapter relate to the link between such conduct and responsibility-attracting outcomes.

Hart and Honoré thought that the best way to understand legal principles of causation was in terms of causal concepts in use outside the law. On the contrary, I have argued that because of law's institutional geography and resources, legal concepts and principles of causation provide a much richer and more detailed account of the relevance of causation to responsibility than is found outside the law. The law is just as likely to influence causal thinking in the moral domain as to be influenced by it. In this way, the law can make a net contribution to society's store of responsibility concepts and practices.

5

Responsibility and Personality

5.1 THREE ISSUES OF PERSONALITY AND RESPONSIBILITY

PARADIGMATICALLY, MORAL AND legal responsibility is attributed to individual human beings in respect of their own conduct. I shall refer to this as "the paradigm of individual responsibility". This chapter is an exploration of the relationship between responsibility, personality and the idea that persons (to borrow Carol Rovane's attractive term) are "human-sized".[1] It deals with three related issues of responsibility arising out of ideas about personality and personhood. The first is "group responsibility" (5.3 to 5.8). I use this term to refer to cases where, for the purposes of attributing responsibility, conduct of two or more human beings is treated as being that of a single non-human entity. The second issue discussed in this chapter is the responsibility of individuals who suffer from what is called "multiple personality disorder" (5.9). This phenomenon raises difficult questions about how to apply notions of responsibility that deal paradigmatically with the typical case of a "single-minded" human. The third issue to be discussed is shared responsibility (5.10). The law recognises various grounds on which responsibility for outcomes can be divided between several entities. Some of these grounds apparently conflict with the paradigm of individual responsibility. For instance, on one view, vicarious liability involves placing on one person responsibility for the conduct of another person.

5.2 APPROACHES TO THE RELATIONSHIP BETWEEN PERSONALITY AND RESPONSIBILITY

Underlying the paradigm of individual responsibility is an association of responsibility with personhood (or "personality"), and an identification of "person" with "human being".[2] It is obvious that not all the senses of "responsibility" that have been identified so far in this book apply only to human beings. Causal responsibility can be ascribed to animals, for instance, and to natural events, such as tornadoes. It is equally clear that legal liability can be attributed to entities, such as corporations, that are not human beings; and that in the moral domain, groups are often treated as proper subjects of responsibility judgments.

[1] Rovane (1998).

[2] This approach has been described as "the thesis of the 'ontological priority' of the individual": Scruton (1989), 254.

But in the philosophical literature there is a strong and persistent strand of thought to the effect that only individual human beings can be *morally* responsible because only individual human beings can be "moral persons". According to this view, (which I shall call "the traditional humanistic approach") the reason why only individual human beings can be moral persons is that only they possess the essential characteristic of moral personhood, namely the capacity for intentional (i.e. "purposive") behaviour, i.e. "intentionality".[3] This capacity is a function of having a (human) body and a (human) mind[4]—although some human beings lack this capacity by reason of (young) age, or bodily or mental infirmity, illness or malfunction.[5]

As applied to group responsibility the traditional humanistic approach rests on the proposition that (non-human) entities which lack a body or a mind (or both) simply *are not* persons in the sense required for being morally responsible. This proposition is not about the proper grounds of moral responsibility, but about the very nature and possibility of moral responsibility. The distinction is neatly captured in Hart's discussion of "capacity responsibility".[6] His view—that "most legal systems . . . have given only a partial or tardy recognition to [certain minimum bodily and mental] capacities as general criteria of legal responsibility"—led him to the observation that failure to incorporate such criteria only threatened the efficacy of a system of legal responsibility. By contrast, he thought, a responsibility system that did not incorporate such criteria "would not, as morality is at present understood, be a morality". The traditional humanistic approach also seems to rule out vicarious liability because it limits a person's responsibility to their own intentional conduct. In its approach to group and vicarious responsibility, the traditional humanistic approach is at odds not only with the law, but also with widespread social practices outside the law. In everyday life, for instance, people frequently attribute responsibility to groups; and many people have no difficulty with the idea that employers should accept responsibility to repair harm done by their employees in the course of employment.

The basic thesis of the chapter is that the main source of conflict between humanistic approaches to the relationship between responsibility and personal-

[3] For a powerful statement of this position see Velasquez (1983), 112–17. Note that in this context, "intentional" is used in a broad sense that embraces the legal concepts of intention, recklessness, foresight and knowledge.

[4] There is, of course, a long philosophical tradition that plays down the significance of the body to personality—*cogito ergo sum*. But my concern here is with responsibility for human conduct, and in this context body and mind are both important. Dennett defines intentionality more broadly so that non-human entities can be "intentional systems": Dennett (1993), ch. 2. Dan-Cohen develops a similar idea in the story of "Personless Corporation": Dan-Cohen (1985), ch. 3. Dan-Cohen acknowledges, however (at 48) that the metaphor of the "intelligent machine" may not be as helpful a paradigm for thinking about responsibility as that of the individual human being. At all events, the intelligent machine metaphor would be much less useful in relation to groups that are not as highly institutionalised and rigidly structured as corporations.

[5] In this way, a human being can be a "person" without being a "moral person".

[6] Hart (1968), 227–30.

ity and social practices of attributing responsibility to groups (for instance) is that the humanistic approach is exclusively agent-focused and takes no account either of the functions of responsibility practices or of the relational nature of responsibility under those practices. The law does not reject the paradigm of individual responsibility because most forms of legal responsibility are ultimately responsibility for human conduct and its outcomes. However, while individual human conduct is a precondition of legal responsibility, it does not mark its boundary. Because law protects not only our interest as agents in freedom of action, but also our interest in security of person and property and society's interest in order and security, the incidence of legal responsibility is not limited in the way the humanistic approach would require. And to the extent that morality is also concerned with interests other than that of agents in freedom of action, we might expect the incidence of moral responsibility not to be limited in the way the humanistic approach would require.

Consider group responsibility, for instance. Human beings are social animals. Group activities are as integral a part of human life as solitary pursuits. By combining in groups,[7] people may, for good or ill, achieve much more than they could by independent activity.[8] Groups can acquire resources and power greater than their individual members could acquire by acting in isolation. Groups may inflict harm on outsiders greater than their individual members could inflict by acting alone. If repairing harm is a function of our responsibility practices, one would expect harm done by groups to attract responsibility in much the same way as harm done by individuals.

5.3 LEGAL PERSONALITY AND THE CORPORATION

Our discussion of the relationship between responsibility and personality begins with a consideration of group responsibility (5.3 to 5.8) and, in particular, corporate responsibility. The legal corporation is what might be called an "abstract entity". The adjective "abstract" indicates that recognition of the corporation is based on observation of, and involves interpretation of, human conduct. The corporation is an entity in the sense that it is treated as different and separate from the human being(s)[9] on whose conduct the recognition process is based. Not all legally recognised abstract entities are corporations in the technical sense. For instance, states are abstract entities in international and domestic law; but typically they are not corporations. On the other hand, the law sometimes attaches significance to group activity without recognising the group as an

[7] For analysis of what a group is see Honoré (1973), 2–14.

[8] It is suggested, for instance, that individuals may be prepared to do things in a group that they would feel constrained from doing if acting alone: Bovens (1998), 125–31.

[9] Originally, legal corporations were conceived as vehicles for group activity: Grantham and Rickett (1998), 8–10. However, now a company need only have one member. This chapter is primarily concerned with group activity.

abstract entity. For instance, under the Public Order Act 1986 (UK), the offence of riot is committed when "12 or more persons who are present together use or threaten unlawful violence for a common purpose".[10] However, a riotous mob is not recognised by the law as an abstract entity—the offence is committed by each of the individuals in the mob, not by the group. As a result of acting in groups, individuals may attract judgments of responsibility to which they would not be subject if they acted independently. The discussion of groups in this chapter will focus on corporations.

The typical corporation involves group activity in two dimensions, as it were. On the one hand, there is contemporaneous conduct of a group of human beings, and on the other a corporation has a continuity of existence over time despite changes in the composition of the group of human beings whose conduct constitutes the activities of the corporation at any one time.[11] The law specifies the procedures that must be followed in order to bring a corporation into existence. A corporation can have legal rights and obligations.[12] Corporations can even take advantage of certain "fundamental rights" enshrined in bills of rights—as they frequently do.[13] A corporation can have prospective responsibilities, and it can be held (historically) responsible. It can make contracts, and commit torts and crimes;[14] it can sue and be sued. As it is summarily expressed, a corporation is a "legal person". It is these various legal attributes that lead to the application of the term "person" to corporations. This marks a fundamental difference between the legal and the humanistic approaches to the relationship between responsibility and personality. Under the latter, responsibility is a function of personality, whereas under the former, personality is a function of responsibility (amongst other things).[15] Corporations are legal persons because they are responsible, not vice versa. [16]

[10] See s. 1(1).

[11] The latter characteristic is shared by "corporations sole".

[12] Corporations may be subjected to legal obligations different from, and more onerous than, those of individual human beings and of abstract entities that do not qualify as corporations: Gower (1997), ch. 5. Such obligations recognise that groups of people acting together may succeed, by virtue of their group activity, in accumulating resources and power beyond the reach of individuals acting independently of one another.

[13] For a sustained argument against according fundamental rights to organisations see Dan-Cohen (1985), chs. 4 and 5.

[14] Indeed, there are many crimes that only a corporation can commit: Lacey (2000b), 28.

[15] Hart (1954).

[16] The same is true of individual human beings. Legal responsibility entails liability to sanctions. The basic function of rules and principles of legal responsibility is to justify the imposition of sanctions. Thus, the characteristic feature of a corporation is that its assets constitute a fund separate from the assets of its members from which its legal obligations can be satisfied. As Stoljar says (Stoljar (1973), 182), the law's prime concern is not to find group persons separate from their members, but rather group assets (see also Hansmann and Kraakman (2000)). Indeed, for legal purposes, the question of whether an abstract entity is a "person" is of no significance as such. In this sense, legal personality is a conclusion, not a premise. Some of the most imaginative and influential writing about corporate responsibility (e.g. Stone (1975); Fisse and Braithwaite (1993)) by-passes issues of personality and examines ways of maximising the punitive, deterrent and restorative effect of corporate responsibility through the design of legal sanctions.

Because they lack body and mind, corporations are often said to be "artificial", not "natural", legal persons. However, we need to be cautious about this contrast between artificial and natural legal persons. A human being is not, *as such*, a legal person.[17] Legal personality is an artefact of legal rules, not of human evolution and reproduction. While it is true that all human beings are recognised by the law, not all human beings have the same legal status, or the same legal rights and obligations. For instance, some human beings lack the legal capacity to commit crimes and to make contracts. In this sense, all legal persons are artificial.

The recognition of abstract entities is not a purely legal phenomenon. For instance, the distinction between a person who holds some office or position and the office or position itself is as common a feature of ordinary social life as of legal discourse. We may well say that the behaviour of Joanna Bloggs, as President of the Newtown Bridge Club, has brought the office of President into disrepute, even though that office is not a legally recognised abstract entity.[18] People often treat the likes of BHP and Microsoft as abstract entities without reference to the niceties of their complex legal structures. In fact, so-called "multi-national corporations" typically have no legal existence as such, but are made up of a dense and complex network of legal corporations. This does not stop us from talking about such conglomerates as if they were single abstract entities.[19] We often treat groups as abstract entities without any belief or implication that they are legal persons: "the Australian people", "the Mafia", "the Skinny-Dippers Swimming Club", and so on. There is, however, a significant difference between the process of recognising abstract entities in the law and the analogous process outside the law. By virtue of the law's institutional nature and resources, a corporation can exist as a legal entity independently of any activity that might meaningfully be described as corporate. "Shelf companies" are corporations that are waiting to be "enlivened" by being made a vehicle for human group activity.[20] In a non-institutional environment, by contrast, the notion of an "inactive" abstract entity having existence independently of group activity makes little sense. In this context it is, as it were, only by the fruits of a group that it can be known.

The law is parsimonious in its recognition of abstract entities.[21] In everyday life, we are much more inclined to treat groups as abstract entities than the law is. To most people, for instance, the distinction between a corporation and a partnership is invisible. To the untrained eye, a large firm of solicitors looks very

[17] Or a moral person. Similarly: Scruton (1989), 255.

[18] i.e. not a corporation sole. The concept of "office" plays an important role in public law, where a distinction is drawn between an employee (a contractual status) and being an officer.

[19] Teubner (1993).

[20] Thus we might say that a shelf company is a "wholly artificial" entity. Once a company becomes a vehicle for group activity, it ceases to be wholly artificial because it embodies a social reality (*pace* Sullivan (1995), 286–7).

[21] For discussion of problems resulting from such parsimony see Collins (1990); Ottolenghi (1990); Austin (1998); Ramsay and Stapledon (2001).

much like a medium-sized company. It would come as a surprise to many people that the company could be sued in its own right but that the partnership could not be, and that the two were subject to different legal regimes of taxation and financial disclosure, for instance.

As in the law, so in other contexts, the recognition of abstract entities is an important element of our responsibility practices. Just as a legal corporation can be held liable for a tort or a breach of contract, so we may judge (for instance) that the Mafia is responsible for a significant proportion of serious crime in Sicily, or that the antics of the Skinny-Dippers Swimming Club are responsible for the traffic jams along the beach-front.[22] In such instances, as in law, the recognition of groups as abstract entities is a function of holding them responsible, rather than vice versa. Because of the law's institutional geography, because legal sanctions are severe and underwritten by state coercion, and because issues of responsibility that enter the legal domain cannot be left unresolved, legal concepts and practices of group responsibility provide a detailed and highly developed model for this approach to the relationship between responsibility and personality.

5.4 LEGAL PRINCIPLES OF GROUP RESPONSIBILITY

5.4.1 Responsibility, personality and rules of attribution

Legal personality is a status based partly on being a subject of responsibility judgments. Because corporations have neither mind nor body, and because the law reflects the paradigm of individual responsibility in which responsibility judgments refer to human conduct and mental states, a necessary precondition of allocating legal responsibility to corporations is a set of rules for attributing human conduct and mental states to corporations. There is no need to give these rules a metaphysical interpretation or significance by talking, for instance, about "the mind of the corporation",[23] or "the corporation's conduct". It is perfectly adequate, and much less mysterious, to treat these rules of attribution as "deeming" rules by which abstract entities are treated as if they had minds and bodies. Viewing rules of attribution in this way reveals the sense in which corporations are "artificial" legal persons. Human beings are not legal persons by virtue of having minds and bodies, but by virtue of legal rules that identify subjects of the law and of legal rights and obligations. However, to the extent that these rules of identification, and the rules defining legal rights and obligations, refer to and presuppose bodily conduct and mental states, human beings can fall within them "naturally". By contrast, corporations can fall within such rules

[22] This example is inspired by Dershowitz (1983), ch. 5.

[23] It is sometimes said that corporate intention is "analogous" to human intention (e.g. Grantham (1998), 68). By contrast, I would say that because they lack a mind, corporations cannot have intentions. But we can attribute human intentions to corporations.

only "artificially", as a result of the attribution to them of human conduct and mental states. Attributing human conduct and mental states to a corporation does not, of course, make that entity a person *in the sense of a human being*—not even an "artificial human being". On the other hand, such attribution does make the corporation a legal person in the sense of *a subject of the law* and of legal rights and obligations.

An important and influential recent statement of the centrality of rules of attribution to the legal concepts of group personality and responsibility is that of Lord Hoffmann in *Meridian Global Funds Management Asia Ltd* v. *Securities Commission*[24] in which the question at issue was whether a fund management company was in breach of a statutory duty to give notice that it had acquired shares in a public listed company:

> "Judges sometimes say that a company 'as such' cannot do anything; it must act by servants or agents. This may seem an unexceptionable, even banal remark . . . But a reference to a company 'as such' might suggest that there is something out there called the company of which one can meaningfully say that it can or cannot do something. There is in fact no such thing as the company as such, no ding an sich, only the applicable rules [of attribution]. To say that a company cannot do something means only that there is no one whose doing of that act would, under the applicable rules of attribution, count as an act of the company".

To the extent that this statement rests on the observation that companies lack body and mind, it is indeed unexceptionable. Companies cannot think thoughts or intend actions or outcomes. Nor can companies do (or omit to do) things, in the way that human beings can, by bodily movements (or abstention therefrom). But it does not follow from the proposition that rules of attribution are essential for the recognition of abstract entities and the construction of group personality, that there is "no such thing" as a company. If it did, it would not logically be possible to say that human conduct could "count as an act of a company". Companies "exist" in two senses. First, like human beings, they are legal persons. Secondly, companies are vehicles for human activity, particularly group activity. Companies do not "exist" solely by virtue of being recognised as legal persons any more than human beings do.[25]

Despite the "banality" of the observation that abstract entities lack mind and body, it is very easy to lose sight of the need for rules of attribution. A common technique for establishing the possibility of group responsibility is to construct corporate intentionality on the analogy of human intentionality, and in the process to lose track of minds and bodies. An example is found in the Australian Commonwealth Criminal Code 1995.[26] So far as concerns the conduct element of offences, the Code's rule of attribution is that conduct of an employee, agent

[24] [1995] 2 AC 500, 506–7.

[25] Teubner (1988). In my terms, Teubner's approach is essentially humanistic. He locates the essence of the (group) legal person in "collective action".

[26] Division 12.

or officer of the corporation acting within the scope of their employment or authority counts as conduct of the corporation. Although the Code does not lay down rules of attribution for determining when a corporation can be said to have "authorised" conduct, or when a person can be said to be an employee or officer of a corporation, there are rules of law available for this purpose. A mental state is to be attributed to a corporation only if the corporation "expressly, tacitly or impliedly authorised the commission of the offence". The Code lays down several criteria for determining whether a corporation authorised the commission of an offence. A corporation may be held to have authorised an offence if (1) a "high managerial agent" of the corporation "engaged in the relevant conduct" with the relevant mental state, and *the corporation* failed to exercise "due diligence" to prevent this; (2) such agent "expressly, tacitly or impliedly authorised" the offence, and *the corporation* failed to exercise due diligence to prevent this; (3) *the board of directors* "carried out the relevant conduct" with the appropriate mental state; (4) *the board of directors* expressly, tacitly or impliedly authorised the offence; (5) *the "corporate culture" of the corporation* "directed, encouraged, tolerated or led to" the commission of the offence; (6) *the corporation* failed to create a corporate culture that discouraged the relevant criminal behaviour.[27] The Code explains the concept of "corporate culture" partly in terms of the conduct of high managerial agents of the corporation.

These criteria of authorisation are riddled with references to the conduct and mental states of abstract entities—the board of directors, the corporation—that are unsupported by appropriate rules of attribution. For instance, the Code does not specify what is to count as conduct of the board of directors, or when a corporation (as opposed to a person) can be said to have exercised due diligence.[28] Nor does it clearly specify what human conduct must be shown to have occurred in order to establish a corporate culture. I am not suggesting that we cannot usefully treat a board of directors as having engaged in conduct, or a corporation as having failed to exercise due diligence; or that we cannot usefully speak of a corporate culture of criminality. The point is that we can only do these things on the basis of attributing human conduct to an abstract entity. Without rules of attribution supporting the use of expressions that treat abstract entities as if they were humans, such talk is meaningless anthropomorphism. The lack of adequate rules of attribution in the Code leaves to the courts the job of providing this essential link between the corporation and the human beings on whose conduct its criminal responsibility is based.

5.4.2 Responsibility and capacity

Capacity responsibility is one of the five elements of Hart's taxonomic account of responsibility concepts, in which it is a precondition of legal and moral liability

[27] Emphases added.

[28] Gobert (1994) and Gobert (1994a) suffer from a similar lack.

responsibility. Hart's discussion of capacity focused on human beings, and was in terms of certain physical and mental abilities. This is not surprising because criminal responsibility (which was Hart's chief concern) is responsibility for bodily movements or the absence thereof (purposively interpreted as conduct—acts and omissions), for mental states accompanying conduct, and for the outcomes of conduct. In this respect, the law reflects the paradigm of individual responsibility. Because corporations lack mind and body, they cannot satisfy this capacity condition of responsibility. Presumably, only conduct and mental states of human beings that do satisfy the capacity condition can be attributed to abstract entities for responsibility purposes. In other words, corporations satisfy the capacity requirement indirectly by virtue of the attribution to them of conduct and mental states of human beings that do satisfy it.

There is another legally relevant notion of capacity that applies only to abstract entities. Being creatures of human group activity, abstract entities are vehicles for the achievement of human goals and purposes. In the case of legally recognised abstract entities, the purposes for which the corporation was established may limit its legal powers or, in other words, its capacity to enter binding legal transactions (such as contracts) under the so-called "doctrine of *ultra vires*". In the case of commercial companies, the main reason for this limitation was "to protect investors in the company by giving them some assurance that the assets of the company would not be used in some wholly unexpected way" by those who managed the company.[29] However, because of the adverse effects of the doctrine on those who entered into non-binding transactions with companies, it has been more or less abolished in many jurisdictions. On the other hand, the doctrine of *ultra vires* is still extremely important in relation to governmental abstract entities, which are discussed further in chapter 8.

5.4.3 Basic legal rules of attribution

There are various legal bases on which human conduct and mental states can be attributed to corporations. The most important are the constitution of the corporation, agency, vicarious liability, delegation and identification.

5.4.3.1 The constitution of the corporation

Typically the "articles of association" of a company will provide that certain decisions of the "primary organs" of the company—the board of directors and the general meeting of shareholders—"shall be" decisions of the company. Also, as a result of court decisions and legislation, rules of attribution may be implied into the constitutions of companies.[30] Because the articles provide only a structural

[29] Treitel (1995), 516. See also Gower (1997), 201–20.

[30] See the example given by Lord Hoffmann in the *Meridian* case (n. 24 above) [1995] 2 AC 500, 506.

skeleton within which the activities of the corporation are carried on, the rules of attribution it contains will not be sufficiently detailed or comprehensive to deal with all situations in which questions of attribution may arise. For this reason, the constitution is supplemented by rules of attribution provided by the doctrines of agency, vicarious liability, delegation and identification. We will consider them in turn.

5.4.3.2 Agency

Rules of agency apply equally to corporations and to human beings, which shows that they are not primarily concerned with the construction of group responsibility. They create a mechanism by which one person—the "principal"—can acquire legal rights and obligations vis-à-vis a second person by virtue of dealings between that person and a third person—the "agent". For instance, if A makes a contract with C as agent for B, the parties to the contract are B and C, not A and C. Both human beings and corporations can be principals and agents.[31] An important difference between a human being and a corporation is that human beings can acquire legal rights and obligations either by their own conduct or through the medium of an agent, whereas corporations, lacking mind and body, can acquire legal rights and obligations only through the medium of human conduct. Thus, if corporation A, acting as agent, makes a contract on behalf of corporation B, as principal, with corporation C, rules of agency are relevant not only to the relationship of agency between A and B and to the creation of the contractual relationship between A and C, but also to the construction of A, B, and C as legal actors and potential holders of legal rights and obligations. By contrast, rules of agency play no part in the construction of human beings as legal actors and potential holders of legal rights and obligations.

5.4.3.3 Vicarious liability

The rules of vicarious liability are concerned not with the creation of rights and obligations but with the allocation of historic responsibility and sanctions for past conduct and outcomes. Like the rules of agency, the principle of vicarious liability can apply both to human beings and to corporations. Vicarious liability attaches to certain types of relationship, the most important being that between employer and employee. For some time it was unclear whether vicarious liability involved attributing one person's conduct and mental states to another person or, by contrast, holding one person legally responsible for another person's breach of the law. Under the former approach, the question to be asked is whether the conduct and mental state attributed to the other person would have made that person legally responsible if they had been that person's

[31] Agency is the basis of partnership—each partner is an agent of all the others.

conduct and mental state. This question cannot meaningfully be asked in relation to corporations lacking, as they do, both mind and body; and this may be one reason why the latter approach is now orthodox: vicarious liability involves holding one person liable for another person's breach of the law.

This point has important implications that deserve some elaboration. When B is held vicariously liable for A's breach of the law, A remains liable as well. In other words, vicarious liability is a form of shared responsibility. In this respect, vicarious liability is different from agency. When A makes a contract with C as agent for B, A is not a party to the contract. The agent makes the contract as the representative, or on behalf, of the principal. This feature of vicarious liability is expressed by saying that whereas B's liability is vicarious, A's is personal. What this means is that A has breached the law, whereas B has not. However, vicarious and personal liability are not mutually exclusive. Imagine that A is employed by B1, a human being, that B1's business is very small, and that B1 is its sole operator and manager. Imagine further that C, another employee of B1, is injured at work in an accident involving the use by A of a tool provided by B1; and that the accident was partly the result of negligence on A's part and partly of negligent failure by B1 to maintain the tool in a safe condition. In such circumstances, B1 may be held vicariously liable for A's negligence, *and also* personally liable for breach of the employer's duty (of care) to provide safe tools.

Now suppose that A's employer, B2, is a corporation rather than a human being; and that the business employs hundreds of people. Still, B2 may be held vicariously liable for A's negligence and personally liable for breach of its own duty. However, being a corporation and lacking mind and body, B2 cannot be held personally liable by virtue of its own conduct, but only by virtue of the conduct of some human being. Thus, rules of attribution are needed to construct the personal liability of B2. These rules are dealt with in 5.4.3.4 and 5.4.3.5. In certain circumstances, they may also play a part in constructing the personal responsibility of human beings. Because B1 was the sole operator and manager of the business in the first example, B1's personal liability for breach of the duty to provide safe tools could be constructed solely out of B1's own conduct. But if B1's business had been larger and B1 had employed a foreman who was responsible for safety on the shop-floor, then a rule of attribution may have been needed to construct B1's responsibility for breach of the duty to provide safe tools.[32] Human beings may choose to discharge their legal duties themselves or through other human beings, whereas the duties of corporations can be discharged only through human beings.

Rules of attribution are relevant to vicarious liability in another way, too. The causal basis of vicarious liability is the provision or creation by the employer of the opportunity for a breach of the law to occur. Corporate employers can create such opportunities only through human conduct; and so

[32] If B1 had failed to take reasonable care in appointing or instructing the foreman, B1's personal liability could have been constructed entirely out of B1's own conduct. But otherwise, reference to the foreman's part in the story would have been necessary for this purpose.

rules of attribution are needed to lay the causal foundation for corporate vicarious liability.

5.4.3.4 *Delegation*

Vicarious liability is an incident of the relationship of employer and employee. B can be vicariously liable for A's tort (for instance) if A is B's employee, and the tort was committed in the course of A's employment. Agency, by contrast, is based on authorisation: A will be B's agent if B has authorised A to act on B's behalf for certain purposes. For instance, B may be bound by a contract made by A with C if B authorised A to enter the contract on B's behalf. An employee may be an agent of the employer; but an employer can be vicariously liable for tortious conduct of an employee even if the conduct was not authorised by the employer. Vicarious liability does not rest on authorisation but on the relationship of employer and employee. If an employer authorises tortious conduct by an employee, the employer may be personally liable as a joint tortfeasor (i.e. for having personally committed a breach of the law by authorisation).

Vicarious liability is liability for another's breach of the law, whereas personal liability is liability for one's own breach of the law. In the paradigm case, a person breaches the law by their own conduct. However, corporations, lacking mind and body, cannot breach the law by their own conduct but only by the conduct of human beings. Sometimes, too (as we saw in 5.4.3.3), a human person's breach of the law may be constructed out of another's conduct. An employer (whether a human being or a corporation) can be (personally) liable for breach of a duty resting on it as employer—such as the duty (of care) to provide safe tools to its employees—as a result of the conduct of another person, even if that person was not an employee, and even though the failure to provide safe tools was not authorised by the employer. The term typically used to describe the principle of attribution at work in such cases is "delegation":[33] for the purpose of deciding whether an employer has breached the duty to provide safe tools, the conduct of any person to whom the task of providing safe tools has been entrusted or allocated can be attributed to the employer.[34]

Delegation-based personal liability (or "direct" liability, as it is sometimes called) is a form of strict liability. An employer can breach the duty to provide safe tools (for instance) by negligently delegating the task to an incompetent person. But even if the employer took all reasonable care in delegating the task, it can still be held liable if the delegate performs the task negligently. The difference between delegation-based personal liability and vicarious liability is that the former rests on attribution to the delegator of conduct of the delegate, not a

[33] Note that I am using this term in the sense it bears in the phrase "non-delegable duty' found in tort law, rather than in the narrower sense found in criminal law cases dealing with licences: Simester and Sullivan (2000), 237–9.

[34] Of course, in the case of a corporate employer, rules of attribution are needed to determine whether the relevant task has been delegated.

breach of the law by the delegate. It is a precondition of vicarious liability that the employee is legally liable, whereas it is not a precondition of delegation-based personal liability that the conduct of the delegate that is attributed to the delegator constitutes a breach of the law by the delegate.[35] In other words, unlike vicarious liability, delegation-based personal liability is not a form of shared liability. In practice, however, the function of delegation-based personal liability (in tort law, anyway) is to extend vicarious liability beyond the relationship of employer and employee to that of employer and independent contractor.

Delegation plays an important part in the civil law of tort. But in England, the House of Lords has apparently held (in the seminal case of *Tesco Supermarkets Ltd* v. *Nattrass*)[36] that it is not a feature of the criminal law. Tesco owned a chain of some 800 supermarkets. In one of its stores, goods were advertised for sale at a price lower than that at which they were actually available. This was a criminal offence for which Tesco was prosecuted. Commission of the offence resulted from failure by a shelf-stacker to inform the manager that the store's supply of cut-priced items had run out, and consequent failure by the manager to remove the offending advertisement. The central management of Tesco had put in place a system to prevent such occurrences, but the system had failed on this occasion. The statute that created the offence expressly contemplated situations in which the conduct of one person (the manager in this case) might lead to another person (Tesco in this case) committing the offence. For such cases, that other person was given a defence that they had taken "all reasonable precautions and exercised all due diligence to avoid the commission of the offence". The Divisional Court held that Tesco could not avail itself of this defence because it had delegated the task of complying with the statute to the store manager, and he had not exercised due diligence. The House of Lords rejected this approach. It held[37] that Tesco (in the guise of its central management) had exercised due diligence by instituting a system to prevent breaches of the statute, and that by so doing it had not delegated its duty of care but discharged it.

Despite this explicit rejection of the principle of delegation, on closer analysis the decision of the House of Lords seems to involve an application of that very principle. In *Tesco* the manager was not prosecuted; but it was accepted that he had committed an offence under the statute. *In effect*, Tesco was held vicariously liable for the manager's offence. *In theory*, however, Tesco's *prima facie* liability for breach of the statute (subject to the defence of due diligence) was personal rather than vicarious. What was attributed to Tesco was not the manager's crime but the manager's conduct. That conduct put Tesco personally in *prima facie* breach of the statute.[38] In other words, Tesco committed an offence

[35] For an example from criminal law see Simester and Sullivan (2000), 237.

[36] [1972] AC 153.

[37] On the basis of the doctrine of identification, which is discussed in 5.3.3.5.

[38] Similarly, in *Director General of Fair Trading* v. *Pioneer Concrete (UK) Ltd* (the *Ready Mixed Concrete* case) [1995] 1 AC 456 the conduct of the employees put the company in contempt of court;

by virtue of having delegated to the manager the task of complying with the statute. So whereas the principle of delegation was not applied to the issue of whether Tesco had exercised due diligence to prevent commission of an offence by the manager, it was applied to the issue of whether Tesco had offered goods for sale in contravention of the statute by reason of the manager's failure to remove the advertisement. The statutory offence had two elements: a *prima facie* liability, for offering goods for sale at lower than their actual price, regardless of fault, and a fault-based defence of due diligence. The principle of delegation was applied to the strict liability element, but not to the fault-based element.

On the basis of the *Tesco* case, we can conclude that in English criminal law, delegation is limited in its operation to strict liability offences.[39] In civil law, by contrast, faulty conduct of one person may be attributed to another, with the result that the latter is held liable for faulty conduct even in the absence of fault on their part. For instance, a delegate's negligent failure to provide safe tools may put the delegator in breach of the delegator's duty of care to provide safe tools, even in the absence of relevant fault on the delegator's part.

The principle of delegation is extremely important in the criminal law because there are many strict liability statutory offences that apply to corporations, and some that can be committed only by corporations. It is in relation to corporations that the delegation principle is most significant because corporations cannot do anything except through human beings.[40] But as we have seen, delegation can also be relevant to individual liability, allowing one individual's conduct to be attributed to another for the purpose of determining the latter's responsibility.

5.4.3.5 *Identification*

It is sometimes said that in English criminal law, vicarious liability operates in relation to strict liability statutory crimes.[41] However, the analysis in 5.3.3.4 suggests that the rule of attribution relevant to such crimes is delegation, not vicarious liability. One person's tort can be attributed to another; and one person's conduct can be attributed to another with the result that the other attracts criminal liability. But one person's crime cannot be attributed to another.[42]

and the absence from the relevant statute of a defence of due diligence deprived it of the escape hatch that Tesco was able to use.

[39] The decisions in *R.* v. *British Steel Plc* [1995] 1 WLR 1356 and *Tesco Stores Ltd* v. *Brent London Borough Council* [1993] 1 WLR 1037 have been interpreted as undermining this proposition (Wells (2001), 101–3; Cartwright (2001), 99–103). I prefer to view them as involving an extension of the doctrine of identification along the lines of Lord Hoffmann's approach discussed in the next section.

[40] Failure to acknowledge this fact mars the discussion in Simester and Sullivan (2000), 239–43, at least in its application to corporations.

[41] Wells (2001), 87–93; Fisse (1968), 199; Fisse (1968a), 537.

[42] According to Fisse, there is a "basal common law principle that D should be held criminally responsible only in respect of his own . . . conduct": Fisse (1968), 202.

In relation to crimes with a fault element (intention, recklessness, knowledge or negligence), a corporation can be liable only if it can be shown that a senior manager had the requisite mental state or was negligent in relation to the criminal conduct. The effect of this rule (which is derived from the *Tesco* case) is that (1) a corporation can be guilty of a crime with a mental element only if a senior manager both committed the criminal conduct and had the requisite mental state; and (2) a corporation can be guilty of a crime of negligence[43] only if a senior manager failed to take reasonable care. The underlying idea is that senior managers are not agents or servants of the corporation. Their conduct and mental states are not attributed to the corporation. Rather senior managers are said, alchemically, to be the corporation. In other words, they are identified with the corporation.[44] In relation to mental states, this is sometimes put by saying that it is only senior managers, responsible for "company policy", who represent the mind of the corporation. "Hands" (lower-level employees) can commit criminal conduct, but only "minds" (senior managers) can have criminal mental states. In relation to negligence, the idea seems to be that a corporation can be at fault only if those who embody it—its senior managers—are at fault.

This doctrine of identification apparently rests on the (fallacious) idea that it is more difficult to attribute a mental state to a corporation than conduct.[45] In fact, because corporations lack body as well as mind, it is no easier to attribute conduct to them than mental states. Underlying the doctrine there also seems to be a judgment that it would be unfair to attribute to a corporation negligence or a mental state of a "lowly" employee, but not the bodily conduct of a lowly employee.[46] This judgment, too, is apparently based on some distinction between body and mind which makes it less objectionable to say, for instance, that a corporation caused harm than to say that it was reckless or failed to measure up to some standard of conduct. But since corporations lack body as well as mind, this distinction seems groundless. By limiting the search for requisite mental states to senior managers, the doctrine of identification significantly reduces the potential scope of corporate criminal liability.

In the *Meridian* case[47] Lord Hoffmann reinterpreted the identification doctrine, by removing the alchemical element, in order to justify attributing to a fund management company knowledge, possessed by relatively junior employees, that the company had (as a result of the employees' actions) acquired shares in a publicly listed company. In his view, whether the mental state of an

[43] The offence in *Tesco* was effectively a crime of negligence.

[44] This is sometimes called the *alter ego* doctrine. It has also been used "defensively" to protect senior managers from liability: Watts (2000).

[45] This idea also underpins the argument in Ouyang and Shiner (1995), 304–9, esp at 307. They seem to favour a regime of strict liability for harmful corporate conduct. But they do not provide a theory of how an abstract entity such as a corporation, that lacks a body, can "act" while, under their account, being incapable of having intentions because of lack of a mind. See also Wolf (1985), 279–83: organisations can be causally responsible because although they lack emotions ("a soul") they have cognitive capacities (despite lack of mind and body).

[46] Both assumptions underpin the discussion in May (1987), 97–9.

[47] See 5.4.1. See also *R.* v. *British Steel Plc* [1995] 1 WLR 1356, 1362–3.

employee could be attributed to the corporation depended not on the employee's status within the company but on whether the "purpose" of the rule in question would be defeated if attribution was not made. This vague criterion gives little indication of the limits of the identification principle. Lord Hoffmann said, for instance, that recklessness of an employee driving a company car on company business could not be attributed to the corporation so as to support a conviction of the company for manslaughter; but he gave no explanation of why not. One can imagine situations in which holding a company liable for its employee's reckless driving might arguably contribute to reducing the death toll on the roads.

Another innovative feature of Lord Hoffmann's approach is that it apparently allows a form of aggregation, by which the elements of a crime can be assembled from the contributions of several humans and attributed to the corporation. His analysis does not seem to require that the duty to give the notice that shares had been acquired should have rested on the employees whose knowledge triggered the duty. In other words, the company's breach of duty was an amalgam of knowledge possessed by two employees, and a failure to act on the part of some other employee. Traditionally, the law has subscribed to an individualist model according to which responsibility will attach to conduct-plus-mental-state only if the person who did the relevant conduct also had the relevant mental state.[48] The form of aggregation contemplated by Lord Hoffmann's analysis should be distinguished from the version, recently rejected by English courts,[49] according to which negligence on the part of several employees of a corporation can, by some sort of transformative process, be put together to produce recklessness on the part of the corporation: 2 + 2 = 5, as it were. By contrast, Lord Hoffmann's version requires no more than an additive process: 2 + 2 = 4, so to speak.

5.5 GROUP RESPONSIBILITY AND DIVISION OF LABOUR

As was just suggested, agency, vicarious liability and identification, as traditionally understood, are concerned with the relationship between a single human being—an agent or an employee—on the one side, and another human being or a corporation, as principal or employer, on the other. This "individualist assumption" about the identity of the agent or employee is challenged by the division of labour that is characteristic of much group activity. One of the ways in which groups can achieve more than their component individuals acting independently is by allocating different parts of the group's activity to different individuals—by division of labour between individuals rather than mere addition of the labours of various individuals. In all but the smallest organisations, division

[48] This model was explicitly adopted in *Attorney-General's Reference (No 2 of 1999)* [2000] 3 WLR 195, 212–13, For a philosophical statement from a traditional humanistic perspective see Velasquez (1983), 120.

[49] Ashworth (1999), 121–2.

of labour is typically accompanied by diffusion of knowledge about the group's activities; no individual working in the group will be fully aware of, or completely understand, the part played by each individual. The additive form of aggregation implicit in Lord Hoffman's approach to the doctrine of identification (see 5.4.3.5) can be seen as a response to division of labour. The transformative version of aggregation that English courts have rejected represents an attempt to deal with the diffusion of knowledge that typically accompanies division of labour in large organisations.

Dan-Cohen vividly describes these two characteristics of group corporate activity (division of labour and diffusion of knowledge) in the following way:

> "The complexity of the large corporation . . . give[s] it a quality of *opaqueness*. The organization may be described as opaque in the sense that its complexity makes it hard to "see through it": it is difficult to trace the acts and decisions of the organization to particular wills and actions on the part of particular individuals".[50]

The opaqueness of large groups may make it difficult to identify a single human being whose conduct or breach of the law can be attributed to a corporation in the way contemplated by the traditional understanding of rules of attribution. This phenomenon has also been called "the problem of many hands".[51]

In some contexts, the doctrine of *res ipsa loquitur* may provide a suitable resolution to problems of proof caused by the opaqueness of groups. For instance, if something goes badly wrong during surgery in circumstances where negligence on the part of a member of the surgical team was more likely than not the cause, and if all members of the team were employees of the hospital, the hospital may be held vicariously liable even if the injured patient cannot identify any particular individual member of the team as more likely than not the negligent party. *Res ipsa loquitur* also plays an important part in imposing on product manufacturers liability for harm caused by manufacturing defects. If a court is satisfied that the defect must have been the result of negligence on the part of some employee of the manufacturer, the manufacturer may be held liable even if the negligent employee cannot be identified. Underlying such reasoning, no doubt, is the individualist assumption that the harm must have been caused by one individual. In practice, however, if all the causal candidates were employees of the one employer, the question of whether the harm resulted from an act of negligence on the part of one individual rather than some lack of coordination between several employees, is unlikely to arise and bar the attribution of vicarious liability to the employer. Of course, the doctrine of *res ipsa loquitur* will not always be available; and when it is not, the opaqueness of groups may well present difficulties of proof.

The context in which opaqueness has been most in issue in recent years is that of major transport accidents resulting in many deaths and serious injuries.[52]

[50] Dan-Cohen (1985), 36 (original emphasis).

[51] Bovens (1998), 45–50.

[52] The *Herald of Free Enterprise* case is a good example: Clarkson (1996), 561; Wells (2001), 47–53.

Such cases bring together two features that are seen as making them particularly problematic. One is nonfeasance in the form of lack of attention to safety "at all levels" in the corporation. As a result, the duties of the various individuals within the organisation in relation to safety may not have been explicitly spelt out or specifically allocated, or appropriate duties may not have been allocated, either explicitly or implicitly, to any individual within the organisation. Another important feature of some such cases is the "public demand" that the seriousness of the incident should be marked by a prosecution of the corporation for manslaughter.

The nonfeasance issue is often referred to in terms of "systemic failure"; and the phenomenon is sometimes described in ways that suggest that the failure was that of the organisation itself rather than of any individual(s) within the organisation. Clarkson, for instance, speaks in this context of "modern corporate decision-making which is often the product of corporate policies and procedures rather than individual decisions".[53] But corporate policies and procedures are developed (or not) and operated (or not) by people. It is important to distinguish between two different questions: one, whether relevant duties had in fact been clearly allocated to specified individuals within the corporation; and the other, whether such duties ought to have been allocated. For the purposes of allocating responsibility to an organisation, it is the latter question, not the former, that is relevant. Although opaqueness may make the first question difficult to answer in particular cases, it presents no problem for answering the second question, which is about the way various individuals within the corporation ought to have behaved, according to interpersonal standards, not how they did behave or what duties they actually had under the corporation's internal rules and procedures. Once it has been decided that someone in the organisation ought to have taken action that would have prevented the harm in question, there seems no need to identify the individual(s). In this respect, opaqueness presents less difficulty for the allocation of responsibility to organisations in cases of nonfeasance than in cases of misfeasance (such as the surgical and product liability examples given earlier in this section).

In fact, in such cases of group nonfeasance, the effect of opaqueness is to block the appropriate allocation of individual responsibility, not corporate responsibility. On the one hand, it may effectively prevent the targeting of particular individuals despite the fact that they were in a position to ensure that appropriate precautions were taken and appropriate systems were put in place. On the other hand, it may result in the targeting of individuals whose conduct was the immediate cause of the harm, even though that conduct would not have occurred, or would not have caused harm, if some larger system had been in operation within the organisation.[54] Because of its effect in blocking the allocation of responsibility

[53] Clarkson (1996), 561. See also Field and Jörg (1991).

[54] Systemic failure thus presents an issue about luck: the individual's conduct has adverse consequences only because of factors outside their control.

to individuals, the opaqueness of large corporations provides important practical and principled arguments for recognising abstract entities as proper subjects of responsibility judgments.

The reason why opaqueness has presented a serious problem in nonfeasance cases is because of the other feature pointed out earlier—namely the public demand that corporations, whose lack of attention to safety causes major disasters, should be prosecuted for the serious offence of manslaughter—coupled with the doctrine of identification. The problem arises regardless of whether the manslaughter is defined in terms of the mental element of knowledge of an unreasonable risk, or in ("objective") terms of obviousness of risk. Senior managers in a large corporation may (for good reasons) have little or no detailed knowledge of risks involved in the day-to-day conduct of the corporation's business. As a result, it may not be possible to say that a particular risk would (or should) have been obvious to a person in the senior manager's position. One response to this situation is to impose on corporations duties of reasonable care to their customers analogous to the employer's duty to provide safe working conditions for employees, and to make breach of such duties a criminal offence. In effect, this is the course that the English Law Commission took in recommending the creation of an offence of "corporate killing".[55]

Unlike the typical safety offence, corporate killing has a fault element defined in terms of breach of interpersonal standards of conduct. This fault element performs two functions. First, it enables the court to single out individuals within the corporation as being (role) responsible for safety regardless of the actual safety policies and procedures of the corporation. Secondly, it justifies the imposition of penalties on the corporation greater than would be justified if the offence lacked a fault element. At the same time, because the relevant duties are imposed on the corporation, the individuals whose negligent conduct is attributed to the corporation cannot be convicted of the offence; and the Commission's draft legislation provides that they cannot be convicted as accessories to the crime. The draft legislation is expressed impersonally in terms of "management failure" and "the way in which [the corporation's] activities are managed or organised". It also specifically provides that a "management failure" may be regarded as the cause of a death "notwithstanding that the immediate cause [was] the act or omission of an individual". The draft legislation specifies no rules of attribution. By effectively imposing a duty of care on the corporation, it implies that delegation is the relevant basis of attribution, as in the case of the employer's duties of care towards employees in tort law. If the relevant duty has not been delegated to anyone, the corporation's liability would be based on failure to act by the human being(s) within the corporation on whom the law imposes the obligation to arrange for the performance of the duty.

[55] Law Commission (1996), Parts VI-VIII; Draft Bill, cl 4.

5.6 THE SCOPE AND FUNCTIONS OF GROUP RESPONSIBILITY

The scope of the potential criminal liability of corporations is more restricted than the scope of their civil liability. It is doubtful whether the principle of vicarious liability is part of English criminal law, whereas it plays a central role in the attribution of tort liability to corporations. It seems that in criminal law, delegation applies only to strict liability offences, whereas in civil law it extends to fault-based liabilities. Identification operates to impose on corporations criminal liability for *mens rea* and negligence, but it is limited in its operation to senior managers.

The relatively narrower scope of the criminal liability of corporations, compared with the scope of their civil liability, reflects the fact that in the criminal law paradigm the core of responsibility is located in the mental states of intention, foresight and knowledge. In civil law, by contrast, liability is typically based on conduct regardless of mental state. The focus on mental states in the criminal law paradigm follows from the common view that moral culpability ought to be a precondition of criminal liability, coupled with the idea that moral responsibility (properly) attaches only to intentional (in the sense of purposive) conduct. It is implicit in the second of these propositions that the core of moral responsibility is found not in conduct but in intentionality: conduct attracts moral responsibility only if it is "intentional". Coupled with the first proposition, the second therefore suggests that criminal liability should always have a mental element. This explains why "moral" objections to corporate criminal liability typically focus on the fact that corporations lack a mind (as opposed to a body), for on this account it is the lack of a mind that ultimately bars moral responsibility. Ironically, it also explains why courts have found it harder to justify imposing on corporations liability for *mens rea* crimes than for strict liability crimes: strict liability is liability for conduct and outcomes regardless of mental state.

However, of course, corporations also lack a body. This fact would seem to provide grounds for objecting to corporate criminal liability based on conduct and outcomes regardless of mental state, just as the lack of a mind provides grounds for objecting to criminal liability based on a mental state in addition to conduct. True enough, because corporations lack both mind and body, corporate liability for crimes with a mental element might seem twice as problematic as corporate liability for crimes without such an element. But if one takes the incorporeality of corporations seriously, that by itself would provide an insuperable barrier to all forms of conduct-based corporate criminal liability, as indeed to conduct-based civil liability.[56] As the basis of objections to the liability of corporations, their incorporeality is surely of universal relevance. It is only by taking into account the social functions of legal responsibility practices and

[56] *Pace* Wolf (1985).

their relational character that we can explain why the incorporeality of corporations is not seen as a universal bar to holding them responsible. From this perspective, the answer to the question of when corporations should be held responsible depends not on their nature but on where to strike the balance between the interests of the group of agents who constitute the corporation in freedom of (group) action against the other interests that responsibility practices seek to protect.

In civil law, the balance between the interests of the victim vis-à-vis those of the agent is generally struck in the same way regardless of whether the agent is an individual or a corporation. In other words, it makes no difference to the rights of the harm-sufferer under the civil law paradigm whether the harm resulted from group action or individual conduct. By contrast, in criminal law, thinking about the responsibility of corporations has been influenced by the humanistic approach to the relationship between responsibility and personality at the expense of the interests of victims in security of person and property and of society in order and security.

5.7 LEGAL AND MORAL GROUP RESPONSIBILITY

The key feature of the legal model of corporate responsibility is a set of rules and principles for attributing human conduct and mental states to abstract entities. These rules and principles also find a place in responsibility practices in the moral domain. Take agency, for instance. Suppose I send my child to the local shop to buy a kilogram of sugar that I urgently need for cooking. I give the child what I believe to be a sufficient amount of money, but it turns out not to be enough because of a recent price increase. The shopkeeper hands over the goods when the child promises to return immediately with the balance. In such circumstances, whatever the legalities of the situation, the child would rightly be treated as my "moral agent", impliedly authorised to undertake, on my behalf, an obligation to pay the balance of the purchase price as soon as possible. This idea of "moral agency" would also apply to groups. So far as vicarious liability is concerned, the example of the parent who feels obliged to pay for repairing a window broken by their child (see 3.6.3.5) shows that this principle of attribution finds a place in reasoning outside the law as well as within it. In practice, of course, people regularly attribute to corporations responsibility for their employees' conduct. The basic idea underlying delegation—that people should not be free to offload responsibility merely by getting someone else to "do their dirty work"—also has strong moral resonance.

The symbiotic relationship between legal and extra-legal concepts and practices of group responsibility is nicely illustrated by recent debates about the criminal liability of corporations for manslaughter in the context of major transport accidents. The widespread demand that corporations be subject to criminal liability in such circumstances reflects a non-legal judgment of group responsibility, based on views about the fair distribution of risks in society, and dependent on an implicit attribution of human conduct to the corporation, despite the problem of many hands. The unwillingness or inability of courts to respond to the demand provoked action from the Law Commission. Its proposal for an offence of corporate killing deals with the problem of many hands by imposing liability for negligent failure to pay sufficient attention to safety. This proposal gives detailed and justiciable content to a popular sentiment that the opaqueness of corporations does not render them morally unaccountable, and to a widespread demand that it should not render them legally unaccountable.

This example illustrates the process by which law can institutionalise and concretise extra-legal judgments of responsibility; and it reveals a way in which morality can make use of law's institutional resources for refinement and reinforcement of its responsibility judgments. It supports the argument that the main difference between law and that part of morality that is concerned with obligations resides in their relative institutionalisation. There is no reason to approach the relationship between law and morality by making an initial assumption that legal rules of attribution of conduct and responsibility to corporations are distorted or artificial competitors to moral principles, as opposed to institutionalised realisations of them.

In fact, the practice of attributing responsibility to abstract entities seems so deeply entrenched in social discourse that it is hard to understand why many philosophers cling so strongly to the traditional humanistic approach. One suggestion is that talk about the responsibility of abstract entities is:

> "at the level of ordinary discourse. A puzzle has been raised at the level of theory about how all that is possible when *ex hypothesi* organizations are a radically different kind of entity from the kind of entity of which . . . predications [of responsibility] are paradigmatically made, namely natural persons. Perhaps such a puzzle seems nonsensical and an affront to common sense. But, as Wittgenstein remarked, 'one can defend common sense against the attacks of philosophers only by solving their puzzles, i.e., by curing them of the temptation to attack common sense, not by restating the views of common sense' ".[57]

In other words, the mere fact that common practice assumes that organisations are morally responsible is no answer to the traditional humanistic approach because it gives no reason for abandoning the view that responsibility is a function of personality, and that personality should be understood in terms of having a mind and body.

My argument is that the "puzzle" of group responsibility can easily be solved by giving proper weight to the functions of "commonsense", "ordinary" responsibility concepts and practices and to their relational character. These features of legal and "ordinary" thinking about responsibility explain why the traditional

[57] Ouyang and Shiner (1995), 296 (footnote omitted). Why should "ordinary discourse" have to justify itself to "theory" rather than vice versa?

humanistic approach is not the basis of social practice in this area. The "theoretical puzzle" about group responsibility is a function of an excessively agent-focused approach.

5.8 MODIFIED HUMANISTIC APPROACHES

Some philosophers, struck perhaps by the gap between the traditional humanistic approach and common social practice, have sought to develop middle positions. Carol Rovane offers what she calls a "revisionary metaphysics" of personhood that creates "the possibility that certain groups of human beings could in principle function as individual agents in their own rights".[58] Her "ethical criterion of personhood" is "being committed to achieving overall rational unity" in practical reasoning. For Rovane, the importance of this criterion is that it severs the link between being a person and being a human being, on which the traditional humanistic approach rests. At the same time, however, it offers an explanation of why the individual human being provides the paradigm of personhood: the ideal of rational unity is a product of reflection on human behaviour.

Because Rovane does not argue that there are actually any group persons—only that they are possible in principle—it is difficult to know whether a large corporation, for instance, could qualify as a person according to her approach. Much depends on what would count as or demonstrate a commitment to overall rational unity. The examples she discusses of possible group persons involve only two or a few people seeking to achieve substantive agreement by the sort of reasoning processes that individual human beings use in deciding what to do. It seems unlikely, for instance, that an organisation that used a voting procedure to resolve substantive disagreement could, on that account, satisfy the criterion of commitment to overall rational unity. Rovane does not discuss the implications of her views for issues of (moral) responsibility. This is significant because she believes that her criterion of personhood not only allows the possibility of group persons, but also of multiple persons within the same human body. Because it has such diverse implications, it would be no simple matter to work out the relationship between responsibility and the commitment-to-rational-unity criterion of personhood.

Philip Pettit also accepts that groups may be persons;[59] but he draws a distinction between what he calls "social integrates" and "social aggregates".[60] In his view, only groups that are social integrates deserve to be treated as "genuine" persons. The distinction between social integrates and social aggregates turns on a contrast between two styles of group decision-making. These can be illustrated by the example of a three-member appellate court. Suppose the issue

[58] Rovane (1998).
[59] Or "agents" or "subjects".
[60] Pettit (2001), ch. 5.

before the court is whether the claimant ought to be awarded damages for personal injury allegedly caused by the defendant's negligence; and that the court has to decide three questions: (1) did the defendant owe the claimant a duty of care? (2) Was the defendant negligent? and (3) did the defendant's negligence cause the claimant's injuries? Suppose that Justice A answers (1) and (2) affirmatively, but (3) negatively; that Justice B answers (1) and (3) affirmatively, but (2) negatively; and that Justice C answers (2) and (3) affirmatively, but (1) negatively. Assuming that all three questions must be answered affirmatively in order for the claimant to succeed, the result will be a unanimous decision against liability, even though each of the questions was answered affirmatively by a majority of the justices. This is because appellate courts adopt an "individual" or "conclusion-driven" mode of decision-making as opposed to a "collective" or "premise-driven" mode of reasoning. In this example, if the court followed a collective decision-making procedure, each of the questions would be answered affirmatively because a majority of the justices answered each affirmatively; and so the claimant would win even though no individual justice decided all three questions affirmatively.

In Pettit's view, the distinguishing feature of a social integrate is that it adopts the collective mode of decision-making. For this reason, he argues, a social integrate satisfies the criterion of commitment to rational unity that (following Rovane) he thinks is definitive of personhood. In Pettit's view, social integrates deserve to be treated as persons separate from their members, because a group that is committed to pursuing collective reasoning may decide on, and be committed to, a course of action that only a minority, or indeed none, of its members favours (except indirectly by accepting the premise-driven decision procedure). In this sense, the group may have an "intention" different from and inconsistent with that of its members.[61]

Pettit's discussion of group personality is embedded in a theory about the relationship between freedom and responsibility. In his view, a person is free to the extent that they are "fit to be held responsible"; and, conversely, a person is fit to be held responsible for their conduct to the extent that their conduct is an exercise of freedom. Pettit gives an account of freedom in terms of what he calls "discursive control", a complex concept which he defines in terms of relationships in which two or more people "attempt to resolve a common, discursive problem—to come to a common mind—by common discursive means".[62] In his view, a social integrate can be free in this sense and, therefore, fit to be held responsible for what it does in exercise of that freedom.

[61] Any voting procedure other than unanimity can commit a group to a decision different from that supported by some of its members. It might be thought that this could justify speaking of a group intention. But Pettit wants to say that only a premise-driven decision-making procedure can produce sufficiently stark discontinuities between group and individual intentions to justity treating the group as different from its members.

[62] Pettit (2001), 67.

For present purposes, Pettit's account has the advantage over Rovane's that it explains how groups that resolve internal disagreements by voting procedures may count as abstract entities separate from their members. However, taken at face value, the criterion of collective reasoning might seem to be a very stringent requirement for group personality. There must be very few groups, one might think, that adopt collective decision-making procedures as their basic *modus operandi*. Appellate courts are certainly not alone in deciding issues by majority voting on conclusions. Nor does the fact that appellate courts decide issues individually rather than collectively discourage people from treating them as having group identity. For instance, the decision of the majority of justices of an appellate bench is treated as the decision of *the court*. In social and political discourse, institutions such as the Supreme Court of the United States and the High Court of Australia are commonly treated as abstract entities with a continuing identity over time. Indeed, the personification of the US Supreme Court is one of the most notable products of the country's constitutional arrangements.

Despite first appearances, however, it may be that a group could satisfy the requirement of collective reasoning even if its basic mode of decision-making was voting on conclusions. As Pettit points out, one of the dangers inherent in conclusion-driven reasoning is inconsistency over time. In the law, the doctrine of *stare decisis*, and the principle that like cases be treated alike on which it rests, are designed to minimise this danger. Although multi-member appellate courts follow a conclusion-driven mode of decision-making, this procedure is constrained by an obligation resting on the various justices to support their conclusions with premises that meet the demand of consistency with the existing body of legal materials, and the requirement of justice that like cases be treated alike. We might argue, therefore, that appellate courts can satisfy Pettit's criterion of personhood because although their synchronic reasoning is conclusion-driven, their diachronic reasoning respects the value of consistency over time.

If this conclusion is acceptable, Pettit's criterion of group personhood is much less stringent that it might appear at first sight. On this interpretation, the criterion would allow groups that follow conclusion-driven majority voting procedures to qualify as persons, provided their members recognised and strove to observe the value of consistency over time. Because consistency over time is prudentially as well as morally valuable, any group that desires a good reputation will be inclined to behave consistently, even if out of pure self-interest. Even so, most of the examples Pettit gives of group behaviour involve very small groups making discrete decisions. It is not clear whether large, complex groups involved in a variety of interrelated activities could meet the criterion of rational unity.

The modified humanistic account that lawyers have found most congenial is that of Peter French. He finds the key to corporate personality in what he calls "the corporation's internal decision structure" ("CID structure"). The CID structure of a corporation, according to French, has two elements "(1) an organizational or responsibility flow chart that delineates stations and levels within the corporate power structure and (2) corporate decision recognition rule(s) (usually embedded in something called 'corporate policy')". "When operative and properly activated, the CID Structure accomplishes a subordination and synthesis of the intentions and acts of various biological persons into a corporate decision".[63] French's CID structure is roughly equivalent to what was referred to in 5.4.3.1 as the "constitution" of the corporation; and this is why his approach is attractive to lawyers. However, whereas I treated the constitution as a source of rules of attribution, French assigns to it the effect of transforming human behaviour into corporate conduct, and of creating a non-human person out of human material. Unlike Rovane and Pettit, French seems happy to give the corporation's constitution this effect provided only that it has the two structural elements he specifies, and regardless of its substantive content. For instance, he does not require that the CID structure should embody a commitment to overall rational unity; or that it should establish a premise-driven decision procedure.

Having been developed with corporations in mind, French's concept of a CID structure is formal and institutional. It does not easily fit cases where responsibility is attributed to groups that lack a developed internal constitution.[64] More importantly for present purposes, French seems to contemplate a corporation's CID structure as being concerned only with macro and meso-level policy and decision-making. It would not, for instance, easily provide the basis for holding a corporation vicariously responsible for negligent driving by a low-level employee of a vehicle owned by the corporation. The same comment also applies to the accounts given by Rovane and Pettit. All three accounts locate the essence of personhood in mental activities, and ignore the bodily aspects of human behaviour. The mental focus of these accounts greatly reduces their potential as foundations of a complete theory of responsibility. In constructing such a theory, it is just as important to be able to attribute bodily conduct to groups as it is to be able to find group mental states.

Despite their recognition of at least the possibility of group responsibility, there is a large gap between these modified humanistic approaches and social practices of attributing responsibility to groups. The reason for this (I would argue) is that modified humanistic approaches, like the traditional humanistic approach, rest (implicitly at least) on the assumption that responsibility is a function of personality. Legal and social practice, by contrast, takes a functional and relational approach to responsibility under which the personality of groups is a function of responsibility (amongst other things).

That ends the discussion of group personality. In the next section I turn to the thorny problem of the responsibility of people who suffer from multiple personality disorder.

[63] French (1979), 143. See also French (1984), chs 3 and 4. It may be that French's approach is not accurately described as humanistic (Ouyang and Shiner (1995)); but this is the way it has been interpreted by lawyers.

[64] For a discussion of its shortcomings as a general theory of group activity see May (1987), chs. 1 and 2.

5.9 DIVIDED MINDS

For the purposes of this brief discussion I shall assume the possibility that a single human being (P) might behave as if their body housed two (or more) distinct human "intentional systems" (let us say P1 and P2), in such a way as to lead us to describe the person as having "a split personality" or "multiple personalities".[65] It is not necessary here to establish criteria that might create such a possibility. The important point is that if we interpret such a possibility in terms of two minds in one body, it would seem to create problems for theories of responsibility based on the idea that the "unit of responsibility", as it were, consists of a single mind in a single body.

Curiously, however, it does not seem as difficult, under the traditional humanistic approach to the relationship between personality and responsibility, to accommodate the possibility that one human body might contain two (or more) units of responsibility, as it is to contemplate the possibility of group persons. The problem with groups is that they lack mind and body. The reason why they lack a mind is (of course) that they lack a brain. But what is important for moral personality is the mind, not the brain. One reason why a human in a persistent vegetative state is not a proper subject of responsibility judgments is that although they have a brain, they lack a mind (at least in the sense required for being responsible). It is not obvious that there is anything in the traditional humanistic approach that rules out the possibility that a human brain might "house" more than one mind. It is also worth noting that from a modified humanistic perspective, Rovane considers that her "ethical criterion of personhood" can accommodate multiple personalities in the one human body.[66] What humanistic approaches would seem to rule out is treating P (as opposed to P1 or P2) as a person.[67] In one sense, P is a body without a mind.

Humanistic approaches, then, may create space for ascriptions of responsibility in cases of split personality. Matters become somewhat more complicated, however, when we go beyond mere ascriptions of responsibility to the implications of multiple personality for moral and legal sanctions. These complications are hidden by the priority that humanistic approaches give to personality over responsibility, and the way they treat responsibility as a function of personality. The difficulties come to the surface if we take a functional and relational approach to responsibility. There is no particular difficulty with "intangible sanctions" such as disapproval and censure. Suppose that P1 does something worthy of disapproval and censure. If we assume that only one of the two personalities can occupy P's conscious mind at any one time, disapproval and censure could be

[65] See Wilkes (1988) 109–28; Rovane (1998), 170; Moore (1984), ch. 11; Sinnott-Armstrong and Behnke (2000). An alternative approach to multiple personality disorder views it as a dissociative disorder which undermines control and, hence, responsibility.

[66] Rovane (1998), ch. 5.

[67] Haji (1997).

directed at P1 without directing them at P2. There may not even be too much of a problem if we assume that both P1 and P2 can be present in P's consciousness at the same time. Many "single-minded" people have different "sides" to their personality, and we generally have no qualms about censuring an individual for conduct that reflects only one of those sides. Split personality can be seen as the most pathological version of the sorts of complexity of behaviour that "normal" people manifest.

The real problems arise out of "tangible" sanctions, such as damages, fines and imprisonment. Because they inhabit the same body, it is not likely to be easy to target such sanctions selectively on P1 rather than P2. If it were the case that the two personalities were never present in P's conscious mind at the same time, it might be possible, in theory at least, to incarcerate P only when P1 was present. If P's life was so bifurcated that P1 and P2 had separate assets, it might even be possible to fine P1 but not P2. In practice, however, any tangible sanction inflicted on P is likely to affect P2 as well as P1 by reason of their presence in one and the same body. One way of dealing with the problem would be to treat split personality as negativing responsibility in the way that automatism, for instance, does. However, this does not seem satisfactory, at least if we assume that at the time of the responsibility-attracting conduct, P1 had conscious control over the body shared with P2. Nor would it seem right to treat the case as one of insanity unless, at the relevant time, P1 met the criteria of insanity.

Another possible solution would be to treat P2 as an innocent bystander, an incidental but inevitable victim of imposing responsibility and sanctions on P1. When sanctions are imposed on "normal" people, others closely associated with them often suffer through no fault of their own. This is an unavoidable price of our responsibility practices which is, perhaps, best taken into account at the level of deciding what sanctions to impose.

It should also be observed that the greatest qualms about imposing sanctions in cases of split personality relate to responsibility for mental states—intention, recklessness and knowledge. Suppose that while in "possession" of the shared body, P1 drives negligently and injures a pedestrian. It is unlikely that we would be tempted to relieve P1 of liability to compensate the pedestrian, even if doing so would indirectly harm P2. Even less, it seems, would multiple personality disorder weigh against strict liability. Moreover, the arguments in favour of modifying our normal responsibility concepts and practices to take account of split personality seem strongest when the issue is whether P/P1/P2 should be punished. In this context, as in others, an account of responsibility that ignores its relational aspects is inevitably incomplete and misleading. Just as the law does not deny a person compensation for harm suffered merely on the ground that the harm was a result of group conduct, neither need it deny compensation merely on the ground that the harm was caused by one persona of a split person. The quandaries about responsibility presented by the possibility of split personality seem most intractable when responsibility is viewed as a function of the agent's personality. When account is taken of the purposes and relational aspects of responsibility concepts and practices, some of the problems presented by split personality seem less difficult to resolve.

5.10 SHARED RESPONSIBILITY

The final topic for discussion in this chapter is shared responsibility.

5.10.1 The relationship between group and shared responsibility

Shared responsibility is a form of individual responsibility. Group responsibility is "collective" in the sense that it falls on the group as an abstract entity, not on the individuals who comprise the group. Under the traditional humanistic approach, there can be no such thing as collective responsibility in this sense because there can be no abstract entities. Thus Velasquez says that even in relation to acts that "can be predicated only of" a group, responsibility must rest on human members of the group.[68] May, by contrast, believes that social groups can be responsible because by group action, people can achieve things that they could not achieve by independent action. But he also thinks that social groups should be conceived of not as abstract entities, but as "individuals in relationships".[69] Thus for him, too, group responsibility is a form of shared responsibility. When it comes to meting out sanctions for group conduct, he thinks that they should be imposed only on the individuals within the group who were personally responsible for what the group did.[70] A central difference between group (collective) responsibility and shared responsibility is that under the former, sanctions are not imposed on the individual members of the group, whereas shared responsibility makes all those who share it individually liable to be sanctioned.

A common objection to collective corporate liability is that imposing financial sanctions on a corporation for its breaches of the law may indirectly impose sanctions on shareholders (i.e. members of the social group that constitutes the company) regardless of whether they are personally guilty of breaches of the law. This objection proves too much. Shareholders are innocent bystanders, not unlike members of the family of a human person who is imprisoned or fined for a criminal offence. The fact that imposing a sanction on one person may have adverse incidental effects on others provides no argument of principle against imposing the sanction, although it is a consideration that can rightly be taken into account in deciding what sanction to impose.[71]

[68] Velasquez (1983), 119.

[69] May (1987), 5.

[70] May (1987), ch. 4.

[71] e.g. *R* v. *Welsh*, *The Times*, 9 January 2001. The full judgments are available at http://www.casetrack.com/ct/casetrack.nsf/bdcde17d2706c4308025677c00506122/. See also Walker and Padfield (1996), para. 4.36.

5.10.2 Joint and concurrent responsibility

Suppose that A suffers certain damage as a result of the combined conduct of several tortfeasors. In such circumstances, a distinction is drawn between joint tortfeasors and concurrent tortfeasors. Where the several tortfeasors act independently of one another, they are concurrent tortfeasors. A simple example would be a three-car road accident attributable to the negligence of the drivers of two of the cars. Where the conduct of the tortfeasors is related in certain ways, they are joint tortfeasors. An obvious example is conspiracy (i.e. agreement) to inflict financial harm by acting unlawfully. Put crudely, whereas concurrent tortfeasors act as individuals, joint tortfeasors act as a group—"in concert" as it is sometimes put. In criminal law, the term "complicity" is used to refer generally to the bases of joint criminal liability.[72]

Where several agents commit a tort jointly, there is only one tort, and the injured person has only one cause of action, no matter how many joint tortfeasors there were. By contrast, where several agents commit concurrent torts, each can be sued for a separate tort. This distinction is now much less important than it once was. Its original significance was that if a claimant sued one joint tortfeasor "to judgment",[73] no claim could subsequently be brought against any other joint tortfeasor, the judgment in the first action having "extinguished" the single cause of action.[74] The judgment in the first claim (it was said) "barred" subsequent claims against joint tortfeasors. In certain circumstances, too, settling a claim against one joint tortfeasor barred claims against the other(s). By contrast, judgment in an action against (or settlement with) one of several concurrent tortfeasors did not prevent the claimant subsequently suing the other(s).[75] The bar on subsequent actions against joint tortfeasors has been abolished in many jurisdictions. It is worth noting that no analogous rule ever existed in criminal law. Even in cases of complicity, each of the involved parties is guilty of a separate offence, and all can be prosecuted either together or separately. This difference between tort law and criminal law may have reflected the greater public interest in the prosecution of criminals compared with the compensation of tort victims. Indeed, in tort law, the bar on subsequent actions applied even if a joint tortfeasor who agreed, or was ordered, to pay damages failed to do so.

The result of all this is that at the level of liability, as opposed to sanctions, it makes no difference whether shared legal responsibility for one and the same event or outcome arises out of group conduct or individual conduct.

[72] Ashworth (1999), ch. 10.

[73] i.e. where the action was terminated by a judgment of a court, whether in favour of or adverse to the claimant.

[74] If the joint tortfeasors were all sued in the same proceedings, they could all be held liable for the tort.

[75] For a fuller account of these and related rules see Cane (1999a), 138–40. For a discussion of the analogous rules in contract law see Treitel (1995), 523–5.

5.10.3 Contributory negligence

Responsibility may be shared not only between various harm-doers but also between a harm-doer and the victim of the harm. This form of shared responsibility is of most importance in tort law, and in the tort of negligence in particular. There is an asymmetry between imposing responsibility on a victim, on the one hand, and a harm-doer on the other. When a harm-doer is held responsible, the cost of the harm will be shifted, whereas when the victim is held responsible, the loss will be left to lie where it fell. This may be important in practice if, for instance, the harm-doer is better insured against incurring liability than the victim is against suffering harm. In principle, however, the "defence" of contributory negligence rests on the straightforward normative principle that a person who fails to take reasonable care for their own safety should not be able to shift responsibility for ensuing harm on to another person.

5.10.4 Secondary responsibility

In many cases of group activity, some parties can be identified as the "principal" agents, and others as "accessories" or "accomplices" or "secondary agents". The sorts of conduct that can attract "accessory liability" can be broadly described as "assistance" and "encouragement". But each of these two terms covers a broad range of conduct, and not all conduct to which they apply will necessarily attract accessory liability. For instance, providing a person with the opportunity to commit a tort is the causal basis of vicarious liability. On the other hand, it is controversial and problematic whether selling an item, which the seller knows will be used to commit a crime or a tort (for instance), will and should attract accessory liability.[76] Similarly problematic and controversial is the extent to which failure to prevent another from committing a breach of the law does and should attract accessory liability.[77] In recent years, this issue has been particularly prominent in the law of tort in the context of attempts to extend the scope of the liability of regulatory and other law-enforcement agencies.

"Encouragement" can range, at one extreme, from the sort of conduct that could provide the principal agent with a defence of duress, through authorisation, inducement, persuasion and the like, to conduct, at the other extreme, that cannot be shown to have borne a causal relationship to the principal's conduct (such as expressing approval of something that the principal intends to do anyway). Obviously, the closer the "encouraging" conduct is to the latter pole, the harder is it to justify attaching accessory liability to it. In criminal law, accessory liability has a double fault element relating, on the one hand, to the principal's

[76] *C.B.S. Songs Ltd* v. *Amstrad Consumer Electronics Plc* [1988] AC 1013; Cornish (1996), 439–40; Spencer (1987).

[77] For philosophical treatments of this issue see May (1992); Bovens (1998), Part III.

conduct and, on the other, to the accessory's conduct.[78] This adds a further layer of complication to this area of the law. The variety and complexity of the issues thrown up by shared legal liability for group activity provides an excellent illustration of the way in which the law's institutional geography and resources enable it to make a net contribution to society's store of responsibility concepts and practices.

5.10.5 Secondary and group responsibility

An interesting analogy can be drawn between the shared criminal liability of individuals for group activity and group criminal responsibility.[79] As we saw in 5.5, the law's traditional stance has been that a corporation can be held criminally responsible only if the relevant conduct can be traced to a single human being. Division of labour and the opaqueness of groups may make this difficult. At first sight, this problem would appear to be even more serious where the issue is not whether the group should be held responsible, but whether responsibility should be shared by its members individually. Surely we would be justified in holding an individual member of a group criminally liable only if the commission of the crime could be traced to them. In practice, however, provided it can be shown of any particular member of the group that they were actually involved in some way in the criminal activity in issue, it is not necessary for the prosecution to establish whether the person was involved as a principal or an accessory.[80] This is because in English criminal law, the liability of an accessory is derivative of that of the principal(s), meaning that the accessory is guilty of the same offence as the principal(s).[81] This approach rests on a form of aggregation: where the commission of a crime has resulted from the activity of a group, the contributions of the group members can be aggregated, and each member can be treated as guilty of the offence.

In this light, the unwillingness of English courts (noted in 5.4.3.5) to recognise aggregation as a basis for attribution of conduct to a corporation is puzzling. The explanation would appear to be that the law of corporate liability is dominated by the humanistic imagery of personality, in which responsibility is a characteristic of individual human beings. By contrast, in cases where no question arises of treating a group as an abstract entity, courts have felt more able to aggregate the conduct of various individuals in a group, and to hold each responsible for the resulting composite conduct and its outcomes. If we are

[78] Ashworth (1999), 438.

[79] Wells (1993), 138–40.

[80] Ashworth (1999), 425–6.

[81] It has been suggested that the derivative theory of accessory liability should be abandoned in favour of an "inchoate" theory: Ashworth (1999), 457–8. Under this approach, an accessory would be guilty of a different offence from that committed by the principal(s). In cases of reasonable doubt as to the part played by each involved person, all could be convicted of an inchoate accessory offence, but none could be convicted of the principal offence.

prepared to hold all the involved members of a group individually responsible for the activities of the group regardless of the precise nature of the involvement of each, is there any reason to refuse to hold the group as a whole responsible? If all members of the group were involved in some way, it is hard to think of any good argument against holding the group, as such, responsible.

What should we think about cases in which only some members of the group were involved? In such cases, would holding the group responsible not entail an unjustified attribution of responsibility to the uninvolved members of the group? This is the basis of the objection, discussed in 5.10.1, that corporate liability adversely affects innocent shareholders. And the answer given there applies here too. The fact that imposing responsibility on A may indirectly harm B even though B is in no way responsible, provides no principled objection to imposing responsibility on A. If it did, we could rarely justify holding anyone responsible, at least in cases where responsibility carries with it a serious tangible sanction. Even if it would be unjust to impose responsibility (and sanctions) directly on a group member who was not involved in the responsibility-attracting events, it does not follow that it would be unjust to impose liability on the group as a whole, even though some members were not involved.

What should we say about the direct attribution of responsibility to uninvolved group members? The answer to this question depends crucially on what is meant by "uninvolved". May, for instance, argues that membership of a group generates special obligations to take reasonable steps to prevent other members of the group doing harm. Individuals may have no obligation to control the conduct of others with whom they have no special relationship. But on this view, people who are related by group membership cannot sit back and stay uninvolved by being inactive, while other members of the group behave badly. Such obligations to control others may be more readily recognised in the moral domain than in the legal. It is one thing to disapprove of a person for failing to prevent harm, but quite another to impose tangible sanctions on that account. Even so, there will be cases in which passive group members can claim to have been truly uninvolved and, on that basis, to be free of moral as well as legal responsibility for what other members of the group do.

5.10.6 Vicarious responsibility

Vicarious liability involves holding one person (A) liable for breach of the law by another person (B). It is a form of shared liability—A shares liability with B. In the typical case, B's personal liability will be responsibility-based. But in such cases, is A's vicarious liability responsibility-based or is it a form of liability without responsibility? The most common view amongst lawyers supports the latter alternative, and explains vicarious liability as a device for allocating and spreading the costs of repairing harm. This approach is congenial to agent-focused accounts of responsibility, under which vicarious liability is problematic because it is a form of strict liability and because it is liability for the conduct of another. But it is not difficult to give an account of vicarious liability as a form of relational activity-based responsibility (3.3.2.1). The main relationship to which vicarious liability attaches is that of employer/employee. Unlike passive strict liability, which is clearly an instance of liability without responsibility, vicarious liability has a foundation in conduct of the person held liable.

Vicarious liability also has a causal basis in the sense that the employment relationship provides the employee with the opportunity to breach the law. From this perspective, the rule that vicarious liability attaches only to conduct "in the course of employment" can be given a causal interpretation as a principle of causal responsibility relevant to determining when an opportunity will be treated as having been provided by the employer. As we saw in 5.10.3, providing the opportunity for a crime to be committed may attract accessory liability if it is done with an appropriate mental state. Providing an opportunity for a tort or a crime to occur may also attract personal (i.e. non-vicarious) tort liability if the person who provided the opportunity was under a duty to take steps to prevent the crime or the tort. But the vicarious liability of the employer is neither a form of liability for assistance, nor a form of personal liability for failing to prevent a tort or a crime. Viewed as a form of activity-based responsibility, it seems to rest on a principle to the effect that those who employ others to further their own projects should bear the cost of breaches of the law for the occurrence of which that employment provides the opportunity. If the employer is doing the employee's business, the employer should accept shared responsibility for what the employee does, for ill as well as good. This principle does not relieve the employee of responsibility:[82] the employee shares responsibility with the employer.

Because vicarious liability is strict and relates to the conduct of another, it is sometimes invoked as a prime illustration of the gap between legal and moral responsibility. This is a mistake. The basic idea of vicarious liability is found in the moral domain as well as in the legal. Indeed, the scope of the moral analogue of vicarious liability seems wider than its legal counterpart. For instance, in law parents are not vicariously liable for their children's torts. By contrast, in some cases, at least, it is thought right for parents to repair harm done by their children. The narrower scope of legal vicarious liability may be thought explicable in terms of the (potentially) onerous nature of legal obligations of repair. The distinction amongst legal sanctions between obligations of repair and punishment may explain the absence of true vicarious liability from the criminal law. It is one thing to require a person to repair harm done by another in breach of the law, but quite a different matter to punish a person for another's wrongdoing.

[82] Some (e.g. La Forest J in *London Drugs Ltd* v. *Kuehne and Nagel* [1992] 3 SCR 299) think that at least in cases where the injured party has had no dealings with the employee but only with the employer, the employer alone should be liable. The argument is strongest where harm is the result of "systemic failings" within a corporation, and the targeted employee's conduct was merely the trigger of the harm-causing incident. See also 5.5.

To be contrasted with vicarious liability is delegation-based personal liability (5.4.3.4). This is not a form of shared liability. It involves attributing conduct of one person (A) to another person (B) regardless of whether A would be held personally liability for the conduct. The basis of such liability is that B has an obligation or duty (a "prospective responsibility" (2.1.2.1)) the discharge or performance of which has been delegated to A. Delegation-based liability is strict (i.e. regardless of fault), but it is more obviously responsibility-based than vicarious liability because the duty or obligation that has been breached rests on the delegator, not on the delegate; and because the act of delegating or entrusting the performance of the duty or obligation to the delegate forges a stronger causal connection between conduct of the delegator and the delegate's breach of the law than that between the conduct of the employer and the employee's breach of the law in the case of vicarious liability.

5.10.7 Assessing shares of responsibility

Where several people share responsibility for an event or an outcome, how should we assess their respective shares of responsibility? This question raises different issues depending on the context in which it arises. For instance, in the allocation of blame (or censure or disapproval), the only issue will be one of relativities—how much blame should be allocated to each person relative to the others? Moreover, because blame is intangible, all we need to decide about each person is whether they were more or less, or no more or less, blameworthy than others. By contrast, where a fixed sum of compensation is to be divided between several responsible parties, not only must the share allocated to each responsible person be relatively fair, but also the shares must add up to one. In yet other cases, where punishment is in issue, not only must the various penalties meted out be fair as between the responsible parties, but they must also be fair relative to the maximum specified (or acceptable) penalty for the conduct in question. But in this last case, the various penalties need not add up in total to the specified maximum. Because of the nature of compensation and tangible punishments (such as fines and imprisonment), it is not enough to say, for instance, that A should pay more compensation than B or receive more punishment than B. Rather, we need to say how much more punishment A should receive, or by how much A's share of the compensation should exceed B's.

In the absence of a generally accepted technique for measuring responsibility, this last task requires the exercise of individual judgment on the part of officials whose job it is to allocate shares of responsibility. In recognition of the intrinsic difficulty of the task, such officials are given considerable discretion. In criminal law, the sentencing process is much less rule-bound than the liability-allocation stage. In civil law, courts possess more or less complete freedom to allocate shares of responsibility, guided only by the injunction to do what is "just and equitable". The most important reference point for the allocation of shares of responsibility in any particular case is a detailed account of what happened, of who did what, and of the outcomes that ensued. Two broad criteria provide some structure for the process: one, the relative fault of the various parties, and the other the relative "causal contributions" of the various parties.[83] The fault criterion can be clearly illustrated by reference to vicarious liability. An employer may be held vicariously liable for an employee's tort even though the employer was completely faultless, and the conduct of the employee who committed the tort was highly culpable. In such a case, as between the employer and the employee responsibility could (in theory at least) be allocated 100 per cent to the employee.

In order to understand the criterion of causal contribution, we need to recall the link between causation and responsibility (see 4.4.1). The issue of allocating shares of responsibility for an event between several people typically arises when the conduct of each was a but-for or NESS condition of the event. Conduct either is such a condition or it is not—there can be no degrees of causal contribution in this sense. But we may, for instance, judge that the thug who administers a beating makes a greater causal contribution to the victim's injuries than a gang member who barracks from the sidelines; and that the latter makes a greater causal contribution than the passer-by who passively looks on in horror, afraid to intervene. Underlying such judgments are what (in 4.4.2) were termed "principles of causal responsibility". Such principles may be relevant not only to deciding whether a person ought to be held responsible or not, but also to deciding how responsible that person is relative to other involved parties.

An important feature of the legal regime for the sharing of obligations to repair adverse outcomes by making a monetary payment (typically compensation) is that the claimant is entitled to proceed against any one or more of the responsible parties, and is not required to sue them all at once or, indeed, at any time. If the claim is brought against one responsible party, that party can be ordered to pay 100 per cent of the amount assessed as due to the claimant, and the claimant is entitled to recover that amount in full from that party. If the claimant proceeds against more than one responsible party at the same time, each of those parties can be ordered to pay 100 per cent of the amount assessed to be due to the claimant, and the claimant is entitled to recover that amount in full from any and all of the parties. The claimant may not recover in total more than the amount assessed as due, but has absolute freedom to recover it from any one or more of the responsible parties. The upshot is that in relation to the claimant, each responsible party is liable in full. The sharing of the liability is a matter between the various responsible parties. If one responsible party ends up paying more than their fair share, they must seek to recover the overpayment from the other responsible party (parties); and it is no answer to a claim for full compensation that the party sued was only one of several responsible parties. This so-called principle of "solidary liability" has a number of important

[83] For a philosophical discussion of these two factors see Goodin (1987).

practical effects. One is to encourage claimants to sue the responsible party (parties) most likely to be able to pay (with the "deepest pocket"). Another is to place the risk that a responsible party will be impecunious or insolvent on the other responsible parties, not on the claimant.

Solidary liability has attracted considerable criticism in recent years. The loudest protests have come from the so-called "reporting professions" such as auditors and surveyors. Such groups are seen as financially desirable targets of litigation, while their "causal contribution" to loss resulting, for instance, from bad investments and shoddy building is often much less than that of the managers of the company or the builder whose activities are the subject of the relevant audit or survey report. This situation has caused greatest anxiety in relation to government agencies, such as building inspectors and banking regulators. In the latter context, a favoured technique for protecting the public purse has been to immunise public bodies from liability in tort for "regulatory failure". The arguments used to justify this approach are not easily applicable to the private sector. Instead, various proposals have been made to replace solidary liability with "proportionate liability", that is, liability proportional to share of responsibility. An effect of implementing such proposals would, of course, be to shift the risk of impecuniosity and insolvency to the claimant. This corollary of proportionate liability is widely seen as unacceptable; and coupled with various technical difficulties, it explains the relative lack of success of proposals to abolish solidary liability.

Solidary liability might appear to be a prime example of a legal doctrine developed for "practical" purposes and lacking any firm "moral" foundation. Certainly, from an agent-focused perspective, it seems difficult to deny that proportionate liability is normatively superior to solidary liability. However, the critical difference between solidary and proportionate liability from the victim's perspective resides in the way they respectively distribute the risk that one or more of the jointly responsible parties will be impecunious or insolvent. If we view shared responsibility relationally, it is certainly not obvious that distributive justice favours proportionate liability over solidary liability.

The choice between solidary and proportionate liability is just one of various issues about responsibility that arise in the context of the allocation of tangible sanctions. Tangible sanctions are much more commonly used in the legal domain than in the moral domain, and so legal materials provide a rich source of illumination about questions that rarely arise in our moral lives. As in so many other areas, here too the law can make a net contribution to society's store of responsibility concepts and practices.

5.11 CONCLUSION

This chapter has explored the relationship between responsibility and personality by discussing shared responsibility, and the responsibility of groups and of people suffering from multiple personality disorder. One approach to the relationship between responsibility and personality is to treat moral responsibility as a function of personality, and personality as a function of human agency. This humanistic approach has obvious affinities with the agent-focused "modern view of responsibility" on which the "will theories" of responsibility, for instance, are based. I have argued that the dissonance between this approach and legal and social responsibility practices is explicable in terms of its lack of attention to the functions of those practices and their relational character. The function of rules and principles of legal responsibility is to justify the imposition of sanctions so as to protect individual and social interests in security and so on. In law, personality is seen as a function of responsibility rather than vice versa. Viewing the relationship between personality and responsibility in this way reveals the law as being much less out of step with morality than proponents of agent-focused accounts of responsibility typically assume it to be. Indeed, whereas, according to the humanistic approach, the law is too ready to impose responsibility on groups, by comparison with social practice, the law seems undesirably unwilling to hold corporations criminally liable. By insisting that responsibility is a function of human agency, humanistic approaches drive a wedge not only between law and morality but also between ethical theory and social practice in the moral domain.

6

Grounds and Bounds of Responsibility

6.1 THE BASIC ARGUMENT AND A PROSPECTUS

THE FOUNDATIONAL ARGUMENT of this chapter is that theories of responsibility that are built solely on the concepts of human agency will give a radically incomplete account of the grounds and bounds of responsibility. This is because they eschew reference to many of the functions of, and many of the interests protected by, responsibility concepts and practices. The only interest which such theories take into account is our interest as agents in freedom of action. Correspondingly, the only function of responsibility concepts and practices that such theories accommodate is that of protecting our interest as agents in freedom of action. This argument is elaborated in 6.2 to 6.4.

This chapter has two main aims. The first is to set out, at a quite abstract level, the most important grounds of legal responsibility (6.5). An aspect of this project will be to map the boundaries between fault-based and strict liability; and within fault-based liability, the boundaries between liability for intention, recklessness and negligence respectively. The discussion in this chapter will be concerned with responsibility under the civil law and criminal law paradigms. The grounds and bounds of responsibility in public law are examined in chapter 8. The second aim of the chapter is to explore (once again, at an abstract level) the bounds of legal responsibility and liability (6.6). Central to this section is an elaboration of the distinction between responsibility and liability that was introduced in 1.1.[1] In 6.6.5.2, I will discuss one of the most important concepts used to mark the bounds of legal liability, namely duty of care in the tort of negligence.

6.2 RESPONSIBILITY, PROTECTED INTERESTS AND THE FUNCTIONS OF LAW

Historic legal responsibility attaches to conduct and consequences; but not all conduct and consequences attract historic legal responsibility. Historic moral responsibility also attaches to conduct and consequences; but not all conduct and consequences attract historic moral responsibility. Both legal and moral historic responsibility have boundaries marked by the rules and principles that determine when conduct and consequences will (and will not) attract historic

[1] See also 2.6 and 3.6.3.5.

responsibility, and that define the grounds of historic responsibility. Agent-focused accounts of historic responsibility typically ground it in the free exercise of human will as expressed in conduct. Concerning the boundaries of responsibility, some will-theorists argue that responsibility attaches, and attaches only, to conduct and consequences that are the product of a mental state—intention, recklessness or knowledge. Others are prepared to extend the bounds of historic responsibility to encompass conduct and consequences that are the product of failure to meet interpersonal standards of conduct (i.e. negligence).

From a legal point of view, such accounts of responsibility are radically incomplete. One reason for this is that agent-focused accounts ignore victims and, consequently, are hard-pressed to provide a convincing analysis of responsibility under the civil law paradigm (and, to a lesser extent, under the criminal law paradigm). However, this is not a necessary feature of will theories. For instance, Ernest Weinrib has developed a theory of civil (or, as he calls it, "private") law which is designed precisely to explain the centrality of victims in the civil law paradigm.[2] According to Weinrib, private law is explicable in terms of two basic ideas. One is corrective justice. Corrective justice can be contrasted with retributive justice on the one hand, and distributive justice on the other. Crudely put, retributive justice is concerned with the allocation of punishment, and underpins the criminal law paradigm of responsibility; distributive justice is concerned with the allocation of benefits and burdens within groups; and corrective justice is concerned with the allocation of obligations of repair. Weinrib's contention is that private law is a system of corrective justice; or, in other words, a system of rights and obligations of repair.

The second component of Weinrib's theory of private law is designed to explain when obligations of repair arise. The building blocks of this part of the theory are essentially the same concepts of human agency and will that figure in agent-focused accounts of responsibility. Weinrib purports to work out the implications of these concepts for responsibility in situations involving "the doing and suffering of harm"—i.e. where one person inflicts harm on another.[3] The result is a theory, most highly elaborated in relation to tort law, that supports liability for intentional, reckless and negligent harmdoing, but rules out strict liability[4] and vicarious liability. Weinrib's willingness to embrace negligence as a ground of responsibility, when many will-theorists reject it, can be explained by the fact that the subject-matter of Weinrib's theory is civil law, not criminal law. However unjustifiable negligence-based responsibility might seem when viewed from the agent's perspective, once proper account is taken of the victim's perspective, a principle that restricted liability for the infliction of harm to intention and recklessness would be seen to adjust the balance of responsibility too far in favour of our interests as agents, and too far against our interests as victims.

[2] Weinrib (1995).
[3] Weinrib (1995), 142–4.
[4] Understood as liability in the absence of fault. But see Cane (1996b), 485–7.

Weinrib's theory of private law shares with agent-focused accounts of responsibility a feature that provides a second reason why both approaches are radically incomplete from a legal point of view: not all conduct and consequences that are the product of intention, recklessness, knowledge or negligence, attract legal responsibility. The grounds and bounds of legal responsibility are not defined solely in terms of "conduct" and "mental states", or in terms of "agency" and "will". Putting the point crudely in terms of Weinrib's analysis of private law, a theory of obligations to repair harm requires an account of what is meant by "harm",[5] as well as an account of the quality of the conduct (e.g. intentional, reckless) that can attract such obligations. Very generally, in legal usage "harm" is defined in terms of interference with legally protected interests of victims which are counterposed to the agent's interest in freedom of action.

At the most abstract level, legally protected interests correlate with the functions of legal responsibility practices. Weinrib expressly rejects this last proposition. One of the foundations of his theory is the contention that private law should be understood and explained purely in terms of its internal structure, and without reference to its functions, which Weinrib considers to be "external" to the practice itself. For him, the defining structural feature of private law is "correlativity"—the fact that in private law, the obligation of one individual is a mirror image of the right of another individual. It follows (in his view) that the grounds and bounds of responsibility in private law are to be found by analysing harmful interactions between individuals in terms of concepts of agency and free will, or what he compendiously calls "Kantian right". In this analysis, what correlates with the agent's harm-causing exercise of freedom of action is not the victim's interest in freedom from harm, but rather the victim's own interest in freedom of choice and action.[6]

In emphasising the structure of private law at the expense of its functions and of the interests (other than freedom of action) that it protects, Weinrib's main targets are theories that seek to explain the grounds and bounds of responsibility under the civil law paradigm in terms of compensation or deterrence.[7] As Weinrib points out, private law cannot be fully explained as a compensation mechanism, because the goal of compensating victims for harm suffered does not explain why one person rather than another should provide the compensation, or why compensation is payable only when losses are caused in certain ways. Conversely, private law cannot be fully explained as a mechanism for deterring undesirable conduct, because the goal of deterrence does not explain why such conduct is often actionable only if it causes loss to another. Furthermore, satisfaction of the deterrence goal does not require that agents compensate their victims—there are other ways of promoting deterrence.

[5] Similarly: Kaplow and Shavell (2001), 1044–50.

[6] Weinrib (1995), 96.

[7] Weinrib also argues that contract law is not explicable in terms of the principles that promises must be kept because this is a unilateral, not a bilateral, principle that does not explain why contract law enforces only some promises: Weinrib (1995), 50–3. See further 6.5.1.3.

Of course, I agree with Weinrib that one-sided, non-relational accounts of responsibility under the civil law paradigm (at least) cannot be adequate. It does not follow, however, that the grounds and bounds of responsibility under the civil law paradigm can be understood without reference to the functions of civil law and to the interests it protects (apart from freedom of action). The reason why compensation and deterrence are incomplete explanations of private law liability is that each looks to only one side of the bilateral relationship that lies at the core of the civil law paradigm—compensation to the victim's side, and deterrence to the agent's side. What is needed for a functional explanation of the bounds and grounds of responsibility under the civil law paradigm are functions of responsibility that refer to both agents and victims or which, at least, are consistent with the correlativity of private law. Justifying the imposition of obligations of repair is a function that meets the former constraint because it requires identification of both the agent on whom the obligation rests, and the beneficiary of the obligation. Justifying the imposition of obligations of repair is, we might say, an intrinsic or internal function of concepts and practices of historic responsibility under the civil law paradigm.[8] Functions that are at least consistent with the correlativity of private law include the coordination of human behaviour, the resolution of certain types of disputes,[9] and the maintenance of social order.

My argument is that at an abstract level, reference to such functions of historic legal responsibility is necessary for a full explanation of the grounds and bounds of historic legal responsibility for conduct and consequences. More concretely, my contention is that a full theory of historic legal responsibility requires an account of protected interests as well as an account, in terms of concepts of agency and will, of the types of conduct that can attract historic responsibility. This is true not only of responsibility under the civil law paradigm, but also of responsibility under the criminal law paradigm. Although victims are not central to the criminal law paradigm, the typical crime involves the infliction of harm by the offender on a victim. A full theory of criminal responsibility requires an account of prohibited harms and, correspondingly, of protected interests, as well as an account, in terms of concepts of agency and will, of the sorts of conduct that can attract criminal responsibility. An exclusively agent-focused account of criminal responsibility ignores many of the functions of, and of the interests protected by, the criminal law.

This argument can be generalised. We cannot fully understand the grounds and bounds of historic legal responsibility without reference to the full range of interests protected by, and the full range of functions of, legal responsibility concepts and practices. Similarly, we cannot fully understand the grounds and bounds of historic moral responsibility without reference to the full range of interests protected by, and the full range of functions of, moral responsibility

[8] Similarly, justification of the imposition of punishments and penalties is an intrinsic function of concepts and practices of historic responsibility under the criminal law paradigm.

[9] For an argument that this is *the* function of tort law see Smith (1987).

concepts and practices. For instance, without a theory of morally protected interests, it would not be possible to distinguish between morality and etiquette. The functions of moral responsibility include justifying the allocation of praise, blame and obligations of repair. As a reaction to conduct and consequences, praise belongs to what we might call the "morality of aspiration", whereas blame and obligations of repair belong to what might be termed the "morality of obligation". The morality of obligation is the non-institutionalised analogue of law. It shares with law functions such as coordinating human behaviour and maintaining social order.[10]

The general argument also applies to what Honoré calls "outcome responsibility".[11] In one sense, outcome responsibility is simply responsibility for the consequences of conduct. But in a different, albeit related, usage, Honoré contrasts outcome responsibility with moral responsibility on the one hand, and legal responsibility on the other. In this sense, whereas (historic) moral responsibility is concerned with the allocation of praise, blame and obligations of repair, and (historic) legal responsibility is concerned with the allocation of punishments and obligations of repair, outcome responsibility is concerned with allocation of the ownership of outcomes.[12] Each person's identity as an individual is partly a product of what they achieve by their conduct, i.e. outcomes. The function of outcome responsibility is to contribute to the establishment and maintenance of the identity of persons as individuals who are able, by their own efforts, to bring about changes in the world. What we are is partly a function of what we do and achieve.

Concerning the grounds and bounds of outcome responsibility, Honoré says, on the one hand, that outcome responsibility is insensitive to both luck and fault.[13] In other words, outcome responsibility is strict responsibility for the consequences of conduct regardless of the role of luck in producing them. On the other hand, Honoré describes outcome responsibility as based on concepts of causation.[14] Hart and Honoré understood "causation" to cover both factual causation (4.3) and principles of causal responsibility (4.4). As was argued in 4.4.2.5, fault plays a part in principles of causal responsibility; and one of the functions of such principles is to strike a balance between sensitivity and insensitivity to luck (see 4.4.2.6). The tension between Honoré's two different accounts of the grounds and bounds of outcome responsibility should be resolved in favour of the latter. Owning all the consequences of our conduct, regardless of the role of luck in producing them, would be just as destructive of our sense of ourselves as agents who can control the world as would owning none of the consequences of our conduct, no matter how small a role luck

[10] Similarly: Hooker (2000), 15–22.

[11] Honoré (1999). Honoré uses the term "outcome" more or less synonymously with "consequences" as defined in 4.1.3, i.e. as covering both definitional and extrinsic consequences.

[12] Cane (2001a)

[13] Honoré (1999), 9.

[14] Honoré (1999), 1, 10.

played in producing them (3.2.1). So far as fault is concerned, there is certainly an important sense in which the bad consequences of a person's conduct are part of their history and profile as an individual, even if the person was not at fault in producing them. But we identify people more strongly with bad consequences of their conduct that are the result of fault on their part than with those that occur without their fault. Production of an outcome by faulty conduct says something about the agent that the production of an outcome without fault does not.

Outcome responsibility is not responsibility for all the consequences of conduct—it has boundaries. The grounds and bounds of outcome responsibility are directly related to its function of contributing to the establishment and maintenance of the identity of persons as individuals who can influence the course of events by their own conduct. Limitless outcome responsibility, just as much as a total denial of outcome responsibility, would destroy our sense of individual identity as effective agents, and it would engender in us a feeling that we were victims, rather than masters, of our fate. To understand the bounds and grounds of outcome responsibility we need to appreciate its psychological function of establishing and maintaining our sense of personal identity as free and effective agents. Putting the same point in different terms: we each have a psychological need for, or interest in, a sense of our individual identity as agents who can effect changes in the world. To understand the grounds and bounds of outcome responsibility we need to take account of that need or interest.

6.3 RESPONSIBILITY, DISTRIBUTIVE JUSTICE AND THE FUNCTIONS OF LAW

As we saw in 6.2, Weinrib's theory of private law locates the grounds and bounds of responsibility under the civil law paradigm in the "internal structure" of private law, and not in its functions. This emphasis on the structure of private law leads Weinrib to the view that private law is concerned solely with corrective justice, and not at all with distributive justice. For him, responsibility under the civil law paradigm is to be understood in terms of bilateral interactions between individuals, not in terms of the distribution within society of benefits and burdens—i.e., in relation to responsibility, of rights and obligations. At one level it is certainly true that historic legal responsibility ignores matters of distribution. For instance, both tort law and criminal law protect property rights regardless of the fairness of the distribution of such rights within society. Similarly, the fact that there is a strong association between material and social deprivation and criminal behaviour is irrelevant to the imposition of criminal liability (although it can be taken into account at the sentencing stage). Lack of concern with distributive justice is also manifest in the law of contract in its attitude to inequality of bargaining power. Pressure arising out of the personal relationship of the contracting parties can provide a basis for avoiding contractual obligations through doctrines such as duress and undue influence.

By contrast, systemic inequalities of bargaining power as between consumers and multi-national corporations, for instance, have traditionally been ignored by the courts in the name of "freedom of contract". In relation to exclusion clauses, the courts did make some attempt to tackle some particularly serious symptoms of imbalance through the doctrine of fundamental breach.[15] But on the whole, it has been left to the legislature to deal with the maldistributive effects of the freedom of contract doctrine and the common law's refusal to examine the "fairness" of contracts.

As these examples show, distributive justice is distinguishable from both corrective and retributive justice; and they reveal the sense in which "the law of obligations" (contract law, tort law, criminal law, and so on) is not primarily concerned with distributive justice. In other ways, however, it is impossible to explain legal responsibility concepts and practices without reference of matters of distribution. First, in Weinrib's account (as was seen in 6.1), corrective justice tells us that wrongful harms should be corrected, but it does not tell us what harms are wrongful. For instance, according Weinrib, justice requires that negligent harms be corrected. Negligent harms are harms against which the reasonable person would have taken precautions. Corrective justice cannot tell us whether any particular harm meets this description.[16] In the famous case of *Bolton* v. *Stone*[17] the issue was whether an obligation should be imposed on a cricket club to compensate a passer-by who was injured by a ball that was hit out of the club's ground onto the adjoining street. Corrective justice, according to Weinrib, tells us that such an obligation ought to be imposed on the club if it was negligent. But the question of whether the club behaved negligently is one of distributive, not corrective, justice, turning ultimately on whether the club was legally free to injure or, conversely, whether the passer-by had a legal entitlement to be free of injury.[18] A neat illustration of this point can be found in recent debates amongst feminist scholars as to whether the test of unreasonableness in the tort of negligence ought to be gender-specific or gender-neutral. Put crudely, some feminists argue that whereas men "take care", women "care for" others in a more empathetic and pro-active way. If this difference were to be reflected in gender-specific standards of care in the tort of negligence, the distributional result would be to make women more vulnerable to findings of negligence than men.[19]

Secondly, law consists largely of rules and principles of general application. Imposing historic legal responsibility involves applying general rules and principles of responsibility to individual cases. Legal responsibility practices and concepts are concerned not only with imposing penalties and obligations of

[15] Guest (1984), 149–52.
[16] Similarly Coleman and Ripstein (1995); Coleman (2001), 31–6, 41–53.
[17] [1941] AC 850.
[18] Cane (1996b), 478–80.
[19] Schwartz (2001), 190. Concerning reasonableness in the criminal law see McColgan (2000), 145–6.

repair in relation to the past, but also and (as was argued in chapter 2) primarily, with establishing norms of behaviour—"responsibilities"—for the future. It is the failure to fulfil such responsibilities that grounds historic responsibility. Legal rules and principles distribute responsibilities within society. When, in *Donoghue* v. *Stevenson*,[20] the House of Lords held, for the first time, that manufacturers owe a duty of care to consumers despite the lack of a contractual relationship between them, it redistributed responsibilities to take care from consumers to manufacturers. Similarly, an important difference between intention-based responsibility, negligence-based responsibility and strict responsibility lies in the way each form of responsibility distributes responsibility for, and the risk of, harm.

It is impossible fully to understand, explain and justify the distributional impacts of legal responsibility concepts and practices without reference to what we might call the "extrinsic" functions of law. For instance, an explanation of *Donoghue* v. *Stevenson* solely in terms of the interaction between Ms Stevenson and the manufacturer of the soft drink that allegedly contained the decomposed remains of a snail, and without reference to the arguments of ethical, social and economic "policy" (such as deterrence, and the relative ability of manufacturers and consumers to guard against product-caused injuries) that led the court to recognise a manufacturer's duty of care, would be seriously incomplete. The extrinsic functions of the law are expressed in such policy arguments. The grounds and bounds of legal responsibility cannot be identified without taking account of the extrinsic functions of law.

This is why it was argued in 2.4.2 that Hart was wrong to draw a sharp distinction between criteria of criminal responsibility (which he identified as concerned with issues of capacity, causation and vicarious responsibility) and the question of whether what was done was a crime. This distinction underpins that between the so-called "general" and "special" "parts" of the criminal law, around which much contemporary theoretical criminal law scholarship is organised. Not surprisingly, the strongest proponents of the latter distinction (such as Michael Moore)[21] are advocates of agent-focused accounts of criminal responsibility couched in terms of conduct and mental states. Such accounts are the criminal law counterpart of Weinrib's corrective justice approach to responsibility in private law. Just as Weinrib's analysis seeks to ground responsibility under the civil law paradigm in corrective justice, without reference to distributive justice, so advocates of agent-focused accounts of criminal responsibility seek to ground responsibility under the criminal law paradigm in some concept of retributive justice, without reference to distributive justice. Corrective justice tells us that wrongful losses should be corrected, but it does not tell us what losses are wrongful. Similarly, retributive justice tells us that wrongful conduct should be punished, but it does not tell us what conduct is wrongful.

[20] [1932] AC 562.

[21] Moore (1997), 30–35; criticised in Lacey (2000).

Theories of responsibility of the sort propounded by Moore and Weinrib strive for a sort of ethical neutrality between different conceptions of right and wrong,[22] a universally and timelessly valid bedrock for responsibility judgments. In eschewing reference to the full range of functions of legal responsibility concepts and practices and to their distributional impacts, such theorists provide only half a theory of legal responsibility. Legal rules that specify what amounts to criminal conduct, and which establish whether liability is based on intention, recklessness or negligence, or is strict—rules, in other words, that define the grounds and bounds of criminal responsibility—cannot be explained solely in terms of the concepts of conduct and mental states, but must be related to the full range of extrinsic functions (ethical, social, economic, and so on) of the criminal law, and to the full range of interests it protects. Such rules are concerned not only with allocating penalties and punishments to individuals for past conduct, but also with establishing for the future responsibilities and prohibitions of general application. It is the breach of such responsibilities and prohibitions that justifies the imposition of historic criminal responsibility. By criminalising some types of conduct but not others, the law establishes a particular pattern of individual entitlements and responsibilities, and a particular pattern of social relationships. Theories that treat historic criminal responsibility solely as a function of the concepts of human agency and will cannot explain its grounds or bounds because they eschew reference to most of the extrinsic functions of the criminal law and to its distributional impact.

The impossibility of explaining the grounds and bounds of legal responsibility without reference to the various functions of law and to ideas of distributive justice is perhaps most obvious in relation to strict liability. Agent-focused theories reject responsibility without fault because they have no resources (other than the concept of factual causation) which could be used to limit its incidence.[23] The grounds and bounds of strict legal liability are defined by reference to ideas such as rights (as in the case of strict tort liability for misappropriation of property), and to achieving a fair balance between the interests of agents and victims (as in the case of outcome-based strict liability). The grounds and bounds of strict liability for harm cannot be identified without reference to the interests that such liability protects and the way it distributes the risk of harm. In chapter 3 I argued that responsibility without fault is not a legal peculiarity, but is found in the moral domain as well. The grounds and bounds of responsibility without fault cannot be explained solely in terms of the concepts of conduct and mental states. To this extent, theories of responsibility that are based

[22] Thus Weinrib (1995), 87: "In Kant's view the relationships of private law are morally intelligible independently of ethical considerations". Again "Kant construes freedom through a process of abstraction from particular ends": *ibid.*, 86.

[23] Weinrib (1995), 181: "Strict liability . . . implies that the very production of external effects—an indispensable part of agency—can itself be a violation of the equality of agents . . . To ascribe liability to an action, regardless of culpability, for whatever harmful effects it has had simply because they *are* its effects, is to hold the agent liable for being active".

on these concepts alone are incapable of explaining important features of both moral and legal responsibility.

I would go further and argue that not only moral and legal responsibility, but also outcome responsibility, cannot be properly understood without recourse to ideas of distributive justice. As was argued in 6.2, outcome responsibility is not entirely insensitive either to luck or to fault. Principles of causal responsibility that underpin outcome responsibility may truncate that responsibility on the ground of bad luck or absence of fault. It follows that certain outcomes of a person's conduct may not "belong" to that person even though they were, in a purely factual sense, caused by the conduct. If such outcomes adversely affect other people, they will end up belonging to the affected person rather than to the agent. In this way, outcome responsibility distributes outcomes amongst individuals.

6.4 PROTECTED INTERESTS, PROSCRIBED CONDUCT AND DISTRIBUTIVE JUSTICE

In 6.2 it was argued that a theory of responsibility requires an account of the full range of interests protected by responsibility concepts and practices, in addition to an account, in terms of agency and will, of unacceptable conduct.. In 6.3 it was argued that a theory of responsibility is not complete without reference to distributive justice. These two points are related. For instance, the principles of responsibility under the civil law paradigm that specify what interests the law protects and what types of conduct it proscribes—or in other words, the elements of "grounds of liability" and "causes of action"—establish a particular social pattern of distribution of rights and obligations and of "legal responsibility resources". Similarly, the catalogue of crimes that make up what was referred to earlier as the "special part" of the criminal law, establish a social pattern of protected interests and proscribed conduct. Theories of responsibility based on the concepts of agency and will deliberately ignore protected interests in an attempt to construct an account of responsibility that is neutral as between different theories of distributive justice. In fact, of course, agent-focused theories of responsibility are not, and cannot be, distributionally neutral. For instance, theories that limit responsibility to intentional or reckless conduct distribute responsibility differently than do theories that encompass negligence-based or strict liability. A principle of responsibility for all and only what one does intentionally is itself a (non-neutral) criterion for the distribution of responsibility. Agent-focused theories seek distributional neutrality by treating agents (or, in Weinrib's case, duets of harmdoers and sufferers) as isolated entities without and beyond social context. Because human beings are social animals, and because responsibility concepts and practices are products of social interaction, even the most exclusively agent-focused theories of responsibility have distributional implications. Any theory of responsibility that fails to address its distributional implications, in terms of protected interests and proscribed conduct, is radically incomplete.

6.5 GROUNDS OF LEGAL RESPONSIBILITY

This section contains an extremely broad-brush survey of the main grounds of legal responsibility, which are identified as breach of promises and undertakings, interference with rights, uttering of untruths, breach of trust, doing harm, creating risks of harm, making gains and contemplating crimes. Each of the grounds of responsibility corresponds to some interest protected by, or to some function of, legal responsibility concepts and practices. In relation to each ground, there is discussion of the incidence of strict and fault-based liability, and within the latter category, of the incidence of intention, recklessness and negligence-based responsibility. The role of fault in responsibility is the main, and often the only, issue addressed by agent-focused theories of responsibility.

A complete exposition of the grounds of legal responsibility would, of course, fill many volumes. The aim here (and in 6.6) is simply to put some flesh on the bones of the arguments made in 6.2 to 6.4. The order of discussion of the various grounds is of no significance. The various grounds are not mutually exclusive, but overlap and interact in complex ways, which cannot be explored here.

6.5.1 Breach of promises and undertakings

6.5.1.1 Promises, undertakings, misfeasance and nonfeasance

Promises and undertakings are means of projecting one's will into the future, of offering assurance that one will behave in a certain way in the future. Breach of promise or undertaking is a pervasive ground of legal (and moral) responsibility, and not just under the rubric of contract law. In tort law, for instance, liability can be founded on the controversial notion of "assumption (or undertaking) of responsibility". Promise and undertaking are important sources of obligation under the rubric of estoppel; and in the law of agency, holding-out and ostensible agency rest on the same basic idea of an assurance about future behaviour. Less obviously, liability for failure to fulfil (prospective) responsibilities that attach to roles (such as professions) and offices (such as that of police constable) is based on the idea that by assuming the role or office, a person (implicitly) offers an assurance that they will fulfil the responsibilities that are attached, by common understanding, to that role or office.

In the legal literature, promise-based liability[24] is often associated with "voluntarily assumed" responsibility as opposed to responsibility that is "imposed by law".[25] In one sense, this association is justified. Such liability typically arises either because a person has freely made a promise; or has freely engaged in an

[24] In what follows I will use the word "promise" and its cognates to refer to the broad concept of making promises and giving undertakings that I have just outlined.

[25] Burrows (1983)

activity, or accepted a role or office, to which (as they know) promise-based responsibilities attach. On the other hand, it is generally true that legal liability, whether or not promise-based, can arise only out of freely undertaken activity. If the law judges conduct not to have been freely engaged in (as it does, for instance, through defences such as duress and automatism), the conduct will not attract legal liability. Moreover, there are many legal obligations that arise out of voluntary conduct but are not promise-based, for instance, the driver's duty of care to other road-users. The critical difference between obligations based on promises and obligations arising out of other types of voluntary conduct is that in the former case but not in the latter, the fact that the relevant conduct was done voluntarily in the knowledge that certain obligations attach to it is part of the reason why the obligation arises.[26]

It might be thought that the reason why the law enforces promises is in order to underwrite the production of the trust that is essential to successful social and economic cooperation and coordination. There is undoubtedly some truth in this observation.[27] However, it is not only promise-based legal liabilities that underwrite the production of trust. For instance, road safety depends crucially on our ability to trust each other to comply with rules of the road and to exercise care; but criminal and civil liability for unsafe conduct on the roads is not promise-based. In my view, the significance of promises as a ground of responsibility lies in the distinction between acts and omissions, misfeasance and nonfeasance. For the sake of individual liberty, in both law and morality there are certain things that we can be (and are) reasonably expected to do only if we have promised to do them; and certain things that we are reasonably entitled to trust others to do only if they have promised to do them.[28] Acting safely on the road is not one of these: it is reasonable to expect and to trust others to do this regardless of whether they have promised to do it, and even if they have promised that they will not do it. The distinction between misfeasance and nonfeasance is not straightforwardly that between doing and not-doing. Misfeasance often involves not-doing—such as not keeping a proper lookout while driving. Rather, nonfeasance is not doing something which a person can reasonably be expected to do only if they have promised to do it, or if they occupy some office or role to which an obligation to do that thing reasonably attaches.

This analysis, if correct, explains why the concept of "voluntary undertaking of responsibility" in the law of negligence has been found problematic. It was originally introduced in the famous case of *Hedley Bryne & Co Ltd* v. *Heller & Partners Ltd*[29] in 1964 as a way of justifying imposition of tort liability for

[26] Raz (1982), 929.

[27] On the limits of contract law as a generator of trust see Collins (1999), esp ch. 5.

[28] Similarly Finnis (1980), XI.2 esp 307–8, 348–50. In Finnis's view, although promises are expressions of will, this does not explain the obligation to keep promises, which is based on principles of "practical reasonableness" and promotion of "the common good". Promises ought to be kept not because they are expressions of will, but because practical reasonableness and the common good require that they be.

[29] [1964] AC 465.

financial loss resulting from reliance on negligent investment advice. Before that decision, tort liability for bad investment advice could only arise if the advice was fraudulent. On the other hand, liability for negligent investment advice could arise if there was a contract for the giving of the advice. The idea behind the concept of voluntary undertaking of responsibility was that if investment advice was freely given without any "disclaimer" of responsibility for its accuracy, the relationship between the giver of the advice and the person who relied on it to their detriment could be treated as "equivalent to contract", even if not technically contractual. The existence of such a "quasi-contractual" relationship was seen as justifying the imposition of liability that would not be justified in its absence.

The problem being addressed by this maneouvre was not that of justifying imposition of liability for nonfeasance—failure to take care in giving investment advice is, like failure to take care when driving, treated by the law as misfeasance. Rather the problem resided in the nature of the harm inflicted—economic loss as opposed to personal injury or property damage. In the law's hierarchy of protected interests, financial interests are seen as deserving less protection than the interest in security of person and property. The concept of voluntary undertaking of responsibility was invented to provide a justification for extending liability for negligent misstatements from personal injury and property damage to economic loss. In more recent years, however, a view has developed[30] that it may be reasonable to impose liability for negligent financial advice and services regardless of any promise or undertaking about the quality of the advice or the services, and even in the face of an express disclaimer by the adviser or service-provider that any such promise or undertaking was being given. The result is not that the incidence of tort liability for financial loss is the same as that for personal injury and property damage, but rather that the concept of promise or undertaking no longer marks the boundary between liability and no-liability in tort for financial harm caused by negligent misfeasance.

6.5.1.2 *Breach of promise and culpability*

I have argued that the normative function of promises is to generate obligations to act that would not exist in their absence. By making promises, people can bind themselves to do things that they would not otherwise be bound to do. This explains why legal liability for breach of a promise is basically strict. If a person promises to do X then, barring impediments beyond their control,[31] they should do it; and the risk that it will not be done should rest on them regardless of fault on their part. Suppose a person promises not "to do X", but "to make all reasonable efforts to do X". Since the promise is to take reasonable care, liability for breach of the promise must be negligence-based, not strict. Many contractual

[30] See e.g. *Smith* v. *Bush* [1990] 1 AC 831.

[31] Allowed for in the doctrine of frustration of contract, for instance.

obligations are of this nature. But in such cases, the promise will typically be *ethically* superfluous to liability for failure to take care. Even if the promisor would be under no obligation to embark upon the project of doing X in the absence of a promise to do so, once the project has commenced, a duty to take care for the interests of the promisee in the execution of it would normally be recognised, both in law and morality, even in the absence of a promise to be careful. It does not follow, however, that the promise to take care is *legally* irrelevant, a point addressed in 6.5.1.3.

In the law of contract, there is a continuing debate about whether a person who deliberately breaks a promise, the breach of which would generate liability regardless of fault, should be liable to some sanction additional to that which would be attracted by non-deliberate breach of the promise (namely, compensation for harm resulting from the breach). In terms of accounts of responsibility based on notions of agency and will, there seems good reason to resolve this debate affirmatively. Freely given promises should be kept, and breaking a promise deliberately is more culpable than breaking it faultlessly. The argument for a negative resolution looks beyond the interests of the promisor and the promisee to a wider social interest. Contracting is a cornerstone of the operation of markets. The *raison d'être* for markets is the efficient allocation of resources. Sometimes (says the so-called "efficient breach" argument) deliberately breaking a contract and paying compensation for harm resulting from the breach is more efficient than performing the contract. Imposing liability over and above an obligation to pay compensation for harm caused would (so the argument goes) discourage such efficient contract-breaking. It is not necessary for present purposes to assess the technical validity of the efficient breach argument or its normative acceptability. The point is that at bottom, the debate about the desirability of exemplary damages for deliberate breach of contract revolves around different views of the function of contract law: is it to give effect to ideas of personal responsibility, or is it to encourage economically efficient behaviour and to discourage economically inefficient behaviour? The efficient breach argument suggests that the answer to this question might depend on the context: the function of contract law in commercial contexts might be different from its role in non-commercial contexts.

6.5.1.3 Promises and contracts

What is the relationship between breach of contract, and breach of a promise, as grounds of legal responsibility? Not all promissory obligations are contractual (6.5.1.1). Conversely, not all contractual obligations are promissory (6.5.1.2). While the main normative function of contracts is to generate obligations to act that would not exist in their absence and to justify the imposition of liability for nonfeasance, there can also be contractual liability for misfeasance (i.e. for negligence) in circumstances where the misfeasance would attract liability even in the absence of a contract. Thus, a negligent breach of contract may also be actionable as a tort. This possibility can create technical problems when rules of contract law (such as those relating to limitation of actions, remoteness of damage and the defence of contributory negligence), that were developed to accommodate contract's prime function of generating obligations to act that would not exist in the absence of a contract, are applied to cases in which the real nub of the complaint is misfeasance rather than nonfeasance. This is because the boundary between the legal categories of contract and tort is not marked by the distinction between nonfeasance and misfeasance. It follows (or so it seems to me) that attempts to explain contractual liability purely in terms of promising are bound to be incomplete. Charles Fried says:

> "The promise principle, which . . . I argue is the moral basis of contract law, is that principle by which persons may impose on themselves obligations where none existed before".[32]

Fried's view of the legal significance of promising is the same as mine, but we differ about the relationship between promise and contract. It is no coincidence, I think, that the index to Fried's book contains no entries for "negligence" or "misfeasance". The moral basis of contractual liability for misfeasance is not the promise principle.[33] Promising is certainly an important ground of legal responsibility, but it is a mistake to identify liability for breach of contract solely with responsibility for breach of promise.

This insight is the core of truth in Patrick Atiyah's challenge to the view that promising as such generates legal (or moral) obligations.[34] The idea that it does is expressed in the rule that the basic measure of compensation for breach of contract is loss of expectation, because the vice of breaking a promise is that it disappoints the legitimate expectations that the promise generated. Atiyah argued that damages for pure loss of expectation are problematic,[35] and that the acquisition of some benefit by the promisor (6.5.6), or the suffering of some loss (other than disappointed expectations) by the promisee (6.5.5) as a result of breach of promise are much more important grounds of contractual liability than is commonly recognised. In his view, the basis of contract law is not a moral principle that promises should be kept, but rather a social practice of enforcing promises for essentially consequentialist reasons.[36] Indeed, he went further and argued that promising is not an independent source of moral or legal obligation.

[32] Fried (1981), 1.

[33] In the fourteenth century, claims for what we would now call contractual misperformance (such as actions against blacksmiths for laming horses while shoeing them) were normally framed as trespass on the case: Ibbetson (1999), 78–80.

[34] Atiyah(1981); Atiyah (1986), Essay 2, esp 39; Atiyah (1995), 444–64.

[35] For a wide-ranging discussion of this problem see Benson (1999). For him, expectation damages are problematic because of a principle of the common law that there can be liability for misfeasance but not for nonfeasance. In my view, there is no such principle, at least of such an unqualified nature.

[36] Atiyah (1981), esp ch. 5.

Atiyah was clearly correct to argue that the acquisition of benefits and the suffering of harm are important grounds of liability for breach of contract. This is reflected in the fact that both "restitution" and "reliance" are recognised as measures of damages for breach of contract. It is also reflected in the fact, for instance, that contracts for the performance of services contain an "implied term" that the service-provider will exercise reasonable care in performing the service. The ground of (contractual) liability for breach of such a term is not promissory: the duty of care would exist even in the absence of a promise to take care. Rather it is grounded in the harm principle (6.5.5). The implied term merely states and reinforces an obligation derived from elsewhere. But (as he acknowledged later)[37] Atiyah went too far when he argued that contract law never does and never should enforce promises. It is not necessary to reject the view that promising is an independent ground of responsibility in order to accept that enforcement of promises, as such, is justified by its consequences.[38] The promise principle cannot provide a complete account of contractual liability; but an account that ignored it would also be seriously deficient.

Weinrib has two arguments against the adequacy of the promise principle as an explanation of contract law. First, it is one-sided in that it does not explain why the law marks the wrongfulness of breaking a promise by requiring damages to be paid to the promisee. Secondly, it cannot explain why only some promises are legally enforceable.[39] The first inadequacy alerts us to the importance of the concept of rights in legal responsibility practices (see 6.5.2); and the second to the importance of paying careful attention to the bounds, as well as the grounds, of responsibility. But Weinrib's objections to Fried's approach do not deny the importance of promise as a ground of legal responsibility (6.6.1).

6.5.2 Interference with rights

Promising can be accommodated within an agent-focused account of responsibility by stressing (as Fried does) its significance as an expression of the promisor's will at the expense of its meaning for the promisee as a source of assurance and legitimate expectation about the promisor's future conduct.[40] Indeed, an account of promising can usefully supplement an agent-focused account of responsibility by explaining how responsibility might attach to inaction as well as to action. By contrast, it is difficult to see what role the concept of rights can play in accounts of responsibility built solely on ideas of agency and will. Rights are correlative to obligations, and therefore inexorably direct our attention away from "the doer" and onto "the sufferer" (to adopt Weinrib's terminology). Rights ground responsibility not in individual freedom *of* will and

[37] Atiyah (1986), 44.
[38] Raz (1982).
[39] Weinrib (1995), 50–3.
[40] Fried (1981), esp 14–17.

agency but in freedom *from* the exercise of individual will and agency. In other words, rights require an account of responsibility in terms of protected interests, not in terms of proscribed conduct.

Rights play a central role in the law, and no account of the grounds and bounds of legal responsibility can be complete without reference to them. In broad terms, there are three types of legal rights: property rights, contractual rights[41] and human rights. These three categories are not mutually exclusive. For instance, property may be classified as a human right.[42] In contemporary legal understanding, human rights are primarily rights of citizens against governments, and so they tend to be embodied in documents of constitutional, as opposed to statutory, status. Although judge-made ("common") law has traditionally offered protection to some of the interests protected by human-rights regimes (such as freedom of speech), it was not until the advent of the international human rights movement, after the Second World War, that English courts came to conceptualise such freedoms as "rights"[43] and to see them as having special force in relations between citizens and governments. In their legal manifestation, by contrast, property and contractual rights are essentially products of the judicial imagination.

In Anglian common law, the law of contract is not only concerned with the creation of contractual rights, but is also the main vehicle for their protection (via liability for breach of contract). By contrast, whereas property law is chiefly concerned with the creation and transfer of property rights,[44] the main vehicle for their protection under the civil law paradigm is the law of tort (under rubrics such as trespass and conversion).[45] For present purposes, the most important characteristic of the legal protection of rights by civil law is strict liability. Rights are strong interests. They create physical and non-physical spaces, and crossing the boundary into such spaces typically[46] attracts legal liability regardless of fault.[47] In this respect, the paradigm right is ownership of tangible property. Adequate protection of the owner's rights—maintaining the distinction between what is yours and what is mine, as it were[48]—requires liability for interference with property regardless of fault.[49] Weinrib's rejection of strict tort liability is descriptively inaccurate and normatively undesirable precisely because he fails to take account of the role of tort law in protecting property

[41] Rights under trusts are, essentially, an amalgam of property and contractual rights.

[42] As under Art. 1 of the First Protocol to the European Convention on Human Rights.

[43] Indeed, English common law conceptualises reputation as a right, and has traditionally recognised speech as a "freedom".

[44] Contract is a major vehicle for the creation and transfer of property rights.

[45] Statutory actions for infringement of intellectual property rights are analogous to tort actions: Cane (1996), 59–73.

[46] But see 6.6.2.

[47] Cane (1996), ch. 2.

[48] "Interferences" with property that do not threaten this distinction are not subject to the strict liability regime. So liability for non-deliberate damaging of property is negligence-based, not strict.

[49] Conversely, the general rule is that failure by the owner to take care of their property provides no defence to liability: Cane (1996), 31.

rights.[50] By contrast, he accepts strict liability for breach of contract because (he says) the effect of a contract is to give the promisee a right "to determine the promisor's action", and this right is a form of property.[51] Weinrib also seems to accept strict (restitutionary) liability to give up "unjust" gains.[52] His explanation for such liability is based on the idea that the defendant's gain rightly belongs to the plaintiff. In other words, restitutionary liability protects property rights. We need not concern ourselves with the descriptive accuracy of this account of restitutionary liability. Its significance, for present purposes, lies in its recognition of the importance of the concept of rights in providing a normative foundation for strict liability.

Criminal law also plays an important role in protecting the institution of property. However, by contrast with civil liability for interference with property rights, criminal liability is not strict.[53] The notion that seems to bind property offences together, says Ashworth,[54] is "dishonesty". In tort law, for instance, it is no defence to liability for taking another's property that the defendant honestly but mistakenly believed it was legally theirs. By contrast, it is not a crime for a person to take property that they honestly (although mistakenly) believed they were legally entitled to.[55] The explanation for this difference lies, I believe, in the fact that the sanctions and stigma that attach to criminal liability are greater than those attaching to civil liability. The property rights of the owner are adequately protected by the right to sue the offender in tort on the basis of strict liability, while the interests of society in the sanctity of property are adequately protected by penalising dishonesty.

Strict liability is a necessary corollary of a system of rights. Accounts of responsibility that rule out strict liability also rule out the legal protection of rights. This is a huge descriptive and normative disadvantage; and the countervailing strengths (if any) of such accounts are by no means clear. Responsibility that cannot accommodate rights is a much diminished affair; and rights without the protection of strict responsibility would be largely rhetorical.

6.5.3 Uttering untruths

It is not surprising that making false statements can ground legal liability under both the civil and the criminal law paradigms. However, this ground of liability cannot be explained non-relationally, by reference only to concepts of agency and will. This is because typically, making a false statement will attract legal

[50] Cane (1996b), 485–7.

[51] Weinrib (1995), 139.

[52] Weinrib (1995), 140–2; Weinrib (2000).

[53] The focus here is on "traditional" property offences. But as Lacey and Wells point out (Lacey and Wells (1998), 254) there are strict liability regulatory offences that protect property interests even though interference with property is not their conduct element.

[54] Ashworth (1999), 374.

[55] e.g. Theft Act 1968 (UK), s. 2(1)(a).

liability only if it provides someone with a reason to behave differently than they would have done if they had known the truth, and they act on that reason. In the typical case, it is impossible to explain why making a false statement attracts legal liability without referring to the conduct of someone other than the person who made the statement. This is as true in criminal law as in civil law.[56]

It may be that in this respect, law and morality diverge a little. Perhaps many people would think intentional (and, possibly, reckless) telling of untruths to be worthy of blame regardless of its effect on the conduct of others. However, such a view is not inconsistent with a belief that inducing a person to act to the detriment of themselves or of some third person, by telling a lie, is worthy of greater disapproval and censure than telling a lie *per se*. Moreover, legal liability for false statements can be negligence-based or even strict. The idea, that carelessly or innocently making a false statement might *per se* attract blame independently of any adverse effect on others, is unattractive.

In civil law, there are three main instances of strict liability for making false statements. One is found in the law of defamation, where it is a corollary of viewing reputation as a right analogous to property. The other two are found in the law of contract. A person may withdraw from ("rescind") a contract which they were induced to enter by an "innocent misrepresentation" made by the other contracting party. And, in accordance with general principle, strict liability attaches to breach of a binding contractual promise that one's statement is true. Normally, however, making a false statement is actionable as such only if the speaker was negligent (at least) in relation to the truth of the statement. Leaving defamation aside, the significance, in this context, of the distinctions between liability for intention/recklessness, liability for negligence, and liability regardless of fault, lies in the scope of liability. The formula for calculating compensation for innocent misrepresentation is (in principle, anyway) less generous to the claimant than that for calculating compensation for negligent misstatements. The latter is less generous than that for calculating compensation for "fraud" (i.e. intentional or reckless falsehood) which is, in turn, less generous than that for calculating compensation for breach of a promise that a statement is true. Another way of putting this is to say that that each of these grounds of liability protects a different interest.

While the law treats making a false statement and breaching a promise that a statement is true as distinct grounds of liability that attract different sanctions, it is nevertheless true, as Atiyah points out, that there is a normative analogy between the two:

> "Promises and statements of fact both create expectations, and both are liable to be relied upon, and to cause loss or disappointment if the speaker lets the other party down".[57]

[56] Ashworth (1999), 413–15.
[57] Atiyah (1981), 103.

On the other hand, (as we have seen) whereas the basic rule is that legal liability for breach of promise is strict, liability for making a false statement is only exceptionally so. Moreover, whereas breach of promise may attract legal liability even if the promisee has not acted in reliance upon it but has suffered only disappointment of the expectations which the promise engendered (6.5.1.3), making a false statement (as was pointed out earlier in this section) will typically attract legal liability only if it has induced someone to behave differently than they would have done if they had known the truth. Atiyah's comment on these facts is worth quoting at length:

> "Doubtless these rules may be dismissed as technical idiosyncracies, but they probably reflect real differences. The fact is that an explicit promise, at any rate, does differ from an ordinary assertion in that the former invites reliance and expectations in a way which the latter does not. Statements are often made in the course of ordinary discourse, and these may in fact be relied upon; but statements do not, as explicit promises do, plainly invite reliance".[58]

The chief interest of these propositions[59] lies not in their validity (which is contestable) but in the fact that Atiyah explains the differences between responsibility for broken promises and responsibility for false statements in terms of their impact on those to whom they are addressed. This is the right approach. Breach of promise and telling untruths are different grounds of responsibility, and the difference between them cannot be fully captured by an analysis based on the parsimonious conceptual resources of "agency" and "will".

6.5.4 Breach of trust

In a technical sense, breach of trust is breach of an obligation arising under a trust. A trust is an arrangement under which an owner of property, the trustee (T), owes a variety of obligations to the beneficiary (B) in relation to the use of the property. As it is put, T holds the property on trust for B.[60] Certain of the obligations of the trustee (such as the obligation not to invest the trust fund in "unauthorised" investments) are strict. Liability for breach of such obligations arises regardless of fault. Such obligations are promise-based; and this explains their strictness. Other obligations of the trustee are obligations to take care not to cause harm to the beneficiary in the management of the trust property.

[58] Atiyah (1981), 105.

[59] They are also of interest for the contrast they suggest between the technical idiosyncracy of the law, and the "reality" of morality. It is surprising to find Atiyah drawing this contrast because he also espoused the view that both morality and law were essentially social, and that the law's treatment of promising was, in some respects, more subtle and nuanced than that of morality. See Atiyah (1981), 68–9 and ch. 5, esp 136–7.

[60] In the present context, we can ignore the distinction between trusts for persons and trusts for purposes. The most important features of the trust are (1) that the trust property is segregated from the rest of the trustee's property; and (2) the trustee's obligations in relation to the use and management of the trust property: Hayton (2001).

Liability for breach of such obligations is analogous to, and in essence indistinguishable from, liability for negligence arising independently of a trust relationship between the agent and the victim of the harm.[61]

A trust relationship in the technical sense is important for present purposes because it gives rise to a type of obligation that would normally not exist in the absence of such a relationship. Just as promising is a means of creating obligations that would not exist in the absence of a promise, so creating a trust is a means of creating obligations that would not exist in the absence of a trust. The type of obligation that is distinctive of a trust is what is generically called a "fiduciary obligation". A fiduciary obligation is an obligation not to take advantage of one's position relative to another, or of one's power over another, to benefit oneself at the expense of the other. In different terms, to breach a fiduciary obligation is to exploit a conflict between one's own interests and those of another. Although a trust relationship in the technical sense is the paradigm "fiduciary relationship", fiduciary obligations can exist in the absence of a trust in the technical sense. For instance, company directors owe fiduciary obligations to the company's shareholders even though the directors do not hold the company's assets on trust for the shareholders.

The fiduciary's obligation not to exploit their position for their own benefit is strict. This fact—an uncomfortable one for agent-focused theories of responsibility—cannot be brushed off as a legal peculiarity. The proscription against betrayal of trust is at least as strong in the moral domain as in the legal. If I acquire[62] some benefit that should have gone to someone under my protection, I should hand it over to my ward regardless of whether its acquisition was in any way my fault. This might be explained in conduct-based terms. Assuming that I knowingly and willingly accepted the role of protector, once I become aware that I have received a benefit that should have gone to my ward, I should hand it over. However, this explanation focuses on the wrong event, namely assumption of the role of fiduciary rather than the acquisition of the benefit. There are, I think, two ways of explaining and justifying the strictness of the fiduciary obligation. Neither refers to the conduct of the fiduciary, but each builds on a recurring theme of this book. The first illustrates the importance of including sanctions in any account of responsibility (2.2, 3.2.4, 3.5.4). Sanctions vary in the degree of stigma attaching to them. For instance, imprisonment carries more stigma than a monetary fine, and both carry more stigma than an order to pay compensation. Remedies carry less stigma than punishments. Arguably, the remedy that carries least stigma is the restitutionary obligation to pay over what (in a colloquial rather than a technically legal sense) "rightly belongs" to other—which, in the contemporary jargon is

[61] Just as liability for breach of a contractual obligation of care is analogous to, and in essence indistinguishable from, liability for negligence arising independently of a contractual relationship between the agent and the victim of the harm (6.1.5.3). As in the latter context, the distinction between trust-based and non-trust-based liability for negligence is significant for technical reasons.

[62] In fact, the legal liability of the fiduciary extends to cases of passive receipt. But such liability, not being conduct-based, is not responsibility-based either.

referred to in terms of "unjust enrichment". As a general principle, the less stigmatic the sanction, the lesser the degree of culpability required to justify its imposition. For instance, it seems very difficult to justify imprisoning a person in the absence of fault, but much easier to justify ordering a person to hand over what rightly belongs to another even in the absence of fault in its acquisition.

The second justificatory explanation for the strictness of the fiduciary obligation points to its source in the relationship of protection on which it is based. Looked at solely in terms of agency and will, responsibility without fault is very difficult to justify. The major insight provided by the distinction between the criminal law and the civil law paradigms of responsibility is that responsibility practices which seem difficult to explain or justify when viewed exclusively from the agent's perspective, take on a very different complexion when viewed relationally. However unfair it may seem from the fiduciary's point of view that the prohibition on benefiting from their position should carry strict liability, when viewed in terms of the nature of the relationship between protector and protected, and from the latter's point of view, the strictness of the protector's obligation is much easier to explain. The agent-focused perspective on responsibility is one-eyed. It views responsibility judgments in purely retributive terms. But responsibility is about correction and distribution as well as retribution. For instance, the obligation to compensate for negligent harm may be correctively just, even if not retributively just; and the obligation to hand over what rightly belongs to another may be distributively just, even if it is neither correctively nor retributively just. Retributive and corrective justice are not co-extensive with the universe of justice. The strict restitutionary obligation of the fiduciary is best explained relationally as a protection for the beneficiary of the fiduciary relationship, and distributionally as a paying-over of what rightly belongs to another.

It does not follow, of course, that the fiduciary's strict restitutionary obligation is relationally and distributionally just. It might be argued, for instance, that a fiduciary obligation of reasonable care would strike a better balance between the interests of the fiduciary and the beneficiary. A strict agency theorist might say that the fiduciary's obligation should only be to refrain from deliberate or reckless exploitation of their position. My point is that such an argument would not deserve to be taken seriously unless the theorist also took account of the interests of the beneficiary and argued that restricting the prohibition to deliberate or reckless exploitation would strike the fairest balance between the interests of the fiduciary and the beneficiary. If this were the argument one could, of course, reject it on corrective or distributional grounds. But at least it is an argument of the right form.

6.5.5 Doing harm

Breach of a promise may attract legal responsibility even if the promisee suffers no harm as a result (other than disappointment of the expectation generated by the promise). More generally, interference with rights may attract legal responsibility even if the right-holder suffers no harm as a result (other than the interference itself).[63] In such cases, the significance of harm is remedial: an obligation (of repair) to pay monetary compensation for breach of a promise or for interference with a right will arise only if the breach or interference causes harm. But causing harm may, as such, attract an obligation to pay compensation even if the harm-causing conduct was neither breach of a promise nor interference with a right.

The commonest basis of legal liability for causing harm, as such, is negligence. This reflects the judgment that a *prima facie* principle of liability only for intentional harm-causing would strike the balance between our interest as agents in freedom of action, and our interest as victims in security, too heavily in favour of the former. Conversely, a *prima facie* principle of strict liability for causing harm would strike the balance too far in the other direction. This distributional perspective explains why liability in the so-called "economic torts"—conspiracy, intimidation, causing loss by unlawful means—is generally based on intention or recklessness. The main function of such torts is to protect the freedom to engage in competitive activity. Liability for negligence would destroy competition. So, too, would general liability for intentional harm-causing; and so liability for causing competitive harm is hedged about by further restrictions.[64]

This pattern of responsibility is incomprehensible from an agency-focused perspective. Viewed from this angle, the dominance of negligence as the standard of responsibility for harm-causing is deeply suspect; but it can easily be explained relationally. The agent-focused perspective simply does not see the competition-based explanation of the role of intention in the economic torts because that explanation depends on viewing the agent's conduct in relationship to that of competitors and, more widely, as part of a network of social interactions in markets.

In circumstances where negligent harm-causing can attract liability, causing harm intentionally can too (*a fortiori*). Since causing harm intentionally is more culpable than causing the same harm negligently, intentional harm-causing may attract more severe sanctions than negligence. Tort liability for negligent misstatement on the one hand and fraudulent misstatement on the other, provide an illustration. This law's judgment that intentional harm-causing is more culpable than negligent harm-causing is certainly consistent with agent-focused accounts of responsibility. However, only an account of responsibility that takes account of sanctions (2.2) as well as conduct can capture the subtlety of the legal position here.

[63] This section is concerned with harm to individuals. Interference with an individual's rights may cause harm even if it does not harm that individual: Raz (1994) cited in Gardner and Shute (2000), 216–17. See also Smith (2000) discussing contractual rights.

[64] Cane (1996), 151–7.

Strict civil liability (in the sense of liability regardless of fault) for causing harm as such is exceptional. Agency theorists are certainly right in saying that such liability cannot be satisfactorily explained or justified purely in terms of agency and will. Instead, recourse must be had to ideas about the fair social distribution of risks and costs of harm. A conclusion that might be drawn from this observation is that strict liability is not a form of "responsibility" at all—or, in other words, that strict liability is not resposibility-based. Unfortunately, this conclusion proves far too much. For instance, it would mean that strict liability for breach of promise was not a form of responsibility either. Similarly strict liability for interference with rights. For those theorists for whom only liability based on intention, recklessness and knowledge is consistent with human free will, it would also mean that negligence liability was not a form of responsibility. Restricting the term "responsibility" in such ways seems neither descriptively accurate, nor normatively attractive.

Doing harm is a ground of responsibility under the criminal law paradigm as well as under the civil law paradigm. The typical crime involves conduct and consequential harm. Whereas the typical standard of civil liability for harm is negligence, the paradigm (and least controversial) basis of criminal responsibility for harm is *mens rea* (intention and recklessness). As in the case of criminal liability for interference with property rights (6.5.2), this reflects the fact that criminal liability carries a greater stigma than civil liability, and that the prime function of responsibility practices under the criminal law paradigm is not the protection of the victim's interests (for instance, by providing compensation for harm suffered) but to protect society's interest in order and security. On the other hand, negligence-based and strict criminal liability for harm is far more common than the theoretical criminal law literature (in particular) might suggest. Because the criminal law paradigm focuses on agents much more than the civil law paradigm, an explanation of such liability in terms of balancing the interests of offenders and victims is unlikely to be convincing.

Ashworth suggests that negligence-based criminal liability may be justified where: (i) the harm is great; (ii) the risk is obvious; and (iii) the defendant had the capacity to take the required precautions. In other words, criminal liability would be acceptable where the agent had breached a personal (as opposed to an interpersonal) standard[65] in relation to "well-known risks of harm".[66] This agent-focused approach seeks to establish that negligent harm-causing can be sufficiently culpable to deserve criminalisation. A different (relational) approach would seek to justify negligence-based criminal liability by arguing that such liability would strike a fair balance between our interest as agents in freedom of action, and society's interest in peace, order, security and so on. Such an approach figures more prominently in discussions of strict criminal liability. For instance, Ashworth discusses an argument in favour of strict liability that is

[65] For this distinction see 3.2.3.

[66] Ashworth (1999), 199.

based on the view that "one of the primary aims of the criminal law is the protection of fundamental social interests".[67] The language of "fundamental social interests" perhaps suggests an analogy between strict criminal liability and strict liability for interference with rights. However, Ashworth interprets the argument as being concerned with deterrence and the minimisation of harm. On this reading, the contention is that strict liability is desirable because it is more effective than negligence liability in minimising harm: it encourages people not only to take care to avoid harm, but also to search for new ways of avoiding harm that is unavoidable given current knowledge, and to abandon the harm-causing activity if such cannot be found.[68]

Understood in this way, the argument for strict criminal liability is essentially the same as that for negligence-based criminal liability. Both are based on developing a scale for measuring the seriousness of offences *from a social point of view*, and on relating the standard of responsibility to the seriousness of the offence—strict liability (regardless of fault) for the most serious, and negligence for offences considered not serious enough to justify strict liability, but too serious to be tied to intention. In the last sentence, the emphasised words are critical. From the individual's point of view, offences involving the infliction of death and serious personal injury must come very near the top of any scale of seriousness; and yet this is a context in which the basic standard of criminal responsibility is intention. By contrast, negligence liability is a feature of harm-causing road traffic offences, and there are very many strict liability offences that do not involve the infliction of serious personal injury. This suggests that social criteria for judging the seriousness of offences may be different from individualistic criteria of offence seriousness.

This suggestion is reinforced when we consider another strand in Ashworth's discussion of strict liability. His view is that in general, it may be easier to justify imposing strict criminal liability on corporations than on individuals:

> "Some corporations operate in spheres of such potential social danger, and wield such power (in terms of economic resources and influence), that there is no social unfairness in holding them to higher standards than individuals when it comes to criminal liability . . . the same cannot be said of individuals, save in exceptional categories such as road traffic offences, where maximum safety is a central issue. Thus the conflict between social welfare and fairness to defendants should be resolved differently according to whether the defendant is a private individual or a large corporation".[69]

The assumption underlying this passage is that an offence may be much more serious from a social point of view than in terms of its impact on any individual. Murder, inflicting grievous bodily harm, and such like, are extremely serious offences from the individual's point of view because of the serious harm they

[67] Ashworth (1999), 168.

[68] Whether strict liability actually has these effects is, of course, an empirical question. Much is likely to depend on the nature and severity of the sanctions attaching to strict liability offences.

[69] Ashworth (1999), 169.

inflict on the individual. Road traffic offences are extremely serious from society's point of view because although the harm inflicted on the individual victim by the typical road traffic offence is much less that inflicted by murder and serious offences of personal violence, the aggregate impact of road traffic offences on social life is arguably much greater than the aggregate impact of murders and offences of serious violence.[70] Similarly, large corporations that engage in dangerous activities have much greater aggregate harm-causing potential than the typical murderer. Whereas negligence-based and strict liability under the civil law paradigm can be understood in terms of a balance between our interest as agents in freedom of action and our interest as individuals in freedom from harm, under the criminal law paradigm what balances our interest in freedom of action is *society's* interest in freedom from harm.

This discussion illustrates a general weakness of agent-focused accounts of responsibility in explaining harm-causing as a ground of responsibility (6.3). In short, they lack an account of what is meant by "harm". They do not distinguish between different types of harm, and they take no account of harm seriousness. As a result, they cannot explain the richness and complexity of the concepts and practices of legal responsibility for harm-causing. The concepts of "harm", "types of harm" and "harm seriousness" are not legal peculiarities, but play a part in responsibility discourse in the moral domain as well. However, because of the functions of law and of its institutional geography and resources, the meanings of these concepts and their implications for responsibility have been worked out in detail in the law. Non-legal analysts of responsibility would do well to pay careful attention to the law in this regard.

6.5.6 Creating risks of harm

Under the civil law paradigm, liability in relation to harm is typically for doing harm, not for creating risks of harm. It is true that a "*quia timet*" injunction may be awarded in a tort action for nuisance before any harm has been done, provided harm is immanently likely; but such awards are comparatively rare. More commonly, injunctions restrain the continuance of harm-causing conduct. On one view,[71] tort liability for defamation is for creating a risk of harm to reputation—a defamatory statement is defined in terms of its likely effect on the mind of the ordinary person, and the claimant does not have to prove harm to reputation. However, the latter rule can be seen as going to proof of harm, not to its existence. An order for specific performance of a contract may address a risk that the contract will not be performed and that harm will be inflicted as a result; but such an order will not issue until the date for performance has passed. Under the doctrine of anticipatory breach, damages may be recovered, before

[70] In light of the events of 11 September 2001 in New York City it is perhaps worth making explicit the implicit disregard in this sentence of war and terrorism.

[71] Held by Jane Stapleton: see Cane (1997), 48 n. 18.

the date for performance has arrived, in a case where the other contracting party has declared that it will not perform when the time comes; but the theory here is that the breaching party's declaration turns a risk of nonperformance into a certainty.

It is also true that from one perspective, the balance-of-probabilities burden of proof in civil law defines causation in terms of a more-than-50-per-cent increase in the risk of harm. However, the effect of this rule is to treat the creation of such a risk of harm as causing the harm. More importantly (as we saw in 4.3.2), there are situations in which damages for harm are calculated by reference to the percentage increase in risk of the harm generated by the defendant's conduct. But such rules do not come into play until it has been proved that the defendant caused some harm to the plaintiff.

Under the civil law paradigm, then, liability for creating a risk of harm is exceptional. This reflects the focus in that paradigm on repair as opposed to prevention. By contrast, there are many criminal offences that penalise precisely the creation of risks of harm, reflecting the greater importance of prevention as a goal of the criminal law relative to civil law. Road traffic offences such as exceeding the speed limit and drunk driving are obvious examples of such offences. The importance of risk creation as a ground of criminal liability may be related to the presumption of innocence. This generally rules out the imposition of anticipatory sanctions such as injunctions and preventive detention. It would make an offence of causing harm by speeding (for instance) more or less useless as a preventive measure.

Risk creation offences are conduct crimes as opposed to result crimes. Can all conduct crimes be understood in terms of risk creation? This is certainly one way of rationalising the inchoate offences of conspiracy, attempt and incitement,[72] at least in cases where the substantive offence in question is a result crime or a conduct crime that can itself be understood as directed against risk-creation. Some offences of ulterior intent[73] and some possession offences[74] also seem susceptible of such treatment.[75] But it may be that certain conduct crimes are best understood not in terms of regulating risks of harm, but of proscribing conduct as such regardless of its harmful properties.[76] Possible examples are the controversial non-statutory crimes of conspiracy to corrupt public morals and conspiracy to outrage public decency.[77]

Conduct crimes are discussed further in 6.5.8.

[72] Ashworth (1999), ch. 11.

[73] Horder (1996).

[74] Ashworth (1999), 111–12.

[75] Note in this regard that prosecuting for a risk creation offence may provide a tactic for overcoming difficulties of proving harm. In this way, standards of criminal responsibility are nested (3.5.1).

[76] This will depend on how "harm" is defined. See, for instance, Gardner and Shute (2000), 216–17.

[77] Robertson (1979), 211–23.

6.5.7 Making gains

Where a gain made by A corresponds to a loss suffered by B, and the making of that gain can be traced to conduct of A, any liability resting on A to return the gain and repair B's loss can be explained in terms of responsibility for doing harm. By contrast, where A's gain and B's corresponding loss cannot be traced to any conduct of A (as where A is the passive beneficiary of a mistaken payment), any liability resting on A to return the gain and repair the loss needs to be explained in terms of the giving and receipt of the gain. A common account of such liability is based on the concepts of agency and will: A should return the benefit because B did not intend A to have it. If B had not been mistaken, A would not have received the benefit. However, this is not an "agent-focused account" of the liability in the sense in which that terms has been used in this book. In such accounts the "agent" is the person on whom the responsibility rests, not the person to whom it is owed. Understanding "agent" in that sense, no agent-focused account of responsibility could explain the liability. Rather we must look to ideas of distributive justice: if a person receives a benefit that they would not have received if the giver had known their identity (for instance),[78] the benefit "rightly belongs" to the giver, not the receiver; and the receiver should give it back. This, anyway, is the *prima facie* legal position. Of course, the issue arises in the moral domain as well; and there, some might want to argue for a different disposition. But no such argument could be couched in terms of the conduct and will of the responsible person.

It is relevant to the standard of liability for (passive) receipt of another's property whether the property was or was not the subject of a trust. Normally, a recipient of trust property will be liable to the beneficiary only if the recipient knew or, at least, ought to have known, of the existence of the trust. By contrast, the recipient's liability to the ("legal") owner of the property (i.e. the trustee where the property is held under a trust) is basically strict. This reflects a difference of function between "property rights" and the rights of a beneficiary under a trust. Although the latter are, in some respects, analogous to property rights, and are sometimes called "equitable property rights", their main function is to enforce standards of honesty and probity in the management of property; and so fault seems the appropriate standard of liability. By contrast, the basic function of (legal) property rights is the exclusive allocation of resources. Strict liability is necessary for the achievement of this function.

Where A makes a gain "at B's expense", but B suffers no corresponding loss, A's liability to B depends on whether A committed some "legal wrong" against B, such as a tort or a breach of trust. This is a complex and confused area of law about which more is said in 6.6.7.

[78] Concerning the relevance of fault on the part of the giver, see Virgo (1999), 161.

The discussion so far in this section has concerned responsibility for gain-making under the civil law paradigm of responsibility. Gain-making is also a ground of criminal responsibility under offences such as theft. Criminal gains typically correspond to harm inflicted by the criminal. But under section 5(4) of the Theft Act 1968 (UK), the passive recipient of a mistaken payment may be guilty of theft of the payment.

6.5.8 Contemplating crimes

In 6.5.6 it was suggested that criminal responsibility for the inchoate offences of conspiracy, attempt and incitement, along with responsibility for possession offences and offences of ulterior intent might, in some instances at least, be understood as grounded in risk creation. However, there is another way of viewing such crimes which emphasises the conduct and mental state of the agent at the expense of the riskiness of what the agent has done.[79] From this perspective, offences in these categories specify circumstances in which contemplating a crime is itself a crime.[80] This approach might be thought preferable simply because it can explain some cases of criminal liability that cannot (easily) be explained in terms of risk creation. However, Ashworth considers it to be preferable in principle as well. His view is that because of the role of circumstantial luck in our lives, the focus of principles of criminal responsibility should be on conduct and mental states, not on consequences.[81] In some cases at least (he says), contemplating a crime can be as culpable as committing it. As Horder puts it in relation to crimes of ulterior intent: "conduct can sometimes be wrong irrespective of whether one can identify a harm done or (objectively) risked, just in virtue of the intention with which one engages in that conduct".[82] Viewed in this way, the category of "offences of crime-contemplation" makes a major inroad on the principle that harm prevention is the basic justification of the criminal law, and a much larger inroad than is made by conduct offences—not involving the infliction of harm—that do not fall into this category (sometimes called "substantive" offences).[83]

[79] The difference between these two approaches finds clear expression in the debate over liability for attempting the impossible: Ashworth (1999), 469–71.

[80] Attempting a civil wrong is not itself a civil wrong. Conspiring to commit a tort or inciting a tort may incur tort liability but only if the "substantive tort" has been committed. A person who facilitates a tort may be liable for it vicariously, but not personally as a tortfeasor. These rules reflect the focus of civil law on reparation.

[81] Ashworth (1999), 487–8.

[82] Horder (1996), 156.

[83] As Ashworth acknowledges (Ashworth (1987), 20), there is a tension between "the proposition that intentions should be more important than outcomes in determining criminal liability and the proposition that the reach of the criminal law should be kept to a minimum".

6.6 THE BOUNDS OF LEGAL RESPONSIBILITY

Agent-focused accounts of responsibility tend to concentrate on the grounds of responsibility. They give little, if any, explicit attention to the question of whether its grounds and its bounds coincide. For instance, one of the results of distinguishing between the general and special parts of the criminal law is that many issues about the bounds (and grounds) of criminal liability are expelled from the responsibility-oriented general part. Rules that define the limits of legal responsibility are divided between elements of *prima facie* liability and answers (3.5.3). As in the case of grounds, this is not the place for a detailed investigation of the bounds of legal responsibility. The aim of this section is to explore some concepts and techniques used to mark the bounds of legal liability, and in the process to provide more illustrations of the inadequacies of agent-focused accounts of responsibility.

6.6.1 For breach of promises and undertakings

As we saw in 6.5.1.3, Weinrib objects to Fried's promise-based account of contractual liability on the ground that it cannot explain why only some promises are legally enforceable. In the law of contract, three markers of the boundaries of the legal enforceability of promises are the doctrine of consideration, requirements of writing, and the notion of "intention to create legal relations". The basic idea behind the doctrine of consideration is that the law should not enforce gratuitous promises, but only promises for which something has been given in return—"bargained-for promises", as they are sometimes called. There are important exceptions to this principle in the doctrine of "estoppel".[84] These exceptions perform two main functions: first, they facilitate mutually advantageous variation of contracts to meet changed circumstances; and secondly, they recognise reasonable reliance on a promise or undertaking as a basis of enforceability.[85] Requirements of writing serve as a sign that promises were seriously made and undertakings seriously given; and as a protection against fraud and the exploitation of a weaker contracting party by a stronger. The requirement of "intention to create legal relations" serves primarily to exclude promise-based social and domestic arrangements from the legal domain.

It may well be that the scope of the legal obligation to fulfil promises is narrower than the obligation of promise-keeping recognised in the moral domain. For instance, there is evidence that business people sometimes knowingly make commercial arrangements that they treat as binding even though they would

[84] Collins (1997), ch. 5.

[85] Reliance is also a basis of responsibility for conduct that takes place before a contract is technically formed: Collins (1997), 165–7.

probably not be legally enforceable.[86] It is probably also the case that gratuitous promises are more likely to be considered binding outside the law than within it; and this must certainly be true of social and domestic promises. In the abstract, this divergence can be explained and justified by arguments about the desirability of placing limits on the deployment of state power to regulate civil society by forcing people to keep their promises and by imposing obligations of repair on them if they do not.[87] Even so, it seems wrong to think that none of the above limits on the deployment of legal sanctions to enforce promise-keeping have moral analogues. For instance, reciprocity and exchange are lynchpins of market activity; and markets can flourish without being regulated by a law of contract created and enforced by organs of the state.[88] "Commercial morality" and the trust that it generates is at least as important as law in the construction of effective markets. This suggests that in recognising the force of reciprocity and exchange as marking a boundary of responsibility, the law is reinforcing non-legal norms rather than departing from them—in relation to commercial contracts, at least.

As for defences to legal liability for breach of promise, frustration allocates the risk that it may not be possible to perform a promise for reasons outside the promisor's control, that is, the risk of circumstantial bad luck. This defence injects only limited sensitivity to luck into contract law because it applies only where a promise has become physically impossible of performance or, at least, extremely onerous.[89] The defence of illegality seeks to prevent contracts being used as vehicles for criminal (i.e. "illegal") or anti-social (as it is sometimes put "immoral") activities. Neither of these defences can be explained in agent-relative terms. The defences that do admit of analysis in such terms are duress, undue influence and mistake. The legal and moral principle that promises should be kept only applies to promises freely given. The presence of these factors derogates from the freedom of any promise they elicit. To this extent, an agent-relative account of promise-based responsibility can account for its bounds. But there is no reason to think that the defence-based bounds of liability for breach of contract that cannot be so explained do not have moral analogues. For instance, it was argued in 3.2.1.1 that because of the ubiquity of circumstantial luck, morality does, and must, exhibit limited, but only limited, sensitivity to it.

6.6.2 For interference with rights

At the level of *prima facie* liability, the bounds of responsibility for interference with rights are set by the classification of particular interests as rights, and by the

[86] Collins (1999), 108–9.

[87] Similarly: Collins (1982), 230.

[88] Collins (1999), 102–10.

[89] The precise impact of the defence cannot be assessed without reference to the remedial scheme attached to it. In England, the provisions of the Frustrated Contracts Act 1946 allow the costs of nonperformance to be distributed between the parties.

scope of such rights. For instance, in Anglian common law, personal liberty is classified as a right (in the Hohfeldian sense of a liberty right or protected freedom, as opposed to a claim right), but personal health and safety is not.[90] So far as liberty is concerned, the scope of the right not to be imprisoned is different from the scope of the right not to be arrested. This is an important point that deserves elaboration.[91] In 6.5.2 it was pointed out that strict liability is typical of the legal protection of rights. It is not the case, however, that fault is totally irrelevant to liability for interference with rights. Whereas imprisonment is unlawful if it is unauthorised by law, an arrest may be lawful, even though unauthorised by law, if the arrester was a police officer and had reasonable grounds to believe (and did believe) that a ground of lawful arrest existed. In other words, the right not to be arrested is narrower in scope than the right not to be imprisoned. This example illustrates the point that recognising interests as rights, and defining the scope of rights, involves the balancing of interests—in other words, it involves judgments of distributive justice. The limited scope of the right not to be arrested, as compared with the right not to be imprisoned, reflects the fact that arrest is a less serious interference with liberty than imprisonment, and a balancing of the interest in personal liberty against the value of summary arrest for the protection of society's interest in the prevention and detection of crime.

In cases where liability for wrongful arrest is fault-based, what is the significance of the classification of personal liberty as a right? How does the interest in personal liberty (which is classified as a right) differ from the interest in personal health and safety (which is not classified as a right, and liability for which is typically fault-based)? The answer lies in the distinction between conditions of *prima facie* liability and answers. Whereas fault is typically a condition of *prima facie* liability for personal injury, absence of fault (in the form of a reasonable belief that a lawful ground of arrest existed) provides a justification for arrest in certain cases. This difference has important practical ramifications for onus of proof. But it also has ideological importance: it creates a presumption in favour of liberty that does not exist in relation to personal health and safety.[92] Other justifications for interference with rights include consent and lawful authority. The distinction between elements of *prima facie* liability and answers is not merely a legal technicality, but reflects an important normative distinction between interests.[93] It is a feature of our responsibility practices that agency-focused accounts cannot explain.

[90] Personal health and safety receive short shrift in human rights documents. For instance, the European Convention on Human Rights (Arts. 2 and 3) prohibits only intentional infliction of death and personal injury. In Feldman's view, a state would be in breach of the Convention for failing to criminalise "intentional murder" but not for failing to criminalise causing death by careless driving: Feldman (1993), 95. The legal position in this regard may be rooted in ideas about the relationship between the body and the self: Gardner and Shute (2000), 202–3.

[91] See also 3.3.2.1.

[92] Whether this order of priorities is defensible is, of course, another matter.

[93] Note, for instance, that absence of consent is generally an element of *prima facie* criminal liability for sexual offences, while in relation to other offences in which it figures, consent is a defence.

6.6.3 For uttering untruths

As was noted in 6.5.1.3 and 6.5.5, breach of promise can generate expectation-based liability even if the promisee suffered no harm as a result of relying on the promise. By contrast, even though a false statement might raise expectations, it will attract responsibility only if harm was suffered as a result of someone's[94] reliance on it (6.5.3). The making of a promise is a "stronger" ground of legal responsibility in the sense that it can give rise to liability for the mere disappointment of expectations. The bounds of liability for promising (including promising that a statement is true) are set more widely than those of liability for uttering untruths.

In cases where liability for false statements can be strict or negligence-based, responsibility will arise only if reliance on the statement was reasonable. At least, this is the rule where the harm suffered in reliance on the statement is purely financial. If a person suffered personal injury (for instance) as a result of relying on a false statement, recovery would probably not be dependent on their reliance being reasonable, although if it was not, the claimant might be met with a successful defence of contributory negligence. There are two important differences to be noted here. First, it is for the claimant to prove that reliance was reasonable, but for the defendant to prove that the claimant was contributorily negligent. Secondly, unreasonableness of reliance negatives liability, whereas contributory negligence justifies apportionment of damages, i.e. division of responsibility between the two parties. These differences cannot be explained in conduct-based terms, but only in terms of protected interests—the interest in bodily health and safety (for instance) receives greater legal protection than purely financial interests.

In cases where the maker of the statement intended it to be relied upon, and knew it was false or was reckless as to its truth (i.e. where the statement was fraudulent), liability can arise regardless of whether reliance was reasonable. This rule, of course, reflects the greater culpability of the speaker in such cases.

6.6.4 For breach of trust

In law, trust is a very "strong" ground of responsibility, drawing, as it does, both on ideas of property and of undertaking. As a result, it has few bounds. There are three basic principles at work here. The first is that in the document that establishes the trust, the parties to the trust—i.e., the "settlor"[95] and the

Ashworth thinks that it would be "odd" if consent were an element of *prima facie* liability for sexual offences (Ashworth (1999), 330–1); but the word "odd" deprives the issue of much of its ideological significance.

[94] i.e. if A suffers harm by relying on the statement, or as a result of B's reliance on the statement.

[95] The person who provides the trust property.

trustee—may agree that the trustee will have power to do things that would, in the absence of agreement, amount to breaches of trust.[96] The trust instrument may also contain what is called an "exclusion" or "exemption" clause, relieving the trustee of liability for breach of trust under specified circumstances. Exclusion clauses are discussed in a little more detail in 6.6.5.5.

The second principle at work here is that a trustee may avoid liability for breach of trust if the beneficiary has freely consented to, or acquiesced in, the breach. However, because of the fiduciary nature of the relationship between the trustee and the beneficiary, conduct of the beneficiary will be effective to relieve the trustee of liability only if the beneficiary was of full and sound mind at the relevant time, and had full knowledge of all relevant facts and of the legal effect of the consent or acquiescence; and if the consent or acquiescence was entirely freely given.[97]

Thirdly, a trustee may apply to a court in advance to sanction conduct that might otherwise amount to a breach of trust. The court also has a discretionary power to relieve a trustee of liability after the event if the trustee acted honestly and reasonably, and ought fairly to be excused from the strict liability that attaches primarily to unauthorised investment of trust property. In England, this excusing power dates from the late nineteenth century, when it was apparently thought to be needed to maintain an adequate supply of suitable trustees.[98] Because the basic liability from which the provision provides relief is strict, there is a danger that the court will take inadequate account of the interests of beneficiaries. From the beneficiary's point of view, unless they have consented to or acquiesced in the breach (in which case the excusing power will not be needed), it is hard to see why they should be deprived of compensation simply because the trustee has acted reasonably. How can the fact that an agent took reasonable care provide an *answer* to a strict liability claim? Isn't the effect to create a fault-based liability with the burden of proof reversed? Courts have struggled to prevent this becoming the reality by stressing the discretionary nature of the excusing power.[99]

6.6.5 For doing harm

6.6.5.1 Types of harm

Fundamental to legal liability for doing harm are distinctions between different types of harm. It is a serious over-simplification to say that doing harm attracts legal responsibility, because the incidence of responsibility for harm depends importantly on the type of harm inflicted. The main types of harm are bodily

[96] Oakley (1998), 699.
[97] Oakley (1998), 702.
[98] Gardner (1990), 154–6, 166.
[99] Gardner (1990), 155.

injury and illness, mental injury and illness, emotional upset (such as anxiety, grief, disappointment, and so on), injury to reputation, physical damage to tangible property, and financial harm. There are many nuances in the law's treatment of these various types of harm, and the discussion that follows will necessarily be somewhat crude. The law distinguishes between types of harm by recognising a sort of hierarchy of protected interests. At the top is the interest in bodily health and safety. In criminal law, for instance, it is offences involving the infliction of death and bodily harm that are considered the most "serious" and, as a result, attract the most severe sanctions. To the extent that tort law is considered to have a prime function, it is to protect the interest in bodily health and safety. In criminal law, offences of damaging tangible property are considered very much less serious than violence to the person. In tort law, by contrast, personal injury and property damage are traditionally bracketed together, and liability for these two types of harm—fault-based liability, anyway—is more or less similar in scope.[100] This difference between criminal and civil liability probably reflects the different basic functions of criminal and civil law, namely punishment and repair, respectively.

From one point of view, the bracketing of personal injury and property damage is surprising. However greatly people value their possessions, they typically value their health and safety more. Indeed, tangible property is often viewed as having no more than financial value; and in the law's hierarchy of interests, purely financial interests rank lower than the interest in bodily health and safety.[101] This ranking is reflected in the fact that promising and undertaking to act for another's benefit is more likely to generate legal liability to repair purely financial harm resulting from failure to do so than is merely doing harm. In other words, the law of contract and the law of trusts are more important sources of legal liability to repair purely financial harm than the law of tort.

The law's approach to mental harm reflects a common idea that injury to and illness of the mind is in some sense less "real", or at least less serious, than injury to or illness of the body. Here is not the place to seek explanations for this view. The point to note is that as medical and social knowledge and understanding about mental illness have increased over the past century or so, the willingness of the law to compensate for mental harm has increased.[102] Nevertheless, a distinction is drawn between what are loosely called "clinically recognised mental illnesses" on the one hand, and emotional upset of various sorts on the other. In tort law, the significance of this distinction is that with certain qualifications, compensation can be recovered for mere emotional upset only if it is an accompaniment of some other compensatable harm (such

[100] This account relates to the current law. Views about the relative importance of various interests may change over time. For instance, in eighteenth century English criminal law, property offences were considered much more serious relative to other offences than they are today. I owe this point to Niki Lacey.

[101] Cane (1996), 12–15. But see Witting (2001).

[102] Mullaney and Handford (1993), 1–7.

as personal injury).[103] By contrast, recognised mental illness may be compensatable even if it is the only harm inflicted on the claimant by the tortious conduct. One qualification is that the tort of assault (as opposed to battery) consists in making a person afraid for their safety. Another arises from the statutory civil liability for "harassment" under the Protection from Harassment Act 1997 (UK).[104] A third qualification is that because the claimant in a defamation action does not have to prove damage to reputation, the tort can be seen as concerned more with the claimant's feelings than their reputation. In contract law, although mere disappointment of expectations may attract liability, normally such expectations are understood in financial terms. Breach of contract does not normally generate an obligation to repair emotional disappointment caused by the breach. Only if the point of the term that was breached was to provide pleasure (as in the case of a package holiday)[105] or to prevent emotional upset (as where a wife employed a solicitor to obtain an order to prevent her husband harassing her)[106] can compensation for emotional upset be awarded.[107]

In the criminal law, clinically recognised psychiatric illnesses count as "bodily harm" for the purposes of the Offences Against the Person Act 1861,[108] and harassment is a crime under the Protection from Harassment Act 1997. But the criminal law goes somewhat further than civil law in protecting against emotional upset short of clinical illness. There are various criminal offences the conduct element of which involves causing fear.[109] There are also crimes that protect people against being offended.[110] The explanation for the wider scope of the criminal law may reside in a feeling that there are certain harms that we should attempt to prevent even though we would not compensate people who suffered them.

The ideas that some harms are more serious than others, that causing certain harms deserves more severe punishment than causing certain others, and that some harms are more deserving of repair than others, cannot be explained in purely agent-relative terms. No theory of responsibility for doing harm—whether legal or moral responsibility—is complete without a definition of "harm" and, without addressing the question of whether distinctions should be drawn between different types of harm. At a very general level, the hierarchy of interests and harms found in the law resonates with judgments commonly made

[103] Such harm is called "non-pecuniary loss" and includes "pain and suffering" and "loss of amenities" (i.e. "loss of the enjoyment of life").

[104] Concerning the meaning of harassment see *Thomas* v. *News Group Newspapers Ltd* [2001] EWCA 1233.

[105] *Jarvis* v. *Swan Tours Ltd* [1973] QB 233.

[106] *Heywood* v. *Wellers* [1976] QB 466.

[107] *Farley* v. *Skinner* [2001] UKHL 49.

[108] *R* v. *Ireland and Burstow* [1998] AC 147.

[109] Ashworth (1987), 9–10.

[110] e.g. Indecent Displays (Control) Act 1981; Williams (1981), chs. 7 and 9.

in non-legal contexts. Here, as elsewhere, there is a complex symbiotic relationship between legal and extra-legal values.[111]

Consider harm to reputation, for instance. Traditionally, the interest in reputation has been given very high value in the law. Thus, in order to recover tort damages for bodily injury, the claimant must prove that the injury resulted from the tort, as well as its nature and extent. By contrast, the law presumes that defamatory statements[112] cause damage to reputation, and does not require the claimant to prove either the existence or the extent of such damage. A defamation claimant who seeks an award of damages for financial loss ("special damage") must prove that they have suffered, or are likely to suffer, financial loss as a result of the defamation; but damages for injury to reputation as such ("non-pecuniary" harm) may also be awarded. In the early 1990s, juries in a number of high-profile English cases awarded amounts of damages for (non-pecuniary) harm to reputation that were very much greater than the maximum amounts awarded (by judges) for non-pecuniary loss (pain and suffering and loss of amenities) in the most serious personal injury cases. It does not follow from this that the juries in question considered the mental anguish of the celebrity defamation claimant to be more serious and worthy of compensation than that of a person seriously and permanently disabled in a road accident (for instance). At the time, juries in defamation actions were given no information about awards for non-pecuniary harm in other defamation cases, let alone in personal injury cases. In response to these cases and the widespread public criticism they attracted, appeal courts said that in future, juries in defamation cases were to be told that damages for injury to reputation as such should be "moderate"; and that in assessing such damages, the jury should take account of the levels of awards for non-pecuniary harm in personal injury cases.

6.6.5.2 Duty of care

One of the most important legal techniques for distinguishing between different types of harm is the concept of duty of care in the tort of negligence. Liability under the rubric of the tort of negligence is based on a very general principle that people ought to take reasonable care for the interests of others.[113] However, the scope of liability for failure to take care varies according to the type of harm resulting from the negligence. This reflects the idea that the degree of constraint on freedom of action imposed by the requirement of care should be proportional to the importance of the interest being protected. The concept of duty of care is also used to distinguish between misfeasance (causing harm) and nonfeasance

[111] For a general theory of the relationship between degrees and types of harm and the seriousness of criminal offences see Von Hirsch and Jareborg (1991).

[112] A defamatory statement is not a statement that actually damages a person's reputation but one that carries a defamatory meaning, i.e. that has the potential to cause damage to reputation.

[113] The defence of contributory negligence gives effect to the broad general principle that people should take reasonable care of their own interests.

(failing to prevent harm), the scope of liability for the former being wider than that for the latter.

Another important function of the duty of care concept is to establish bounds of legal liability that are not related to ideas of personal responsibility. One example of such a boundary is the immunity of judges from liability for things said and done in their judicial capacity. Another is found in the concept of justiciability as deployed in tort actions against government bodies.[114] This concept gives effect to the constitutional doctrine of separation of powers by identifying decisions and conduct that are considered to fall within the province of the executive and, therefore, not to be suitable subjects for review by courts. The idea of justiciability operates in two distinct ways. There are some areas of "high policy" government activity (such as defence) which probably enjoy a complete immunity from liability in tort. In other areas, the government's decision-making discretion is recognised by modifying the standard of care applicable in a negligence action to require "extraordinary" negligence rather than "ordinary negligence" (3.3.1.3).

Bounds of legal liability such as these cannot be explained in either agent-relative or victim-relative terms. Rather they recognise that individual conduct and personal responsibility practices both have a social context, and that a person's role in the social order and the responsibilities attached to that role (owed to society as a whole) may affect the legal obligations of repair owed to individuals affected by their conduct. Such bounds negative legal liability, not responsibility, nor even a non-legal obligation of repair. A government that successfully claims immunity from legal liability may nevertheless acknowledge responsibility for its conduct and even an obligation to repair its consequences. Giving effect to concepts of personal responsibility is a major function of the law, but not its only function. Not only can there be legal liability without responsibility (as in the case of passive receipt of a mistaken payment, for instance), but there can also be responsibility without legal liability. The essential difference between responsibility and liability lies in their relationship to sanctions. The major function of legal responsibility concepts and practices is to justify the imposition of sanctions—punishment and obligations of repair. In other words, the major function of legal responsibility concepts and practices is to justify the imposition of legal liability. Liability entails sanctions, but responsibility does not. So there can be responsibility without liability. Legal immunities, such as that of the judge, block liability and hence sanctions; but they do not negative responsibility. An important function of the duty of care concept is to specify when legal responsibility for negligent conduct will not attract liability or sanctions.

It is a notable feature of much theoretical analysis of tort liability for negligence that it focuses on the concepts of negligent conduct and causation and largely neglects the duty of care concept. This is true of both deterrence-based

[114] See further 8.4.1. and 8.5.1.

economic analysis of law[115] and of responsibility-based "corrective justice theories".[116] Although these two approaches are seriously at odds with one another, their neglect of duty of care (it seems to me) springs from essentially the same source. In 6.3 we saw that Weinrib denies the distributional function and impact of private law. It is exactly with matters of distributional justice that the duty of care concept is concerned. Similarly, it is a fundamental tenet of much economic analysis of law that the function of law is the promotion of efficiency, regardless of matters of distribution. Moreover, just as corrective justice theories typically focus on the bilateral relationship between the "doer and the sufferer of harm" (to adopt Weinrib's terminology), so in economic analysis of tort law, efficiency is judged in a restricted, bilateral framework that ignores larger social cost-benefit calculations.[117] Neither the tort of negligence, nor private law, nor law more generally, can be explained solely in terms of deterrence or corrective justice. Both represent functions of law, but not its only functions. Law is also concerned with how resources, risks and responsibility are distributed, and with the wider social implications of the way disputes between individuals are settled. This is obviously true of statute law, but is equally true of judge-made law.

6.6.5.3 Answers

As would be expected, most answers to criminal liability for doing harm are agent-relative: insanity, duress, self-defence, and so on. The only major victim-relative answer is consent. By contrast, the most important answers (both in theory and in practice) to civil liability for doing harm are victim-relative: contributory negligence, assumption of risk and illegality. The only significant agent-relative defence is automatism. This pattern reflects, of course, the different orientations of the criminal law and the civil law paradigms of responsibility respectively. Amongst victim-relative answers, contributory negligence limits the agent's responsibility by allocating some responsibility to the victim; while assumption of risk and illegality do not negative the agent's responsibility, but deny that the victim has cause for complaint—i.e. they block liability but do not negative responsibility. Amongst agent-relative answers, excuses (such as insanity) negative responsibility, but justifications (such as self-defence) do not. In other words, some answers set bounds to responsibility (and hence to liability), while others set bounds to liability (without negativing responsibility). As noted in 6.6.5.2, answers that block legal liability (and hence sanctions) but do not negative responsibility leave open the question of whether some non-legal sanction might be justifiably imposed. Legal sanctions are typically more

115 e.g. the index to Posner (1992) contains no entry for "duty of care".

116 e.g. Weinrib treats "duty of care" as a technique performing the same function as "proximate causation": Weinrib (1995), 158–70.

117 Cane (1982), 43–4.

severe than sanctions in the moral domain, and so the blocking of the former does not settle the appropriateness (or otherwise) of the latter.

6.6.5.4 *Limitation of Liability*

This topic is not relevant exclusively to the boundaries of responsibility for doing harm. But this is a convenient context in which to consider it, and the following discussion will be framed in terms of liability for doing harm. Where the doer and the sufferer of harm are in a relationship with one another before the harm occurs, they may agree between themselves that if harm does occur, the doer will not be liable for it, or that the sanction attaching to the doer's liability will be less than application of the relevant legal rules would require. Such an agreement obviously does not affect the agent's responsibility, but only the legal liability and sanctions that can attach to it. In effect, the agreement provides the agent with a total or partial immunity from legal liability and sanctions.

Agreements to limit or exclude liability can only be effective in relation to civil liability. In the criminal context, prospective grants of immunity from prosecution would, no doubt, be considered contrary to "public policy"; and retrospective grants of immunity, as well as plea bargaining (effectively, a limitation of liability) are widely considered undesirable.[118] This partly reflects the greater social interest in imposing sanctions on the criminally responsible than on the civilly responsible. But it also recognises the danger that undue pressure may be put on offenders to plead guilty in return for a lesser sentence. Agreements to limit or exclude civil liability have been seen to pose a similar and similarly serious social problem in dealings between consumers and businesses, where consumers frequently have little "real" choice whether to agree to a limitation or exclusion of liability or not. Therefore, English legislation (for instance) has erected significant barriers to the enforcement of such agreements by businesses against consumers.[119]

6.6.5.5 *Limitation periods*

Although they are not exclusively relevant to liability for doing harm, here is also a convenient place to say something about limitation periods. They were discussed in 2.5, and there is no need to repeat the discussion here. Suffice it to say that limitation periods block legal liability and sanctions, not responsibility. The passage of time has a similar effect in the moral domain. It does not erase responsibility. But by justifying a shift from the present to the past tense—"was", rather than "is" responsible—it signals the inappropriateness of imposing a sanction (or any further sanction, such as continuing disapproval) on the agent.

[118] Concerning prospective immunity see *The Queen on the Application of Mrs Dianne Pretty* v. *Director Public Prosecutions and the Secretary of State for the Home Department* [2001] UKHL 61. Concerning plea bargaining see 7.2.3.

[119] e.g. Unfair Contract Terms Act 1977 (UK).

6.6.6 For creating risks of harm

Victim-relative answers are obviously not available in respect of criminal liability for creating risks of harm. The other points that need to be made in this context relate to offences of crime contemplation, and are considered in 6.6.8.

6.6.7 For making gains

Here we need to take account of two variables. The first is whether or not the recipient's gain corresponds to a loss (i.e. harm) suffered by the claimant; and the second is whether the recipient was active or passive (i.e. whether there was a causal connection between the receipt of the gain and conduct of the recipient). Where the recipient was passive, any liability to give up the gain cannot be based on principles of personal responsibility, which attaches to conduct. The bounds of such liability are, therefore, not strictly relevant to the present discussion. As in the case of responsibility-based liability, these bounds are defined partly by the elements of *prima facie* liability to restore gains (mistake and ignorance on the part of the payer, for instance) and partly by answers (change of position by the recipient, for instance). Liability for passive receipt can only arise in cases where the recipient's gain corresponds to a loss suffered by the claimant, i.e. where the claimant is the payer. Because the recipient's liability is not responsibility-based, its measure is neither the payer's loss nor the recipient's gain, but the coincidence of loss and gain. The recipient's obligation, we might say, is to "restore", not to "compensate". Where the only loss suffered by the claimant corresponds to a gain made by the recipient, the effect of imposing an obligation to compensate would be the same as that of imposing an obligation to restore. But because an obligation to compensate can extend to losses that do not correspond to gains made by the recipient, it would not be appropriate to impose such an obligation on a passive recipient who, by definition, could not have caused such losses.

Where the cause of the recipient's gain was conduct of the recipient, any liability to give up the gain will be responsibility-based. Such liability may take the form of an obligation to restore a gain that corresponds to a loss suffered by the claimant, but it may also take the form of an obligation to "disgorge" a gain that does not correspond to loss suffered by the claimant where e.g. the source of the gain was a third party. There has been much debate about the proper bounds of liability to disgorge gains that do not correspond to loss suffered by the claimant.[120] Under present English law, such liability can arise only in three types of case: where a person has interfered with or exploited another's property without the latter's consent; where a trustee or fiduciary has abused a position of

[120] e.g. Cane (1996), 302–7; Cane (1996c), 312–23; Weinrib (2000); Gordley (2000).

trust; and where a person has consciously sought gain by conduct that constitutes a tort for which punitive damages are available. These instances suggest a more general principle, namely that liability to disgorge attaches (or should attach) only to interference with very highly valued interests (such as property), and to conduct that is particularly reprehensible and deserving of disapproval. This principle could be explained on the basis that it is harder to justify stripping a person of gains that have not harmed the claimant than to justify requiring them to compensate for losses. In principle, therefore, conduct should be liable to attract an obligation to disgorge gains that do not correspond to loss suffered by the claimant only if it would also attract an obligation to compensate for harm caused by it to the claimant. It would not follow, however, that conduct would be liable to attract an obligation to disgorge merely because it was liable to attract an obligation to compensate. Disgorgement is a more onerous obligation than compensation, and so conduct might be liable to attract the latter obligation but not the former.

As for answers, a distinction needs to be drawn between liability to restore gains that correspond to losses and liability to disgorge gains that do not correspond to loss suffered by the claimaint. Because conduct that is liable to attract an obligation to disgorge would (or should) also be liable to attract an obligation to compensate for losses (whether or not the losses correspond to gains made by the recipient), answers to claims for compensation will also be applicable (in theory at least) to claims for disgorgement. There are no answers peculiar to claims for disgorgement.

By contrast, there are several answers peculiar to restoration claims. One is found in the doctrine of "*bona fide* purchaser for value without notice". This answer is typically relevant to cases where a person actively acquires money or property belonging to the claimant from someone other than the claimant. In crude non-technical terms, it is available where a person buys property without knowing, or having reasonable grounds for knowing, that it is rightfully the claimant's. In effect, the answer turns *prima facie* strict liability for active receipt into fault-based liability.[121] Another answer to restoration claims is change of position, which may be available where the recipient has, for instance, consumed what was received or has given it away. Like *bona fide* purchase, this answer is only available to innocent recipients; but unlike the former, it is potentially available to donees and passive recipients as well as purchasers. Whereas a successful plea of *bona fide* purchase allows the recipient to keep the gain, change of position is available only if (and to the extent that) the recipient no longer has it.

Answers to restoration claims are explicable in distributional terms. In the case of *bona fide* purchase, the requirements of purchase and lack of knowledge serve to tip the balance of distributive justice as between the claimant and the

[121] For this reason, it may be treated as an element of *prima facie* liability rather than as an answer: Tettenborn (1996), 23–5, 245.

recipient (i.e. the purchaser) in the latter's favour, thus protecting the security of commercial transactions. However, the answer is more freely available against claims by beneficiaries under trusts than against claims by "legal" owners. This is because the prime purpose of a trust is to protect beneficiaries from unconscionable dealings with trust property, which *bona fide* purchase is not. By contrast, the prime function of "legal" property rights is to provide security of resource allocation; and for this purpose, strict liability is required, at least as a general rule. Security of property is more basic than security of commerce because the latter depends on the former. The distributive justification for the change of position answer is simple: a person cannot restore a gain to the provider if they no longer have it; and they cannot fairly be required to provide a substitute if they were ignorant, both at the time of receipt and of disposal of the gain, that it was not rightly theirs.[122] It is one thing to require a person to give up what is not rightfully theirs, but quite another to require them, if they no longer have it, to replace it out of what is rightfully theirs. The latter needs stronger justification than the former.

Finally, note that in criminal law there are no answers peculiar to liability for gain-making.

6.6.8 For contemplating crimes

Both the category of risk creation offences (such as speeding (6.5.6)) and that of crime contemplation offences (such as attempt (6.5.8)) can be viewed as criminalising conduct on the ground that it creates a risk of some other conduct or event. There is, however, a crucial difference between the two categories. In terms of offence seriousness, contemplating a crime is treated as roughly equivalent to committing it.[123] By contrast, creating a risk of harm (by speeding, for instance) is treated as less serious than causing injury (by speeding, for instance).[124] One of the uses of crime contemplation offences is to provide prosecuting authorities with a way of overcoming problems of proving that contemplated criminal conduct actually occurred. There is a resulting tension between crime contemplation offences and the presumption of innocence—a person found guilty of contemplating a crime may be treated more or less as if they had committed the contemplated crime, even in the absence of proof that the contemplated crime was committed by them or by anyone. For this reason, establishing the boundaries of responsibility for crime contemplation poses difficult questions about the proper scope of the criminal law.[125] One problem

[122] Virgo (1999), 722–3.

[123] Those who think that people who merely contemplate crimes are less culpable than those who commit them generally favour reflecting this difference in principles of sentencing, not of responsibility.

[124] This is one way in which consequences can be important to responsibility.

[125] For general discussions see Ashworth (1987) and Ashworth (1999), ch. 11.

arises out of the abstractness of the conduct elements of the inchoate offences of attempt, conspiracy and incitement. Another (which has received most attention in relation to attempt) is whether intention to commit the contemplated offence should be a condition of liability for contemplating the offence.[126]

6.7 CONCLUSION

In this chapter I have argued that accounts of responsibility that are built solely on the concepts of agency and will cannot explain the grounds and bounds of responsibility because they ignore many of the functions of responsibility practices, especially their distributive function. The distinctions between the various grounds of legal responsibility examined in 6.5 rest ultimately on arguments of distributive justice. The same is true of the bounds of responsibility examined in 6.6. The discussion in that section also emphasised the importance of sanctions in understanding the grounds and bounds of responsibility, because it lies at the heart of the distinction between responsibility and liability.

[126] Horder (1994).

7

Realising Responsibility

7.1 THE "LAW IN THE BOOKS" VS THE "LAW IN ACTION"

ONE OF THE major themes of this book is that responsibility is the product of a set of social practices and not merely the outworking of a set of concepts through which we can understand and interpret human behaviour. The discussion so far of legal responsibility practices has identified those practices more or less with legal rules and principles, especially common law rules and principles made by courts. It has assumed that we can understand legal responsibility practices by understanding the rules and principles of responsibility found in the written legal sources—the "law in the books", as it is often called. It is clear, however, that various important social phenomena that are widely understood as legal responsibility practices do not involve straightforward or accurate application of legal rules and principles of responsibility. For instance, the vast majority of claims for legal compensation for death and personal injury are settled out of court, many without a formal legal claim for compensation being made.[1] Moreover, it is likely that a large proportion of personal injury claims are settled on terms different from those that would be embodied in the court's order, if the claim in question were tried by a court. Although the relevant legal rules provide a framework within which the settlement process takes place, that process involves bargaining "in the shadow of the law"[2] rather than fact-finding according to legal rules of evidence and proof, followed by application of the letter of the law to the facts as found. Phenomena such as settlement out of court are often described as "the law in action".

Out-of-court settlement of personal injury claims involves the application of legal responsibility rules and principles by subjects of the law. The typical result is a greater or lesser degree of divergence between the responsibility imposed (and accepted) in the name of the law, and responsibility according to law. There are also instances where such divergence results from the conduct of legal officials. For instance, there is much evidence that regulatory authorities typically use criminal prosecution as an enforcement technique only in cases of egregious fault, even in circumstances where the offence in question is one of strict liability (7.3). In this instance, whereas the law imposes responsibility regardless of fault, the practices of the enforcement authorities are based on the principle of "no legal liability without fault". One aim of this chapter is to explore the

[1] Similarly, most cases that enter the criminal justice system are dealt with informally.
[2] This famous phrase comes from Mnookin and Kornhauser (1979).

implications for accounts of responsibility of enforcement practices, such as these, that drive a wedge between rules and principles of responsibility on the one hand, and the "realisation of responsibility" on the other.

A second aim of this chapter is to examine the implications of insurance for theories of responsibility. Insurance is a pervasive concomitant of modern systems of legal responsibility. Indeed, without freely-available liability insurance, the legal system could not operate as it does to provide compensation for personal injury, property damage, and so on. And yet at first sight, allowing obligations of repair to be discharged by the proceeds of an insurance policy might seem to derogate from the very idea of *personal* responsibility for one's conduct and its consequences.

7.2 SETTLEMENT

7.2.1 The nature of settlements

One of the distinguishing characteristics of the legal domain is the presence of institutions that interpret, apply and enforce rules and principles of responsibility. Courts are amongst these institutions. Courts also resolve disputes about the existence and extent of legal responsibility; and in the process they can make rules establishing prospective responsibilities and the conditions of historic responsibility. From one perspective, courts are part of the machinery of government. This is particularly so in relation to their rule-making function; but regulating the resolution of disputes between citizens amongst themselves,[3] and between citizens and government,[4] is also an important governmental function that contributes to social stability and cooperation. From another perspective, however, courts can be seen as a facility provided by government to citizens to "adjudicate" disputes that cannot be resolved by agreement between the parties to the dispute.[5] Courts are not the only form of third party dispute resolution available to resolve legal disputes. Parties to a dispute may agree to abide by the decision of the third party, usually known as an "arbitrator" or (in the USA) a "private judge". The parties choose not only the arbitrator, but also the rules according to which the dispute is to be settled. Typically, those rules are the relevant rules of a particular legal system chosen by the parties; but the parties are free to modify those rules if they wish.

Arbitration of disputes is similar to adjudication in that the dispute is resolved according to the decision of a third party. It differs from adjudication in that the power ("jurisdiction") of the arbitrator to resolve the dispute rests

[3] This is the area of private law.

[4] Public law and criminal law are relevant here. There may also be legal disputes between government bodies; but this complication can be ignored for present purposes.

[5] It is in this image of courts that the independence of the judiciary assumes importance, especially in cases where one of the parties is a government body.

on the agreement of the parties, whereas judicial process can be (and is typically)[6] initiated by one party acting unilaterally. Arbitration differs from adjudication also in the fact that it is the prior agreement of the disputing parties that makes the decision of the arbitrator binding, whereas court decisions are binding by virtue of the (political and social) authority of the state. The authority of the state is ultimately underwritten by its coercive power. Of course, not all non-judicial, consensual third party dispute resolution qualifies as "arbitration". Arbitration is legally recognised and legally underwritten in the sense that recourse is available to the coercive power of the state in order to enforce decisions of arbitrators.

Settlement is similar to arbitration in that both are based on agreement between the parties in dispute. A fundamental difference between arbitration and settlement as techniques of dispute resolution is that settlements involve agreement between the parties about the substance of the dispute as opposed to a mechanism for resolving it—i.e. in the case of arbitration, by submission to a third party. The job of the arbitrator, as of a court, is to resolve disputes according to pre-established rules; and, if necessary, to interpret the rules, to fill in gaps, and to make new rules, in order to reach a resolution of the dispute. The decision of a court may be subject to appeal on the ground that the court has misinterpreted the law or made some other legal error; and the decision of an arbitrator may, in exceptional cases, be challenged in a court for "error of law". The parties to an arbitration can choose not only the arbitrator, but also the law according to which their dispute is to be settled; and in this respect, arbitration differs from adjudication—the parties to a dispute that is submitted for adjudication by a court cannot ultimately choose the law to be applied by the court. However, arbitration and adjudication share the feature that the validity and enforceability of the decision reached by the arbitrator or adjudicator (as the case may be) depends, in principle at least and to a greater or lesser extent, on conformity of that decision with a specified set of rules and principles. Arbitration and adjudication are both mechanisms for resolving disputes according to rules and principles that are specified before, or at the time of, submission of the dispute to the decision-maker.

This is not true of settlements of legal disputes, even if a third party is involved in the settlement process in some way, as a mediator or a conciliator, for instance. It is true, of course, that the parties to a settlement of a legal claim will recognise that pre-existing (legal) rules are relevant to the resolution of their dispute. If this were not so, it would not be possible to identify the dispute as a legal one. A legal dispute is one to which legal rules are recognised to apply. It is also true that in the sense in which it is being used here, a settlement involves resolution of a legal dispute by reference to legal rules that are recognised as applying to it. Parties to a legal dispute may decide to resolve their dispute without reference to those

[6] The jurisdiction of the International Court of Justice is frequently the result of voluntary submission by both parties.

rules.[7] An agreement to resolve a legal dispute without reference to relevant legal rules would not be a settlement in the sense we are concerned with here.[8] However, a crucial difference between settlement on the one hand, and both arbitration and adjudication on the other, is that (as a general rule) the bindingness of a settlement does not depend in any way on congruence between its terms and the relevant rules of law; and a settlement cannot be challenged by the parties to it on the basis of lack of congruence between its terms and the relevant rules of law.

This point about settlements should not be confused with that made in 2.3 about the relationship between criteria of responsibility on the one hand, and rules of evidence and proof on the other. For instance, proving that A intended to kill B presupposes a concept of "intention"; but it also requires rules of evidence to allocate the risk of epistemological uncertainty. Similarly, proving that A negligently injured B presupposes a concept of "negligence"; but it also requires rules of evidence to allocate the risk of epistemological uncertainty. The point I am making here is not that a settlement between A and B, under which (for instance) A agrees to pay compensation for injury suffered by B (allegedly as a result of A's negligence), may be based on an agreement between A and B that B *has proved that* A was negligent, as opposed to an agreement that A *actually was* negligent. In this respect, a settlement is no different from a court decision: a court decision in favour of B against A would depend on B *proving that* the injuries suffered resulted from A's negligence, not on their having *actually resulted* from A's negligence. Rather the point is that a settlement under which A agreed to compensate B for injury suffered by B (allegedly as a result of A's negligence) would be legally enforceable (as a valid contract) regardless of whether it was based on an agreement between the parties that B could prove (or had proved) the injuries to be a result of A's negligence. By contrast, it would be contrary to law for a court to award B damages against A regardless of whether B could prove that A had caused the injuries; but this does not undermine the enforceability of a settlement made on such a basis.

A good illustration of the point is found in the world-wide, multi-billion dollar settlement between the Dow Corning Corporation and some 170,000 women who claimed to have suffered various forms of personal injury as a result of receiving silicone breast implants manufactured by Dow Corning. A court-approved settlement was reached despite the fact that the claimants did not prove a causal connection (as defined by law) between the more serious injuries suffered and the implants; and despite the fact that the available scientific evidence suggested that no such connection could have been proved.[9] Similarly,

[7] See e.g. Collins (1999), ch. 14: parties in long-term business relationships may deliberately choose to ignore legal rights and obligations in settling their contractual disputes in order to preserve the relationship.

[8] In practice, it may not be easy to distinguish between an agreement to settle a legal dispute regardless of legal rights and obligations and a settlement that is intended to give effect to the parties' legal rights and obligations but does not do so: Collins (1999), 335.

[9] Rabin (2000), 2061–2.

Janet Alexander has argued, on the basis of US experience, that the initiation of class actions in respect of breaches of securities regulations may provoke large settlements in favour of claimants regardless of whether any breach could be shown to have occurred.[10]

Putting the point at its most stark, an agreement that purports to resolve a legal dispute may give rise to legal rights and obligations (i.e. prospective responsibilities) regardless of whether it gives effect to the legal rights and obligations of the parties in relation to the matters in dispute (in terms of historic responsibility). So, for instance, by virtue of a settlement agreement, a person may be subject to a legal obligation to repair harm based on responsibility for that harm, regardless not only of whether they were responsible for the harm, but also of whether they could be proved (applying legal rules of evidence designed to allocate the risk of epistemological uncertainty) to have been responsible for the harm. The question this raises is whether, and if so in what sense, the practice of settling legal claims without recourse to a third-party, legally underwritten, dispute-resolution mechanism, can rightly be called a "legal responsibility practice". This is a fundamentally important question because we know, for instance, that the vast majority of personal injury claims are settled without recourse to such a dispute-resolution mechanism. With rare exceptions,[11] all such settlements give rise to legally enforceable rights and obligations regardless of whether the terms of the settlement are consistent with the legal rules and principles of responsibility relevant to the matters in dispute. Is the law's willingness to enforce settlements about legal responsibility, regardless of whether the settlement gives effect to legal rights and obligations, an example of the law adopting standards "for its own practical purposes" that morality would reject?

Before attempting to answer this question (in 7.2.4), it is important to say a little more about what we know of how the settlement process works (7.2.2) and about common arguments for and against settlement (7.2.3).

7.2.2 The dynamics of the settlement process

The main components of judicial dispute resolution are fact finding, law interpretation, law application and law making. Of course, not all of these components are present in every case where a court resolves a dispute. Most judicial

[10] Alexander (1991).

[11] In some cases, settlements are binding only if they are approved by a court. This process gives the court the opportunity to refuse approval if the terms of the settlement are seriously inconsistent with relevant legal rules and principles. If a public authority accepted obligations under a settlement that were inconsistent with applicable rules of law, the settlement might be open to challenge under rules concerned with controlling the exercise of public powers—but this statement is highly speculative. Because settlements are binding contracts, it may be possible for standards of fairness to be applied to the settlement process by interpretation of the terms of the contract: *Bank of Credit and Commerce International SA (in compulsory liquidation)* v. *Munawar Ali* [2001] 2 WLR 735.

dispute resolution involves only fact finding and law application. But disputes about responsibility can turn on any of these matters. The parties may disagree about what the relevant facts of their dispute are; about which legal rules and principles are applicable to their dispute; about the correct interpretation of those rules and principles; about how some gap in the law, revealed by their dispute, should be filled; or about how some ambiguity or lack of clarity in the law should be resolved. They may also have different opinions about how a court would resolve their points of disagreement. It is in the space created by uncertainty about how a court would resolve the dispute, coupled with difference of opinion on this point, that negotiation and bargaining between the parties may take place.

For instance, suppose a claimant estimates that the best possible result that could be expected from going to court is a compensation award of $100,000, and that the worst possible result to be expected is a compensation award of $80,000. And suppose that the defendant's estimates of the best and worst possible results that could be expected from going to court are $70,000 and $90,000 respectively. Suppose, further, that for some reason, no settlement takes place and the case goes to court, the result being an award of compensation of $75,000.[12] If there is an area of overlap between the estimates made respectively by the two parties of the possible range of outcomes that could be expected from going to court (as in this example), the area of overlap represents the space for negotiation. In this case, it would make sense for both claimant and defendant to settle for an amount between $80,000 and $90,000 in order to avoid the risk of a worse outcome (less than $80,000 in the claimant's case, and more than $90,000 in the defendant's case) by going to court. If there is no area of overlap between the parties' respective best and worst estimates of the outcome of going to court, it is not in the interests of either party to settle.[13] In this example, too, we can see that even if the parties had settled somewhere within the area of overlap, their settlement would not have coincided with the value of the claim as authoritatively decided by the court. Even if parties settle within the area of overlap, the settlement figure might not be that at which a court would value the claim.

As this illustration suggests, many settlements involve compromise.[14] From the claimant's point of view, it might be worthwhile to accept something less than their estimate of the best possible outcome of going to court, in order to be free of the risk of an even worse outcome. Conversely, it might be worthwhile for the defendant to offer more to the claimant than their estimate of the best possible outcome of going to court, in order to be free of the risk of an even worse

[12] In this example, I am ignoring the impact of costs, which complicates the picture. Establishing responsibility costs money, and the question of how these costs should be borne admits of a variety of answers.

[13] Once again, ignoring the issue of costs.

[14] But not, of course, if the parties agree about their respective legal rights and obligations.

outcome. But there is another factor to be taken into account. The illustration I have given assumes that each party knows the strength of the other's case. In reality, this will often not be so because neither party will know precisely what relevant information the other possesses. This creates the possibility that one party (A) may be able persuade the other party (B) that B's case is weaker than B thinks, or that A's case is stronger than B thinks; and, as a result, that it would be sensible for B to settle for less (or more, as the case may be) than their estimate of the worst possible outcome of going to court. Provided A's bargaining behaviour does not give B a basis for attacking the settlement agreement on the ground, for instance, of actionable misrepresentation, the settlement will be valid and enforceable. This illustrates the importance to the outcome of settlement negotiations of the relative bargaining abilities and strengths of the two parties. The outcome of settlement negotiations about legal responsibility may diverge from what a proper application of legal rules of responsibility would require, not only because of the uncertainties of litigation, but also because of the ability of one party to persuade the other party that the risks of litigation are greater than they think.

Another "weapon" available to parties in settlement negotiations is delay. Typically, delay will be more disadvantageous to one party than to the other; and this fact may be exploited to "encourage" the former to accept a settlement worse than their estimate of the worst possible outcome of going to court. There are various legal techniques available to discourage undue delay. Some operate only after legal proceedings have been commenced; and a significant proportion of legal claims are settled without this ever happening. Moreover, it is questionable whether the techniques available are adequate to neutralise delay as a settlement tactic. Yet another factor that often affects one party to settlement negotiations more than the other is the personal impact of the claim. In the typical personal injury case, for instance, the process of making a legal claim is likely to be much more emotionally upsetting for the injured plaintiff than for the defendant, whose claim will be handled by an insurance company without any, or any significant, personal participation by the defendant. In such a case, the plaintiff will feel much more pressure than the defendant to resolve the claim quickly regardless of the terms of the agreement. These and other factors (such as differences of experience and skill amongst lawyers handling settlement negotiations on behalf of the parties) can all operate to produce divergence between the outcome of settlements of legal claims and the outcome that would be reached if the claim went to court and the relevant legal rules and principles of responsibility were authoritatively applied. In the nature of things, the actual incidence and extent of such divergence is a matter of speculation. As far as I am aware, there is no methodologically rigorous evidence on this matter. However, the theoretical arguments that support the existence of divergence are so powerful, and the conviction that it does exist is so widespread, that its possibility deserves to be taken seriously when thinking about the relationship between legal and moral responsibility.

7.2.3 For and against settlement

The arguments for and against settlement vary somewhat according to context. Let us first consider settlement of private law claims arising, for instance, out of torts and breaches of contract. There are two main arguments in favour of settlement as opposed to litigation of such claims. The first rests on the idea that it is intrinsically better and more desirable that people should settle disputes by mutual agreement and accommodation than by having recourse to a third party to impose a solution.[15] The second main argument in favour of settlement is economic: litigation is expensive; and (so it is assumed) the aggregate administrative cost of resolving, by litigation, claims that are currently settled would be greater than the cost of resolving them without recourse to litigation. Such arguments are widely accepted by courts. For instance, one of the reasons commonly given in support of so-called "bright-line" liability rules and against vague standards such as "reasonableness" is that they facilitate out-of-court settlement of legal disputes. More broadly, Harris and Veljanovski argue that rules governing remedies for breach of contract should be designed for use by contracting parties in settlement negotiations, not by judges in litigation.[16]

The commonest argument against settlement of private law claims and in favour of litigation is that the outcome of the settlement process depends, to a much greater extent than the outcome of a full trial does, on factors other than the "legal merits" of claims—most notably, the relative resources and bargaining strengths of the parties. Put tendentiously, the argument is that "justice" ought to be administered, not negotiated. Its force comes from the assumption that the settlement process is likely to produce outcomes that do not give accurate effect to the legal rights and obligations of the parties. Court decisions may produce such outcomes, of course. But in that case, there is typically the possibility of appeal. Whereas the "deviant" court judgment is considered a mistake, "deviant" settlements are accepted by the law as enforceable contracts. Another argument against settlement is that in some cases, it may deprive a court of the opportunity to clarify the law or to make new law. This argument rests on the idea that courts are not merely government-sponsored facilities for resolving private disputes. They also have an important public law-making and law-interpreting function with which settlement may interfere. It is true that courts

[15] Collins takes this argument further in relation to settlement of contractual disputes: "We must question whether there is any independent value in the assertion and enforcement of the law of contract between parties to a commercial dispute in circumstances where they agree in the light of their interests to apply different standards. Just as the parties are free to remake their deal by agreed modification in order to respond to changes in circumstances, so too they can be granted the facility to alter their legal entitlements retrospectively by a settlement in order to further their business interests" (Collins (1999), 335–6). Collins sees settlement as a means by which parties can avoid strict vindication of contractual rights (351). For this reason, he argues (somewhat inconsistently) for legal regulation of the process of resolving consumer's contractual complaints (352–5).

[16] Harris and Veljanovski (1983).

are not the only, or the most important, law-making institutions. But they are the most important law-interpreting institutions;[17] and law making in the context of specific cases provides an important supplement to legislative law making that proceeds without reference to specific cases. In some areas of the law (such as tort law) rule making through adjudication is the prime mode of norm generation.

When we move to public law disputes between citizen and government,[18] several more arguments against settlement emerge.[19] One points to the public's interest in the dispute arising from the fact that one of the parties to the dispute is the government (in some guise). Secondly, in such cases, any inequality of bargaining power between government and citizen will more likely than not be in favour of the government. Thirdly, to the extent that the matters in dispute raise issues of public interest and importance, it is desirable that those issues be resolved in a public forum rather than by private negotiation between the disputants. Disputes between citizen and government are more likely to involve such issues than disputes between citizen and citizen. This is so even where the non-government party is an individual (such as a social security claimant). It is even more so where the non-government party is an interest group or other type of representative claimant. The point here is not that settlement might deprive the court of the opportunity to interpret existing law or make new law, but rather that even if the dispute involves only the straightforward application of established law, it may be important that this be done by public "administration of justice" rather than private "negotiation of justice". For instance, it may be important that factual disputes, relevant to whether a breach of the law has actually occurred, should be publicly resolved. The point was made well by Alexander in relation to class actions based on alleged breaches of securities regulations:

> "If securities class actions are systematically resolved without regard to whether a violation was committed, this dysfunction is not a matter of concern only to the parties to the lawsuit. Both substantive law and the judicial process are supposed to make behavior conform to the norms expressed in the law . . . substantive accuracy *is* important".[20]

The area in which settlement is most controversial is criminal law. Various practices involve negotiation between offenders and law-enforcement authorities over whether or not a trial will take place—formal police cautioning, charge bargaining, fact bargaining and plea bargaining.[21] For the sake of simplicity, the

[17] This is because their interpretations are authoritative. In practice, of course, non-authoritative interpretations by police and others who apply and enforce the law may be equally, if not more, important.

[18] Or a private entity performing a "public function" such as regulation of economic or social activity.

[19] Fiss (1984).

[20] Alexander (1991), 569 (emphasis in original). In addition to the "injustice" of such settlements, Alexander identifies a range of undesirable social and economic effects which are not germane to the present discussion.

[21] Ashworth (1998), chs. 5 and 9.

following discussion will be limited to plea bargains, under which the defendant pleads guilty in return for a lower sentence than would probably be received in the event of a conviction after a plea of not guilty.[22] In England, plea bargains are encouraged by lack of restriction on the entering of guilty pleas, and on the practice of sentence-discounting in cases where a guilty plea is entered. The basic argument in favour of settlement in this context is put powerfully by Easterbrook (discussing plea bargaining):

> "plea bargaining helps defendants. Forcing them to use their rights at trial means compelling them to take the risk of conviction or acquittal; risk-averse persons prefer a certain but small punishment to a chancy but large one . . . Compromise also benefits prosecutors and society at large. In purchasing procedural entitlements with lower sentences, prosecutors buy that most valuable commodity, time. With time they can prosecute more criminals . . . The ratio of prosecutions (and convictions) to crimes would be extremely low if compromises were forbidden".[23]

The arguments against settlement of criminal cases are to some extent sensitive to factors (such as the way lawyers are remunerated) that vary from one jurisdiction to another. In general terms, however, the arguments are of two types: principled and pragmatic. As a matter of principle, it is thought undesirable that criminal guilt should be decided by negotiation as opposed to the decision of a court. Ashworth, for instance, invokes the presumption of innocence, the privilege against self-incrimination, and the right to a fair trial under Article 6(1) of the European Convention of Human Rights in his attack on plea bargaining.[24] Pragmatic objections to plea bargaining focus on factors such as structural inequalities between defendants as a group and prosecutors as a group, and the possibility of conflict between the interests of prosecutors and the public interest, on the one hand, and between the interests of defendants and their lawyers on the other.[25] Principled objections would stand even if the only defendants who ever pleaded guilty were actually guilty, and even if the sentences agreed upon never differed from the sentence that would have been imposed after a full trial by more than an announced discount for pleading guilty. By contrast, pragmatic objections rest on assumptions such as that plea bargaining results in more convictions of innocent defendants than do trials, or that it results in departures from the principle of proportionality in sentencing which, in turn, undermine the purposes of the criminal law, such as retribution

[22] A phenomenon that deserves consideration in this context is "diversionary conferencing". This practice is conducted under the umbrella of the complex and multi-faceted concept of "restorative justice". Offenders who plead guilty, instead of being sentenced by a court, may take part in a meeting with the victim and other interested parties (such as relatives and friends) to negotiate how to deal with the crime and its effects. Proponents of this technique consider it to have various social and psychological advantages over traditional modes of handling offenders. See generally Braithwaite (1999).

[23] Easterbrook (1992), 1975.

[24] Ashworth (1998), ch. 9.

[25] Ashworth also points out that cautioning deprives victims of the possibility of receiving compensation under a compensation order: Ashworth (1998), 159, 169–70.

and deterrence. In reality, people who object to plea bargaining on grounds of principle typically object to it for pragmatic reasons as well; and they typically advocate its abolition. By contrast, some who find it acceptable, and even desirable, in principle argue for regulation of the process to improve the fairness of its practical operation.[26]

7.2.4 Settlement and responsibility

For present purposes, let us make two assumptions. The first is that courts enforce legal principles of responsibility accurately. In other words, let us assume that when a court holds a person civilly (not) liable or criminally (not) guilty, that person really is (not) liable or (not) guilty according to the relevant rules and principles of legal responsibility. The second assumption to be made is that the settlement process suffers from no defects, such as inequality of bargaining power, and that all settlements are the product of free, fully informed and mutually advantageous bargaining. Although these assumptions are obviously not universally justified, they enable us to isolate the basic point at issue. In cases where there is uncertainty about how a court would resolve a dispute, and where the parties disagree about what a court would do, the terms of any settlement they reach may diverge from the result of an accurate application of legal rules and principles of responsibility even if the settlement process operates perfectly. Nevertheless, the settlement will be legally valid and enforceable. This raises the question of whether the risk of divergence between the outcomes of settlements and accurate applications of legal rules and principles of responsibility—which is inherent in the settlement process in cases of uncertainty and disagreement[27]—should lead us to deny to settlement the status of a "responsibility practice"?

It may help in answering this question to consider the fact that whereas various pragmatic objections are made to settlement in both the civil and the criminal contexts, it is only settlements of criminal cases that attract serious objections of principle. Why is this? One answer, I think, lies in the fact that we conceptualise responsibility differently under the civil law paradigm and the criminal law paradigm respectively. Our view of criminal responsibility is heavily influenced by notions of individual agency and will. Responsibility under the criminal law paradigm is agent-focused—a function of the offender's conduct and mental states. A process that carries an inherent risk of imposition of criminal sanctions that do not accurately reflect individual responsibility seems deeply suspect. By contrast, responsibility under the civil law paradigm is much more relational, focusing on protected interests as much as sanctioned conduct. From this perspective, responsibility can be viewed as much as a resource for

[26] Scott and Stuntz (1992). See also Schulhofer (1992), Easterbrook (1992) and Scott and Stuntz (1992a).

[27] And which, in practice, may be very large.

victims as a function of agency. Put crudely, civil responsibility may be viewed as an asset; and like most other assets, as tradeable. On this basis, there is no objection in principle to bargains about civil responsibility. By contrast, criminal responsibility is not viewed as an asset belonging to the public (for the protection of whose interests the criminal law primarily exists);[28] and for this reason it can be doubted whether criminal responsibility is a proper subject for bargains between offenders and the public's representatives—criminal prosecutors.

The value of the distinction between responsibility as an asset and as a function of agency is confirmed by a consideration of regulatory criminal law. For present purposes, we can define regulatory law as law the prime function of which is to control economic and commercial activity so as to minimise the harm it causes to the environment, for instance, or to the health and safety or workers, or to the financial interests of investors.[29] One of the tools used for this purpose is the criminal law. Many regulatory criminal offences are offences of strict liability (although often subject to fault-based defences). There is good reason to think that regulatory crimes are viewed rather differently than offences of personal violence, for instance, and property offences (such as theft). Crudely put, there is a feeling in some quarters that regulatory crime is not "real crime". This is reflected in the fact that an alternative to criminal prosecution for many breaches of regulatory statutes is the imposition of a penalty by an administrative body (as opposed to a court) without anything resembling a trial. It is also reflected in the fact that many regulatory bodies apparently view criminal prosecution not as a means of enforcing personal responsibility, but rather as a resource to be used as part of a larger strategy of achieving the harm reduction goals of the regulatory regime in question.[30] This suggests that although the responsibility in question is technically criminal, it is perceived as more akin to civil responsibility, the beneficiary and asset-holder being the public rather than any particular individual.

A second reason why civil responsibility and criminal responsibility are viewed differently may be as follows. The main beneficiary of the criminal law is society as a whole. This is why victims are marginal to the criminal justice process. The public interest protected by the criminal law is in order and security. The criminal law serves to announce community standards of acceptable behaviour and to reinforce those standards by imposing sanctions on those who fail to comply with

[28] For the view that "conflicts" belong to victims see Christie (1977). Christie's argument has supplied one of the intellectual and ideological pillars of the restorative justice movement.

[29] Regulatory criminal law may be defined more broadly to cover any offence the *actus* of which is not considered *reus*, and the function of which is purely instrumental. This definition begs the question I want to discuss. Whether an offence is regulatory in this sense is an evaluative question that may be answered differently at different times. For instance, driving under the influence of alcohol is probably viewed today as much more reprehensible than it was 30 or 40 years ago. (I owe this point to Niki Lacey).

[30] Richardson (1987).

them. Public prosecution of criminal offences, and the public trial of offenders in court, play a central role both in achieving the goals of the criminal law in relation to the regulation of behaviour, and also in reassuring the public that community standards are being upheld, and that social order and security are being protected. Avoidance of trial by settlements between offenders and prosecutors undermines the public element of the criminal process. This interest in the public, official and authoritative enforcement of responsibility also explains unease about settlement of claims against government bodies that we noted earlier.

The point is not that the public has no interest in the resolution of legal disputes between citizens. The very fact that a dispute is legally regulated, and that it falls within the jurisdiction of a public court, indicates that there is some public interest in its resolution. The orderly and peaceful resolution of private disputes is itself a benefit to society at large. Resolution of private disputes by public courts also has the social benefit of generating common law rules and principles—"precedents" as they are loosely called. Still, disputes between citizens may be considered to "belong" to the parties in a way that disputes between citizens and the state do not.

Even if this is accepted, however, does it help us to answer the question posed earlier, namely whether settlement can be counted as a "responsibility practice", or whether, on the contrary, the prevalence of settlement seriously weakens the link between law and responsibility? Consider civil cases first. From the claimant's perspective, the question is whether treating responsibility as an asset tradeable by its "beneficiary" is in some sense inconsistent with the very nature of responsibility. There seems no reason to answer this question affirmatively. Outside the law, people are not *required* to enforce obligations of repair that they allege are owed to them, either in full or at all. Enforcement is not intrinsic to the idea of responsibility. If it were, the moral domain would not be so devoid of enforcement institutions as it is. If the beneficiary of an obligation of repair sees some advantage in taking the risk that what they receive under a settlement will be less than a court would award them, a decision to do so is just as open in morality as in law. Moreover, such a decision does not alter the nature or reality of the responsibility in issue.

From the defendant's perspective, the question is whether the status of settlement as a responsibility practice is undermined by the risk, inherent in settlement, that a defendant may incur a legal obligation to the claimant more onerous than that which a court would impose if the case went to trial. Once again, there seems no good reason to answer this question affirmatively. Both within and outside the law, one way of incurring an obligation is by freely accepting it. A settlement is a contract, and contract is a device by which people can assume responsibilities they did not previously have. On the assumption that the settlement process is free of imperfections, there is no reason to object to its outcome on responsibility grounds simply because the obligation of repair accepted by the defendant under the terms of the settlement is more onerous than that which a court would have imposed if the case had gone to trial.

Moreover, the willingness of a defendant to accept an obligation *to repair* an adverse outcome does not affect the nature of their responsibility *for* that outcome.

What should we say about settlement of criminal cases? Although it seems that criminal responsibility is not viewed as an asset belonging to the public, a decision that the overall balance of social advantage lies in not dealing with every instance of alleged criminal conduct in strict accordance with accepted rules and principles of responsibility seems no more problematic in this context than the decision not to enforce alleged civil responsibility strictly in accordance with the law. Enforcement is not intrinsic to responsibility, and a decision not to enforce does not alter the nature or reality of the responsibility in question. However, this line of reasoning is more problematic from the criminal defendant's point of view because even under the assumptions we are making, there is a risk that the defendant will end up worse off as a result of settlement than they would have been if the case had gone to trial. This is also true in the civil context, of course. But a process that carries the risk of being punished more than the law requires might be thought qualitatively more objectionable in responsibility terms than one that carries the risk of agreeing to do more to repair harm than the law requires. The risk that an innocent person will be punished (or that a guilty person will be punished too much) is inherent in the very process of settling criminal cases. Punishment carries a stigma that obligations of repair do not. Punishment is intrinsically undesirable in a way that repairing harm is not, and it calls for justification in a way that repairing harm does not.

It might be argued, then, that settlement of criminal cases is intrinsically objectionable in responsibility terms in a way that settlement of civil cases is not. If this argument is accepted, its implications are fundamental. If settlement of criminal cases (with its inherent risk that people will be punished more than the law requires and allows) is to be justified, it will have to be accepted that the enforcement of criminal responsibility (i.e. retributive justice) is not the only legitimate goal of the criminal justice system, nor the only justification for punishment. A classic objection to utilitarian theories of punishment is that they might, in some extreme case, justify deliberate punishment of the innocent. But analysis of the process of settling criminal cases shows that the problem of justifying punishment of the innocent may arise in mundane cases as well. Even assuming that the settlement process is without imperfections, a system that allows guilty pleas and encourages them with a sentence discount creates a non-negligible risk of punishment of the innocent. In such a system, being able to justify unintentional punishment of the innocent is not an optional extra for a theory of punishment, but an essential precondition of its acceptability. The need to be able to justify punishment of the innocent becomes greater when we drop the empirically invalid assumptions that courts always apply the rules and principles of criminal responsibility correctly and never punish the innocent; and that the settlement process is free of defects. It becomes even greater again when we consider how much it would cost to eliminate the risk of punishing the innocent, and the impact this expenditure would have on the achievement of goals of the criminal justice system other than retributive justice, and of other valued social objectives.

7.3 SELECTIVE ENFORCEMENT

An implication of the argument in 7.2 is that enforcing principles of personal responsibility is an important value in both the legal and the moral domains, but that it is not the only legal or moral value, and it should not be (and is not) pursued regardless of the cost to other values. Completely faithful adherence to rules and principles of personal responsibility may come at a cost not only to other legal and moral values (such as deterrence of illegal or immoral behaviour), but also to wider social and economic values, such as health and education. Putting the point crudely, in a world of limited resources, the more that is expended on ensuring accurate enforcement of personal responsibility, the less there will be available for achieving other valued social goals. In other words, enforcing personal responsibility raises issues of distributive, as well as of corrective and retributive, justice.[31] It is important to bear this in mind when assessing the significance of the phenomenon of selective enforcement of legal responsibility.

As should be clear by now, my basic argument is that selective enforcement is not objectionable in itself. People to whom obligations are owed are not required to enforce them, either in the moral or the legal domain. The fact that only some negligent injuries are made the subject of legal action, or that only some criminal offences are prosecuted, is not intrinsically problematic. Indeed, responsibility-related factors that mitigate sentence—such as motive and the amount of harm inflicted—may also underpin decisions not to prosecute. Objections to selective enforcement are typically not responsibility-based. For instance, it has frequently been observed that whether personal injuries are made the subject of legal action or not depends to a significant extent on the context in which they were suffered. A very high proportion of personal injury actions arise out of road and work accidents, even though such injuries form a much smaller proportion of the injuries that could, in principle, attract legal liability. It is also widely accepted that levels of prosecution of "white-collar" and "regulatory" crime are significantly lower than levels of prosecution of "traditional" crimes, such as personal violence and theft. It is often alleged, too, that enforcement of the criminal law is, for instance, racially discriminatory. At the same time, it is universally assumed (implicitly, at least) that even if "full enforcement" were possible in practice, it would not be desirable because of its expense. The optimal level of enforcement is that at which the costs and

[31] This is an important reason why Weinrib's corrective justice theory of tort law, for instance (see 6.2–6.3) is inadequate.

benefits of enforcement are in equilibrium, so that the benefits of any increase in enforcement would be outweighed by its cost.

Even so, there is a well-documented phenomenon that deserves some discussion from the point of view of responsibility. On the one hand, many "regulatory" statutory criminal offences are offences of strict liability (although often subject to a fault-based defence). On the other hand, empirical investigation of the enforcement practices of certain regulatory authorities has shown that prosecutions for strict liability regulatory offences are rare,[32] and that a characteristic of cases in which prosecutions are brought is egregious fault on the part of the defendant.[33] Does this have any responsibility-related significance? First, it is important to remember that legal strict liability is liability regardless of fault, not liability in the absence of fault. So there is no incongruity in prosecuting egregiously faulty defendants on a strict liability basis. Secondly, if there is no objection in principle to selective enforcement of responsibility, there could be no objection to singling out for prosecution those most at fault. Indeed, of all possible principles of selection, this might seem the most justifiable. There are at least two possible interpretations of the phenomenon.[34] One is that the regulatory authorities in question view prosecution for regulatory offences not in terms of personal responsibility for conduct and outcomes, but as a tool available for furthering the aims of the relevant regulatory scheme.[35] The fact that the tool is so rarely resorted to demonstrates that the regulators think that there are much better tools available to them. This interpretation arguably reflects the view that regulatory crime is not "real crime", and supports the interpretation of fines for regulatory offences as activity taxes rather than punishments (see 3.6.3.5), in other words, as mechanisms of (re)distribution rather than retribution.

Another possible (and contrary) interpretation of the phenomenon under consideration is that the regulatory authorities in question view the relevant regulatory crimes as real crimes, and fines imposed on regulatory offenders as punishments rather than taxes; and that this is why they are loath to prosecute in the absence of serious fault.[36] Under this interpretation, the practice of selective enforcement can be seen as giving effect to the responsibility-based objection to strict criminal liability that it is inappropriate to impose the stigma that attaches to punishment on a person whose conduct was faultless (see 3.6.3.5). In this way, this instance of selective enforcement can be seen not only as presenting no challenge to responsibility-based principles of retributive justice, but as correcting the legislature's departure from those principles. The effect of such selective enforcement can, however, also be understood in distributive terms. Fault-based and strict liabilities distribute risks, harms and responsibilities in different ways.

32 Prosecutions are expensive and resources are scarce.
33 Richardson (1987). For a more recent overview see Cartwright (2001), ch. 7.
34 Another is "agency capture", as to which see Ogus (1994), 57–8, 94–5, 106–7.
35 Richardson (1987).
36 Hawkins (1984), 161–71.

By prosecuting strict liability only in cases of egregious fault, selective enforcement establishes a different pattern of distribution from that mandated by the legislature. From this perspective, the acceptability of selective enforcement must be tested according to principles of distributive justice.

This last point can be generalised, I think. There is no objection, based on principles of retributive justice, to selective enforcement of the criminal law because there is no requirement that responsibility always be enforced. But patterns of selective enforcement may be open to objection on distributive grounds if, for instance, they are racially discriminatory or they seriously undermine social goals of the criminal law, such as deterrence, without providing any countervailing social benefit. Similarly, there is no objection, based on principles of corrective justice, to settlement of civil claims because there is no requirement that principles of responsibility always be enforced. But patterns of settlement of civil claims may be objectionable on distributive grounds if, for instance, they are systemically affected by inequality of resources. The principle that like cases be treated alike is a principle of distributive justice, not of corrective or retributive justice. In order to understand and assess any system of responsibility we need to pay attention not only to the rules and principles according to which responsibility is attributed, but also the principles and practices that determine the way it is distributed. This is one of the senses in which an account of responsibility must be relational in order to be accurate and complete.

7.4 SPREADING LEGAL RESPONSIBILITY

7.4.1 The importance of insurance in civil law

In this section, I consider the implications for theories of responsibility of what I will loosely call the spreading of responsibility. The terminology is loose because what is spread is not responsibility but the financial costs of responsibility. There are two main ways in which the financial costs of legal responsibility can be spread—liability insurance and self-insurance. Liability insurance spreads the costs of responsibility amongst a pool of potentially responsible parties. Self-insurance involves passing on the costs of responsibility to some group such as the responsible party's customers (in the form of higher prices), employees (in the form of lower wages) or shareholders (in the form of lower dividends).[37]

[37] Thus I am distinguishing self-insurance from simple absence of insurance ("going bare"). A defendant who is neither insured nor has the ability to pass on the costs of liability may end up in bankruptcy. In that case, the plaintiff will typically rank as an unsecured creditor, and will have to bear a greater or lesser extent of the liability costs. This result is, of course, inconsistent with responsibility rules and principles. This is why it is important to distinguish between self-insuring and going bare. The former is a way of meeting the costs of liability, whereas the latter can be used as part of a strategy for evading such costs.

Liability insurance is a relatively recent phenomenon. It started to become common only towards the end of the nineteenth century. It has had a fundamental impact on the law, most particularly in the context of tort liability for personal injuries. The tort system of compensating for personal injuries, as we know it today, could not exist in the absence of widespread liability insurance. For instance, the typical defendant to a tort action arising out of a serious road accident could not personally pay the amounts of damages that are routinely recovered by claimants in such cases. In relation to personal injuries suffered on the road and at work, liability insurance (or the provision of a financial guarantee in lieu) is compulsory. As a result, the great majority of tort claims for personal injuries arise out of work and road accidents, even though these causes of injuries account for a much smaller proportion of the total number of potential personal injury tort claims. Given that the vast majority of personal injury tort claims are settled out of court by negotiation, there is a sense in which the tort system of compensating for personal injuries is best understood as an insurance-based administrative system incorporating a facility for recourse to a court when negotiations fail. Even in areas where liability insurance is not compulsory (that of commercial contracting, for instance), the civil liability system depends on liability insurance (or self-insurance) for its efficacy. Since the vast majority of all civil liability claims are settled out of court, the whole civil liability system can be viewed as an administrative compensation regime incorporating a facility of recourse to a court to resolve disputes arising out of the negotiating process.

7.4.2 Insurance and interpretations of tort law

In relation to personal injury tort claims, in particular, the importance of liability insurance has led many observers to argue that tort law can no longer be understood as a system of rules and principles of personal responsibility (assuming it ever was such a system), but must be viewed primarily as a means of compensating for harm, and of spreading the cost of that compensation widely and thinly throughout society. Pursuing this interpretation, vicarious liability is seen to be a loss-spreading device rather than an outworking of ideas of personal responsibility. From this perspective, tort law is viewed as a system of distributive justice, not a system of corrective justice. A different interpretation of tort-law-cum-liability-insurance (or perhaps more accurately, "insurance-cum-tort-law") focuses on defendants rather than plaintiffs, and speaks in terms of "cost internalisation", "enterprise liability" and "deterrence". According to this view, tort law is primarily a system for achieving the socially optimal incidence of injury-causing events and the socially optimal level of injury costs. The key concept in this approach is not responsibility for injuries but capacity to avoid or prevent accidents and to minimise accident costs. This "economic" interpretation of tort law views it not as a mechanism for distributing injury costs but rather for achieving "efficiency"—i.e. the optimal utilisation of social resources.

In descriptive terms, both of these approaches suffer from serious shortcomings. In principle, tort law does not purport to compensate for personal injuries as such, but only for personal injuries that are caused in certain ways. Conversely, tort law does not purport to provide incentives to avoid injuries—it concerns itself with conduct that has actually caused injuries, and not with potentially injury-causing conduct.[38] In practice, we know that tort law does not even compensate all those whose injuries fall within its terms; and such evidence as we have casts serious doubt on the deterrent efficacy of tort liability even in those classes of case that fall within its terms. Reactions to such facts depend on the ideological predilections of the observer. So far as compensation is concerned, some people favour replacement of the tort system with some system of public provision (social security),[39] while others prefer first party private insurance.[40] In order to further deterrence, liberal individualists favour fine-tuning of tort law to improve its deterrent potential, while communitarians prefer public regulation. By contrast, "corrective justice theorists"[41] insist that tort law is still best understood as a system of rules and principles of personal responsibility, and that the compensatory and deterrent shortcomings of the tort system are of no account provided the rules and principles of tort law are correctively just.

How does each of these interpretations of tort law accommodate liability insurance? As noted, the compensatory account of tort law is a reaction to the prevalence of liability insurance. Under it, liability insurance is not only compatible with responsibility for tortious conduct, but is a necessary precondition for performance of the main function of such responsibility, namely providing, and spreading the cost of, compensation for harm.[42] The theory underlying the deterrence interpretation of tort law is that requiring compensation to be paid for harm caused creates a financial incentive to prevent similar harm in the future, provided this could be done at less than the cost of paying compensation. By this mechanism, harm causing is reduced to its socially optimal level—people will spend money on harm prevention to the point where reducing harm any further would be more expensive than compensating for it. In theory, liability insurance is compatible with this cost-benefit objective provided, anyway, that the premium for the insurance accurately reflects the risk that the insured will incur liability.

Proponents of corrective justice accounts of civil law—and of tort law in particular—typically see no incompatibility between liability insurance and their preferred interpretation of the law. Here is what Weinrib says:

[38] The possibility of obtaining an injunction to restrain potentially harm-causing conduct is not inconsistent with this statement because an injunction will issue only if the court is satisfied that the conduct in question would certainly or very likely cause harm. An injunction does not provide an incentive to avoid harm. Rather it aims to prevent harm by prohibiting conduct.

[39] e.g. Cane (1999).

[40] e.g. Atiyah (1997).

[41] e.g. Weinrib (1995).

[42] Schwartz (1990), 359–62.

"corrective justice is applicable in the modern world despite the fact that the prevalence of liability insurance means that the defendant personally does not compensate the plaintiff for the loss. Corrective justice goes to the nature of the obligation; it does not prescribe the mechanism by which the obligation is discharged. Liability insurance presupposes liability, and it is that liability which is intelligible in the light of corrective justice. Nothing about corrective justice precludes the defendant from anticipating the possibility of liability by investing in liability insurance".[43]

At first sight, Weinrib's approach is puzzling. Corrective justice accounts of tort law are rooted in ideas of personal responsibility. From the proposition that civil liability is a function of personal responsibility, it might seem to follow that the cost of liability should rest on the person held responsible for the liability-attracting event. Through liability insurance, a person can shift much of the cost of liability onto others who were not personally responsible for the liability-attracting event. In this way, it might be argued, liability insurance undermines personal responsibility. The view that provided the allocation of liability is consistent with corrective justice, it does not matter how the liability is "discharged", seems to ignore the possibility that liability insurance might so undermine corrective justice as to cast doubt on whether tort law can be understood as its vehicle.

Schwartz identifies various "fairness-based" justifications for liability insurance.[44] One is that it enhances freedom of contract: "the goals of ethics are generally advanced if individuals are allowed, in a voluntary way, to enter into contracts that they know will be binding on them".[45] A second fairness-based justification for liability insurance identified by Schwartz views it as a cushion against liability for bad luck[46] and against the risk of errors in the adjudication of liability.[47] Thirdly, Schwartz thinks that provided premiums are risk-related, liability insurance can further retributive justice by making "the defendant's financial burden proportional to the level of improper risks that his conduct occasions"[48] and by spreading the costs of liability amongst all risk-creators, and not just those whose risky conduct actually causes harm. Fourthly, Schwartz points out, liability insurance "fares just fine"[49] to the extent that tort liability is justified in terms of compensatory justice. None of these justifications helps much in explaining why Weinrib thinks that liability insurance is compatible with his account of corrective justice. The first makes some sense of his view about liability insurance quoted above; but being entirely agent-focused, it also suggests inconsistency between that view and his insistence that private law must be understood correlatively. The second and third justifications are agent-

[43] Weinrib (1995), 135, n. 25. See also Weinrib (1985).

[44] Schwartz (1990), 321–36.

[45] Schwartz (1990), 323. For Schwartz, the element of voluntariness is essential to the fairness of liability insurance: compelling people to buy liability insurance "weakens the . . . ethical . . . arguments in [its] favor": Schwartz (1990) 326, n. 55.

[46] Schwartz seems to assume that fairness requires complete sensitivity to luck. I disagree: see 3.2.

[47] Schwartz (1990), 323–5.

[48] Schwartz (1990), 328.

[49] Schwartz (1990), 328.

focused, and the fourth is victim-focused; and so they are all incompatible with the correlativity account of private law. The retributive justice justification is incompatible with Weinrib's account in another way too, because it appeals to the spreading of risks amongst actors who have not caused harm. Indeed, the propensity of liability insurance to impose liability costs regardless of causation would seem to make it deeply problematic for Weinrib,[50] who insists on the centrality of causation of harm to the concept of corrective justice.[51]

The key to understanding Weinrib's position is the distinction between tort law and the tort system. His view is that tort law—in the sense of judge-made[52] legal doctrine—must be understood "internally" as a set of rules and principles of personal responsibility, without reference to its social effects or "external purposes", such as compensation and deterrence. Because the incidence and availability of liability insurance generally play no part in tort doctrine, Weinrib can ignore the impact of insurance on the practical operation of tort doctrine—in other words, on the realisation of tort liability in the tort system. Schwartz, by contrast, is interested in the tort system—tort law in action—and in its goals and effects. He concludes, therefore, that any account that ignores the impact of liability insurance will be "unsound".[53] But in directing this criticism at Weinrib, Schwartz wrongly attributes to him concern with the extent to which corrective justice is realised in the operation of the tort system. Weinrib's account of tort law is deeply philosophical in its concentration on concepts and its disregard of how those concepts might be, and are, operationalised. Weinrib's version of corrective justice has nothing to say about liability insurance because its only concern is the internal conceptual logic of the set (or sets) of rules and principles we call "private law". If Weinrib were offering corrective justice normatively (or descriptively, for that matter) as a goal of tort law, liability insurance might be seen to undermine the achievement of that goal so seriously as to make the corrective justice account of tort law totally implausible. Indeed, it is precisely the mismatch between the concepts of personal responsibility that underlie tort doctrine and the realisation of those concepts in the tort-cum-liability-insurance system that has generated the most powerful critiques of, and the deepest dissatisfactions with, tort law as a social institution for dealing with injury and illness.

7.4.3 A relational and functional account of the relationship between responsibility and liability insurance

As was suggested in 7.4.2, insurance against civil liability looks troublesome from a responsibility point of view because it enables the cost of liability for

[50] Similarly Schwartz (1990), 334.

[51] e.g. Weinrib (1995), 11–12.

[52] Weinrib would consider statutory compulsory insurance provisions not to be part of tort doctrine in the relevant sense.

[53] Schwartz (1990), 364.

harm to be offloaded onto parties who were not responsible for the harm. Indeed, it has been said that "[a]t the beginning of the nineteenth century, liability insurance would have been . . . considered immoral".[54] If the law had adopted this approach, the growth of the liability insurance industry would have been seriously impeded, and the enactment of statutes requiring car users and employers to buy liability insurance would, no doubt, have been significantly delayed. As it was, while liability insurance contracts in respect of deliberate wrongs were generally regarded as illegal and unenforceable, no legal barriers were put in the way of insurance against negligence-based and strict liability.[55] As the responsibility-based argument against liability insurance would lead us to expect, this has undermined the responsibility-based analysis of tort liability for personal injuries to the point where the High Court of Australia has held that even liability to pay punitive damages may be insured against,[56] despite the fact that such liability requires *mens rea*. The court supported this rule by arguing that punitive damages "serve to assuage any urge for revenge felt by victims and to discourage any temptation to engage in self-help likely to endanger the peace". The court also appealed to the expressive function of punitive damages which, it seemed to think, was unaffected by insurance.[57]

In principle, one would expect the position regarding insurance against criminal liability to be somewhat different. After all, the criminal law paradigm is agent-focused; and it might be thought that there is a fundamental ethical (if not logical) incoherence in the idea that the risk of being punished should be insurable. But here too, while it is clear that insurance against liability for crimes that require *mens rea* is illegal, there is doubt as to whether insurance against negligence-based and strict criminal liability is similarly unenforceable.[58]

In a crude way, drawing the line between insurability and uninsurability by distingushing between liability based on *mens rea* on the one hand, and negligence-based and strict liability on the other, might seem consistent with the idea that "moral" responsibility requires culpability, and with an agent-focused, choice-based interpretation of culpability: a person should not be allowed to offload the burden of culpability-based responsibility onto non-responsible parties by insurance or passing-on. By contrast, under this approach there would be no responsibility-based objection to insurance against (or passing-on of) the costs of legal liability that cannot be justified in terms of choice-based culpability (assuming that the liability itself is justifiable).

However, drawing the line between insurability and uninsurability in this way does not seem right in relation either to civil liability or criminal liability. For one thing, the distinction between liability for *mens rea* on the one hand,

[54] Schwartz (1990), 314, n. 5.

[55] Treitel (1995), 395–7. A detailed and still useful (though dated) discussion of the relevant US law is McNeely (1941).

[56] *Lamb* v. *Cotogno* (1988) 164 CLR 1.

[57] (1988) 164 CLR 1, 9–10.

[58] Treitel (1995), 394–5.

and negligence-based and strict liability on the other ignores the nested nature of criteria of legal liability (3.5.1). The relevant point so far as a person's responsibility is concerned is not the legal basis of liability, but whether the person held liable was actually at fault or not; and if at fault, in what way (intentionally, recklessly or negligently).

More substantively, so far as civil liability is concerned, the distinction is problematic because it classifies breaches of the law in an agent-focused way, ignoring the essentially relational nature of responsibility under the civil law paradigm. From the claimant's point of view, the harm to be repaired is the same regardless whether it was caused intentionally, recklessly, negligently or without fault. Why, then, should the law (in the name of an inappropriate model of responsibility) make it more difficult in practice for the victim of intentional or reckless harm to recover compensation than it is for the victim of negligent or faultless harm, by allowing liability for the latter, but not for the former, to be insured against? In 3.4 we saw that *mens rea* requirements play two roles in tort law. Their independent function is to justify the imposition of liability where none would attach in its absence (as in relation to the so-called "economic torts"). Their ancillary function is to justify the awarding of remedies that would not be available in their absence (as in relation to the tort of deceit). Neither of these functions requires that tort liability for *mens rea* should be uninsurable. This is obvious in relation to the ancillary function—here, the presence of *mens rea* justifies enhanced protection for the claimant's interests. It makes no sense to undermine this enhanced protection by prohibiting insurance of the enhanced liability. By its independent function, *mens rea* restricts the scope of tort liability for social reasons, so as not to discourage competition, for instance. But such reasons do not require or justify banning insurance against liability in cases that fall within the scope of liability so defined, because the main function of such liability, as of civil liability generally, is to justify the imposition of obligations of repair. Liability insurance facilitates the fulfilment of such obligations.

The effect of liability insurance may be to blunt the expressive and deterrent effects of civil liability. But this is not a strong argument against allowing it because rules and principles of responsibility under the civil law paradigm (even those that require *mens rea*) are not primarily (or well) designed to stigmatise defendants and to deter unacceptable conduct; and because if it were not allowed, civil law could not effectively perform its main function of repairing harm. Liability insurance is a positively desirable adjunct to civil law responsibility rules and principles because it enables injurers to fulfil obligations of repair that would otherwise be beyond their resources. It does not follow from this that rules of civil liability should take account of whether the defendant was insured against liability or could have bought such insurance. Liability insurance is a responsibility-compatible, claimant-friendly adjunct to civil liability. But civil liability is not a function of either insurance or insurability.[59]

[59] Cane (1996), 421–9; Stapleton (1995).

For Honoré, liability insurance is not only compatible with strict tort liability, but also plays an essential part in justifying it.[60] His argument is based on the idea that proportionality between proscribed conduct and sanction is as much a requirement of civil law as of criminal law. His view is that tort liability can be justified even in the absence of *mens rea* because imprisonment is not available as a sanction for breaches of civil law. But because the financial burden of repairing harm can be very great, some variety of fault is generally a precondition of tort liability. In his opinion, liability without fault that imposes heavy financial burdens can only be justified if the costs of liability will be spread by insurance. Several objections can be made to this line of argument. First, it involves assessing the fairness of civil liability in an excessively agent-focused way. The importation of the proportionality principle into civil law gives too little weight to the reparative function of civil law. Secondly, Honoré seeks to justify strict tort liability in terms of its impact on agents rather than in terms of the protection it gives to the interests of victims and society (3.6.3.5). Thirdly, by making loss-spreading ability relevant to liability, Honoré's argument fatally undermines the potential of strict liability to repair harms by leaving it open to potential defendants (in the absence of a legal requirement to insure) to avoid liability by "going bare".[61] Because of the relational nature of responsibility under the civil law paradigm, liability insurance should be viewed essentially as a protection for claimants, not for defendants. The critical normative question in this context is not whether potential defendants should be allowed to insure against liability but whether they should be required to do so.

Drawing the line between insurability and uninsurability by distinguishing negligence-based and strict liability from liability for *mens rea* does not seem right in relation to criminal liability either. The analysis in 3.6.3.1 challenged the choice-based view that negligence is not culpable, and that negligence-based criminal liability is objectionable in principle. If negligent conduct is thought sufficiently culpable to attract criminal liability, it is at least arguable that since criminal liability for *mens rea* is not insurable, negligence-based criminal liability should not be insurable either. It may be that only "gross" negligence deserves the stigma of punishment—of serious punishment, anyway. However, even if fines for negligence are seen as carrying little or no stigma, but rather as being designed to provide incentives to take care, their impact would be blunted by insurance. Since the offender's means are relevant to the assessment of criminal fines, and since they are payable to the state rather than to any victim(s) of the crime, there seems no good reason why they should be insurable, and good reason why they should not be, even if they carry no stigma. In this respect, criminal liability for negligence should be distinguished from civil liability for negligence. Because the main function of rules and principles of responsibility under the civil law paradigm is to justify the imposition of obligations of repair,

[60] Honoré (1995a), 88–90.
[61] i.e. by not insuring.

liability for negligence should be insurable even though negligence is culpable. By contrast, criminal law sanctions for negligent behaviour are not reparative, but deterrent (even if not retributive). The reason they should not be insurable is that this would be likely seriously to blunt their deterrent (and retributive) effects.

As for strict criminal liability, it was argued in 3.6.3.5 that punishing the faultless *is* objectionable, and that the better interpretation of fines levied in the absence of fault is that they are a sort of activity tax. If this is correct, then insurance against strict criminal liability seems unobjectionable on the basis that its likely effect would be to internalise the cost of liability to a risk pool defined in terms of the offending activity. Since taxation is a (re)distributive mechanism, there can be no objection in principle to spreading its burden amongst a group sharing tax-attracting characteristics with the taxpayer.

I have argued that the choice-based account of the relationship between liability insurance and responsibility under the civil law paradigm is inadequate because it ignores the main function of rules and principles of civil responsibility, namely to justify the imposition of obligations of repair. Its defect in relation to responsibility under the criminal law paradigm is analogous: it ignores the main function of rules and principles under that paradigm, namely to justify the imposition of retributive and deterrent sanctions (punishments and penalties). There certainly does seem to be a fundamental ethical inconsistency between these functions of rules and principles of criminal responsibility and tolerance of liability insurance. People should not be allowed to offload deserved punishments and penalties onto others who do not deserve it. So the fundamental question in this context concerns when the imposition of criminal sanctions is justified. For choice theorists, *mens rea* is a precondition of criminal sanctions being justified. Some people would say that negligence sometimes deserves a criminal sanction. In the view of many people, punishment cannot be justified in the absence of fault. To the extent that criminal sanctions can be imposed in situations where they cannot be justified, they should be (and in practice, typically are) interpreted as a sort of activity tax. The purpose of activity taxes is to regulate the incidence of the activity in question. So long as the tax is internalised to the relevant activity, there can be no objection to the spreading of the burden of the tax beyond the taxpayer personally.

7.5 CONCLUSION

The purpose of this chapter has been to consider the relationship between judge-made rules and principles of responsibility—"the law in the books"—and certain practices through which those rules and principles are implemented—"the law in action" we might say. In various ways, the practices of settlement out of court, selective enforcement and liability insurance generate discrepancies between, on the one hand, what the law says about when people are responsible and about the sanctions that appropriately attach to that responsibility; and, on the other hand, the responsibility and sanctions that are actually realised and imposed. So far as settlement and selective enforcement are concerned, the general conclusion is that neither is, *per se*, objectionable in responsibility terms because responsibility is a resource, and the resource-holder is under no obligation to utilise that resource. This conclusion rests ultimately on the idea that responsibility rules and principles are social practices, and that they are best understood functionally. The basic functions of legal responsibility rules and practices are to justify the imposition of sanctions—reparative, retributive, restorative, and so on. Settlement and selective enforcement may be objectionable if they generate distributional injustice in the allocation of such sanctions. But the mere fact that the full potential of responsibility rules and principles to fulfil these functions is not realised is not, in itself, objectionable. However important corrective and retributive justice (for instance) may be, they are not worth pursuing at any cost to the achievement of other valued objectives.

So far as liability insurance is concerned, my relational and functional analysis concluded that it is not inconsistent with responsibility under the civil law paradigm—whether the responsibility is based on *mens rea* or negligence, or can arise without fault—because it furthers the primary reparative goal of civil law. By contrast, I concluded that liability insurance is inconsistent with the primarily retributive, expressive and deterrent functions of sanctions under the criminal law paradigm, but not with sanctions that are effectively activity taxes.

8

Responsibility in Public Law

8.1 THE PUBLIC LAW PARADIGM

THE MAIN SOCIAL function[1] of principles of responsibility under the civil law paradigm is to prevent and repair harm to individuals. Under this paradigm, the basic distributive question is how to balance the interest we each have in freedom of action against the interest we each have in security of person and property. The main social function of principles of responsibility under the criminal law paradigm is to punish and deter seriously unacceptable behaviour. Under this paradigm, the basic distributive question is more complex than that under the civil law paradigm. Against the interest we each have in freedom of action has to be balanced, on the one hand, the interest we each have in security of person and property; and on the other hand, society's interest in order and security. The importance of this social interest under the criminal law paradigm is reflected in the very small role played by victims in the criminal process, and also in the fact that not all crimes involve invasion of an individual's interest in security of person or property.

The social functions of principles of responsibility under the paradigm with which this chapter is concerned (which I shall call the "public law paradigm") are essentially similar to functions of principles of responsibility under the civil law and the criminal law paradigms—chiefly to prevent harm and deter certain types of conduct (see 8.4.3). But the distributive issue that the public law paradigm presents is different. The public law paradigm is centrally concerned with the performance of public functions.[2] On the one hand, public law deals positively with

[1] Their basic normative function is to justify the imposition of sanctions designed to achieve this social function. I have adapted the distinction between normative and social functions from Raz (1973).

[2] There are some serious complications lurking in the distinction between public (i.e. governmental) entities and public functions. A common view is that non-governmental entities may and do perform public functions, and that governmental entities may and do engage in non-public activities. According to this view, the province of public law should be defined in terms of public functions. Another view is that everything done by government is "public" in some sense because in everything it does, government's obligation is to serve the public interest: governments have no interests of their own. This approach finds expression in the Human Rights Act 1998, which applies to all activities of "public authorities"; but only to other actors to the extent that they are performing public functions (Oliver (1999), 226–7). The two approaches start from different points. The former ("British") approach rests on a principle of equality of government and nongovernment before the law, while the latter ("Continental") approach starts with the proposition that government should be treated differently from its citizens. The difference is further discussed later in this section, and in 8.3, 8.4.1 and 8.4.2.

the functions, structure, organisation and processes of public functionaries; and on the other hand, it is concerned negatively with regulating, controlling and reviewing the exercise of public functions by defining and enforcing the obligations of public functionaries. For present purposes we can define public functions as functions that are (meant to be) performed on behalf of and in the interests of the public (in the sense of society as a whole) rather than on the functionary's own behalf (self-interestedly), or on behalf of and in the interests of any particular individual or group.[3] Whether a function is public in this sense or not is a normative question. Least controversially public is the provision of certain "public goods", i.e. goods (in the sense of "benefits") that cannot effectively be provided to some without being provided to all[4], such as national defence.[5] The last twenty years have witnessed major changes in views about whether the provision of particular non-public goods—most notably, perhaps, public utilities such as gas, electricity, clean water and telecommunications—is a public function or not. Public law defines what are public functions for its purposes, and public law principles of responsibility provide an answer to the distributive question of how to balance the public's interest in the promotion of the public good through the performance of public functions,[6] against the interests of citizens in freedom of action, security of person and property, and the promotion of their well-being as individuals or as members of some group within society (as opposed to society as a whole).

Perhaps the most famous legal discussion of this question is that of the Victorian jurist, A.V. Dicey.[7] His basic view can be encapsulated as the "equality principle". Dicey believed that in its dealings with citizens, government should be subject to the same law as governed dealings between citizens amongst themselves. Thus, he argued that government should be liable to be sued for torts and breaches of contract (for instance) in the "ordinary courts". He was deeply opposed to a system (such as the French) in which public functionaries were judged according to special rules administered by special courts. His fear was that special laws could be and were used to justify privileges and immunities for public functionaries that were not also enjoyed by citizens. He apparently did not conceive of the possibility that special laws might be used to

[3] Similarly Sorell (2000), 91; Walzer (1973), 162–3. This definition is neutral as between the two views outlined in the previous note. Under the first view, functions are classified by their nature, whereas under the second view, only functions performed by non-government entities are so classified because all functions performed by government are public regardless of their nature. This latter view puts more weight on the distinction between the state and civil society than does the first view. It is, therefore, ironical that Oliver, who seeks to destabilise the public/private distinction, should be a proponent of the second view: Oliver (1999), esp 110–16.

[4] The classic discussion of public goods is Samuelson (1954). He defined them in terms of non-excludability and non-competitive consumption (one person's enjoyment of the good does not diminish anyone else's enjoyment of it). Subsequent work has emphasised non-excludability.

[5] A classic example of a public good the provision of which many people would consider not to be a public function is free-to-air television.

[6] However that interest is defined. The "public interest" is, of course, a highly contested concept.

[7] Dicey (1885).

impose additional obligations on public functionaries. Dicey's work was vulnerable to criticism on various grounds,[8] and despite its huge and continuing influence on public law thinking, many of his views are now deeply unfashionable. His genius lay in his ability to spot and clearly articulate fundamental issues. Of those he uncovered, that concerning whether and to what extent the law should treat government differently from the way it treats "citizens" is perhaps the most basic and important.[9]

Dicey's view of public law followed what (in 2.4.1) I have called the "private model" of the role of the courts in holding public functionaries accountable. According to this model, public law is primarily concerned with the basic distributive question of how to balance the public interest in the performance of public functions against the interests of individual citizens in freedom of action and security of person and property. The beneficiaries of public law principles of responsibility under the private model of the judicial role are individuals. By contrast, under what I have dubbed the "public model" of the role of the courts in holding public functionaries accountable, public law principles of responsibility protect the interests of the public and of sections of the public. Under this model, the distributive question is not how the costs and benefits of the performance of public functions should be divided between the public on the one hand, and individual citizens on the other, but rather how those costs and benefits should be divided between various sections of the public. Under this model, the "public interest" in the performance of public functions is conceived as a balance between various sectional interests; and public law principles of responsibility impose certain constraints within which public functionaries must operate in striking that balance.

The private model of the judicial role is reflected in the fact that public functionaries are, in general, liable to be sued for breaches of civil law. It is also reflected in the fact that individuals may have "standing" to enforce public law principles of responsibility through the courts. The public model of public law is reflected in the fact that groups (and individuals) may have standing to enforce public law principles of responsibility as representatives either of the public as a whole or of some section of the public.[10] Indeed, the law of standing provides a sort of litmus test of the extent to which public law principles of responsibility fit into the private or the public model of public law. For instance, in recent years there has been a deep ideological divide amongst members of the US Supreme Court over the extent to which interest groups should be accorded standing independently of a showing of injury suffered personally by individual members of the group.[11] English public law is arguably more willing to accord standing to groups than either side of the US debate.[12]

[8] Cosgrove (1980), chs. 4 and 5.

[9] On this issue he has modern supporters. See e.g. Harlow (1980); Hogg and Monahan (2000), iii, 1–4.

[10] Cane (1995).

[11] A recent illustration is *Friends of the Earth Inc* v. *Laidlaw Environmental Services Inc* (2000) 528 US 167.

[12] Cane (1995a).

The public law paradigm of responsibility, then, addresses two distributive questions: first, how to balance the public interest in the performance of public functions against the interests of individual citizens; and secondly, how to balance the (competing) interests of various sections of the public in the performance of public functions. The first aim of this chapter is to consider briefly what the law says about which functions are public—in other words, the province of public law. The second aim is to examine the way the law goes about answering the two distributive questions posed under the public law paradigm—in other words, to examine the grounds and bounds of public law responsibility. The third aim of the chapter is to explore the relationship between the law's approach to dealing with these distributive issues and non-legal ways of thinking about them. Before attempting these tasks, however, it is necessary to say something about the institutional framework of public law.

8.2 THE INSTITUTIONAL FRAMEWORK OF PUBLIC LAW

In a crude way,[13] it is possible to see legal principles of responsibility for conduct of individual citizens engaged in on their own behalf, or on behalf of other individual citizens ("private law"), as law made by the government to regulate the lives of the governed. One of the legal tasks of government is to provide principles of responsibility that determine how risks and costs generated by such conduct are to be distributed. By contrast, public law may be seen as law made by the government to regulate the performance of public functions. Not all public functionaries are government entities. For instance, non-government bodies are involved in regulation of financial and commercial activity. But government is the major repository of public functions, and non-governmental public functionaries can be viewed as delegates of government, at least in the sense that they are performing functions that could appropriately be performed by government. So public law can be viewed, in effect, as law made by government to regulate governmental activities. One of the legal tasks of government is to provide principles of responsibility that determine how risks and costs generated by the performance of public functions are to be distributed.

Addressing the potential for conflicts of interest and abuse of power inherent in this situation (in which those who wield power are also centrally involved in regulating its exercise) provides the rationale for various constitutional principles and ideals, including separation of powers, checks and balances, representative and responsible government, and the rule of law in its formal or procedural sense. Such principles and ideals are designed in large part to ensure that in exercising public functions, public functionaries do not seek to further their own personal interests, and that they do not (in arriving at a conception of what the public interest requires) give undue weight to the interests of some

[13] Crude because it suggests a simplistically positivistic theory of the nature of law.

section of society to which they belong, or with which they identify, or which they represent. Fundamental to understanding the public law paradigm of responsibility is an appreciation of the interaction between such constitutional fundamentals and the institutional architecture of government. Amongst polities there are, of course, various architectural styles, and my discussion will deal only with Westminster-style governmental systems.

In Westminster systems the relationship between the executive and the legislature is one of greater or lesser intimacy, while that between the executive and the legislature on the one hand, and the judicial branch on the other is one of considerable distance. Put crudely, in Westminster systems, the executive more or less controls the legislature. At the same time, compared with the executive, the legislature is relatively immune from control by the courts, even in polities that have a constitutionally entrenched bill of rights. There are more grounds on which actions of the executive can be challenged in court than on which acts of the legislature can be so challenged. This is because in a democracy, the main avenue of accountability for parliamentary legislation is to the people through the ballot box. The executive's control over the legislature provides it with opportunities, that it might not otherwise have, to cast over its activities the blanket of legislative immunity from review by the courts. Widely drafted statutory provisions excluding judicial review provide a good example.

The position of the courts vis-à-vis the executive is compromised by their ambiguous location in the architectural scheme of things. In relation to private law, the courts can, and typically are, seen as a more or less independent dispute-resolving and law-making facility provided by government for its citizens. In relation to public law, by contrast, the fact that the courts constitute a branch of government threatens their legitimacy in at least two ways. From the citizen's perspective, it raises a doubt about their impartiality as between citizen and government. From the perspective of the other branches of government, it raises the spectre of judicial usurpation of functions that rightly belong to them. An important device for dealing with the second of these threats is the trichotomous distinction between law, fact and policy. The role of courts in the constitutional order is to enforce (and, to a lesser extent, to make) law. By defining the category of "law" narrowly relative to "fact" and "policy", and by leaving the executive relatively free of control on matters of fact and policy, the courts attempt to minimise the risk of attracting accusations of overstepping the proper bounds of their constitutional role.

An argument often used by courts to justify defining their role, as reviewers of the performance of public functions, in terms of a relatively narrow concept of "law" is that there are other avenues of review available to enforce non-legal standards of propriety on government. In the discussion so far in this book, the highly institutionalised domain of law has been contrasted with the largely non-institutionalised domain of morality. As a picture of civil society, this account is accurate enough. Outside of the law, there are relatively few norm-enforcing institutions in civil society. In the public domain, by contrast, there is a plethora of institutionalised mechanisms for policing compliance with non-legal norms.[14] There is, no doubt, a domain of public "morality" that is devoid of institutions of the types that are characteristic of law. But there is, in between public law and public morality, a normative domain in which formal institutions of various sorts play significant policing and enforcement functions. We might collectively call them "institutions of non-legal accountability", and their job that of "enforcing norms of non-legal responsibility". The most venerable, and in constitutional terms, the most important, of such institutions is parliament in its guise as scrutineer of government conduct under the principles of "responsible government" and "ministerial responsibility". In Westminster systems, ombudsmen tend to operate under this umbrella as agents of parliament, as do general audit offices.[15]

The upshot is that whereas in the context of civil society, legalisation of norms is the most important technique for engaging formal institutional mechanisms of policing and enforcement, in the public realm law has various competitors for "regulatory space". A major argument of this book so far has been that law and morality chiefly differ not in terms of the account they respectively give of what it means to be responsible, but rather in terms of what obligations they respectively impose. The same point holds, I would argue, in the public realm. The various normative sub-systems, both institutionalised and non-institutionalised, found there establish different sets of obligations (prospective responsibilities), but operate with a common store of concepts of what it means to be responsible. It follows that the focus of analysis in this chapter will be on the grounds and bounds of responsibility in public law, not on what it means to be responsible.

8.3 THE PROVINCE OF PUBLIC LAW

I have defined the province of public law in terms of the concept of public functions. I have defined public functions as functions that are judged as being appropriately performed on behalf of the public rather than on behalf of the functionary or of some particular individual or group. It is because public functions are so judged that they are seen to raise questions about how risks and costs generated by their performance should be distributed between the public and citizens on the one hand, and between various sections of the public on the other hand. This definition of public functions and of the province of public law is not intended as an account of the currently relevant law in any jurisdiction, and here is not the place to attempt to give such an account. For one thing, the distinction between public and private functions is used in various contexts, and it is by no means clear that the distinction is drawn in the same way in all of

[14] See e.g. Hood et al. (1999).

[15] See e.g. White and Hollingsworth (1999).

those contexts. The definition is simply an attempt to identify the criterion that seems to provide the ultimate foundation of the distinction between public and private functions. For present purposes, three comments will suffice.

First, because the criterion of publicness is a normative one, the basic issue it addresses is whether the function in question is appropriately performed in a representative capacity by the functionary on behalf of the public. For purposes of legal principles of responsibility, the basic issue is whether performance of the function in question appropriately raises a question about how risks and costs generated thereby should be distributed between the public and citizens, and between various sections of the public. Not all functions performed by government are public in this sense. In other words, for the purposes of legal responsibility, not all conduct of public functionaries is treated as being done in a representative capacity on behalf of the public. For instance, if a civil servant driving a car on government business negligently injures a pedestrian, the legal liability of the driver and, vicariously, of the government, will be assessed according to the same rules of tort law as would apply if the driver had been a citizen driving the car for their own purposes. In other words, the case will not be seen as appropriately raising an issue about how the costs of the accident should be distributed between the public and the injured pedestrian. Rather, the driver and the government will be treated in law as having been acting on their own behalf and not on behalf of the public, and the distributive issue will be how to distribute the costs of the accident between the pedestrian and the driver/employer. There is obviously a sense in which a civil servant driving a car on government business is acting on behalf of the public, if only because the activity is funded out of the public purse. But the question in the present context is whether what is being done is judged appropriately to raise an issue about how the costs of the activity should be distributed between the public and citizens or between sections of the public.

The second point to make is this. It has often been observed that some commercial corporations have larger turnovers than some nation-states, and that their activities can affect the public or sections of the public just as much as, if not more than, some of the activities of governments. And yet, the activities of such corporations are treated, for purposes of legal responsibility, as private rather than public. The suggestion here is that because such activities affect large numbers of people in significant ways, they should be treated by the law as public, i.e. as being conducted on behalf of the public and as appropriately raising issues about the distribution of their costs between the public and individuals, and between sections of the public. In other words, the argument is that when engaged in commercial activities that affect large numbers of people, corporations should be treated as public functionaries.

In assessing such arguments, several factors seem relevant. On the one hand, there are obvious and significant differences between the sort of commercial activities that proponents of such arguments have in mind and governmental activities. For one thing, the activities of private commercial corporations are typically not funded out of the public purse; and for another, commercial corporations do not have access to state mechanisms of coercion in aid of achieving their objectives. On the other hand. although such factors play an important part in supporting classification of certain functions as public, for responsibility purposes the critical issue is whether the function in question is seen as appropriately raising the distributive issues already mentioned. Nor is the fact that the functionary is not a governmental body in any way conclusive against classification of its functions as public. The performance of functions that are uncontroversially public may be delegated to non-government bodies, and there is no logical reason why a function that has never been performed by government should not be treated as public if its performance is thought appropriately to raise the distributive issues that are distinctive of public functions. Because the concept of "public function" is a normative one, commercial activities of non-governmental corporations could be treated as public. If they were, distributing risks and costs generated by such activities would be seen as raising issues of distribution as between the public and individual citizens, and as between sections of the public, as opposed to issues of distribution as between individual and individual.

The third point to be made about the province of public law is this: in the past twenty years in various countries, many activities carried on by government functionaries have been transferred to non-government entities through privatisation and outsourcing. In relation to some of these activities, many public lawyers have seen this process as one of transferring the performance of public functions from a government to a non-government functionary. Consequently, they have argued, public law principles of responsibility should continue to govern the performance of such functions. By contrast, the ideology underlying at least some of these developments has, I believe, rested on a conviction that the functions in question are not appropriately classified as public, and that their performance is not appropriately subjected to public law principles of accountability. This difference of opinion is, of course about a normative question; and for the purposes of legal responsibility, it is for the law to decide how the question should be answered in relation to any particular function. It goes without saying that the fact that a particular function was once, but is no longer, performed by government does not determine its character as public or private any more than the fact that a particular function has never been performed by government determines its character. To repeat yet again, the legal criterion of publicness is a function of certain distributional issues.

8.4 GROUNDS OF PUBLIC LAW RESPONSIBILITY

8.4.1 Civil liability

Historically, government enjoyed various protections from civil liability for torts, breaches of contract, and so on. But now the common law's starting point is perhaps more accurately described as a principle of equality.[16] In its pure form, the equality principle states that the government should be subject to the same liability rules as its citizens. The principle has two limbs: government should enjoy no immunities from or defences to liability not also enjoyed by citizens; and government should be subject to no liabilities to which citizens are not subject. However, the principle is rarely stated in this pure form. It is typically qualified by the words "as nearly as possible" or the like. The basic justification for the qualification is that government may legitimately coerce citizens to act or refrain from acting in ways determined by the government in order to further community goals at their expense. This legal power of legitimate coercion is not possessed by any ordinary citizen, no matter how great their *de facto* power over other citizens may be. Government is different from its citizens in having power which they do not have, and in having responsibilities to the community as a whole which they do not have. The phrase "as nearly as possible" recognises that in order to control the exercise of the legitimate coercive powers of government we may be justified in imposing certain liabilities on government which do not also rest on its citizens; and that in order to enable it to fulfil its responsibilities to society as a whole, we might be justified in relieving government of certain liabilities to which citizens are subject. The phrase also indicates, however, that departures from the equality principle ought to be the minimum necessary to achieve an acceptable level of control over the exercise of government power consistently with giving government sufficient freedom to further the public interest.

Expanded in this way, it becomes clear that equality before the law is a formal principle. It instructs us to treat government in the same way as citizens are treated to the extent that government is the same as its citizens; but beyond that, to treat it differently. Under the equality principle, actual equality of treatment is not the ideal to be aimed at. The goal is the "right" mix of equal and unequal treatment.

The equality principle has traditionally been stated as being concerned with the relative legal positions of government on the one hand, and citizens on the other. One of the most important developments of the last thirty years in thinking about public law is the realisation that there is a difference between what might be called "the tasks of government", on the one hand, and what governments actually do, on the other. The "tasks of government" are those tasks that are thought appropriately performed on behalf of the public—what I have earlier called "public functions". We now understand that not everything that governments do is done in performance of public functions, and that not all public functionaries are government entities. It follows, I think, that the equality principle must be rephrased in terms of "public functionaries" rather than in terms of "government". Public functionaries have powers and obligations that do not

[16] Allars (1996). In England, the pivotal incident in the change of direction was the enactment of the Crown Proceedings Act in 1947. The process began much earlier in Australia: Aronson and Whitmore (1982), ch. 1.

attach to things done in performance of "non-public" functions (whether by citizens or government); and one way of recognising this is to make appropriate modifications to the way that rules and principles of civil liability (that were developed in a non-public context) apply to the performance of public functions.

Here it is neither necessary nor feasible to explore in detail the way legal rules and principles of civil responsibility are modified in their application to public functionaries. A few examples will suffice. In the law of contract, the doctrine of executive necessity may provide a public functionary with a defence to a claim for breach of contract.[17] It is in the law of tort that the implications of the equality principle have been given most attention. There, various technical devices have been utilised to protect public functionaries from civil liability. One is the rule that breach of a statutory duty is not actionable in tort unless the duty was designed to protect individuals rather than the public generally. Another is the recognition of immunities. Judges and magistrates enjoy wide or even total immunity from tort liability in exercising their judicial functions; and police officers enjoy wider freedom from tort liability for arrest than do ordinary citizens.[18] In the tort of negligence, the concepts of "proximity" and "justice and reasonableness" have been utilised to create immunities from civil liability by denying the existence of a duty of care.[19] At the level of standard of care, public functionaries may be protected by requiring them to meet a lower standard of reasonable conduct than is demanded of ordinary citizens (so-called "*Wednesbury* unreasonableness": 3.3.1.3). Each of these devices provides a conceptual framework for distributing risks and costs generated by performance of public functions differently from those of non-public activities.

On the other side of the coin, there is one traditional head of tort liability that only applies to the performance of public functions, namely misfeasance in a public office.[20] Liability for this tort can attach only to conduct that is unlawful in the public law sense—see 8.4.3—and so it can be seen as creating a ground of legal liability to which the conduct of citizens is not subject. However, it seems that liability can arise under this tort only if the agent knew that their conduct was unlawful or, at least was aware that it might be unlawful; and only if the agent intended to harm the victim or, at least, was aware that their conduct created a risk of harm. In other words, this is a *mens rea* tort, requiring either intention or recklessness in relation both to the quality of the conduct in question and to the harm caused. As a result, the tort imposes no more onerous obligations than do "non-public" torts, such as intimidation, that require unlawful conduct

[17] Seddon (1999), §§ 5.2–5.9

[18] This is because police officers have wider powers of arrest than do ordinary citizens. But ever since the famous case of *Entick* v. *Carrington* (1765) 19 St Tr 1030 the law of tort has played an important role in protecting citizens against unlawful interference with person and property by public officials.

[19] Cane (1996a), ch. 12.

[20] The antecedents of this head of liability can be found in the famous right-to-vote case of *Ashby* v. *White* (1703) 2 Ld Raym 938.

and *mens rea*. More importantly, perhaps, repeated attempts by litigants to persuade courts to abandon the *mens rea* requirement, so that misfeasance in a public office would generate liability (simply) for causing harm by conduct unlawful in the public law sense, have failed. Courts have apparently taken the view that such a development would be inconsistent with a basic tenet of English law that damages are not available as a remedy for public law illegality "as such".[21]

Damages have traditionally been seen as a "private law" remedy, i.e. as a remedy for harm caused by non-public activity. There is a strong bias in public law in favour of preventative as opposed to reparative remedies—mandatory and prohibitory orders and "quashing" of potentially harmful decisions, as opposed to compensation. In general, unless the harm done by a public functionary is actionable as a tort, breach of contract or other private law wrong, the law will not compensate for it. The unavailability of damages as a remedy for breaches of public law (as such) generates one of the most important distributional differences between public law and private law responsibility regimes. It imposes a significant temporal limit on the enforceability of public law principles of responsibility: once harm has been done, effective legal remedies cease to be available (unless the harm is actionable in private law).

Courts have not clearly spelled out reasons for the bias against damages in public law, and elsewhere I have argued that it is difficult to justify.[22] There have been important developments in recent years suggesting that the bias is weakening. Most significantly, perhaps, human rights documents may contain provision for the payment of compensation to persons whose rights have been infringed. Human rights are traditionally conceived of as rights against government, and they are designed precisely to protect the interests of individuals against those of the community as a whole, and of minorities against those of the majority. In other words, a central function of human rights documents is to adjust the distribution of risks and costs generated by the performance of public functions favourably to individual citizens and minority groups. To the extent that human rights are enforceable by citizens against public functionaries but not against other citizens,[23] this development represents the imposition of greater obligations on public functionaries than rest on those conducting non-public activities. On the other hand, to the extent that citizens may suffer harm as a result of unlawful performance of public functions that would not qualify as breach of a human right, the development falls short of providing a cause of action for compensation for harm resulting from the unlawful performance of public functions.

Finally, some words about attribution of responsibility for torts committed by public functionaries. An element of every tort is human conduct. If a non-human

[21] Cane (1999b). The damages liability of Member States for breaches of European law is liability for public law illegality as such.

[22] Cane (1996b).

[23] Oliver suggests that English courts will develop a "family of constitutional torts", such as invasion of privacy, actionable only against public authorities: Oliver (1999), 177, 237–8.

entity, such as a corporation, or the state, is to be held liable for a tort, this must be on the basis of attribution to it of conduct of a human being.[24] The legal rules of attribution were discussed in chapter 5 in the context of constructing the legal responsibility of groups. The basic rule is that an employer is "vicariously" liable for the torts of its employees committed in the course of employment, while the employee is "personally" liable. In general, this rule applies even when the employee is a public functionary, and even when the employer is the state. There is a rule that an employer is not vicariously liable for torts committed by an employee exercising an "independent discretion".[25] Its basis is obscure, but it seems to rest on the idea that employees who exercise public functions (such as police officers) are not subject to the detailed control of their employer in doing so. At all events, the rule was widely criticised in the second half of the twentieth century, and it has been abolished, or its scope has been limited, by statute in many jurisdictions. At least in relation to government employees, it certainly seems strange to argue that the employer should not be vicariously liable for the torts of an employee on the basis that the employee, in performing a public function, was serving the public, not the employer. After all, the employer *is* the public, at least in the sense of representing and acting on behalf of the public. Even where the employer is not a government entity, so long as the public function is a function of the employer, it seems right that the employer should be vicariously liable, even if the employee enjoys considerable operational freedom. The obligation of the employer and, hence, of the employee, is to exercise the function in the public interest, not in the interest of either the employee or the employer.

The rule that public functionaries are personally liable for torts committed by them in the course of exercising their functions[26] follows from the combined application of the equality principle and basic concepts of personal responsibility. Hogg speaks approvingly of "powerful symbolism" in the equal treatment of "public and private employees".[27] By contrast, Pannam argues that personal liability of public employees was developed to overcome the traditional immunity of government from tort liability, and that it only makes sense against that (now-vanished) background.[28] Although the personal liability of employees remains the basic rule in the private employment context, there are signs of unease. The related rule, that the employer held vicariously liable has a right of indemnity against the employee, has been subjected to judicial and statutory encroachment.[29] The Supreme Court of Canada has held that a contractual clause limiting the liability of the employer for negligence also protects the

[24] Similarly: Hogg and Monahan (2000), 13–15.

[25] Trindade and Cane (1999), 720; Hogg and Monahan (2000), 125–7.

[26] Government employees are, of course, also personally liable for torts committed in the course of employment even if the tort was not committed in the exercise of a public function; and the (government) employer is vicariously liable for such torts.

[27] Hogg (1989), 145.

[28] Pannam (1966).

[29] Trindade and Cane (1999), 744–5.

employee.[30] One of the judges (La Forest J) went further and argued that in "commercial" contexts, the employee should be immune from liability for negligence, and that the employer alone should be liable for torts committed by employees in the course of employment. It is not uncommon for public employees to be protected by statute from personal liability for torts committed in "*bona fide*" performance of their functions. Such clauses are designed to protect public employees exercising public functions.[31] However, if the employee is not liable personally, the employer cannot be liable vicariously. Unless the statutory provision preserves the liability of the employer, there will be no-one the victim can sue. Such a result runs contrary to the spirit of the decision of the House of Lords that in principle, the government can be sued vicariously for misfeasance in a public office.[32] If the law is prepared to hold the government liable for deliberate wrongdoing by its employees in exercise of public functions, it should surely not allow it to escape liability for *bona fide* exercise of those functions.

The problem here lies in conceptualising the liability of the government for performance by its employees of public functions as being vicarious rather than personal (or "direct").[33] Treating the government's liability for tortious exercise of public functions as direct would involve imposing the obligation to perform public functions non-tortiously on the government rather than on its human functionaries, in the same way that the duty to provide safe tools rests on the employer and not on the person to whom the task of providing safe tools is delegated. In the case in which the US Supreme Court first awarded damages for breach of the Constitution by a federal agent,[34] the court overcame a statutory provision protecting the agent from personal liability by imposing direct liability on the government.[35] If the liability of the employer for torts committed by public functionaries were conceptualised as direct rather than vicarious, it could extend even to purely self-interested conduct by public functionaries committed under cover of their public office. Such conduct might fall outside the scope of vicarious liability by reason of being insufficiently related to the performance of the function—outside the scope of the functionary's employment, in traditional terms. Holding employers of public functionaries directly liable even for self-interested abuse of the functionary's position could be justified as an appropriate distribution of the costs of the performance of public functions as between the public and individual citizens. Even if it is not considered fair that an employer should be held liable for conduct of a rogue employee purporting to act on the employer's behalf, it may be considered fair in the case of a rogue employee purporting to act (as the employer is obliged to act) on behalf of the public.

[30] *London Drugs Ltd* v. *Kuehne & Nagel* [1992] 3 SCR 299.

[31] Trindade and Cane (1999), 715–16; Kneebone (1998), 244–59.

[32] *Racz* v. *Home Office* [1994] 2 AC 45.

[33] See 5.4.3.4.

[34] *Bivens* v. *Six Unknown Named Agents of the Federal Bureau of Narcotics* 403 US 388 (1971).

[35] The New Zealand Court of Appeal acted similarly in *Simpson* v. *Attorney-General (Baigent's Case)* [1994] 3 NZLR 337.

Concerns about the fairness of imposing liability on employees for torts committed in the course of employment well illustrate the importance of observing the distinction between responsibility and liability. Relieving the employee of legal liability does not negative their personal responsibility; but there may be good reasons why personal responsibility should not be translated into legal liability. Conversely, it might be thought that the best arguments for direct liability of employers of rogue public functionaries are not based on principles of responsibility, but on ideas of fair distribution of the costs of the performance of public functions.

8.4.2 Criminal liability

Traditionally, there was only one "public tort"—misfeasance in a public office—that could be committed only by a public functionary;[36] and there is no head of tort liability that can only be committed against a public functionary. In criminal law, the picture is quite different. There is a significant number of criminal offences that can only be committed by public functionaries.[37] Examples are corruption offences, and offences involving the disclosure of secret information obtained in the course of public employment. There are also offences that can only be committed by military personnel, such as desertion and mutiny.[38] An important function of such offences is to punish and deter self-interested conduct by public functionaries. Criminal liability is the most severe and serious form of legal liability, and it is particularly appropriate in relation to self-interested abuse and exploitation of their power and position by public functionaries.

On the other hand, there are offences that can only be committed against the public. In this regard, it is useful to distinguish between interests that are directly protected by the criminal law, and interests that are indirectly protected. Offences such as murder and rape, for instance, directly protect an interest in personal security, but they also indirectly protect society's interest in order and security. "Victimless" crimes, such as "possession" offences, attempts, and so

[36] The damages liability of Member States for breaches of EC law may be conceptualised as a form of tort liability; and damages liability for human rights violations is often referred to as liability for "constitutional torts".

[37] This section deals only with municipal law. International criminal law is in a rather rudimentary state of development. The best-established international crimes are "war crimes", and these are typically committed by public functionaries purportedly acting on behalf of their "citizens". Such crimes, as well as so-called "crimes against humanity", are committed against individuals in their capacity as members of social or ethnic groups, or nations. To date, prosecutions for such crimes have been against individuals. Firm, clear principles of state responsibility for crime are yet to be established: Bassiouni (1980), 7–12. See generally Bassiouni (1986–7), Weiler et al. (1989). For more recent consideration see Abi-Saab (1999), Gaja (1999) and Pellet (1999), Jørgensen (2000) and Balint (2001), 140–2. For some reflections on the public/private distinction in international law see Chinkin (1999).

[38] Many of these crimes are statutory. For an account of common law crimes that can be committed only by public functionaries see Finn (1978).

on, indirectly protect society's interest in order and security. Offences of the type I have in mind here directly protect some interest of the public, and indirectly protect society's interest in order and security. Examples include treason, espionage, bribery of public functionaries, electoral offences, social security fraud, evading taxes, assaulting law enforcement officers, interference with the administration of justice, and so on. The criminal law may also directly protect the public interest through the sentencing process. For instance, under the New South Wales Crimes Act 1900 the maximum penalty for assault occasioning actual bodily harm is five years' imprisonment (section 59); but for assaulting a police officer in the execution of duty thereby occasioning actual bodily harm, the maximum penalty is seven years' imprisonment (section 60(2)). In such a case, the basic five-year penalty can be seen as directly protecting the victim's interest in bodily security and indirectly protecting the public's interest in order and security; and the two-year premium can be seen as directly protecting the public's interest in the performance of a public function.

Not only are there heads of criminal liability designed to protect the integrity of the performance of public functions, but there are also circumstances in which conduct that would constitute a criminal offence if done by a citizen will not attract criminal liability if done by a public functionary.[39] For instance, law enforcement officers have legal powers (of summary arrest, for instance) that narrow the scope of their potential criminal liability for violence to the person relative to that of ordinary citizens. Public functionaries may also enjoy immunity from criminal liability for offences committed in the course of officially authorised covert operations.[40]

In short, the public interest in the proper performance of public functions is directly protected by a dense web of criminal offences directed against both conduct of citizens and conduct of public functionaries. On the other side of the coin, the public interest in the effective performance of public functions (such as law enforcement) is also protected by selectively shielding public functionaries from criminal liability. However, beyond that shielded area, public functionaries are subject to the criminal law in precisely the same way as citizens. For instance, there are many offences—most particularly, regulatory offences—that apply equally to government and to citizen, by virtue of the fact that government engages in many activities that citizens also engage in. Not all of the activities of government involve the exercise of public functions. Government bodies may commit environmental offences in their capacity as property owners; and they may commit health and safety offences in their capacity as employers.[41] The equality principle is of even greater constitutional importance in this context than in relation to civil liability.

[39] For a discussion and a proposal for reform of the law concerning the liability of law enforcement officials (as opposed to ordinary citizens) for the use of force see Rogers (1998).

[40] See e.g. Australian Commonwealth Crimes Act 1914, s. 15I.

[41] We can, for present purposes, leave aside the special position of the Crown, as to which see Hogg and Monahan (2000), 313–17.

Criminal liability for the performance of public functions is predominantly personal, i.e. it rests on individual public functionaries, not on their employers. It is important to distinguish two different issues here. The first concerns the construction of one person's criminal liability out of the criminal responsibility of another. Unlike the position under the civil law paradigm, there is no general principle of vicarious liability for criminal offences, and vicarious criminal liability is rare. The second issue concerns the construction of group legal responsibility by the attribution to abstract entities of the criminal conduct or the criminal responsibility of a human being. All crimes involve human conduct, and if non-human public functionaries are to be held criminally liable, this must be on the basis of attribution of the criminal conduct or responsibility of a human being. More particularly, if "government" is to be held criminally liable, whether for crimes designed to protect the integrity of the performance of public functions, or for other crimes, this must be on the basis of the conduct of some human being acting on behalf of the government. The construction of group criminal liability was discussed in detail in chapter 5, and there is no need to reiterate the discussion here. The question that must be addressed is whether the fact that a crime is committed in the course of performing a public function, or is committed by a public employee in the course of employment, requires a different approach to the relationship between personal liability on the one hand, and vicarious or group responsibility on the other, than the one adopted in the non-public context in the earlier discussion.

Central to answering this question must be a recognition of the agent-oriented nature of responsibility under the criminal law paradigm . Under the civil law paradigm, vicarious liability is the basic rule because the focus of that paradigm is on reparation of harm, and vicarious liability increases the chance that harm will be repaired by providing the victim of a breach of civil law with an additional target. From this point of view, if the possibility of suing the tortfeasor is of no practical importance (because the party vicariously liable is in a better position to repair the harm), the fact that the party primarily responsible for the harm (the tortfeasor) may never be held legally liable is of no great moment. By contrast, the focus of the criminal law paradigm of responsibility is on expressing disapproval of and deterring unacceptable conduct. From this perspective, it seems much more important that the agent be held criminally liable, at least in addition to the agent's principal. At the same time, where the criminal conduct occurred within the course of the agent's employment (as this phrase is understood in the civil law of vicarious liability), it might be thought of considerable symbolic and political importance that the principal should not be allowed to disassociate itself from the criminal activity. It is all to easy for political superiors to disown responsibility for what is done in their name, or in the name of the public, and leave an individual public agent to take the rap.

Dennis Thompson argues against government criminal liability for conduct of public employees on the basis that in order to justify punishing the government, we would have to treat it as a moral agent, just like its citizens. But if we did that, he says, we would have to accord to government the sort of freedom of action we accord to citizens. In particular, we would have to free government from the constraint of justifying everything it does in terms of the public interest.[42] Thompson's argument is a complex one. It rests on the idea that governments have no "private life"; or, as Oliver puts it, that government has no interests of its own.[43] So whereas, for citizens, everything that is not prohibited by law is permitted, for government, nothing is permitted that is not authorised by law. As a formula for determining the rights and powers of government, this dictum has obvious attractions. But in the context of responsibility, it seems to imply that we must give up the equally attractive principle of reciprocity that underpins the equality principle. In order to make the point more concrete, consider the case of government contracting. There is certainly a case for arguing that government should not enjoy such extensive freedom of contract as the citizen, and that its exercise of the power to make contracts should always be constrained by the requirements of the public interest. On the other hand, there is also a case for arguing that when government breaches a contract, it should be liable as if it were a citizen, unless it can positively justify what it did in terms of the requirements of the public interest. In other words, the position in relation to powers and rights on the one hand, and responsibilities on the other, is not symmetrical. The same arguments that support a presumption against equality in the former context support a presumption in favour of equality in the latter.

From my point of view, there is another objection to Thompson's argument, which is that it rests on what, in chapter 5, I called the humanistic approach to group responsibility. Thompson believes that in order to justify subjecting government to criminal responsibility, we must treat it as a moral person. On the contrary, I would argue that if there are good functional reasons to hold the government liable for crimes committed by its agents, we are justified in doing so. The powerful functional case for government criminal liability is that it makes it harder for governments to offload on to individual public agents responsibility for what is done in the name of the government or the public. In fact, Thompson is not opposed to the imposition of sanctions on government organisations that are implicated in criminal activity; but he thinks that such sanctions should not be seen as punishment but as "political" measures that need not respect the same constraints, and do not carry the same stigma, as punishments. Downgrading a sanction from the criminal to the political category is a serious matter, and hardly justified by what seems to me the unnecessary and unjustified conclusion that if government is to be treated like its citizens in respect of criminal responsibility, it must be accorded the same powers and rights as citizens. In reality, the desirable position is that in respect both of powers and rights and of responsibilities, government should be treated in some respects like its citizens and in other respects differently.

[42] Thompson (1985), 225–6.
[43] Oliver (1999), 112–16.

Why is the criminal law much more heavily implicated in the legal control of the performance of public functions than the civil law? The answer, I think, lies in the fact that the public law paradigm of responsibility is, like the criminal law paradigm, agent-focused. Public law is centrally concerned with the exercise of public power. This explains why damages have not traditionally been seen as a remedy for breaches of public law—the main function of principles of responsibility under the public law paradigm (as we will see in 8.4.3) is to ensure that public functions are performed in accordance with law, not to repair harm done by misperformance or nonperformance of public functions.[44] Public law differs from criminal law in respect of available sanctions and also by virtue of the fact that whereas criminal law is normally enforced by the state, the former is normally enforced by citizens. Under rules of "standing", citizens may seek to enforce public law in order to protect their own personal interests (under the private model of the judicial role in holding public functionaries accountable) or as representatives of the public as a whole or of some section of the public (under the public model). Rules of standing, which define the interests that are protected by public law, are separate from, rather than integral to, the grounds of public law responsibility, which set limits on public power. This marks an important contrast between the public law paradigm and the civil law paradigm. Under the latter, principles of responsibility define not only the conduct to which responsibility attaches, but also the interests they protect. This contrast reflects the different focus of the two paradigms—civil law on repair of harm and public law on ensuring that public powers are not exceeded or abused. The development of damages as a public law remedy involves re-orientation of the focus of public law away from control of public power as such, to the repairing of harm resulting from abuse and excess of public power.[45]

8.4.3 Judicial review

The archetypal proceeding for the enforcement of civil law responsibility is the claim for damages by one citizen against another. The archetypal proceeding for enforcing criminal law responsibility is the prosecution of a citizen by the state. The archetypal proceeding for enforcement of public law responsibility is the application by a citizen for judicial review of a decision of a public functionary. The judicial function involved in judicial review is the supervisory function. Oliver describes this function in terms of:

[44] "Public law is not at base about rights, even though abuses of power often do invade private rights; it is about wrongs—that is to say, misuses of public power": *R* v. *Somerset County Council, ex parte Dixon* [1998] Env LR 111, 121 per Sedley J.

[45] Heightened emphasis on reparation in this context may be compared with the increased concern for victims of crime that underpinned important developments of the latter half of the twentieth century, such as criminal injuries compensation schemes and the restorative justice movement. Both may be seen as part of a larger change in social and legal attitudes to and norms of responsibility.

> "identifying the limits of the powers of bodies, especially those which interfere with the liberties of individuals or with broad public interests, and laying down the rules for the exercise of decision-making powers".[46]

The main sanctions available in judicial review proceedings are orders to prohibit the carrying out of an illegal decision, orders requiring a functionary to act in accordance with the law, orders "quashing" an illegal decision (i.e. depriving it of legal effect), and declarations of the legal rights, powers and duties of the functionary.[47] Public law sanctions are referred to as "remedies", indicating that like civil law sanctions, they are designed to provide some benefit to the applicant for judicial review. On the other hand, like criminal law sanctions, they do not directly address harm suffered by the applicant, but rather the nature and quality of the respondent's (i.e. the defendant functionary's) conduct. Responsibility under the public law paradigm is a sort of hybrid of civil law and criminal law concepts of responsibility.

It is neither necessary nor desirable to provide here a detailed account of the grounds of public law responsibility. A short summary will suffice. The grounds of public law responsibility are based on a set of principles of good decision-making. They can be divided roughly into two categories, procedural and substantive. The substantive grounds are traditionally conceptualised in terms of a trichotonomous distinction between issues of law, issues of fact and issues of policy. A decision of a public functionary may attract public law sanctions if it is based on an error of law, an error of fact or a policy mistake. Policy mistakes are understood in terms of striking a wrong balance between competing interests in the subject-matter of the decision being challenged. The procedural category must be understood broadly. The so-called rules of natural justice are designed to avoid conflicts of interest and to secure participation of affected parties in decision-making processes.[48] There are various grounds of judicial review that regulate the basis on which decisions are made. Decision-makers must not "fetter" their decision-making power by agreeing in advance to make a particular decision without reference to all relevant circumstances existing at some later time. On the other hand, a decision-maker must not act inconsistently by treating like cases differently. A functionary to whom a decision-making power has been allocated must not allow someone else to make the decision either actually or effectively. Decisions must be justifiable in terms of the purposes for which the decision-making power exists, taking account of relevant considerations and ignoring irrelevant ones.

The main function of rules and principles of responsibility under the public law paradigm is to set legal boundaries to the exercise of decision-making powers by public functionaries. Looked at from the other side, as it were, their

[46] Oliver (1999), 25.

[47] Cane (1997a).

[48] On the importance of procedure in non-legal ideas of decision-making legitimacy see Tyler (1990).

function is to create protected spaces within which public functionaries are free to make what they consider to be the best decision in the public interest. Public functions, it will be recalled, are functions that are meant to be performed on behalf of and in the interests of the public, not in the interests of the functionary or of particular individuals or groups within society. In 8.4.2 it was argued that the criminal law plays an important part in protecting the public from self-interested abuse of power by public functionaries. Principles of judicial review also play a part here—self-interested exercise of a public decision-making power would fall foul of the rule that irrelevant considerations must be ignored. But in practice, principles of judicial review are more centrally directed against the exercise of public decision-making powers in the interests of particular individuals or groups within society. Rules directed against the pursuit of "improper purposes", the taking into account of "irrelevant considerations" and the making of "unreasonable" decisions all play a part in securing that in formulating a conception of the public interest, public functionaries do not give undue weight to the interests of particular individuals or groups.

Guarding against favouritism to a particular group is of special importance. The grounds of public law responsibility that are directed to this end do not, as such, apply to parliamentary legislation. This exemption is an aspect of parliamentary legislative supremacy. Competing visions of the public interest entail different distributions of risks and resources as between various sections of society. In party-based democracies, political groups compete for the right to favour certain groups in society over others by giving effect to one particular vision of the public interest, primarily through legislation. Subject to constitutional constraints, the main mechanism of accountability for the way this power is used is the electoral process. By contrast, in administering the law (and in making subordinate legislation) the basic obligation of the government is to give effect to the balance between the interests of various social groups that has been struck in legislation. The administrative process is at one remove from democratic accountability through the ballot box, and so public law principles of responsibility constrain administrators from the sort of favouritism to particular groups that can only be legitimised through elections. Another way of making this point is in the language of "agency". In an important sense, the legislature is agent of the public, and administrators exercising public functions are agents of the legislature. The public controls its agent through the electoral process, while compliance by administrators with the terms of their agency is enforced by a variety of mechanisms, one of which is public law. The rules and principles of judicial review can be interpreted as a technique for enforcing the terms of their agency against public functionaries.[49]

Because public law principles of responsibility mark boundaries within which public functionaries must operate, most grounds of judicial review generate strict liability. For instance, it is no answer to a claim for a judicial review remedy on

[49] Bishop (1990).

the ground that a decision-maker made an error of law, for the decision-maker to say that the error was made without fault. The only ground of judicial review that rests on a notion analogous to concepts of fault in civil or criminal law is that of "unreasonableness" and its relative "proportionality". These grounds entail that the decision-maker failed to weigh the competing interests affected by the decision according to an objective standard.

The various principles of judicial review are seen as appropriate and desirable constraints on the exercise of public decision-making power. This is not to say that all of these principles are exclusively applicable to decision-making by public functionaries. As Oliver shows, the origins of some of these principles can plausibly be traced to non-public contexts, and in recent times some have been applied to decision-making by one citizen affecting another (in the area of employment, for instance).[50] Oliver concludes on this basis that there are no distinctive constraints on the exercise of public decision-making power; in her words, that there is no public-private divide. This conclusion is both descriptively hyperbolic and normatively problematic. There can be no objection to requiring citizens to be "considerate" (as Oliver puts it)[51] in exercising power over other citizens in areas such as employment. It remains true, however, that the constraints embodied in the grounds of judicial review are peculiarly appropriate and necessary constraints on the exercise of public power because public power is underwritten by the state's monopoly of legitimate coercive power.

Julia Black's discussion of self-regulation is suggestive in this regard.[52] Self-regulation of economic and social activity is, in many instances, an activity of such public importance that it should be conducted in accordance with (at least some) principles of considerate decision-making even if, in particular instances, it is not underwritten by the coercive power of the state. If it is so underwritten, there is a strong case for subjecting it to the full range of public law constraints, even though it is not conducted by government officials. Principles of responsibility under the public law paradigm constrain the exercise of the state's monopoly of legitimate coercion. But the limits of that coercion do not mark the outer boundary of public law because some activities are of such public importance and impact that they are rightly subjected to (at least some) principles of public law even if they are not underwritten by state coercion.

This argument also suggests why some government activities should be subject to the same principles of responsibility as apply in dealings between citizen and citizen. When a government department makes a contract for the purchase of paper clips (for instance), enforcing performance of the contract by the supplier is, and should be, no more underwritten by state coercive power than it would be

[50] Oliver (1999). The analogies between public law principles and the law of trusts (Oliver (1999), 187–94) have been emphasised in recent decisions of the High Court of Australia, especially by Gummow J. See, for instance, *Bateman's Bay Local Aboriginal Land Council* v. *Aboriginal Community Benefit Fund Ltd* (1998) 194 CLR 247.

[51] Oliver (1999), 200.

[52] Black (1996).

if the purchaser were a private individual or corporation. Principles of public law become relevant and essential when government claims to be entitled to use the strength that comes from monopoly control of legitimate coercive power to force citizens to behave in ways that other citizens could not lawfully force them to behave, or to resist a claim by a citizen that another citizen could not lawfully resist. Collapsing the distinction between public law principles of responsibility and private law principles of responsibility threatens the vitality of an essential protection for citizens against the monopolistic coercive power of the state.

8.5 BOUNDS OF PUBLIC LAW RESPONSIBILITY

8.5.1 Civil liability

Historically, certain government entities—most notably the Crown—enjoyed immunity from tort liability on what might be called "constitutional" or "political" grounds. The twentieth century saw the demise of this type of immunity. Now, to the extent that public functionaries are protected from tort (and other forms of civil) liability by immunities, they are functionally based. For instance, so-called "good faith" clauses, that provide immunity for "*bona fide*" exercise of statutory functions, have been interpreted as applying only to the exercise of what I have called "public functions".[53] Judges enjoy wide immunity from tort liability for things said and done in the course of exercising their judicial functions. This immunity does not protect judges *qua* judges, but as officials performing a function that is thought to require a degree of protection from potential interference by third parties that justifies immunity from the risk of being sued (let alone being held liable) in tort.

Functionally-based immunities from and defences to civil liability claims play two main roles. One is to protect public functionaries from liability to pay damages. Decisions that are immunised from civil liability may not be protected from challenge by means of judicial review. In such cases, the importance of protection from civil liability lies in the remedies that only civil liability can provide, notably damages. The other main function of protections for public functionaries from civil liability is to mark the boundaries of law as a source of monetary recompense. Governments typically run various more or less formalised *ex gratia* compensation schemes, and complaint to an ombudsman may yield monetary recompense even if the ombudsman has no power to order that it be paid, but only to recommend payment. In short, immunities from civil liability should not be interpreted as based on a judgment that public functionaries should be unaccountable, but only that civil law principles of accountability are not the appropriate ones, either because of the content of the principles, or because of the remedies that attach to them, or because of some characteristic of the bodies—the courts—that enforce those principles.

[53] Kneebone (1998), 244–59.

As regards the last of these considerations, there are three main characteristics that are typically seen as generating significant limitations on the appropriateness of court-administered rules and principles of responsibility: expertise, procedure and constitutional function. Courts define the areas of their special expertise in terms of making and applying law and of finding facts. To the extent that complaints about decisions made by public functionaries cannot be characterised as concerning law or fact, courts are less willing to entertain such complaints. The limitations of adversarial court procedure for dealing with multi-faceted, "polycentric" issues of "policy" provide another reason for judicial restraint in reviewing public decisions.[54] Thirdly, constitutional notions of separation of powers suggest that when one branch of government "checks and balances" the activities of another, it should take care not to usurp the power of the other. The constitutional task of holding another branch accountable is fundamentally different from acting as a "surrogate" of that other branch.

A basic point to observe here is the important distinction between responsibility and liability. The fact that public functionaries may be protected from legal liability for harm caused by the performance of public functions does not mean that they do not bear responsibility for that harm. However, legal liability is only one mechanism for enforcing responsibility for such harm, and there are other institutionalised mechanisms in the public realm that may be available to fulfil this function. There are more non-legal institutions of accountability in the public realm than in civil society. The institutional geography of the public realm is an important factor in setting the bounds of the legal liability of public functionaries.

8.5.2 Criminal liability

Although the law recognises that the public interest justifies giving public functionaries some protection from the criminal law that applies to citizens as such, there is a background unwillingness to create significant areas where the criminal law does not run. So, for instance, although courts generally recognise the right of parliament to regulate its own internal affairs, this does not extend to dealing with criminal offences committed within the curtilage of parliament. Neither "the Crown"[55] nor ministers of the Crown[56] enjoy immunity from criminal liability by virtue of their status.

8.5.3 Judicial review

For present purposes, the bounds of responsibility under the public law paradigm can be treated as coincident with the bounds of judicial review. The function of

[54] Allison (1994).
[55] *Cain* v. *Doyle* (1946) 72 CLR 409.
[56] *Connor* v. *Sankey* [1976] 2 NSWLR 570, 599–600 per Street CJ.

the boundaries is to regulate the relationship between the courts and the other branches of government on the one hand, and between legal and non-legal accountability on the other. First, concepts such as "non-justiciability" and "political questions" are used to mark out issues of policy which are thought completely unsuitable for judicial consideration by way of judicial review of administrative action. Conversely, some concept such as "maladministration" is used in contradistinction to "illegality" to define the jurisdiction of ombudsmen. Secondly, there are limits related to the timing of judicial review. Public law claims are, of course, subject to time limits (limitation periods). In addition, there are various rules that serve to ensure that judicial review applications are not made prematurely in such a way as to deprive the decision-maker of a full opportunity to resolve the case.[57] Another relevant idea is that because the prime judicial function is to resolve disputes, courts should be wary of making purely advisory statements of law in anticipation of a dispute or after any dispute has been resolved.[58]

Thirdly, the concept of standing is of central importance in defining the scope of accountability via judicial review. Rules of standing determine who may enforce public law rules and principles of responsibility. "Narrow" rules of standing allow public law to be used to protect the interests of individuals against undue harm and encroachment resulting from the exercise of public functions. "Broad" rules of standing allow public law to be used to protect groups and the public generally against abuse and excess of public powers. Whereas the grounds of public law responsibility define public law illegality, the rules of standing define the interests protected against public law illegality. The practical and ideological importance of the distinction between narrow and broad standing rules can be well illustrated by reference to actions designed to secure the proper enforcement of environmental law by regulators. Whereas broad standing rules may enable the beneficiaries of environmental regulation (citizens) to use the courts to challenge decisions (or inaction) by regulatory agencies, narrow rules tend to allow only the subjects of regulation ("polluters") access to the judicial process.

Fourthly, statutory ouster clauses may impose significant limits on the use of law to control the exercise of public functions. In England, courts have tended to interpret such clauses narrowly in order to minimise their negative impact on the scope of judicial review, on the basis of a principle that citizens' access to the courts is of fundamental constitutional importance. Ultimately, however, in the absence of constitutionally entrenched limitations on the power of the legislature to oust judicial review, courts must give effect to clearly worded statutory provisions, even if their effect is to immunise administrative decisions from being judicially reviewed.

The effect of these various boundary principles is not to negative responsibility according to public law principles, but to block the enforcement of those

[57] Beatson (1998).
[58] Cane (1997a), 265–8.

principles—in other words, to block liability. In some cases, this may produce an accountability vacuum, but in many cases the effect is to create space for other accountability mechanisms to operate. Of course, alternative mechanisms may themselves be less than perfect, and this may influence judicial thinking about the appropriate scope of judicial review. For instance, the relative ineffectiveness of ministerial accountability[59] to parliament in Westminster systems sometimes plays a part in judicial reasoning in favour of expansive rather than restrictive enforcement of public law principles of responsibility.[60]

The most important general point arising from this discussion is that the bounds of liability for breaches of public law principles of responsibility are primarily a function of judgments about what might generically be called "comparative institutional competence". In private law, this idea plays a role in defining the grounds of responsibility. For instance, the so-called "Bolam" test of professional negligence[61] rests on a judgment that lawyers (i.e. judges) should be hesitant about setting standards of sound medical practice (for instance). Similarly, in public law, the so-called "*Wednesbury*" test of unreasonableness[62] rests on a judgment that courts should be hesitant to interfere with the policy decisions of executive government. In these cases, the effect of considerations of comparative institutional competence is seen in the adoption of relatively "permissive" standards of responsibility. In this section we have seen how ideas of comparative institutional competence underpin rules and principles that limit the area of operation of legal principles of responsibility rather than "watering down" those principles.

8.6 PUBLIC LAW RESPONSIBILITY AND "THE PROBLEM OF DIRTY HANDS"

In this final section of the chapter I want to consider what light, if any, the discussion so far can shed on the relevance of the public/private distinction in the moral domain. Public functionaries have powers that permit and enable them to give effect to their conception of the public good. Public law imposes certain constraints on the exercise of public powers. Public law principles of responsibility are agent-focused in the sense that their main concern is to limit and control the making of decisions by public functionaries. In this respect, the focus of the public law paradigm of responsibility is different from that of the civil law paradigm, the prime concern of the latter being with preventing and repairing harm. On the other hand, the public law paradigm of responsibility is agent-focused in a different sense from that in which the criminal law paradigm is

[59] For a careful analysis of the role of fault in the doctrine of ministerial responsibility see Woodhouse (1994), Part Two. Uncertainty and imprecision of the rules and principles of ministerial responsibility (Woodhouse (1994), 284–5) illustrate a relative disadvantage of accountability regimes that lack the institutional resources of the legal system.

[60] Woodhouse (1994), 277–80.

[61] Trindade and Cane (1999), 454–5.

[62] Cane (1996a), 208–12.

agent-focused. Criminal law principles of responsibility are primarily concerned with individual agency—with what it means to be human and to possess free will. By contrast, the public law paradigm of responsibility focuses on processes and institutions of social decision-making. It places certain constraints on public functionaries that are designed to prevent them ignoring or giving too little weight to certain interests (of individuals and groups) in formulating their conception of the public interest. This difference is reflected in the fact that liability under the public law paradigm is generally strict. The public law paradigm is less concerned than either the criminal law paradigm or the civil law paradigm with the rights and interests of individuals as agents and victims, and more with the aggregate good of society—the "public interest".

In this way, the public law paradigm of responsibility resonates with a persistent theme in the philosophical literature dealing with the ethics of public life. This theme is that consequentialist considerations play, and rightly play, a larger part in practical reasoning in public life than in interactions between individuals. The most famous proponent of this idea was Macchiavelli. Macchiavelli's approach is open to two competing interpretations.[63] One is that doing the best for the public interest sometimes requires public functionaries to act immorally.[64] Another is that "there is a specific morality appropriate to political activity and that its deliverances outweigh considerations of 'ordinary' or 'private' morality".[65] Modern theorists tend to prefer the latter approach. Robert Goodin, for instance, argues that utilitarianism is best understood as a statement of what morality requires at the social as opposed to the individual level;[66] and Thomas Nagel argues that private morality is much more "agent-centred" than public morality.[67]

It may be, however, that this is a false dichotomy bred of a failure to distinguish two distinct issues. We have seen that public law has two concerns. One is whether and how principles of responsibility (under the civil law and criminal law paradigms) that were developed to regulate interactions between individuals need to be modified when applied to conduct of public functionaries acting as such. Public law gives public functionaries certain immunities from civil and criminal liability, and it does this on the basis that sometimes the demands of the public interest require and justify the infliction of harm on individuals that would not be acceptable if inflicted in the name of the agent's individual interests. As we have seen, such legal immunities from civil and criminal liability do not negative responsibility. The position in "morality" is analogous. We may be prepared to contemplate behaviour for the sake of the public interest that would not be acceptable if done to further the agent's own interests—to allow public

[63] Coady (1991).

[64] A problem with this interpretation is that it apparently assumes that "morality" is only concerned with "private life": Coady (1991), 374.

[65] Coady (1991), 374.

[66] Goodin (1995), ch. 1. The same basic idea is developed in a very different way in Kaplow and Shavell (2001).

[67] Nagel (1978); Hampshire (1978), 49–50.

functionaries to "dirty their hands", as the saying goes. But the behaviour does not cease to be regrettable.[68] The force of the immunity from principles of interpersonal responsibility lies precisely in the recognition of a normative dilemma; and the dilemma does not disappear by being resolved in one way or the other.

The second concern of public law is how to limit and control decision-making by public functionaries acting as such. In this context, using principles of responsibility developed with reference to interpersonal transactions as a benchmark for the conduct of public functionaries seems less than satisfactory. In deciding how to exercise their public powers, we want and expect our public functionaries to cast their gaze beyond the impact of their actions on particular individuals, and to aggregate the costs and benefits across different sectors of society. Indeed, we demand of our public functionaries an impartiality that is inconsistent with attending to the impact of their decisions on specific individuals. The same is true in the ethical domain. Deciding what is best for the group as a whole requires the downgrading of the interests of individuals that would be quite unacceptable in dealings between individual and individual.

In ethics, as in law, there are two strands in our thinking about politics and public life. One is that public functionaries should be subject to the same rules of behaviour to which they subject their citizens. The other is that for the sake of society as a whole, public functionaries must be free to treat citizens in ways that citizens should not be free to treat each other. It is with this balance between the individual and the social perspectives that public law and the ethics of public life are both concerned.

Some people—both lawyers and others—would argue that the dichotomy between public and private life is a false one. Oliver, for instance, maintains that the values to which public law principles of responsibility give expression also underpin rules of law that regulate dealings between citizens.[69] Similarly, Coady argues that certain "moral situations", to which principles of "public morality" are relevant, may occur in many areas of life, and not just the political.[70] Legal objections to the public/private dichotomy rest, to some extent at least, on a desire to promote the application of public law principles to the performance of certain functions regardless of whether they are performed by government or by non-government entities, and even regardless of whether their performance is publicly funded or underwritten by state coercion.[71] Coady, by contrast, sees the critical characteristic of political activity as being its "collaborative" nature. This seems to me to get close to the heart of the matter, although I would put the point slightly differently. Politics is pre-eminently an activity concerned with social life as opposed to interpersonal life. The central question in politics is how to do the best for society. The interests of individuals and social sub-groups operate as side-constraints on public decision-making, whereas the interests of

[68] Walzer (1973) makes a similar argument.
[69] Oliver (1999).
[70] Coady (1991).
[71] Black (1996).

individuals are central to practical reasoning at the interpersonal level. Treating individuals as "statistics" is acceptable and desirable in public decision-making to an extent that it is not in interpersonal transactions.

While prime concern with the social is central to politics, it is not unique to it. In "ordinary life" we often have to make decisions, on behalf of a group and about the life of the group, that will affect individual members of the group differently, and some more beneficially (or detrimentally) than others. Such situations raise ethical questions analogous to those that arise in political life. This is why principles of responsibility analogous to those at work in public law (and morality) can seem appropriate to situations that may arise outside politics. For instance, principles of fair procedure that are primarily identified with public law have also been applied to decisions about membership of private groups such as trade unions. It does not follow from this that no distinction should be drawn between public and private life, public and private morality, public and private law. Although public decision-making is but a species of the genus "social decision-making", it is perhaps the most important species and the species the exercise of which most needs to be carefully and closely controlled. Three reasons may be suggested in support of this conclusion. First, the group affected by political decision-making is typically larger and more heterogeneous than groups affected by social decision-making in the non-political realm. Secondly, public decision-making is funded by money raised by compulsion. Thirdly, the decisions of public functionaries are underwritten by state coercion.

8.7 CONCLUSION

Principles of responsibility under the civil law and criminal law paradigms were developed primarily in the context of interpersonal relations. In terms of what it means to be responsible, principles of responsibility under the public law paradigm can be explained in terms of concepts developed in those paradigms. What distinguishes the public law paradigm of responsibility is its prime focus on society. Public law principles of responsibility are ultimately directed to protecting the interest that all citizens share in the well-being of their society, and to balancing this against the interests of citizens in freedom of action, security of person and property, and the promotion of their well-being as individuals and as members of groups within society.

In the last part of the chapter I used the analysis of principles of responsibility under the public law paradigm and of the relationship between the public law paradigm on the one hand, and the civil and criminal law paradigms on the other, to offer a new perspective on the philosophical debate about the distinction between public and private morality and the problem of "dirty hands". I suggested that the tension found in public law between subjecting public functionaries to the same rules of responsibility as govern the lives of citizens and treating them differently is also found in our thinking about the ethics of public life.

9

Thinking about Responsibility

WHAT DOES IT mean to say that we are responsible, and what are our responsibilities? Although these two questions have received much attention in this book, the point of the project has not been to provide answers to them. Doing this would require a library of books. Rather my aim has been to suggest fruitful ways of thinking about answering them. In this final chapter I want briefly to restate the approach to thinking about responsibility that has been adopted in this book. This is worth doing because it can usefully be applied to analysing not only responsibility but also other "complex concepts" (see 1.1.1), such as right, duty and property, that are used in practical reasoning both in the law and outside it.

The analysis of responsibility in this book is underpinned by seven interrelated methodological recommendations. The first is to think about responsibility *socially*—i.e. as a set of social practices of taking responsibility and of holding people responsible—rather than naturalistically. Naturalistic thinking about responsibility, as I understand it, implies that if we look hard and long enough, we will discover "the truth" about what it means to be responsible and about what our responsibilities are. The recommendation to think about responsibility socially does not involve a rejection of this view, or an assertion that study of social practice can tell us all there is to know about responsibility. I am agnostic about this. My view is simply that in the absence of agreement as to what the truth about responsibility is, social practice provides us with an extensive and extremely rich data set about responsibility. By observing social responsibility practices, we are able to explore aspects of responsibility (such as sanctions) which rarely, if ever, receive detailed consideration in the methodologically naturalistic literature.

The second recommendation is to think about responsibility *contextually* rather than abstractly. One of the most significant developments in legal scholarship in the latter half of the twentieth century was the "law in context" movement.[1] An intellectual premise of work in this genre (a premise now so widely accepted that its novelty in the late 1960s is hard to recapture) is that law should not be viewed as an autonomous universe of discourse or a closed analytical system, but as part of the normative life of a society. The founders of the movement identified as one of the defects of much legal scholarship of the time an excessive abstractness and lack of awareness of and sensitivity to the relationships between legal doctrine—"the law in the books", as it was often referred to—and

[1] Twining (1991).

the operationalisation of that doctrine in the legal system, and its impact on society more widely—"the law in action". The law in context movement was the English version of American legal realism, and part of a larger intellectual trend that also manifested itself in "post-modernist" writings in other disciplines such as philosophy and history. Of course, these trends have not swept all before them. In particular, much that is written about responsibility today is analytical and abstract; and a significant proportion of legal literature (both academic and practitioner-oriented) is of the analytical "black-letter" variety. But at least it can be said that many flowers are blooming in the methodological landscape.

"Context" is, of course, an extremely vague term. All I mean to convey by it is that much can be gained by thinking about responsibility in relation to a particular society and a particular time, and in relation to particular social activities and problems, and particular value systems. My approach does not entail the view that responsibility can only be understood contextually, and that there is nothing to be learnt from contextually indeterminate abstract analysis of responsibility or from careful analysis of legal doctrine. I do assert, however, that we cannot learn all there is to know about responsibility without thinking about it contextually. A useful analogy can be drawn with "human rights". A degree of abstractness and universality is fundamental to the very idea of human rights. At the same time, the idea that social context can be ignored in deciding concrete issues about human rights is, at least, highly controversial. It follows from my approach that the analysis of responsibility in this book should not be treated as making claims larger than can be justified by reference to its chosen context.

Thirdly, a central recommendation of this book is to think about responsibility *legally*. Law has institutional resources (for the making, interpretation, application and enforcement of rules and principles of responsibility, and in its literature) that non-legal responsibility practices lack; and many issues of responsibility that can be left unresolved in daily life must be confronted when they enter the legal system. I recommend that careful attention be paid to legal responsibility practices not primarily because of their content, but because of the institutional features of the law. Looking at responsibility from a legal perspective is fruitful not because of the answers the law gives to the questions, "what does it mean to say we are responsible?" and "what are our responsibilities?". Rather, studying the law directs our attention to aspects of these questions (such as the relationship between responsibility and sanctions) that are often not discussed in non-legal analyses of responsibility.

Emphasising the institutional features, as opposed to the substance, of legal responsibility practices has led me to characterise "morality" in institutional terms. From this perspective, the important differences between law and morality lie in the way each comes into existence and is recorded, and in the way each is interpreted, applied and enforced. This, of course, is very different from the approach to morality which sees it as a source of ultimate values—as opposed to law, which is conventional. It is not part of my argument that there are no ultimate responsibility values, no "truth" about what it means to be responsible and about what our responsibilities are. Nor is it part of my argument that morality does not embody such truths. Rather, my argument is that in the absence of agreement about what moral responsibility is and what our moral responsibilities are, it is not sensible to treat the relationship between morality and law as that of critical standard to conventional practice, or to assume that when the law clashes with moral views about responsibility, the truth must lie in the moral as opposed to the legal position. In support of this view I have argued that there are important similarities between moral and legal reasoning about responsibility, and that the relationship between law and morality is symbiotic. Assuming that there are ultimate truths about responsibility, this book has challenged the view that these truths are more likely to be found in non-legal social practices than in the law, or in theoretical, non-contextualised reflection on the human condition than in social responsibility practices.

Fourthly, I recommend thinking about responsibility *functionally*. Both within the law and outside it, concepts and principles of responsibility do not exist (purely) for their own sake but as part of a complex set of practices of taking responsibility and holding responsible. Even if it makes sense to conceive of responsibility independently of any purpose it serves, many important aspects of responsibility can be perceived only by viewing responsibility teleologically. From this perspective, there is no single answer to the questions of what it means to be responsible and what our responsibilities are. Because concepts and principles of responsibility serve various functions, there are various functionally specific answers to these questions. The functions of responsibility can be described in a number of ways. In 2.5 I suggested a fourfold analysis in terms of ontological, explanatory, normative and evaluative functions. The normative function correlates with the question of what our responsibilities are (chapter 6). The explanatory function correlates with the issue of causation (chapter 4); and the evaluative function correlates with the idea of historic responsibility (2.1.1 and 2.1.2). By reason of law's institutional resources, legal practices can throw considerable light on all of these functions and can supplement extra-legal understandings of responsibility in all of these areas.

In particular, I have stressed the value of studying legal responsibility practices for the light they cast on the relationship between responsibility and sanctions, and between what it means to be responsible and the determination of whether, in particular circumstances, individuals are responsible in this sense for their conduct and its consequences. In law, the main function of rules and principles of responsibility is to justify the imposition of punishments and obligations of repair, and the awarding of remedies and reparations. Fairness in the performance of this function requires fair rules and procedures for determining what people's responsibilities are and for allocating historic responsibility. Determination of historic responsibility in particular cases and the allocation of sanctions are often seen as "practical matters" that have little to do with the truth about responsibility. My argument is that approaches to responsibility that marginalise or ignore these issues are not only incomplete but also morally deficient. Law provides an excellent case study for understanding these aspects of responsibility. For instance, by attending to the distinction between responsibility and liability (to incur sanctions), it was possible to cast light upon the relationship between responsibility and culpability in the moral domain (3.6.3.5).

Fifthly, I have recommended thinking about responsibility *relationally*. Much of the legal and philosophical literature about responsibility is agent-focused. This suggests a view of responsibility as a state in which atomised human individuals may find themselves. Perhaps the largest dividend of thinking about responsibility legally is to alert us to the fact that it is about human relationships, not about humans as isolated agents; and perhaps the biggest pay-off from thinking about responsibility functionally is to show us that it has as much to do with repairing adverse outcomes as with punishing bad conduct. This insight is primarily expressed in the distinction I have drawn between the civil law and the criminal law paradigms of responsibility. It is impossible to understand many of the features of legal responsibility (and, hence, of responsibility more generally) without acknowledging that responsibility is not only about the relationship between agents and their conduct, but also about the relationship between agents and the outcomes of their conduct. Viewed against the background of criminal law, the relationship between responsibility and outcomes is problematic because notions of responsibility in criminal law are significantly agent-focused—surprisingly so given that the *actus reus* of the typical crime consists of conduct and its outcome, not conduct alone. But viewed against the background of civil law, the idea that we could understand what it means to be responsible and what our responsibilities are without reference to outcomes is obviously ridiculous.

There is very little theoretical literature, either legal or philosophical, about responsibility that takes account—let alone proper account—of the importance of outcomes. This is because most of this literature takes criminal responsibility as the paradigm not only of legal responsibility but also of moral responsibility. For what it is worth, my view is that whatever the "truth" about responsibility, it is impossible, having observed the distinction between civil law and criminal law and taken it seriously, to think that all there is to know about responsibility resides in exclusively (or even predominantly) agent-focused theories of responsibility.

Sixthly, I have recommended thinking about responsibility *distributionally*. This point is a corollary of drawing the distinction between what it means to be responsible, on the one hand, and what our responsibilities are, on the other. Answers to the second question are often left out of theories of responsibility. This phenomenon is reflected, for instance, in the distinction between the so-called "general part" of the criminal law, concerned with "responsibility", and the "special part", which tells us what sorts of conduct are criminal. It is also reflected in the concentration on issues of capacity and intentionality in philosophical discussions of responsibility. Within such frames of reference, it is relatively easy (although deeply unsatisfactory) to ignore distributional issues and to account for responsibility in terms of agent-focused ideas such as retributive justice, and in terms of corrective justice, which is the traditional antithesis of distributive justice. But as soon as the question of what our responsibilities are is factored into an account of responsibility, it is impossible to ignore the way rules and principles of responsibility distribute risks, rights and obligations amongst individuals and groups. Viewed functionally, responsibility is itself a resource that people can use to protect their interests, and the way that resource (and, conversely, the burden of responsibility) is distributed is an important part of any account of responsibility. In chapter 8, for instance, I argued that the distinction between public and private law (and between public and private morality) is explicable not in terms of the issue of what it means to be responsible, but in terms of what our responsibilities are.

Finally, in chapter 7 I recommended thinking about responsibility *operationally*. This perspective is a corollary of and supplements the functional approach to responsibility. Acceptance that responsibility concepts and practices have functions prompts questions not only about the fit between the content of concepts and principles of responsibility and those functions, but also about the extent to which those functions are realised in practice. Adopting this perspective on responsibility also supplements the distributional approach because questions about the enforcement of responsibility raise issues of distributive justice. But the matters discussed in chapter 7 are important even if a purely non-functional, naturalistic approach is taken to responsibility. It is difficult to see why we should be interested in responsibility at all unless it has some point. The desire to understand the truth about responsibility grows, one assumes, out of a need or a desire to discover the meaning of life and what it means to be human. From that perspective it surely matters how and to what extent concepts of responsibility are realised in our lives. If responsibility matters, then it matters whether and to what extent our lives are regulated in conformity with it.

These seven recommendations for thinking about responsibility are the product of a lawyer's reflection on the rich and varied philosophical and theoretical literature about responsibility. They offer ways of getting the most out of taking law seriously in the search to understand responsibility. Of course, taking law seriously cannot tell us all there is to know about responsibility, if for no other reason than that the functions of responsibility in law are not all of the functions of responsibility. Most particularly, law has nothing to say, directly at least, about the ontological function of responsibility. It may be that naturalistic, agent-focused accounts of responsibility are most valuable for the contribution they can make to our understanding of responsibility as a component of personal identity. If this is so, it would explain the limitations of such accounts, and it would reinforce the value of looking to the law to enrich our understanding of functions of responsibility that find detailed and elaborately documented expression there.

References

ABI-SAAB, G. (1999), "The Uses of Article 19" 10 *European J of International Law* 339–51

ALEXANDER, J.C. (1991), "Do the Merits Matter? A Studty of Settlements in Securities Class Actions" 43 *Stanford LR* 497–598

ALLARS, M. (1996), "Tort and Equity Claims Against the State" in P.D. Finn (ed.), *Essays on Law and Government, Vol 2: The Citizen and the State in the Courts* (Sydney), 49–100

ALLISON, J. (1994), "The Procedural Reason for Judicial Restraint" *Public Law* 452–73

ARENELLA, P. (1989), "Character, Choice and Moral Agency: the Relevance of Character to our Moral Culpability Judgments" 7 *Social Philosophy and Policy* 59–83

—— (1992), "Convicting the Morally Blameless: Reassessing the Relationship between Legal and Moral Accountability" 39 *UCLA LR* 1511–1622

ARONSON, M. and WHITMORE, H. (1982), *Public Torts and Contracts* (Sydney)

ASHWORTH, A. (1987), "Defining Criminal Offences Without Harm" in P. Smith (ed.), *Criminal Law: Essays in Honour of J.C. Smith* (London) 7–23

—— (1993), "Taking the Consequences" in S. Shute, J. Gardner and J. Horder (eds.), *Action and Value in Criminal Law* (Oxford)

—— (1994), *The Criminal Process: An Evaluative Study* (Oxford)

—— (1996), "Driving Up the Tariff" 8 *Archbold News* 5–8

—— (1998), *The Criminal Process: An Evaluative Study* (Oxford)

—— (1999), *Principles of Criminal Law* (Oxford, 1999)

—— (2000), *Sentencing and Criminal Justice,* 3rd edn. (London)

—— and BLAKE, M. (1996), "The Presumption of Innocence in English Criminal Law" *Criminal LR* 306–17

ATIYAH, P.S. (1981), *Promises, Morals and the Law* (Oxford)

—— (1986), *Essays on Contract* (Oxford)

—— (1995), *An Introduction to the Law of Contract*, 5th edn. (Oxford)

—— (1997), *The Damages Lottery* (Oxford)

AUSTIN, R.P. (1998), "Corporate Groups" in R. Grantham and C. Rickett (eds.), *Corporate Personality in the 20th Century* (Oxford)

BAIER, K. (1970), "Responsibility and Action" in M. Brand (ed.), *The Nature of Human Action* (Glenview, Ill), 100–16

BALINT, J. (2001), "Law's Constitutive Possibilities: Reconciliation and Reconstruction in the Wake of Genocide and State Crime" in E. Christodoulidis and S. Veitch, *Lethe's Law: Justice, Law and Ethics in Reconciliation* (Oxford) 129–49.

BANDALLI, S. (1998), "Abolition of the Presumption of *Doli Incapax* and the Criminalisation of Children" 37 *Howard Journal of Criminal Justice* 114–23

BASSIOUNI, M.C. (1980), *International Criminal Law: A Draft International Criminal Code* (Alphen aan den Rijn)

—— (1986–7), *International Criminal Law, Vol 1 (Crimes)* (Dobbs Ferry); *Vol 2 (Procedure)* (Dobbs Ferry); *Vol 3 (Enforcement)* (Dobbs Ferry)

BEATSON, J. (1998), "Prematurity and Ripeness for Review" in C. Forsyth and I. Hare (eds.), *The Golden Metwand and the Crooked Cord: Essays on Public Law in Honour of Sir William Wade* (Oxford), 221–52
BEAUMONT, J. (2000), "Mistake and Strict Liability—Part I" *New LJ* 382–3
BELL, J. (1983), *Policy Arguments in Judicial Decisions* (Oxford)
BENSON, P. (1999), "Contract" in D. Patterson (ed.), *A Companion to Philosophy of Law and Legal Theory* (Oxford), 24–56
BISHOP, W. (1990), "A Theory of Administrative Law" 19 *J of Legal Studies* 489–530
BLACK, J. (1996), "Constitutionalising Self-Regulation" 59 *Modern LR* 24–55
BLACKMAN, D.E. (1981), "The Mental Element in Crime and Behaviourism" in S. Lloyd-Bostock (ed.), *Law and Psychology* (Oxford) 113–25
BODENHEIMER, E. (1980), *Philosophy of Responsibility* (Littleton, Colorado)
BOVENS, M. (1998), *The Quest for Responsibility: Accountability and Citizenship in Complex Organisations* (Cambridge)
BRAITHWAITE, J. (1982), "Challenging Just Deserts: Punishing White-Collar Criminals" 73 *J of Criminal L and Criminology* 723–63
—— (1987), "Negotiation versus Litigation: Industry Regulation in Great Britain and the United States" *American Bar Foundation Research J* 559–74
—— (1999), "Restorative Justice: Assessing Optimistic and Pessimistic Accounts" 25 *Crime and Justice: A Review of Research* 1–127
—— and ROCHE, D. (2001), "Responsibility and Restorative Justice" in G. Bazemore and M. Schiff (eds.), *Restorative Community Justice: Repairing Harm and Transforming Communities* (Cincinnati), 63–84
BRATMAN, M. (1987), *Intentions, Plans and Practical Reason* (Cambridge, Mass)
BROWNLIE, I. (1998), *Principles of Public International Law*, 5th edn. (London)
BRUDNER, A. (1987), "A Theory of Necessity" 7 *Oxford J Legal Studies* 339–68
—— (1993), "Agency and Welfare in the Penal Law" in S. Shute, J. Gardner and J. Horder (eds.), *Action and Value in Criminal Law* (Oxford), 21–53
BURROWS, A.S. (1983), "Contract, Tort and Restitution—A Satisfactory Division or Not?" 99 *Law Quarterly R* 217–67
—— (1993), *The Law of Restitution* (London)
CALABRESI, G. (1975), "Concerning Cause and the Law of Torts: An Essay for Harry Kalven Jr" 43 *U of Chicago LR* 69–108
CANE, P. (1982), "Justice and Justifications for Tort Liability" 2 *Oxford J of Legal Studies* 30–62
—— (1995), "Standing up for the Public *Public Law* 276
—— (1995a), "Standing, Representation and the Environment" in I. Loveland (ed.), *A Special Relationship? American Influences on Public Law in the UK* (Oxford), 123–50
—— (1996), *Tort Law and Economic Interests*, 2nd edn. (Oxford)
—— (1996a), *An Introduction to Administrative Law* (Oxford)
—— (1996b), "Corrective Justice and Correlativity in Private law" 16 *Oxford J of Legal Studies* 471–88
—— (1996c) "Exceptional Measures of Damages: A Search for Principles" in P. Birks (ed.), *Wrongs and Remedies in the Twenty-First Century* (Oxford), 301–25
—— (1997), *The Anatomy of Tort Law* (Oxford)
—— (1997a), "The Constitutional Basis of Judicial Remedies in Public Law" in P. Leyland and T. Woods (eds.), *Administrative Law Facing the Future: Old Constraints and New Horizons* (London), 242–70

—— (1998), "Retribution, Proportionality, and Moral Luck in Tort Law" in P. Cane and J. Stapleton (eds.), *The Law of Obligations: Essays in Celebration of John Fleming* (Oxford), 141–73

—— (1999), *Atiyah's Accident, Compensation and the Law*, 6th edn. (London)

—— (1999a), "Multiple Torts, Contribution and the Dynamics of the Settlement Process" 7 *Torts LJ* 137–54

—— (1999b), "Damages in Public Law" 9 *Otago LR* 489–517

—— (2000), "Fleeting Mental States" *Cambridge LJ* 273–83

—— (2000a), "Mens Rea in Tort Law" 20 *Oxford J of Legal Studies* 533–56

—— (2000b), "Fault and Strict Liability for Harm in Tort Law" in W. Swadling and G. Jones (eds.), *The Search for Principle: Essays on Honour of Lord Goff of Chieveley* (Oxford), 171–206

—— (2001), "The Temporal Element in Law" 117 *LQR* 5–10

—— (2001a), "Responsibility and Fault" in P. Cane and J. Gardner (eds.), *Relating to Responsibility: Essays for Tony Honoré on his Eightieth Birthday* (Oxford), 81–110

—— (2001b), "Distributive Justice and Tort Law" (manuscript on file with author)

CARTWRIGHT, P. (2001), *Consumer Protection and the Criminal Law* (Cambridge)

CHAYES, A. (1976), "The Role of the Judge in Public Law Litigation" 89 *Harvard LR* 1281–1316

CHINKIN, C. (1999), "A Critique of the Public/Private Dimension" 10 *European J of International Law* 387–95

CHRISTIE, N. (1977), "Conflicts as Property" 17 *British J of Criminology* 1–15

CLARKSON, C.M.V. (1996), "Kicking Corporate Bodies and Damning their Souls" 59 *Modern LR* 557–72

COADY, C.A.J. (1991), "Politics and the Problem of Dirty Hands" in P. Singer (ed.), *A Companion to Ethics* (Oxford), 373–83

COHEN, G.A. (1989), "On the Currency of Egalitarian Justice" 99 *Ethics* 906–44

COLEMAN, J. (2001), *The Practice of Principle: In Defence of a Pragmatist Approach to Legal Theory* (Oxford)

—— and RIPSTEIN, A. (1995) "Mischief and Misfortune" 41 *McGill LJ* 91–128

COLLINS, H. (1982) "Counsel to Philosophers" 45 *Modern LR* 225–30

—— (1990), "Ascription of Legal Responsibility to Groups in Complex Patterns of Economic Integration" 53 *Modern LR* 731–44

—— (1997), *The Law of Contract*, 3rd edn. (London)

—— (1999), *Regulating Contracts* (Oxford)

CONAGHAN, J. (1996), "Tort Law and the Feminist Critique of Reason" in A. Bottomley (ed.), *Feminist Perspectives on the Foundational Subjects of Law* (London)

COOPER, P.J. (1988), *Hard Judicial Choices* (New York)

CORNISH, W.R. (1996), *Intellectual Property*, 3rd edn. (London)

COSGROVE, R.A. (1980), *The Rule of Law: Albert Venn Dicey, Victorian Jurist* (London)

CRAWFORD, J. (1999), "Revising the Draft Articles on State Responsibility" *European Journal of International Law* 435–60

CRISP, R. (2000), "Particularising Particularism" in B. Hooker and M.O. Little (eds.), *Moral Particularism* (Oxford), 23–47

CROSS, R. and TAPPER, C. (1995), *Cross and Tapper on Evidence*, 8th edn. (London)

DAN-COHEN, M. (1985), *Rights, Persons and Organizations: A Legal Theory for Bureaucratic Society* (Berkeley)

DAN-COHEN, M. (1992), "Responsibility and the Boundaries of Self" 105 *Harvard Law Review* 959–1003
DAVIDSON, D. (1963), "Actions, Reasons and Causes" 60 *J of Philosophy* 685–700
DAVIES, P.L. (1997), *Gower's Principles of Modern Company Law* (London)
DAVIS, L.H. (1994), "Action (1)" in S. Guttenplan (ed.), *A Companion to the Philosophy of Mind* (Oxford), 111–17
DENNETT, D.C. (1984), *Elbow Room: The Varieties of Freewill Worth Wanting* (Cambridge, Mass)
—— (1993), *The Intentional Stance* (Cambridge, Mass)
DERSHOWITZ, A.M. (1983), *The Best Defense* (New York)
DICEY, A.V. (1885), *An Introduction to the Study of the Law of the Constitution*, 10th edn., E.C.S Wade (ed.), (London)
DOWNIE, R.S. (1969), "Collective Responsibility" 44 *Philosophy*, reproduced in May and Hoffman (1991), 47–51
DUFF, R.A. (1987), "Codifying Criminal Law: Conceptual Problems and Presuppositions" in I.H. Dennis (ed.), *Criminal Law and Justice* (London), 93–108
—— (1990), *Intention, Agency and Criminal Liability* (Oxford)
—— (1993), "Choice, Character and Criminal Liability" 12 *Law and Philosophy* 345–83
—— (1996), *Criminal Attempts* (Oxford)
DWORKIN, R. (1975), "The Original Position" in N. Daniels (ed.), *Reading Rawls: Critical Studies of* A Theory of Justice (Oxford), 16–53
—— (1981), "What is Equality? Part 2: Equality of Resources" 10 *Philosophy and Public Affairs* 283–345
EASTERBROOK, F.H. (1992), "Plea Bargaining as Compromise" 101 *Yale LJ* 1969–78
FEINBERG, J. (1970), *Doing and Deserving* (Princeton)
—— (1978), "Voluntary Euthanasia and the Inalienable Right to Life" 7 *Philosophy and Public Affairs* 93–123
FELDMAN, D. (1993), *Civil Liberties and Human Rights in England and Wales* (Oxford)
FIELD, S. and JÖRG, and N. (1991), "Corporate Liability and Manslaughter: Should We be Going Dutch? *Criminal LR* 156–71
FINN, P. (1978), "Official Misconduct" 2 *Criminal LJ* 307–25
FINNIS, J. (1980), *Natural Law and Natural Rights* (Oxford)
—— (1991), "Intention and Side-Effects" in R.G. Frey and C.W. Morris (eds.), *Liability and Responsibility: Essays in Law and Morals* (Cambridge), 32–64
—— (1995), "Intention in Tort Law" in D.G. Owen (ed.), *Philosophical Foundations of Tort Law* (Oxford), 229–47
FISCHER, J.M. (1999), "Recent Work on Moral Responsibility" *Ethics* 93–139
—— and ENNIS, R.H. (1986), "Causation and Liability" 15 *Philosophy and Public Affairs* 33–40
—— and RAVIZZA, M. (1993), "Introduction" in J.M. Fischer and M. Ravizza (eds.), *Perspectives on Moral Responsibility* (Ithaca, NY)
—— and —— (1998), *Responsibility and Control: A Theory of Moral Responsibility* (Cambridge)
FISS, O.M. (1984), "Against Settlement" 93 *Yale LJ* 1073–89
FISSE, B. (1968), "The Elimination of Vicarious Liability in Regulatory Offences" 42 *Australian LJ* 199–207, 250–60
—— (1968a), "Vicarious Liability for the Conduct of Independent Contractors" *Criminal LR* 537–44

—— (1983), "Reconstructing Corporate Criminal Law: Deterrence, Fault and Sanctions" 56 *So Cal LR* 1141–1246

—— and BRAITHWAITE, J. (1993) *Corporations, Crime and Accountability* (Cambridge)

FLEMING, J.G. (1988), *The American Tort Process* (Oxford)

—— (1998), *The Law of Torts*, 9th edn. (Sydney)

FLETCHER, G.P. (1993), "The Nature of Justification" in S. Shute, J. Gardner and J. Horder (eds.), *Action and Value in Criminal Law* (Oxford), 175–86

FRENCH, P.A. (1979), "The Corporation as Moral Person" 16 *American Philosophical Quarterly*; reprinted in May and Hoffman (1991), 133–49

—— (1984), *Collective and Corporate Responsibility* (New York)

FRIED, C. (1981), "The Artificial Reason of the Law or: What Lawyers Know" 60 *Texas LR* 35–58

—— (1981a), *Contract as Promise* (Cambridge, Mass)

GAJA, G. (1999), "Should All References to International Crimes Disappear from the ILC Draft Articles on State Responsibility?" 10 *European J of International Law* 365–70

GALLIGAN, D.J. (1978), "Responsibility for Recklessness" *Current Legal Problems* 55–80

GARDNER, J. (1998), "Crime: in Proportion and in Perspective" in A. Ashworth and M. Wasik, *Fundamentals of Sentencing Theory: Essays in Honour of Andrew von Hirsch* (Oxford), 31–52

—— (2001), "Obligations and Outcomes in the Law of Torts" in P. Cane and J. Gardner (eds.), *Relating to Responsibility: Essays for Tony Honoré on his Eightieth Birthday* (Oxford), 111–43

—— and MACKLEM, T. (2001), "Compassion without Respect? Nine Fallacies in *R* v. *Smith*" *Criminal LR* 623–35

—— and SHUTE, S. (2000), "The Wrongness of Rape" in J. Horder (ed.), *Oxford Essays in Jurisprudence, Fourth Series* (Oxford), 193–217

GARDNER, S. (1990), *An Introduction to the Law of Trusts* (Oxford)

GLAZEBROOK, P.R. (1978), "Situational Liability" in P.R. Glazebrook (ed.), *Reshaping the Criminal Law* (London)

GLOVER, J. (1970), *Responsibility* (London)

GOBERT, J. (1994), "Corporate Criminality: Four Models of Fault" 14 *Legal Studies* 393–410

—— (1994a), "Corporate Criminality: New Crimes for the Times" *Criminal LR* 722–34

GOLDBERG, J.C.P. (1999), "Rights and Wrongs" 97 *Michigan LR* 1828–56

GOLDMAN, A.I. (1994), "Action (2)" in S. Guttenplan (ed.), *A Companion to the Philosophy of Mind* (Oxford), 117–21

GOODIN, R.E. (1987), "Apportioning Responsibilties" 6 *Law and Philosophy* 167–85

—— (1995), *Utilitarianism as a Public Philosophy* (Cambridge)

GORDLEY, J. (2000), "The Purpose of Awarding Restitutionary Damages: A Reply to Professor Weinrib" 1 *Theoretical Inquiries in Law* 39–58

GRANTHAM, R. (1998), "Commentary on Goddard" in R. Grantham and C. Rickett (eds.), *Corporate Personality in the 20th Century* (Oxford), 65–70

—— and RICKETT, C. (1998) "The Bootmaker's Legacy to Rickett Company Law Doctrine" in R. Grantham and C. Rickett (eds.), *Corporate Personality in the 20th Century* (Oxford), 1–10

GUEST, A.G. (1984), *Anson's Law of Contract*, 24th edn. (Oxford)

HACKER, P.M.S. (1973), "Sanction Theories of Duty" in A.W.B. Simpson (ed.), *Oxford Essays in Jurisprudence, Second Series* (Oxford), 131–70

HAJI, I. (1997), "Multiple Selves and Personality" 3 *Legal Theory* 249–71

HAMILTON, V.L. (1980), "Intuitive Psychologist ot Intuitive Lawyer: Alternative Models of the Attribution process" 39 *J of Personality and Social Psychology* 767–72

HAMPSHIRE, S. (1978), "Public and Private Morality" in S. Hampshire (ed.), *Public and Private Morality* (Cambridge), 23–53

HAMPTON, J. (1992), "Correcting Harms Versus Righting Wrongs: The Goals of Retribution" 39 *UCLA LR* 1659–702

HANSMANN, H. and KRAAKMAN, R. (2000), "The Essential Role of Organizational Law" 110 *Yale LJ* 387–440

HARLOW, C. (1980), " 'Public' and 'Private' Law: Definition Without Distinction" 43 *Modern LR* 241–65

HARRIS, D.R. and VELJANOVSKI, C.G. (1983), "Remedies Under Contract Law: Designing Rules to Facilitate Out-of-Court Settlements" *Law and Policy Quarterly* 97–127

HART, H.L.A. (1954), "Definition and Theory in Jurisprudence" 70 *Law Quarterly Review* 37–60

—— (1961), *The Concept of Law* (Oxford)

—— (1968), *Punishment and Responsibility* (Oxford)

—— (1982), *Essays on Bentham: Jurisprudence and Political Theory* (Oxford)

—— and HONORÉ, T. (1985), *Causation in the Law*, 2nd edn. (Oxford)

HAWKINS, K. (1984), *Environment and Enforcement: Regulation and the Social Definition of Pollution* (Oxford)

HAYDON, G. (1978), "On Being Responsible" 28 *Philosophical Quarterly* 46–57

HAYTON, D. (2001), "Developing the Obligation Characteristic of the Trust" 117 *Law Quarterly Review* 96–108

HEIMER, C.A. and STAFFEN, L.R. (1998), *For the Sake of the Children* (Chicago)

HERMAN, B. (1993), *The Practice of Moral Judgment* (Cambridge, Mass)

HOGG, P. (1989), *Liability of the Crown*, 2nd edn. (North Ryde, NSW)

—— and MONAHAN, P.J. (2000), *Liability of the Crown*, 3rd edn. (Scarborough, Ontario)

HOLMES, O.W. (1881), *The Common Law* (M. deW. Howe, ed, Cambridge, Mass, 1963)

HONORÉ, A.M. (1966), "Law, Morals and Rescue" in J.M. Ratcliffe (ed.), *The Good Samaritan and the Law* (Garden City, NJ), 225–42

—— A.M. (1973), "Groups, Laws and Obedience" in A.W.B. Simpson (ed.), *Oxford Essays in Jurisprudence, Second Series* (Oxford), 1–21

HONORÉ, T. (1991), *Are Omissions Less Culpable?* in P. Cane and J. Stapleton (eds.), *Essays for Patrick Atiyah* (Oxford), 31–52

—— (1993), "The Dependence of Morality on Law" 13 *Oxford J of Legal Studies* 1–17

—— (1995), "Necessary and Sufficient Conditions in Tort Law" in D.G. Owen (ed.), *Philosophical Foundations of Tort Law* (Oxford), 363–85

—— (1995a), "The Morality of Tort Law—Questions and Answers" in D.G. Owen (ed.), *Philosophical Foundations of Tort Law* (Oxford), 73–95

—— (1999), *Responsibility and Fault* (Oxford)

—— (2001), "Appreciations and Responses" in P. Cane and J. Gardner (eds.), *Relating to Responsibility: Essays for Tony Honoré on his Eightieth Birthday* (Oxford), 219–39

HOOD, C., SCOTT, C., JAMES, O., JONES, G. and TRAVERS, T. (1999), *Regulation Inside Government—Waste-Watchers, Quality Police and Sleaze-Busters* (Oxford)

HOOKER, B. (2000), "Moral Particularism: Wrong and Bad" in B. Hooker and M.O. Little (eds.), *Moral Particularsim* (Oxford), 1–22
HORDER, J. (1996), "Crimes of Ulterior Intent" in A.P. Simester and A.T.H. Smith (eds.), *Harm and Culpability* (Oxford), 153–72
—— (2000), "On the Irrelevance of Motive in Criminal Law" in J. Horder (ed.), *Oxford Essays in Jurisprudence, Fourth Series* (Oxford)
HUSACK, D. and VON HIRSCH, A. (1993), "Culpability and Mistake of Law" in S. Shute, J. Gardner and J. Horder (eds.), *Action and Value in Criminal Law* (Oxford), 157–74
HUTTER, B.M. (1988), *The Reasonable Arm of the Law? Law Enforcement Procedures of Environmental Health Officers* (Oxford)
—— (1997), *Compliance: Regulation and Environment* (Oxford)
IBBETSON, D. (1999), " 'The Law of Business Rome': Foundations of the Anglo-American Tort of Negligence" 52 *Current Legal Problems* 76–109.
JAMIESON, D. (1991) "Method and Moral Theory" in P. Singer (ed.), *A Companion to Ethics* (Oxford), 476–87
JØRGENSEN, N.H.B. (2000), *The Responsibility of States for International Crimes* (Oxford)
KAGAN, S. (1986), "Causation, Liability and Internalism" 15 *Philosophy and Public Affairs* 41–59
KAHAN, D.M. and NUSSBAUM, N.C. (1996), "Two Conceptions of Emotion in Criminal Law" (1996) 96 *Columbia LR* 269–374
KAPLOW, L. and SHAVELL, S. (2001), "Fairness Versus Welfare" 114 *Harvard LR* 961–1388
KEANE, A. (2000), *The Modern Law of Evidence*, 5th edn. (London)
KENNY, A. (1978), *Freewill and Responsibility* (London)
KILLINGLEY, J. (1997), "Some Egonomic Challenges for Fault-Based Compensation Systems" in R. Baldwin (ed.), *Law and Uncertainty: Risks and Legal Processes* (London), 39–53
KNEEBONE, S. (1998), *Tort Liability of Public Authorities* (Sydney)
LACEY, N. (1998), "Contingency, Coherence and Conceptualism: Reflections on the Encounter between 'Critique' and 'the Philosophy of the Criminal Law' " in A. Duff (ed.), *Philosophy and the Criminal Law: Principle and Critique* (Cambridge), 7–59
—— (2000), "Review of M.S. Moore, *Placing Blame: A General Theory of the Criminal Law*" 63 *Modern LR* 141–8
—— (2000a), "Partial Defences to Homicide: Questions of Power and Principle in Imperfect and Less Perfect Worlds" in A. Ashworth and B. Mitchell (eds.), *Rethinking English Homicide Law* (Oxford), 107–31
—— (2000b), "Philosophical Foundations of the Common Law" in J. Horder (ed.), *Oxford Essays in Jurisprudence, Fourth Series* (Oxford), 17–39
—— (2001), "Responsibility and Modernity" 9 *J of Political Philosophy* (forthcoming)
—— (2001a), "In Search of the Responsible Subject: History, Philosophy and Social Sciences in Criminal Law Theory" 64 *Modern LR* 350–71
—— and WELLS, C. (1998), *Reconstructing Criminal Law*, 2nd edn. (1998) (London)
LAW COMMISSION (1996), *Legislating the Criminal Code: Involuntary Manslaughter* (London)
LEIGH, L.H. (1982), *Strict and Vicarious Liability: A Study in Administrative Criminal Law* (London)
LEWIS, H.D. (1948), "Collective Responsibility" 24 *Philosophy*, reproduced in May and Hoffman (1991), 17–34

LLOYD-BOSTOCK, S. (1979), "The Ordinary Man and the Psychology of Attributing Cases and Responsibility" 42 *Modern LR* 143–68

—— (1983), "Attributions of Cause and Responsibility as Social Phenomena" in J. Jaspars, F.D. Fincham and M. Hewstone (eds.), *Attribution Theory and Research: Conceptual, Developmental and Social Dimensions* (London), 261–89

—— (1984), "Fault and Liability for Accidents: The Accident Victim's Perspective" in D. Harris *et al*, *Compensation and Support for Illness and Injury* (Oxford)

LOUGHLIN, M. (1999), "The State, the Crown and the Law" in M. Sunkin and S. Payne (eds.), *The Nature of the Crown: A Legal and Political Analysis* (Oxford), 33–76

MACCORMICK, N. (1994), *Legal Reasoning and Legal Theory*, rev. edn. (Oxford)

MACKIE, J.L. (1977), *Ethics: Inventing Right and Wrong* (Harmondsworth)

MARKESINIS, B.S. and DEAKIN, S.F. (1999), *Tort Law*, 4th edn. (Oxford)

MAY, L. (1987), *The Morality of Groups: Collective and Group-Based Harm and Corporate Rights* (Notre Dame)

—— (1992), *Sharing Responsibility* (Chicago)

—— and HOFFMAN, S. (1991) (eds.), *Collective Responsibility: Five Decades of Debate in Theoretical and Applied Ethics* (Savage, Maryland)

MCCOLGAN, A. (2000), "General Defences" in D. Nicolson and L. Bibbings (eds.), *Feminist Perspectives on Criminal Law* (London)

MCDONALD, A. (1995), "Proximate Cause in Insurance Law: Fire Following Earthquake" 25 *Victoria University of Wellington LR* 525–55

MCFEE, G. (2000), *Freewill* (Teddington)

MCNEELY, M.C. (1941), "Illegality as a Factor in Liability Insurance" 41 *Columbia Law Review* 26–60

MILLER, D. (1976), *Social Justice* (Oxford)

MINOW, M. (1998), *Between Vengeance and Forgiveness: Facing History After Genocide and Mass Violence* (Boston)

MNOOKIN, R.H. and KORNHAUSER, L. (1979), "Bargaining in the Shadow of the Law: the Case of Divorce 88 *Yale LJ* 950–97

MOORE, M.S. (1984), *Law and Psychiatry: Rethinking the Relationship* (Cambridge)

—— (1993), "Foreseeing Harm Opaquely" in S. Shute, J. Gardner and J. Horder (eds.), *Action and Value in Criminal Law* (Oxford), 126–55

—— (1996), "*Prima Facie* Moral Culpability" 76 *Boston University LR* 319–33

—— (1997), *Placing Blame: A General Theory of the Criminal Law* (Oxford)

MORSE, S.J. (1993), "Diminished Capacity" in S. Shute, J. Garnder and J. Horder (eds.), *Action and Value in Criminal Law* (Oxford), 239–78

MULLANEY, N.J. and HANDFORD, P.R. (1993), *Tort Liability for Psychiatric Damage* (Sydney)

MUREINIK, E. (1988), "Dworkin and Apartheid" in H. Corder (ed.), *Essays on Law and Social Practice in South Africa* (Cape Town), 191–217

NAGEL, T. (1978), "Ruthlessness in Public Life" in S. Hampshire (ed.), *Public and Private Morality* (Cambridge), 75–91

—— (1979), *Mortal Questions* (Cambridge)

NICOLSON, D. (2000), "What the Law Giveth it also Taketh Away" in D. Nicolson and L. Bibbings (eds.), *Feminist Perspectives on Criminal Law* (London)

NORRIE, A. (1993), *Crime, Reason and History* (London)

—— (2000), *Punishment, Responsibility and Justice* (Oxford)

NUSSBAUM, M. (2000), "Why Practice Needs Ethical Theory: Particularism, Principle and Bad Behaviour" in B. Hooker and M.O. Little (eds.), *Moral Particularism* (Oxford)

OAKLEY, A.J. (1998), *Parker and Mellows: The Modern Law of Trusts*, 7th edn. (London)
O'CONNELL, D.P. (1970), *International Law, Vol One* (London)
OGUS, A.I. (1994), *Regulation: Legal Form and Economic Theory* (Oxford)
OLIVER, D. (1999), *Common Values and the Public Private Divide* (London)
OTTOLENGHI, S. (1990), "From Peeping Behind the Corporate Veil, to Ignoring It Completely" 53 *Modern LR* 338–53
OUYANG, G. and SHINER, R. (1995), "Organizations and Agency" 1 *Legal Theory* 283–310
PANNAM, C.L. (1966), "Tortious Liability for Acts Committed under an Unconstitutional Statute" 5 *Melbourne University LR* 113–57
PELLET, A. (1999), "Can a State Commit a Crime? Definitely, Yes!" 10 *European J of International Law* 425–34
PENNOCK, J.R. (1960), "The Problem of Responsibility" in C.J. Friedrich (ed.), *Responsibility* (New York), 3–27
PERRY, S.R. (2001), "Honoré on Responsibility for Outcomes" in P. Cane and J. Gardner (eds.), *Relating to Responsibility: Essays for Tony Honoré on his Eigthieth Birthday* (Oxford), 61–80
PERRY, T.D. (1976), *Moral Reasoning and Truth* (Oxford)
PETTIT, P. (2001), *A Theory of Freedom: From the Psychology to the Politics of Agency* (Cambridge)
—— (2001a), "The Capacity to Have Done Otherwise: An Agent-Centred View" in P. Cane and J. Gardner (eds.), *Relating to Responsibility: Essays for Tony Honoré on his Eightieth Birthday* (Oxford), 21–35
—— (2001b), "Embracing Objectivity in Ethics" in B. Leiter (ed.), *Objectivity in Law and Morals* (Cambridge), 234–86
POSNER, R.A. (1992), *Economic Analysis of Law,* 4th edn. (Boston)
—— and RASMUSEN, E.B. (1999), "Creating and Enforcing Norms, with Special Reference to Sanctions" 19 *International R of Law and Economics* 369–82
POSTEMA, G.J. (1986), *Bentham and the Common Law Tradition* (Oxford)
RABIN, R.L. (2000), "Reassessing Regulatory Compliance" 88 *Georgia LJ* 2049–84
RAMSAY, I.M. and STAPLEDON, G.P. (2001), "Corporate Groups in Australia" 29 *Australian Business LR* 7–31
RAWLS, J. (1972), *A Theory of Justice* (London)
RAZ, J. (1973), "On the Functions of Law" in A.W.B Simpson (ed.), *Oxford Essays in Jurisprudence, Second Series* (Oxford), 278–304
—— (1975), *Practical Reasons and Norms* (London)
—— (1979), *The Authority of Law: Essays on Law and Morality* (Oxford)
—— (1982), "Promises in Morality and Law" 95 *Harvard LR* 916–38
—— (1986), *The Morality of Freedom* (Oxford)
—— (1994), *Ethics in the Public Domain: Essays in the Morality of Law and Politics* (Oxford)
RICHARDSON, G. (1987), "Strict Liability for Regulatory Crime? The Empirical Research" *Criminal LR* 295–306
RIDEOUT, R.W. (1996), "The Limited Liability of Unincorporated Associations" 49 *Current Legal Problems (Part 2)* 187–205
RIPSTEIN, A. (1999) *Equality, Responsibility and the Law* (Cambridge)
ROBERTSON, G. (1979) *Obscenity* (London)
ROBINSON, P.H. and DARLEY, J.M. "The Utility of Desert" 91 *Northwestern University LR* 453–99

ROGERS, J. (1998), "Justifying the Use of Firearms by Policemen and Soldiers: A Response to the Home Office's Review of the Law on the Use of Lethal Force" 18 *Legal Studies* 486–509

RORTY, R. (1979), *Philosophy and the Mirror of Nature* (Princeton)

—— (1982), *Consequences of Pragmatism* (Brighton)

ROSENBERG, D. (1995), *The Hidden Holmes* (Cambridge, Mass)

ROVANE, C. (1998), *The Bounds of Agency: An Essay in Revisionary Metaphysics* (Princeton)

SAMUELSON, P.A. (1954), "The Pure Theory of Public Expenditure" 36 *R of Economics and Statistics* 387–9

SCHEFFLER, S. (1992), "Responsibility, Reactive Attitudes and Liberalism in Philosophy and Politics" 21 *Philosophy and Public Affairs* 299–323

SCHULHOFER, S.J. (1992), "Plea Bargaining as Disaster" 101 *Yale LJ* 1979–2009

SCHULTZ, T.R. and SCHLEIFER, M. (1983), "Towards a Refinement of Attribution Concepts" in J. Jaspars. F.D. Fincham and M. Hewstone (eds.), *Attribution Theory and Research: Conceptual, Developmental and Social Dimensions* (London)

SCHWARTZ, G.T. (1990), "The Ethics and Economics of Tort Liability Insurance" 75 *Georgia LR* 313–65

—— (2001), "Feminist Approaches to Tort Law" 2 *Theoretical Inquiries in Law* 175–209

SCOTT, R.E. and STUNTZ, W.J. (1992), "Plea Bargaining as Contract" 101 *Yale LJ* 1909–68

—— and —— (1992a), "A Reply: Imperfect Bargains, Imperfect Trials and Innocent Defendants" 101 *Yale LJ* 2011–15

SCRUTON, R. (1989), "Corporate Persons" *Proceedings of the Aristotelian Society (Supplementary Vol LXVII)* 239–66

SEARLE, J.R. (1964), "How to Derive and 'Ought' from an 'Is' " *The Philosophical R* 43–58

—— (1983), *Intentionality* (Cambridge)

—— (1995), *The Construction of Social Reality* (London)

SEDDON, N. (1999), *Government Contracts, Federal, State and Local* (Sydney)

SHAVELL, S. (1987), *Economic Analysis of Accident Law* (Cambridge, Mass)

SHAVER, K.G. (1985), *The Attribution of Blame: Causality, Responsibility and Blameworthiness* (New York)

SIMESTER, A.P. (2000), "Can Negligence be Culpable?" in J. Horder (ed.), *Oxford Essays in Jurisprudence (Fourth Series)* (Oxford), 85–106

SIMESTER, A.P. and SULLIVAN, G.R. *Criminal Law: Theory and Doctrine* (Oxford)

SIMPSON, A.W.B. (1973), "The Common Law and Legal Theory" in A.W.B. Simpson (ed.), *Oxford Essays in Jurisprudence (Second Series)* (Oxford), 77–99

SINNOTT-ARMSTRONG, W. and BEHNKE, S. (2000), "Responsibility in Cases of Multiple Personality Disorder" in J.E. Tomberlin (ed.), *Philosophical Perspectives, 14, Action and Freedom*, 301–23

SMILEY, M. (1992), *Moral Responsibility and the Boundaries of Community* (Chicago)

SMITH, S.A. (2000), "Towards a Theory of Contract" in J. Horder (ed.), *Oxford Essays in Jurisprudence, Fourth Series* (Oxford), 107–29

SMITH, S.D. (1987), "The Critics and the 'Crisis': A Reassessment of Current Conceptions of Tort Law" 72 *Cornell LR* 745–98

SOLAN, L.M. and DARLEY, J.M. (2001), "Causation, Contribution and Legal Liability; An Empirical Study" 64 *Law and Contemporary Problems* 265–98

SORELL, T. (2000), *Moral Theory and Anomaly* (Oxford)

Spencer, J.R. (1987), "Trying to Help Another Person Commit a Crime" in P. Smith (ed.), *Criminal Law: Essays in Honour of J.C. Smith* (London), 148–69

Stapleton, J. (1995), "Tort, Insurance and Ideology" 58 *Modern LR* 820–45

—— (2000), "Perspectives on Causation" in J. Horder (ed.), *Oxford Essays in Jurisprudence, Series IV* (Oxford), 61–84

—— (2001), "Unpacking Causation" in P. Cane and J. Gardner (eds.), *Relating to Responsibility: Essays for Tony Honoré on his Eightieth Birthday* (Oxford), 145–85

Stein, P. and Shand, J. (1974), *Legal Values in Western Society* (Edinburgh)

Stoljar, S.J. (1973), *Groups and Entities: An Inquiry into Corporate Theory* (Canberra)

Stone, C.D. (1975), *Where the Law Ends: the Social Control of Corporate Behaviour* (New York)

Strawson, P.F. (1962), "Freedom and Resentment" 48 *Proceedings of the British Academy* 187–211

Sullivan, G.R. (1995), "Expressing Corporate Guilt" 15 *Oxford J of Legal Studies* 281–93

—— (1996), "The Attribution of Culpability to Limited Companies" *Cambridge LJ* 515–46

Sumner, L.W. (1987), *The Moral Foundation of Rights* (Oxford)

Sunstein, C.R. (1996), *Legal Reasoning and Political Conflict* (New York)

Taylor, C. (1995), "A Most Peculiar Institution" in J.E.J. Altham and R. Harrison (eds.), *World, Mind and Ethics: Essays on the Ethical Philosophy of Bernard Williams* (Cambridge), 132–55

Terry, H.T. (1924), "Duties, Rights and Wrongs", 10 *American Bar Assoc J* 123–8

Tettenborn, A. (1996), *Law of Restitution in England and Ireland*, 2nd edn. (London)

Teubner, G. (1988), "Enterprise Corporatism: New Industrial Policy and the 'Essence' of the Legal Person" 36 *American J of Comparative Law* 130–55

—— (1993), "The Many-Headed Hydra: Networks as Higher-Order Collective Actors" in J. McCahery, S. Picciotto and C. Scott (eds.), *Corporate Control and Accountability* (Oxford), 41–60

Thompson, D.F. (1985), "Criminal Responsibility in Government" in J.R. Pennock and J.W. Chapman (eds.), *Criminal Justice (Nomos XXVII)* (New York), 202–40

Thompson, J.J. (1984), "Remarks on Causation and Liability" 13 *Philosophy and Public Affairs* 101–33

—— (1986), "A Note on Internalism" 15 *Philosophy and Public Affairs* 60–6

Treitel, G.H. (1995), *The Law of Contract*, 9th edn. (London)

Trindade, F. and Cane, P. (1999), *The Law of Torts in Australia*, 3rd edn. (Melbourne)

Twining, W. (1991), "Reflections on Law in Context" in P. Cane and J. Stapleton (eds.), *Essays for Patrick Atiyah* (Oxford), 1–30

Tyler, T.R. (1990), *Why People Obey the Law* (New Haven)

Velasquez, M.G. (1983), "Why Corporations are Not Morally Responsible for Anything They Do" 2 *Business and Professional Ethics*, reprinted in Hoffman and May (1991), 111–31

Virgo, G. (1999), *The Principles of the Law of Restitution* (Oxford)

Von Hirsch, A. and Jareborg, N. (1991), "Gauging Criminal Harm: A Living-Standard Analysis" 11 *Oxford J of Legal Studies* 1–38

Waldron, J. (1999), *Law and Disagreement* (Oxford)

—— (2000), " 'Transcendental Nonsense' and System in the Law" 100 *Columbia LR* 16–53

WALKER, N. and PADFIELD, N. (1996), *Sentencing: Theory, Law and Practice*, 2nd edn. (London)

WALLACE, R. J. (1994), *Responsibility and the Moral Sentiments* (Cambridge, Mass)

WALLACE, G. and WALKER, A.D.M. (1970), "Introduction" in G. Wallace and A.D.M. Walker (eds.), *The Definition of Morality* (London), 1–20

WALZER, M. (1973), "Political Action: The Problem of Dirty Hands" 2 *Philosophy and Public Affairs* 160–80

WARNOCK, G.J. (1971), *The Object of Morality* (London)

WATTS, P. (2000), "The Company's *Alter Ego*—An Imposter in Private Law" 116 *Law Quarterly Review* 525–30

WEILER, J.H.H., CASSESE, A. and SPINEDI, M. (eds.) (1989), *International Crimes of State* (Berlin)

WEINRIB, E.J. (1985), "The Insurance Justification and Private Law" 14 *J of Legal Studies* 681–7

—— (1995), *The Idea of Private Law* (Cambridge, Mass)

—— (2000), "Restitutionary Damages as Corrective Justice" 1 *Theoretical Inquiries in Law* 1–37

WELLS, C. (1993), *Corporation and Criminal Responsibility* (London)

—— (2001) *Corporation and Criminal Responsibility*, 2nd edn. (Oxford)

WHITE, J. (1999), "Analogical Reasoning" in D. Patterson (ed.), *A Companion to Philosophy of Law and Legal Theory* (Oxford), 583–90

WHITE, F. and HOLLINGSWORTH, K. (1999), *Audit, Accountability and Government* (Oxford)

WILKES, K.V. (1988), *Real People: Personal Identity without Thought Experiments* (Oxford)

WILLIAMS, B (1976), "Moral Luck" *Proceedings of the Aristotelian Society, Supplementary Volume L* 115–35

—— (1981), *Obscenity and Film Censorship* (Cambridge)

—— (1985), *Ethics and the Limits of Philosophy* (Cambridge, Mass)

WITTING, C. (2001), "Distinguishing between Property Damage and Pure Economic Loss in Negligence: A Personality Thesis" 21 *Legal Studies* 481–514

WOLF, S. (1985), "The Legal and Moral Responsibility of Organizations" in J.R. Pennock and J.W. Chapman (eds.), *Criminal Justice (Nomos XXVII)* (New York), 269–86

WOODHOUSE, D. (1994), *Ministers and Parliament: Accountability in Theory and Practice* (Oxford)

WRIGHT, R.G. (1996), *Does the Law Morally Bind the Poor? or, What Good's the Constitution When You Can't Afford a Loaf of Bread?* (New York)

YOUNG, R. (1991), "The Implications of Determinism" in P. Singer (ed.), *A Companion to Ethics* (Oxford), 534–42

ZANDER, M. (2000), "The Criminal Standard of Proof: How Sure is It? *New LJ* 1517–19

ZEDNER, L. (1994), "Reparation and Retribution: Are They Reconcilable? 57 *Modern LR* 228–50

—— (1996), "England" in A. Eser and S. Walther (eds.), *Wiedergutmachung im Kriminalrecht* (Freiburg), 110–227

Index

Abi-Saab, 264
abstraction:
  levels of, 22–7
academics, 8, 13
accountability, 30
agency, 4, 23, 39, 58, 63, 70–1, 76, 93–4, 105, 107, 152, 183, 189, 198, 200, 224
  agent-focused approach, 49–50, 55–6, 63, 92, 94–5, 99–100, 108–9, 119, 123, 125, 130, 136, 138–9, 145, 165, 179–84, 186, 188–90, 196, 201–4, 206, 208, 211–12, 218–19, 235, 244–8, 266, 268, 275–6, 282–3
  moral agency, 163
Alexander, 229, 233
Allars, 259
Allison, 273
analogy, 25–8
Anglian legal systems, 7, 10, 16, 25, 38, 42, 51, 61, 63, 197, 212
answerability, 30
answers, 90–2, 219–20
Aquinas, 59
arbitration, 226–8
Arenella, 3, 72
Aronson, 259
Ashworth, 1, 19, 34, 37, 39, 69, 71, 74, 77, 85–7, 97, 104–5, 120, 133, 138, 158, 172, 174, 198–9, 204–5, 207, 209, 213, 216, 223, 233–4
Atiyah, 62, 195–6, 199–200, 243
attribution:
  rules of, 148–58, 161, 163–4, 168, 177, 262, 266
attribution theory, 18, 22
Austin, 30, 147
automatic behaviour, 100
autonomy, 105, 110

Baier, 30, 32–3, 35
Balint, 264
Bandali, 72
Bassiouni, 264
Beatson, 274
Beaumont, 48
Behnke, 169
belief, 81, 104–5
Bell, 18
Benson, 195
bill of rights, 255
Bishop, 270
Black, 271, 277
Blackman, 47
Blake, 85–6
Bodenheimer, 105
Bovens, 33–4, 145, 159, 173
Braithwaite, 15, 36–7, 61, 87, 146, 234
Bratman, 17
Brownlie, 42–3
Brudner, 50, 69, 107
burden of proof, *see* proof
Burrows, 1, 191
but-for test, 120–3, 128–34, 136, 140, 178

Caja, 264
Calabresi, 116
can, 75, 85, 114
Cane, 1, 7, 26, 34, 39, 42, 47, 61, 68–70, 72, 76, 80, 86–7, 90–1, 94, 105, 126, 172, 182, 185, 187, 197–8, 203, 206, 215, 219, 221, 243, 247, 253, 260–3, 269, 274–5
capacity, 65, 72, 74, 76–7, 90, 97–8, 114, 144, 150–1, 282
Cartwright, 156, 240
causation, 5, 69, 84, 113–41, 185
  as interpretation, 118–19, 128
  attributive element of legal causation, 128–36
  causal over-determination, 121–2, 130, 133
  chain of causation, 135
  definition of, 118, 129, 131–3
  factual element of legal causation, 120–7
  in law and morality, 136–44
  nature of legal causation, 115–20
  ordinary/extraordinary distinction, 134–6
  temporal orientation of, 116–17
character, 102–4
Chayes, 38
Chinkin, 264
choice, 5, 95–111
  and automaticity, 100–2
Christie, 236
civil claims:
  settlement of, 5
civil law paradigm, 5, 50–1, 53, 77, 94, 99–100, 119–20, 162–3, 182–4, 186, 188, 204, 206–7, 209, 219, 235–6, 247–9, 251, 266, 268, 275–6, 282
civil society, 255–6
Clarkson, 159–60
Coady, 2, 276–7

Cohen, 68
Coleman, 187
Collins, 69, 147, 192, 210–11, 228, 232
common law, 7–11, 16, 18, 21, 24–6, 28, 45, 62, 105, 187, 197, 212, 225, 237, 258, 264
  democratic deficit of, 9, 20
  legitimacy of, 8–9, 18
  providing understanding of complex concepts, 9–10, 12–14, 24–5, 28, 44–5, 49, 283
common sense, 9, 17–19, 118, 128, 164
community values, 17, 236
complex concepts, 2–3, 8–9, 15, 24, 28, 279
  legal versions of, 9
Conaghan, 72
conduct, 78
consent, 212–14
consequences:
  definitional consequences, 78, 83, 104, 114–15
  extrinsic consequences, 78, 104, 114–15
  see also outcomes
considerate decision-making, 271
constitutional torts, 261, 264
contract, 191–6, 210–11
Cooper, 38
Cornish, 173
corporate responsibility, 5, 36, 40–2, 145–68, 176
  humanistic approach to, 144–6, 163–5, 169, 171, 180, 267
  models of, 163–8
  modified humanistic approach to, 165–8
corporations, 52, 257–8, 262
  constitution of, 151–2, 168
  corporate killing, 161, 164
  criminal liability of, 157–8, 163, 205
  identification, 157–8
  internal decision structure, 167–8
  opaqueness of, 159–61, 164
  see also corporate responsibility
Cosgrove, 253
cost allocation, 5
courts, 6, 226–30, 232–3, 255
  appellate courts, 166–7
  constitutional role, 255
  expertise of, 273
  private model of, 253
  public model of, 253
  requirement to reach decision, 9, 12, 127
Crawford, 43
criminal law, 85, 92–4, 103–4, 138, 202
  distinquished from tort law, 100
  enforcement of, 5
  international criminal law, 264
  offences against the public, 264
  regulatory criminal law, 236, 239–41
criminal law paradigm, 5, 50, 53, 77, 87, 94, 99, 119–20, 123, 162, 182, 188, 202, 204, 206, 219, 235–6, 246, 251, 266, 268, 275–6, 282
criminal liability:
  contemplating crimes, 209, 223–4
  group criminal liability, 266
  within public functions, 264–8
criminal prosecution, 225
Crisp, 93
Cross, 92
culpability, *see* fault

Dan-Cohen, 104–6, 110, 144, 146, 159
Dancy, 21
Darley, 14–15, 118
Davidson, 131
Deakin, 60–1
deceit, 89
declaratory theory, 7
deduction, 25–6
delegation, 154–6, 161, 177
democracy, 255
democratic deficit, 9, 20
Dennett, 22, 24, 47, 66–7, 74–6
Dershowitz, 148
determinism, 23–4, 66
Dicey, 252–3
dishonesty, 19, 81, 198, 208
dispute resolution, 22, 24–8
distributional neutrality, 190
distributive issues, 251–4, 257–8, 264, 270, 282–3
due diligence, 92
Duff, 47, 69, 103
duty, 1, 279
duty of care, 188, 196, 217–19, 260
Dworkin, 68

Easterbrook, 234–5
economic approach, 11, 60–2, 84, 117, 219, 242–3
EC law, 264
efficiency, 242
enforcement, 283
  selective enforcement, 225–6, 239–41
Ennis, 137–9
equality, 259
equality before the law, 259
ethical domain, 277
ethical neutrality, 189
evidence, 45–9
  see also proof
excuses, 90

false statements, 198–200, 213
fault, 30, 65, 78–87, 89, 94, 106, 110–11, 156–7, 161, 185–6, 190, 194, 197, 199, 212, 225, 247–8

Feinberg, 2, 9, 55, 107
Feldman, 212
fiduciary obligation, 201
Field, 160
Finn, 264
Finnis, 15, 59, 81, 95, 102, 192
Fischer, 24, 66, 95, 137–9
Fiss, 233
Fisse, 36–9, 146, 156
Fleming, 38
Fletcher, 90
foreseeability, 134–6, 144
freedom of choice, 66, 100
free market individualism, 62
free will, 4, 23–4, 67, 183
French, 167–8
Fried, 26–7, 195–6, 210

gains:
  making, 208–9, 221–3
Galligan, 80
Gardner, 50, 72, 99, 108, 203, 207, 212, 214
general principles, 93–4
Glazebrook, 133
Glover, 75
Gobert, 150
Goldman, 100
Goodin, 178, 276
Gordley, 221
government, 42, 51–2, 55, 218, 251–3, 258–9, 266–7, 271–2, 277
  British/Continental approaches to, 251–3
  liability for employees, 262–4, 266–7
Gower, 151
Grantham, 145, 148
group responsibility, 23–4, 40–3, 143, 145–68, 174–5
  distinct from shared responsibility, 171
  scope and functions of, 162–3
groups, 266, 278
  as social integrates, 165–7
  division of labour, 158–62
  opaqueness of, 174
Guest, 187
Gummow J, 271

Hacker, 30
Haji, 169
Hamilton, 140
Hampshire, 276
Hampton, 50
Handford, 215
Hansmann, 146
hard cases, 19
Harlow, 253
harm, 214–20
  doing harm, 202–6
  risks of, 206–7, 221
  types of harm, 136, 214–17
Harris, 232
Hart, 4, 11–12, 14, 20, 29–33, 35, 54, 61, 63, 79, 95–8, 105, 113, 117–18, 128–9, 131, 135, 137, 141, 144, 146, 151, 188
Hawkins, 6, 240
Haydon, 30, 32–3
Hayton, 200
Heimer, 33
Herman, 107
historic responsibility, 31, 34–5, 38–9, 44, 57, 60–3, 114, 140, 152, 181–5, 187–8, 281
  as pathological form of legal responsibility, 35
Hoffmann, Lord 149, 151, 156–9
Hogg, 253, 262, 265
Hohfeld, 212
Hollingsworth, 256
Holmes J, 48, 74
honesty, *see* dishonesty
Honoré, 14–15, 30, 32, 36, 55, 57, 68, 73, 75–6, 85, 105–7, 113, 117–18, 122–3, 128–9, 131, 135, 137, 141, 145, 185, 248
Hood, 256
Hooker, 21, 70, 93, 185
Horder, 87, 207, 209, 224
Husack, 104
Hutter, 6

Ibbetson, 195
immunities, 90
inadvertent behaviour, 101
indifference, 80
induction, 25–8
institutions of law, 6–12
  law-applying, 6–7
  law-enforcement, 6–7
  law-making, 6–7
institutions of morality, 10–12
insurance, 5, 226, 241–9
  absence of insurance, 241
  against criminal liability, 246, 248–9
  and tort, 242–5
  justification for liability insurance, 244–5
  liability insurance, 241–50
  responsibility and liability insurance, 245–50
  self-insurance, 241
intention, 46–8, 62, 65, 79, 81, 86, 88, 93, 95–7, 99, 105, 144, 157, 162, 170, 182, 199, 203–4, 209, 282
internal point of view, 11
international law, 42–3

Jamieson, 16, 22
Jareborg, 217
Jörg, 160
Jørgensen, 264

judges, 61
  judicial dispute resolution, 226–30
  judicial functions, 260
  judicial law-making, 7–10, 17–19, 21, 25
judicial reasoning, 8–9, 17, 27
  institutional constraints affecting, 20–1
  see also legal reasoning
judicial review, 255, 268–75
justice, 232–3
  compensatory justice, 244
  corrective justice, 68, 182, 186–8, 202, 219, 239, 241–5, 283
  distributive justice, 68–9, 127, 179, 182, 186–90, 202, 208, 219, 224, 241–2, 283
  natural justice, 269
  restorative justice, 37–8, 61, 87, 234, 236, 268
  retributive justice, 182, 187–8, 202, 238–9, 241, 244–5, 283
  social justice, 70
justification, 90

Kagan, 138
Kahan, 87
Kant, 23, 189
Kaplow, 8, 12, 183, 276
Keane, 104
Kenny, 12, 47
Killingley, 101
Kneebone, 263, 272
knowledge, 81, 104–5, 144, 157, 170, 182
Kornhauser, 225
Kraakman, 146

Lacey, 22, 44, 48, 54, 87, 103, 146, 188, 198, 215, 236
La Forest J, 176, 263
law:
  and morality, 54–5, 110, 164, 280
  as illuminating subject of study, 3, 179
  domain of law, 6, 255
  extrinsic functions of, 188–9
  functions of, 60–2
  institutional characteristics, 5
  institutional resources of, 12, 15, 24–5, 28, 44–5, 49, 63, 113, 129, 141, 164, 206, 280–1
  law in context, 279–80
  nature of, 3
  regarded as artifical, 2
law and economics, *see* economic approach
law in action, 225, 249–50, 280
legal domain, 20–1, 26–7, 30, 60, 71, 75–6, 92, 94, 98–9, 104, 127, 129, 140, 179, 201, 239
legal liability, 1, 30, 60, 78–85
  and culpability, 65
  answers to *prima facie* liability, 90–2
  civil liability, 74, 258–64, 272–3
  criminal liability, 74, 85–7, 109–10, 273
  legal criteria of, 78, 88–94
  shared liability, 155
  solidary liability, 178–9
  vicarious liability, 106–7, 109, 118, 131, 144, 152–6, 162–3, 175–7, 182, 242, 262–4, 266
  without causation, 132–3
legal persons, 147–9
legal personality, 40–1
legal reasoning 1, 3–4, 6, 16–28, 281
  criteria of good legal reasoning, 21
  see also judicial reasoning
legal responsibility, 34–5, 41, 56, 190
  analysis of, 3–4
  bounds of, 188, 210–214
  functions of, 189
  grounds of, 188, 191–209
  paradigms of, 5, 49–53
legal sources, 225, 249–50, 279
legislation, 7–10, 27
Leigh, 88
Lewis, 2, 57–8, 60
liability, *see* legal liability
limitation agreements, 220
limitation periods, 58–60, 220, 274
Lloyd-Bostock, 9, 18, 21–2, 45, 106, 137
Loughlin, 42
luck, 5, 65–78, 84–5, 106, 110–11, 137–8, 160, 185, 190, 244
  circumstantial luck, 67, 69–71, 130, 135–9, 209, 211
  dispositional luck, 67, 72–8, 98, 137–8

Macchiavelli, 276
MacCormick, 17
Mackie, 23, 55
Macklem, 72
Markesinis, 60–1
markets, 194
May, 157, 168, 171, 173, 175
McColgan, 187
McDonald, 128
McFee, 66, 95
McNeely, 246
meaning of life, 283
mens rea, 37, 49, 162, 204, 246–9, 260–1
mental states, 47–8, 78, 85–7, 92, 94, 99, 102–4, 110, 119, 129, 148, 150–3, 157, 162, 168, 170, 182, 189, 209, 235
metaphysics, 24, 165
Miller, 21
Minow, 59
Mnookin, 225
Monahan, 253, 262, 265
Moore, 54, 100, 104, 135, 169, 188–9
moral domain, 10–11, 14–16, 20–1, 28, 39, 56–7, 71, 75–6, 89, 92, 94, 98–9, 104, 106, 123, 127, 132, 140–1, 179–80, 201, 206, 208, 237, 239, 255, 282

morality, 34, 45, 74–6, 280
and legal reasoning, 15–28
definition of, 6
folk-morality, 18
institutional characteristics, 5
nature of, 3
objective quality of, 12, 19
popular contrasted with legal, 14–15
public morality, 256
public/private distinction, 5
relationship with law, 2–28
moral particularism, 93
moral rationality, 19–28
moral reasoning, 3–4, 6, 8, 281
analytical moral reasoning, 16–17, 27
practical moral reasoning, 16–17, 19, 27
moral responsiblity, 1, 23, 29–30, 41, 45, 51, 54, 74, 76, 98, 104, 106–7, 144, 162, 185, 190, 246, 282
choice-based account of, 95–111
requirement of intentionality, 95–7
Morse, 77
motives, 71–2, 82, 87, 90, 92–4, 102–4
Mullaney, 215
multiple personality, 143, 165, 169–71
Mureinik, 20

Nagel, 2 , 276
negligence, 5, 23, 46, 53, 65, 72–4, 79–80, 85–6, 89, 95, 97–9, 101–2, 111, 133, 137, 157, 162, 182, 187–8, 192–4, 197–9, 201, 203–6, 213, 217–19, 246–8, 263, 275
contributory negligence, 91, 173, 195
NESS test, 120–3, 128–34, 136, 140, 178
Nicolson, 70
normative domains, 3, 5
Norrie, 70–2, 81, 87, 93–4, 102–4, 110
Nussbaum, 21, 87

Oakley, 214
obligation of repair, 108–11, 120, 124, 126, 137, 140, 182, 184–5, 226, 237–8, 248–9
O'Connell, 43
Ogus, 240
Oliver, 251–2, 261, 267–9, 271, 277
omissions, 132
ordinary language, 128–9, 131, 137
Ottolenghi, 147
outcomes, 5, 65, 76, 78, 84, 108–9, 114–15, 117–18, 126, 138, 140, 151, 282
grounds and bounds of outcome responsibility, 185–6
outcome responsibility, 106–8, 185, 190
Ouyang, 157, 164, 168

Padfield, 77, 87, 104, 171
Pannam, 262
paradigm of individual responsibility, 143–5, 148, 151
Pellet, 264
Pennock, 31
Perry, S, 76
Perry, T, 19–21
personality, 5
relationship with responsibility, 143–5, 163
personhood, 168
revisionary metaphysics of, 165
Pettit, 12–13, 75, 100, 165–8
philosophical perspective, 2–5, 17–19, 22–3, 26, 49, 65, 92, 95, 113, 144, 158, 164, 178, 276, 282–3
police, 6, 260, 262
Posner, 11, 42, 45, 73, 219
Postema, 7, 9, 26
practical reasoning, 2, 12, 16–17, 19, 27, 98–9, 114, 276, 278–9
pragmatism, 62
promises, 191–6, 199–200, 210–11, 213
proof, 45–9, 91–2, 123–7, 207, 214, 228
property, 1, 87, 197–8, 208, 279
proportionality, 271
protected interests, 183–4, 190, 197
public functions, 251–2, 254, 256–60, 262, 265, 268
public interest, 252–4, 262, 265, 267, 269–70, 276
public law, 233, 251–78
and damages, 260–1, 268
bounds of responsibility, 272–5
equality principle, 252, 259, 262, 265, 267
grounds of public law responsibility, 258–72
institutional framework of, 254–6
problem of dirty hands, 275–8
province of, 251–2, 254, 256–8
public law paradigm, 5, 42, 51–3, 55, 251–5, 268–9, 271, 275–6, 278
public/private distinction, 5, 252, 256–8, 264, 271–2, 277
punishment, 99, 109–10, 120, 137, 140, 177, 238–9, 248–9

Rabin, 229
Ramsay, 147
Rasmusen, 11, 45
Ravizza, 24, 66, 95
Rawls, 68
Raz, 11, 14, 56, 70, 192, 196, 203, 251
reactive fault, 36–9
reasonableness, 187, 232, 271, 275
reasonable person, 72–3, 79, 111
reasons, 102–4
reasons for action, 108
recklessness, 46, 65, 80–1, 86, 93, 95, 99, 105, 144, 157, 170, 182, 199, 204
remoteness of damage, 119, 130

res ipsa loquitur, 46, 159
responsible person, 33
responsibility, 212
 as a virtue, 33–4
 as fundamental legal concept, 1
 capacity responsibility, 29–30, 35–6, 63, 65, 144, 150–1
 causal reponsiblity, 29–30, 36, 129–36, 178, 185
 choice theory of responsibilty, 105
 civil responsibility, 49–50, 75
 compared with liability, 1–2, 60–2
 contextual approach, 22, 24–5, 279–80
 conventional responsibility, 4
 criminal responsiblity, 45–6, 49–50, 54, 70–2, 75, 151, 188, 207
 degrees of, 44
 distinction with liability, 30 , 109
 functional approach, 281–3
 grounds and bounds of, 5, 189
 heterogeneous nature of, 24–5
 intention responsibility, 55–6
 joint and concurrent, 172
 legal distinct from moral, 1–2
 legal responsibility, 29–30, 144
 liability responsibility, 29–30, 35
 methodological approach, 279–83
 ministerial responsiibility, 275
 modern approach to, 23–4, 39–40
 naturalistic account of, 4, 40–3
 operational responsibility, 283
 ontological function of, 283
 paradigms of responsibility, 63
 personal responsibility, 39–40
 political responsiblity, 52–3
 practical responsibility, 48–9
 prospective responsibility, 30–5, 38–9, 44, 55, 57, 61, 63, 256
 reactive responsibility, 36–9
 relational aspect of, 49–56, 70, 108–9, 145, 163, 168–71, 198–200, 202, 204–6, 235, 241, 247–8, 282
 relationship with duty, 31, 33–4
 responsibility and causation, 113, 128, 178
 responsibility and culpability, 94–7
 responsibility and liability, 224, 264, 273, 282
 responsibility and luck, 65–78
 responsibility discriminations, 89
 responsibility tapestry, 13
 role responsibility, 29, 32–3, 35
 secondary responsibility, 173–5
 shared responsibility, 40, 43, 143, 153, 171–9
 shares of responsibility, 177–9
 task responsibility, 30
 taxonomies of, 4–5, 29–43, 113
 temporal element, 31–9
 theoretical responsibilty, 48–9
 type of control relevant to, 67–9
 vicarious responsibility, 39–40, 168
responsibility practices, 4–5, 13, 18, 24–5, 28, 43–63, 66–7, 78, 117, 127, 139, 141, 145, 148, 162, 179–80, 183, 187, 189–90, 218, 225, 235, 237, 279–81, 283
 evaluative function of, 57, 60
 explanatory function of, 57
 functions of 56–60
 normative function of, 57–8
 ontological function of, 57
 relational aspects, 97, 99–100
Richardson, 236, 240
Rickett, 145
rights, 1, 87, 183, 196–8, 211–12, 232, 268, 279, 283
 and balancing of interests, 212
 contractual rights, 197–8
 human rights, 197, 261, 280
 legal rights, 197
 property rights, 87, 197–8, 208
Ripstein, 68–9, 79, 82, 187
risk distribution, 5, 108, 122, 128–9, 164, 204, 240–1, 257–8, 260
Robertson, 207
Robinson, 14–15
Roche, 37
Rogers, 265
Rorty, 4, 58
Rosenberg, 48
Rovane, 143, 165, 167–9

Samuelson, 252
sanctions, 30, 43–4, 49–50, 57–8, 63, 71, 76–7, 87, 92–4, 104, 110, 113, 123, 137, 140, 146, 152, 170–1, 179, 198, 201, 203, 224, 248–50, 268, 280–2
 public law sanctions, 269
Scheffler, 68
Schleifer, 18, 95, 122
Schulhofer, 235
Schultz, 18, 95, 122
Schwartz, 187, 243–6
Scott, 235
Scruton, 143, 147
Searle, 10, 101
Seddon, 260
separation of powers, 218, 254, 273
settlement, 225–3, 235–9
 arguments regarding, 232–5
 in criminal law, 233–9
 settlement negotiations, 230–1
Shand, 104
Shavell, 8, 13, 48, 73–4, 183, 276
Shaver, 18, 47–8, 77, 113, 118
Shiner, 157, 164, 168
Shute, 203, 207, 212
Simester, 73–4, 89, 102, 154–6
Simpson, 8

Sinnott-Amsrrong, 169
Smiley, 23, 104, 113, 116, 132
Smith, S.A., 203
Smith, S.D., 184
social context, 22, 24–5, 279–80
social practice, 18, 279
social values, 53–6, 62–3, 117
Solan, 118
Sorell, 252
Spencer, 173
split personality, 169–71
Staffen, 33
standards of conduct, 78, 83
standing, 52, 253, 268, 274
Stapleton, 62, 118, 122, 128–9, 136, 147, 206, 247
Stein, 104
Stoljar, 146
Stone, 146
Strawson, 24
strict liability, 5, 46, 48, 65, 82–7, 91, 105–11, 154, 156–7, 182, 189, 197, 200–2, 204–6, 212, 214, 225, 246–9, 270
  and luck, 84–5
  grounds and bounds of, 189
  incidence of, 85–7
  selective enforcement of, 240–1
  varieties of, 82–4
strict responsiblity, 24, 39–40
  four categories of, 39
Stuntz, 235
Sullivan, 89, 102, 147, 154–6
Summer, 2, 11
Sunstein, 17, 26
supererogation, 34
syllogistic reasoning, 21

tapestry model, 6, 13, 28
Tapper, 92
tax, 249
Taylor, 34
Terry, 78
Tettenborn, 222
Teubner, 147, 149
Thompson, D, 266–7
Thompson, J, 107, 137–9
tort law, 62, 86, 242–5
Treitel, 151, 172, 246
Trindade, 26, 34, 69–70, 72, 80, 90, 262–3, 275
trust, 208, 222–3
  breach of, 200–2, 208, 213–14
Twining, 279
Tyler, 270

utilitarian theories, 238, 276

Velasquez, 2, 45, 105, 144, 158, 171
Veljanovski, 232
victims, 50, 55–6, 62–3, 94, 99, 110, 119, 123, 125, 130, 136, 163, 179, 182, 218–19, 236, 245, 268
Virgo, 1, 208, 223
von Hirsch, 104, 217

Waldron, 10, 14
Walker, 6, 77, 87, 104, 171
Wallace, G, 6
Wallace, R, 66, 75, 95–9, 101–3
Walzer, 252, 277
Watts, 157
Weiler, 264
Weinrib, 23, 61, 182–4, 187–90, 196, 198, 210, 219, 221, 239, 243–5
welfare economics, 13
welfare state, 62
Wells, 110, 156, 159, 174, 198
Wertheimer, 2
White, F, 256
White, J, 25
Whitmore, 259
Wilkes, 22, 169
Williams, 34, 107, 216
will theories, 182
Wittgenstein, 164
Witting, 215
Wolf, 106, 157, 162
Woodhouse, 275
Wootton, 61
Wright, 70

Young, 24

Zander, 124
Zedner, 49–50, 70